MARION DAVIES

MARION DAVIES

A BIOGRAPHY BY
FRED
LAWRENCE
GUILES

McGRAW-HILL BOOK COMPANY

New York   St. Louis   San Francisco
Düsseldorf   London   Mexico   Sydney   Toronto

2 3 4 5 6 7 8 9   BP BP   7 9 8 7 6 5 4 3 2

Design: Robert Aulicino
Art Direction: Harris Lewine

Acknowledgment is made to the following for their kind
permission to publish or reprint material from copyright or
otherwise controlled sources:
Miss Alice E. Head (her memoirs *It Could Never Have
Happened*); The Bodley Head Ltd of London (Charles Chaplin's
My Autobiography); Chappell & Company, Inc. (the song
Sonny Boy—Copyright © 1928 by De Sylva, Brown & Henderson,
Inc. Copyright renewed, assigned to Chappell & Company, Inc.
Used by permission of Chappell & Company, Inc.);
Doubleday & Company, Inc. (*Past Imperfect* by Ilka Chase,
The Gay Illiterate by Louella O. Parsons, *Memoirs of a Star* by
Pola Negri, and *The Honeycomb* by Adela Rogers St. Johns);
Greenbaum, Wolff & Ernst (*A Peculiar Treasure* by Edna Ferber,
Copyright 1938, 1939, by Edna Ferber, Copyright © 1960,
by Morris L. Ernst, et al., Trustees, Copyright © Renewed 1966 by
Edna Ferber); E. P. Dutton & Company, Inc. and Harold
Matson Company, Inc. (from the book *The Life and Good Times of
William Randolph Hearst* by John Tebbel. Copyright, 1952,
by John Tebbel. Published by E. P. Dutton & Company, Inc. and
used with their permission and that of Harold Matson Company,
Inc.); Holt, Rinehart and Winston, Inc. (*Hollywood Rajah* by
Bosley Crowther, Rinehart and Winston as publishers);
Houghton Mifflin Company (*Twenty-One Years* by Randolph S.
Churchill); The Macmillan Company (*A Preface to Morals* by
Walter Lippmann, © 1929 by the Macmillan Company;
renewed 1957 by Walter Lippmann); Simon & Schuster, Inc.
(*A Child of the Century* by Ben Hecht, Copyright © 1954 by
Ben Hecht); Pantheon Books, a Division of Random House, Inc.
(*Hard Times* by Studs Terkel, Copyright © 1970); Charles
Scribner's Sons (*Citizen Hearst* by W. A. Swanberg); Gloria
Vanderbilt Cooper (*Without Prejudice* by Gloria Vanderbilt, Sr.);
Anita Loos (*A Girl Like I*, published by Random House, Inc.);
Time/Life Syndication Service (editorial on Hearst, Copyright *Life*
Magazine, © 1951 by Time, Inc.);
To publish photographs of Marion Davies, her family, friends
and colleagues: Charles Lederer, William "Buster" Collier,
and Marie Glendinning;
For the other photographs, material and assistance, a special
acknowledgment to the executors and heirs of the estate
of Marion Douras Brown.

Library of Congress Cataloging in Publication Data
Guiles, Fred Lawrence. Marion Davies.
1. Davies, Marion, 1897-1961.
PN2287.D315G8   791.43'028'0924 [B]   79-38936
ISBN 0-07-025114-2

FOR ANITA LOOS,
NADINE JACKSON,
AND CARLOS MacMASTER

CONTENTS

INTRODUCTION
She Was a Daisy, But No Susan Alexander
ix

PART ONE
Nearly the End, and the Beginning
1

PART TWO
The New Pollyanna
75

PART THREE
Life and Sudden Death in Hollywood
143

PART FOUR
San Simeon—The Great Days
179

PART FIVE
Mr. Shaw's Favorite Blonde
241

PART SIX
Citizen Kane and the Yellow Peril
309

PART SEVEN
The Mood Is Blue
347

Appendix
375

Bibliography
405

Index
407

INTRODUCTION:
She Was a Daisy,
but No Susan Alexander

The year 1918 saw the end of one war, the most terrible and devastating in history up to that time, and the beginning of another—the war against oppression in most corners of the world, paralleled by a blithe disregard for the shaking timbers beneath their feet among the oppressors. The most powerful molder of public attitudes in America, publishing giant William Randolph Hearst, managed with considerable success to plead the cause of some of the oppressed in banner headlines while dancing a bearlike waltz (and he was a graceful bear indeed on a ballroom floor) in one of his many villas, castles, and townhouses.

In such an unreal *mise en scène*, one has to seek some familiar touchstones—such as love and devotion—to keep the fairy dust from obscuring the vision. These virtues undoubtedly contributed much toward involving Hearst increasingly in a secondary career, filmmaking, which for more than twenty years took up a substantial amount of his time and energy. With most of the implements needed for success at hand—great wealth, enormous publicity machinery, and a larger talent for packaging his own fantasies than many film historians later would concede —he made the attempt to elevate the woman he loved, Marion Davies, to those rarefied and lonely heights where Pickford, Lillian Gish, and, later, Garbo resided. Although she did become a star, the campaign misfired and only served to create an impression, and a false one, that Maid Marion, chatelaine of San Simeon (as Arthurian a setting as any Camelot), needed help to get by in her career.

There are numerous film buffs and critics whose thinking about the film career of Marion Davies has been formed *ex parte* by the mystique surrounding the celebrated film inspired by Hearst's life, Orson Welles' *Citizen Kane*. They will be disappointed to learn that she was no Susan Alexander, not the "terrible actress who was forced upon the public by her megalomaniac lover"—a description of Marion often voiced by these rather careless scholars and drawn directly from the character of Kane's second wife in the movie. Studio executives Thalberg, Mayer, and Jack Warner, as well as directors Vidor, Leonard, Walsh, LeRoy, Goulding, and others who guided her through such films as *Peg O' My Heart, The Patsy, Show People, Blondie of the Follies*, and *Going Hollywood* considered her a talented comedienne and mime. Marion Davies was a significant leading lady for more than fifteen years with a reputation for being dependably funny and poignant in each of her films. The critics, including Mordaunt Hall of *The New York Times*, loved her zest and the little note of pathos she brought to her comedy. She had several cycles of successful films, the low points all miscalculations of Hearst's, for he was running her career as well as her life.

Fame, then, was legitimately hers, but she was a mistress by default. Despite her numerous denials, she wanted marriage desperately and she was the world's busiest matchmaker. Accepting the emoluments of screen stardom in lieu of a ring, her career became her only escape from the onus of being a back-street girl dragged into the limelight by her reckless lover. The wryly comic note was that, once there, she was oversold by him as a kind of madonna.

Marion Davies does not figure very strongly in the annals of Hearst as a maker of history. He already had done his controversial turn of helping to drag the United States into war against the Spanish long before he met Marion. She remained very much in the background at San Simeon during the 1932 Democratic convention when—from his California mountaintop —he helped put across the candidacy of Franklin Delano Roosevelt. It was, like nearly all of his ultimate political decisions, a compromise, but what is significant is that these historical events were *thirty-four years apart* and Hearst continued influencing American history and opinion for almost two decades more. But Marion was something more than an eyewitness to thirty-five years of her lover's powerful role in American life. She sustained —through her laughter and encouragement—a man who was something less than a titan physically as he moved beyond his middle years.

Hearst's way of life was a Cecil B. De Mille epic realized, a little grander than the imaginings of Sir Walter Scott. While at first he seemed some monstrous throwback to the age of feudalism, Marion changed all that. Hearst's lifelong debauch in the Western world's treasures and relics found a focus and inspiration in her. The infectious wit and luminous charm of Marion gave his castle enterprises a redeeming panache.

Marion Davies realized that her life story would be a social document of some importance. The very name conjures up an image of the film queen *in excelsis* presiding with her lover over an Americanized Versailles; the sunny blonde pal of kings and the world's great who would go out of their way while in the United States to see Hearst's castle *and* Marion herself, an attraction of far greater interest to them than Miss Liberty turning green in New York Harbor or any First Lady of this century. At least one attempt to set down the facts about her life was aborted (Was she fearful of the consequences?), but even if she had succeeded in completing her memoirs, they would have to be suspect. She had moved in a world more improbable than anything in Lewis Carroll's pages and she was chronically addicted to dressing up the truth despite her personal lack of that preoccupation with self so common among actresses.

A generation removed from the actress, I grew up in Iowa and New Jersey in a kind of perpetual twilight that was my life from Saturday matinee to Saturday matinee. My senses were really engaged only when I was settled back in some movie cavern watching Janet Gaynor or Colleen Moore or Marion Davies, who was a special favorite of mine, in their comic or bittersweet romances. Those three stars were uniquely representative of the silent film's golden age, ranging from Janet Gaynor's purity of heart (an innocent gamine nearly destroyed by tragic circumstances) through Marion Davies's impishness (her beaux could expect a practical joke or two before the final embrace) to Colleen Moore's emancipated flapper. Then came the great sound revolution and I was relieved to hear the unique Davies voice (I was to learn how drinking could improve a woman's voice some years later) as she sang and danced briefly in an early showcase of Metro stars, *The Hollywood Revue of 1929.*

We were never to meet, Miss Davies and I, and I was to return to my precocious obsession with her personality rather late in life, after a casual suggestion by Anita Loos, who once had been a neighbor of Marion's at Santa Monica and a frequent visitor at San Simeon.

I especially would like to thank Charles Lederer for devoting many hours to discussing details of Marion Davies's life and career, for helping me make contact with those who knew her best, and for answering dozens of questions posed by my interviews with others; Captain Horace G. Brown for giving me not only enriching details about Miss Davies's last decade but the resolute will to make the book uncompromising as well as compassionate; Miss Dorothy Mackaill for journeying from Hawaii to San Francisco to meet with me simply out of her respect for Miss Davies; and Mrs. Eleanor Boardman d'Arrast for seeing me numerous times, making suggestions and corrections and maintaining an interest in the project from the beginning to the end.

The substance of this book has been taken from old letters, cables, verses, and snatches of conversations and memories recalled by those mentioned above as well as Anita Loos, Eileen Percy Ruby, Fifi D'Orsay, Marie Glendinning, Tom Kennington, Floretta Mouser, Lloyd Pantages, Bing Crosby, Buster Collier, Cobina Wright, Sr., Frances Marion, Kay Gable, Diana Fitzmaurice Cousins, William Haines, Patricia Lake, Mrs. Herman Mankiewicz, Vera Burnett, Ann Davis, Faith Grant, Anne Shirley Lederer, Howard Strickling, Ben Lyon, Harriet Parsons, Gregson Bautzer, and two of Marion's directors, King Vidor and Mervyn Le Roy. I am profoundly grateful to all of them. A debt is owed, too, to the library staffs of the Academy of Motion Picture Arts and Sciences and to the Lincoln Center Museum and Library of the Performing Arts, to Professors Irwin Blacker and Howard Suber for supplying background material on the filming of *Citizen Kane;* to Philip Chamberlain of the Los Angeles County Art Museum for loaning me the facilities to screen Miss Davies's films and helping collate the credits which can be seen in the Appendix; to Robert Board, archivist and documentarian of Marion Davies memorabilia; to Madeline Milgroom for her perceptive eye and patience as she typed the final manuscript; and to Richard Simonton, Jr., for supplying additional screening facilities.

October 1971   FRED LAWRENCE GUILES

PART ONE

NEARLY THE END, AND THE BEGINNING

I

They were gathering for the death watch. Marion could see the black Cadillacs pulling into the cobbled courtyard from her office window, where she so often stood to glance out when car doors slammed. An unfashionable room composed of unmatching desks, a settee, and a couple of chairs, it was Marion Davies' retreat in her hilltop mansion in Beverly Hills. When she was not in her own bedroom on the second floor, where she usually remained until early in the afternoon, most often she could be found in the small office or in its adjoining kitchen. Her intimate friends—nearly all of them "girlfriends," survivors from her movie and *Follies* days—would be brought there to chat, with Marion herself running to the oversized refrigerator fetching ice cubes for their drinks.

Although she was "a good sport," as game as anyone in Hollywood in dealing with adversity, her staff knew that despite all the cheerful little stories passed along to her gossip columnist friends Hedda Hopper and Louella Parsons, her waking hours were not filled to the brim with charitable activities (although she was the most generous woman in the film colony) or with family visits. Her days for a long while had been unhappy and uneventful, rendered so terribly alike through their emptiness that she scarcely saw the attractive scenery any more—those landscaped terraces leading down to a reflecting pool, the carefully assembled period rooms, her collection of Fragonards and other French and Dutch paintings—and the faces of those around her, employees and a small band of faithful friends, most of whom would set aside one afternoon a week as their time "to visit Marion," several of them in cahoots so that their visits would not conflict. Her life had become very much like the decomposing early Davies films now mouldering in the storage vaults, some of it nearly white with lost detail with close-up figures often out of focus. It was, oddly enough, beginning to resemble that of Mary Pickford, who, more than anyone, had inspired Hearst through her success to launch Marion as a film star. The ladies had become the closest of friends, and when the film community changed and became alien to them, each withdrew and deliberately obscured the reality of what was outside their mansion walls.

But the evening of August 13, 1951, was becoming radically different from the more than 1500 other evenings Marion had spent in her pseudo-Italian villa. It was shaping up as a day of reckoning and she was terrified. As the most accepted and certainly the wealthiest mistress of all time, she was losing her companion finally to the one force that could break them apart—Death. Her lover through thirty-five years, three castles, several townhouses, villas, and smaller palaces (real estate cannot be ignored in writing about these lives), two world wars, near financial ruin, was a wasted wreck of a man in the north wing of the second floor of the mansion. William Randolph Hearst, a giant historically and physically through much of his lifetime, was dying now in his eighty-ninth year.

"We never talk about death," Marion would say when cornered about it. It was something to be kept at bay, the pariah of conversational topics, and not simply because the master of the household was running out of time. The guests at San Simeon, Hearst's castle headquarters 250 miles northward for nearly a quarter of a century, and at Wyntoon, his wooded play park and estate near the Oregon line, were cued to avoid its mention. Doubtless the taboo had its beginnings long ago, in 1919, when his mother Phoebe died. There were a number of times when death had crashed its way past the polite barricades —all in a row it claimed most of Marion's family beginning in 1928, and then again on that Christmas day in 1936 when Hearst's great friend and most loved employee Arthur Brisbane was taken.

But *taken where*? Hearst's keen perceptions about the hopes and fears of men—that same insight that made him a shrewd manipulator of the news—had made him deeply suspicious about immortality. He liked churches and cathedrals, but they could be bought and dismantled and reassembled (and he had bought a number of them in whole and in part) and he found them just as effective in new sites as before. He preferred his surroundings to be cloisterlike not because he felt closer to God in such an ambience but because he hoped that someday he might be persuaded to a firmer belief—by the sight of some long-gone saint on the wing perhaps?

So it was easy to see why Hearst had taken such a fanatical interest in any and all scientific experiments involving geriatrics and longevity. Aldous Huxley had visited San Simeon on one or two occasions, coming away with the germ of a novel. *After Many a Summer Dies the Swan* told of a humorless megalomaniac tycoon who employed scientists at his mountain castle in a "crash program" to discover how life could be prolonged. If Hearst was Huxley's source in creating the character of Jo Stoyte, he was repaid for his hospitality to Huxley by a rare instance of unkindness. But the preoccupation with survival, the setting, and the megalomania were accurately recorded.

Ambrose Bierce, the acidulous Hearst columnist and dark-omened author of the nineties, once said of his employer, "Never just, Mr. Hearst is always generous." Now as he lay dying, the well-paid secretaries, house staff, nurses, and well-subsidized family members, both Hearsts and Dourases (Douras was Marion's real surname), gathered around their benefactor. The Dourases who came and went that night were few, winnowed down by death over the years. Although Hearst had been older than all of Marion's relatives except her father, who was just ten years Hearst's senior, through a regimen that had included regularly taking the baths at Bad Nauheim, restricted intake of alcohol, and—lately—the ministrations of heart specialists, he had survived all but Marion's sister Rose, Rose's daughter Pat, Marion's beloved nephew Charles Lederer, son of her late sister Reine, and Marion herself, who would live only another ten years. Probably the Hearst line was sturdier. It was certainly more careful. Hearst had lost none of his five sons, although one of them would follow him in seven years, and his indomitable wife Millicent would live on and on.

Some of those on the scene had arrived earlier in the week. The top management of the Hearst Corporation, Richard Berlin, Jacob D. Gortatowsky, and Martin Huberth, had come to see their "Chief" quite unexpectedly. At least Marion had not been forewarned. Hearst was still on his feet part of the time when they got there. He would walk about the upstairs rooms with Marion at his elbow between sessions in a rocking bed, a device believed at the time to help poor circulation. Whether these men had come because Hearst's doctors believed the end near or whether they were summoned by Hearst is unknown. Certainly they attempted to discuss with him the future of the publishing empire.

Once the men were in the house, Hearst had appeared agitated nearly all of the time. The arrival of his second oldest son, William Randolph, Jr., the most powerful publishing figure among his boys, failed to relieve his anxiety, and for Bill, the circumstance of having to confront the old man at death's door with the urgent matters of the corporation, paramount among them the question of what to do to eliminate Marion from any control, could only have been a painful ordeal. Bill must have been haunted by the memory of Marion smiling at him across the table over countless dinners in California, Mexico, Europe, and even Africa. In the past, he seemed to have liked her genuinely, but along with his brothers he had been lectured in gallantry toward his father's mistress. It had become an obsessive topic with Hearst once he knew that his remaining life might be measured in weeks or days. And Marion's doubts about Bill's loyalty to her had become painful conviction by that final night.

The other sons began to arrive. Their father had had an accident, a stroke, while being shaved by his lady barber in his bathroom (he had an old-fashioned barber chair there). Bill gravely shook hands with each one: David and Randolph, the twins born to Millicent Hearst in 1915 just before their father's alliance with Marion had been formed, and then George, the eldest, but passed by as heir to the publishing empire in favor of Bill because George's gift for spending money and enjoying life far exceeded his business capacities. George immediately sought out Marion to pay his respects and offer what comfort he could. A man with his father's sensual appetites to an exaggerated degree, he was chronically overweight and in matrimonial difficulties. But Marion never once had put him down because of his weaknesses. Her loyalty to those who loved her was total and redemptive. This would make her shock more staggering when all the sons but George cut her dead immediately following their father's death. "They turned on me like vipers!" Marion said. But George would not, ignoring his brothers' advice to stay away from Marion. The other four sons found her illicit role in their father's life a handy implement in their self-righteous disavowal of her. Despite her many generous acts in their behalf, it was easy to dismiss her as a woman who had been paid handsomely to sleep with their father. Just as a small example of her role as their intermediary in the past, Marion had sneaked more than one of them up the back stairs to Hearst's rooms when he had ordered the staff to deny them entry.

As young men, the Hearst sons had shared a real camaraderie with Marion and called her "Daisy," a pet name given her by Constance Talmadge, who now had joined Marie Glendinning, a petite former actress and Marion's sponsor on the stage, in standing by Marion during those most difficult hours of her life. Constance was probably Marion's closest friend, much closer than any of Marion's sisters had been. Like Marion, she had come from a family dominated by women. Along with two of her sisters, Norma and Natalie, she had become a leading lady in silent films. Norma had possessed the sober beauty of a Dresden china figurine and always had seemed incapable of really enjoying the rewards of the great fame and wealth that were hers for over a decade. According to Anita Loos, Constance or "Dutch," as she was called by her friends, once had suitors as celebrated and as varied as Irving Berlin, Richard Barthelmess, and Irving Thalberg. In her own memoirs, Miss Loos writes that "the boy genius Irving Thalberg used to pace a Beverly Hills sidewalk night after night, his gaze fastened on the light in Dutch's window. And where was Dutch? Having left her lamp burning to make Irving think she was studying a script, she sneaked out the back door to join a movie clique that spent its free time in clowning. Dutch only wanted to be where the laughs were." So Constance was a soul sister to Marion, a kindred spirit who would be needed when Marion's world collapsed—as it surely would—at any moment.

Marion's own clownish nature, her outrageous parodies of friend and foe, and her ebullience in general had had a tonic effect upon Hearst throughout their years together. Before his final illness, when Marion was not so dedicated to getting through her crashing boredom, Marion and Hearst were very much alike in the simple joy they took from just being alive. They were *now people* long before the phrase held any special meaning. With Constance and Marie to sustain her, Marion made a valiant effort that final night to revive a spark of her old self before stupefaction finally set in. She sat beside Hearst in the terrible quiet of his room, forcing herself to recall and laugh about old memories. She was not even sure that he could hear her when she began, holding his hand and dredging up tales of Flo Ziegfeld, of being shadowed by gendarmes in Paris, of losing a gold watch he had given her in a snowdrift. His eyes were closed, his breathing shallow, and he seemed to be dozing, but then Marion would strike some richly humorous vein of memory and Hearst would smile faintly. When at last he seemed to be sleeping, Marion was afraid to stop talking. "I had this funny feeling," she said later, "that if I stopped, then he would stop—you know, breathing. I just kept rattling on for a while. But he was still alive when I left the room. I watched his chest and I knew."

Lights blazed all that night and "the Beverly house," as the stucco villa was called by Marion and Hearst, had some of the forbidding gloom of a Wagnerian set. Especially at night, the windows seemed like apertures and it looked far more like a fortress than a home, but that was the taste of the man. Hearst had lived the life of an old French king, paying lip-service to democracy in about the same way the Bourbons had looked into the muted anguish of the peasants. He would be leaving an indelible mark on his country's history—his power had been enormous; his life-style so contemptuous of the ordinary God-fearing American monogamist, his legend would haunt a string of writers from his minions and admirers to satirists such as Huxley.

And below the death suite, his court had gathered in a kind of dread fraternity, waiting for the end and watching the lady of the household insulate herself from what was happening with liquor. "Booze," as it was labeled in Marion's mid-twenties show-business argot, seldom made her undesirable company. Now her drinking was a grim, fascinating encore performance for the men gathered there. None of them could have been surprised. She never had carried liquor well, but she persisted, often to an embarrassing degree. And by now her brain had got used to this regular assault upon it, repeatedly had thrown back the enemy—insensibility—and, perhaps as compensation, usually had made her wit even sharper than when she was sober.

This night was an exception, and an understandable one. Marion was drinking neat scotch in quantities that suggested she really was hoping for unconsciousness. Halfway through that interminable night, she turned to her friend Marie Glendinning, whose own affection for scotch was formidable. "I shouldn't be drunk tonight, Marie," she said, but Marie patted the hand that held the glass and told her, "You need it, darling. Drink up."

Marion, who had held out until the last possible moment in her insistence that the doctors had to save Hearst, now was letting the drinks take over because Hearst had said three words before her final vigil at his bedside: "Stop the bed." Marion had known what that meant. It meant simply that Hearst had given up to death and wanted that foolish rocking device stopped so that he might die peacefully.

That Hearst now was dying in the home of his mistress was
a far more scandalous fact in the East among Millicent's crowd
than it was in the film community where it was happening. The
last humiliation for his wife would be the one that would cut
most deeply. Yet it stemmed from an old sorrow, an accommoda-
tion of years ago. Hearst had defied public morality and opinion
then and he had got away with it through sheer audacity,
through a *noblesse oblige* he had insisted was his through many
years. Hearst's image even had been enhanced by his liaison with
Marion to some members of the film colony.

This view of their affair had less to do with local permissive-
ness than with Marion's own public image. She had no known
enemies, unless you counted one or two members of the Hearst
hierarchy who saw her as a potential threat to the publishing empire. She was "a good woman," famous for her charities and
denied marriage because of Hearst's decision never to abandon
his wife totally. Among Marion's friends, it was believed that
Hearst had tried many times to get a divorce from Millicent, but
she adamantly had refused—something difficult to believe in
light of his connections and influence in the state of New York
where she lived. (Hearst was a nearly pure example of post-
Victorian duality. With Millicent, he had moved with real society as dutiful husband and father; with Marion, he had moved
with those who amused him. But he managed both without sub-
terfuge, down front and center on the world's stage. He never
had courted favorable public opinion, in fact at times had seemed
to be courting calumny and taking a perverse satisfaction in it.)

Nephew Charlie Lederer was among those sitting with Marion during that long night of waiting. By midnight, fatigue had
caught up with everyone, the tension palpable, conversation dangerous. It was around that hour when Charlie was sure he overheard one of the Hearst sons answer Marion's inquiry about his
well-being with an unexpected outburst: *"Why should you care,
you whore!"* One of Marion's omnipresent nurses swore later
that she, too, had heard the remark. Whoever said it, it would
have been unforgivable except that Marion did not seem to hear
it or pretended not to. Her fear that night was too overwhelming
to penetrate, even by an offense of such magnitude as that.

And fear was an unusual emotion for Marion. She had been
a woman who was famous for her daring. Life for her—before
Hearst's last few years of invalidism—was not meant to be simply endured and if she seemed to have been in quest of an elusive

goal, it was Joy that she sought. Sometimes it was caught for a few delicious moments during a boisterous frolic around the pool at San Simeon, when for example famed screen lover Rudy Valentino began strutting around with one hand on his hip and his other hand limp and fluttering in an outrageous parody of the man many men in America thought him to be; or when Marion was riding the roller coaster at Venice Amusement Park.

It was not merely death that frightened Marion now. She had spent nearly a lifetime keeping Hearst comfortable, laughing and joking with him and often being an enchanting hostess in one of the castles he kept improving for her as chatelaine. But with Hearst gone, what could she possibly do with her life? Her fears for the future were visible in her eyes and in the occasional shudders that convulsed her. Hearst had provided for her in every way except in preparing her for his likely departure in advance of hers. He had given her no instructions in how to live without him because, until nearly the end, he somehow imagined that he could outwit death.

Their life-styles, as in marriages of long standing, had blended. He had taken something from hers, a great deal in fact, and she had taken enough from his to leave her rudderless when death caught up with him. Much of Marion's exuberance and zest for life—always bubbling beneath the surface even when subdued—was to die on that day in mid-August. She was only fifty-four.

In the gray light of dawn, Marion appeared haggard and near collapse. The sons and the Hearst executives had gone to bed down the slope in the guest house. Dr. Eliot Corday, Marion's physician, tried to persuade her to go to her bedroom where she could be sedated. She roused herself to fight the suggestion. Marie Glendinning then proposed that nephew Charlie, who had gone home around one A.M., be sent for. Everyone close to Marion knew that Charlie was her favorite person after Hearst. "Charlie can talk her into it, if anyone can," Marie said, and Dr. Corday agreed.

Charlie Lederer was awakened around six in the morning when his wife, the actress Anne Shirley, told him that he was wanted at the Beverly house. Close friend and frequent traveling companion to Hearst since his school days and a brief career as a Hearst reporter, Charlie was distraught over his friend's imminent death and what it would do to Marion. The only son of her sister Reine who had died in 1938, he had inherited some of his aunt's love of the ridiculous, but both Hearst and Marion had taken special pride in his more serious side—he had become almost as successful a screen writer and *farceur* (*His Girl Friday*) as Marion once had been as a screen star, and entirely on his own. ("You can't say the same for me," Marion would say a bit wryly.)

Urged along by Charlie, Marion was led to her bedroom between six-thirty and seven A.M. "I can't sleep," she protested. "W.R. might need me." But Dr. Corday promised that if Hearst awakened and called for her, he would have her on her feet "in two seconds flat." Marion consented and then changed her mind, then again consented and this occupied the better part of half an hour until finally the doctor got her into bed. With her back exposed as she pressed her face into the pillow, Dr. Corday gave her a strong barbiturate by hypodermic injection. Within minutes, she was deeply asleep.

Later, there would be published rumors of a conspiracy on the part of the Hearst sons and executives to drug Marion in a desperate move to get her out of their way when death came. Since Dr. Corday worked as an associate of Dr. Myron Prinzmetal (Hearst's specialist), a suggestion to him from the Hearst side might have been carried out. But her state of exhaustion gave the incident equal, if not stronger, justification. Adding an oddly humorous note to the drama—and unintentionally on her part— Marion later would insist that Dr. Corday had given her the injection by stealth, when she was "stooped over to pick up a telegram from the floor."

Around nine-thirty that Monday morning, one of Hearst's day nurses entered his room to find him in a spasm of coughing. He seemed to be choking on his own mucus. The woman rushed out of the room to find a doctor. Although he was a man who feared death with a consummate passion, perhaps because his strongest faith was in himself, there was no living creature at his bedside at that moment except his dachshund Helena. She had been moving from room to room in the Hearst suite, upset by the commotion in the house, and just happened to be in the bedroom.

There was a flurry as nurses and doctors converged on the master suite, and Floretta Mouser, who had been Marion's night nurse for three years, came to the hall doorway of Marion's bedroom to see if she could determine what had happened. Mrs.

Mouser was more companion than nurse, although she did have to support Marion when she walked because of those undependable legs. The nurse would sit through most of her nightly vigils while Marion chattered about her *Follies* days or her career as a Metro leading lady; only rarely would she talk about anything but her dwindling family and her working days. Sometimes, Mrs. Mouser and Marion would watch the late-late movie on television. Marion had come to believe that TV had supplanted the movies as the public's favorite diversion. Then occasionally she would read a mystery—in snatches, and mulling over aloud the possibilities of who had done it, often over a drink. "Theater people are like that when they're not working," Mrs. Mouser commented some years afterward. "They stay up all night and go to bed at dawn."

When Mrs. Ann Davis, the day nurse, arrived, Mrs. Mouser was sitting upright in a bedside chair. She was exhausted by the tensions of that night but she was far too worried to relax. "I think Mr. Hearst is very bad," she told Mrs. Davis.

"You haven't heard?" Mrs. Davis asked. "Mr. Hearst is dead. I saw them bringing him down just now as I came up the stairs."

The Hearst sons had been summoned from the guest house, and executives Berlin, Huberth and Gortatowsky had joined them as they walked silently into the master bedroom to look upon their father one last time. Then someone had proposed that an undertaker be called without delay. There is no doubt at all about the dispatch with which the body was removed from Marion's home. Alive, Hearst was there out of his own will and choice, but the unprotesting corpse was something else.

Marion slept through the early morning, unaware that a hearse had been sent for. The vehicle pulled into the courtyard slightly more than an hour after Hearst had been pronounced dead. The body was taken to Pierce Brothers Mortuary in Beverly Hills, embalmed at once and put into an expensive bronze casket. Early in the afternoon, it was airborne, on its way from Lockheed Air Terminal in Burbank to San Francisco for the funeral and burial services.

Charlie Lederer was the first of Marion's family to return to the house. Probably if he had known how soon Hearst's death would follow the difficulty of getting Marion to bed, he would not have bothered to drive the mile or two back to his own house. When he started up the stairs, Richard Berlin appeared at the bottom and shouted after him, "You're not wanted here." But Charlie ignored the remark and continued on.

"Don't go into Mr. Hearst's room," Berlin warned him—this being a few minutes before the hearse arrived—and Charlie turned and said, "I'll go anywhere I damn please in this house."

Charlie hurried to Marion's room, where she was still in her drug-induced slumber. He couldn't bear to tell her himself what had happened, so he asked one of her nurses to find Dr. Corday.

"I asked where he was," Marion said to a reporter later that day, "and I was told he was dead. His body was gone, whoosh, like that. Old W.R. was gone. The boys were gone. Do you realize what they did? They stole a possession of mine. He belonged to me. I loved him for thirty-two years and now he was gone. I couldn't even say good-bye."

Then she asked that Helena be brought to her room, and she sat for a long time holding Hearst's dog and singing snatches of an old tune:

> Little old lady in a big red room,
> Little old lady in a big red room . . .

II

Friends began to gather around Marion, joining Marie Glendinning and Constance Talmadge. They came singly and in twos and threes to sit with her in the parlor across from what had been Hearst's exquisite wood-paneled library, rising two stories high and the only room in the house approaching the splendor of San Simeon. Files in the library already had been sealed by a court deputy at the request of the Hearst estate. The breakdown in relations between Marion and the Hearst empire which Hearst had feared and attempted to prevent was now a reality. Home delivery of Marion's complimentary copies of the Los Angeles *Herald* and *Express* was stopped on Monday morning before the funeral plans had been announced in San Francisco.

Marion's sister Rose, Rose's daughter Patricia (married to television's *Dagwood*, Arthur Lake), Charlie Lederer with his wife Annie—all the immediate family she had—came by that afternoon, but not as a group; and Marion, who was extraordinarily close to her own family, was too numb to take much comfort from their presence. Those friends who came were nearly all from the film colony: Mary Pickford; columnist Hedda Hopper, a woman of intense loyalties and equally intense peeves who would broadcast Marion's most personal decisions during the next decade; Lloyd Pantages of the movie theater family and once a guest of Marion's and Hearst's on a junket through Europe; his sister Carmen Pantages Considine; Kay Spreckels, married to Adolph Spreckels and a few years later to become the last Mrs. Clark Gable; silent star Norman Kerry and his wife Kay English. And then there was Cobina Wright, Sr., a woman of considerable pluck and dignity and, like Mrs. Spreckels, spunkily defensive toward Marion during this testing of loyalties. Mrs. Wright, a former society leader in New York, was even then doing her syndicated social column for the Hearst press and had been not only a close friend to Hearst and Marion, but to Millicent as well. "I didn't care at the time what the Hearst family would think of my visiting Marion," Mrs. Wright recalled. "She needed her friends, and I was one of them."

There was a steady stream of delivery wagons from local florists coming up the winding drive. At one point, there were three such small trucks in the cobbled U-shaped courtyard. The housekeeper saw that only a few were kept—in rooms not used by Marion, since she hated cut flowers because they reminded her of funerals, of which she felt she had more than her share. Most of these tokens of sympathy were dispatched to local hospitals, including her own Children's Clinic into which she had poured something over a million and a half dollars.

No one told Marion that she could not go to the funeral, but she was a woman sensitive to the emotional atmosphere around her. Excepting George, who had asked if there was anything he could do for her, the Hearst family had let the door slam shut after the coffin had passed through. None of her close friends even mentioned the possibility of her going to San Francisco, where the services were to be held. "Why should I?" she asked a reporter who had come to the house. "Why should I go through that kind of dramatics when I had him alive all these years?"

Louella Parsons, her ample body swathed in black silk, paid Marion a brief sympathy call. She alone seemed to be unsure about Marion's intentions regarding the services. "I didn't tell her a thing," Marion said later. "I let her figure that one out for herself." But her presence was painful and—in her "widow's black" —a needless reminder to Marion both of "the dramatics" she wished to avoid and of the obvious fact that Louella was still very much a part of the Hearst publishing family, while she had been banished in a most ungracious fashion.

By this time, Marion and Louella were like members of a large family who find they really don't care much for each other and assume company manners when together. This change in their relationship—so contrary to the sisterly closeness of the early years—was a convenience for Louella, who could say in all honesty from then on (to any Hearst executives who might ask) that she didn't see much of Marion anymore.

A number of the friends consoling Marion that afternoon believed that her long affair with Hearst was "the romance of the century." If they were referring to dollars spent (tens of millions), the flamboyantly romantic settings (Arthurian down to the knight's armor standing in the corners at San Simeon), the possessiveness of Hearst and his near manic jealousy, or its longevity, perhaps they were right.

But as with most love affairs of any duration, there was considerable self-deception present. Marion would sit down within the year with a journalist named Stanley Flink and attempt to recall the details of her life as America's most durable mistress. When discussing the death of Thomas Ince and the rumor that Hearst had shot him, she would say that Hearst had been "the most innocent, naive, kindest person that you'd ever want to meet in your life. He wouldn't have harmed anybody," and within the bounds of her experience, this was close to the truth. Despite the veneer of sophistication she had acquired over the years by putting notables at their ease in the castle and in her own beach palace, there was a sentimental streak in Marion (Irish perhaps?) that responded to Hearst's projection of himself as a man of good-will and near-cloying sweetness. But she was forgetting the one or two occasions when Hearst had detectives following her (when he was in the East and was convinced that she was having an outside affair) and she was pretending to have been taken in by his agreeableness whenever he was with those whose company he enjoyed. After weeks of sitting before Mr. Flink's tape recorder recalling what memories she could and inventing those she could not, she agonized over having told too much about Hearst and became afraid that she might have done harm to his memory. The taping sessions were stopped and the project with Mr. Flink quietly terminated.

Hearst himself was often quite candid with reporters and

was impatient with anyone who suggested that he was benign. In
1935, he told a writer to beware of tranquillity. "It proclaims the
toppling-over stage," he said. "It is the sleep that precedes dissolu-
tion. . . . About the time anybody really desires tranquillity he
gets it permanently—in death." And there were a few—those
who had been Marion's confidantes and recalled an element of
fear in her of Hearst—who would lend authority to a belief that
her life with Hearst was not nearly as tranquil as she painted it
in those self-deluding memoirs.

But Hearst did want to be liked. He wanted to be loved, and
as a man who attacked life's problems with all the fury of a hur-
ricane, he was not satisfied until all those close to him conceded
that he *was* lovable. Many friends at San Simeon and Wyntoon
never once saw him lose his temper. Orphans not only made him
weep, but they would be supplied with food, clothing and, often,
an education. Animals, especially dogs, were to be looked after
and protected from harm.

When Marion's mother had died in 1928, Hearst got Marion
on the phone at her mother's Beverly Hills home and calmed her
down a little by asking if he could be a "mother" to her. Marion
thought that his gesture was beautiful, and he was being perfectly true to the image he had of himself as Marion's Galahad,
but he had not always been so kind in his dealings with Millicent,
with his sons when they had upset him, with certain of his employees, or with a few political figures who had riled him. It was
almost as though Hearst was atoning for sins past in his behavior
toward Marion, her family, his favorite writers such as Louella
Parsons and Adela Rogers St. Johns, and his key executives.

John Randolph Hearst, the son least involved with Marion,
had flown out from New York with his mother. Millicent was
supported through the funeral and graveside ceremonies by her
sons. She carried herself with her usual dignity, and there were
some who would criticize this "performance"—those who believed that Hearst genuinely had wanted his freedom. Perhaps he
did. He certainly went through the motions—for Marion's sake.
But there is a strong possibility that Millicent knew otherwise,
and that whatever bitterness had existed between the couple was
buried with Hearst. A mostly absent husband had become a dead
American whose place in history must have redeemed for Millicent much of the humiliation she had endured earlier. The charade was over.

Marion remained in the seclusion of her bedroom much of the time, but she emerged once to say, "Let me know when the funeral takes place. I want to say my prayers." One of her friends recalled that she had told someone whom she knew to be friendly with Millicent, too, "Please tell Mrs. Hearst not to forget to wear her widow's weeds."

There were 1200 mourners inside San Francisco's Grace Cathedral near the summit of Nob Hill and nearly as many curious onlookers outside. Flags were flown at half-mast in New York City, where Hearst twice had run an unsuccessful race for mayor, although in one of them he had been the victim of fraud at the polls. His obituary in *The New York Times* ran to three pages.

Reporters and photographers glanced anxiously at the hundreds of Hearst friends getting out of the two-block-long line of limousines. A photo of Marion Davies dressed in black as she reached Grace Cathedral certainly would make the front pages. But the newsmen looked in vain and had to content themselves with less dramatic shots of the mighty American figures arriving for the services: Former President Hoover, Governor Earl Warren, Bernard Baruch, Arthur Hays Sulzberger, L. M. Giannini, Joseph Schenck, Roy Howard, and Colonel Robert McCormick.

Hearst always had seemed a character larger than life. Now he was entering the mythology of the nation. "The Chief" had been highly regarded by many of the men in his farflung publishing enterprises and feared by a few who had witnessed some sudden Hearstian fit of displeasure, but the general public had ambivalent feelings about him. In the public mind, he was the man who had fostered—possibly even invented—"yellow journalism," the sensational headlines and mud-slinging exposés to bolster circulation. To some film scholars, to American liberals who had not got to know the man as had Thalberg, Mayer, Selznick, and other movie moguls, and to many intellectuals, including a few who had been his guests, he was also the supreme vulgarian hero of *Citizen Kane*—a ruthless and eccentric egoist, bent upon power and carving out a feudalistic empire along some remote coastline of the United States. There was a question in many minds as to whether his mistress, Marion Davies, was his victim or his cherished, very public inamorata. He was, of course, all of these things and, in years past, Marion was both willingly caged in the most gilded environment conceivable—and a bubbling, free spirit withal.

It was not surprising that, with Hearst's death, a kind of gauze had dropped between Marion and reality, and it was not to be lifted perceptibly during those last ten years of her life. She seemed to be marking time, simply enduring each day—an impression shared by most of the few friends she still saw—former screen star Eleanor Boardman, both friend and tenant, who had made Marion's gatehouse into a charming French maisonette, Marie Glendinning, Eileen Percy Ruby (once Douglas Fairbanks's leading lady), Constance Talmadge and Aileen Pringle, whenever one or the other was in town, Mary Pickford, Kay Spreckels, and the Kerrys. To those few surviving members of her family, she seemed slightly more animated, but then she had always saved a reserve of energy to give to her family, since after Hearst they always had come first.

Sometimes she would seem very nearly her old self when she was visited by someone she had not seen for a long time or whose company was especially diverting. Such guests might be an old intimate from her working years in Hollywood like Dorothy Mackaill, the ex-Ziegfeld girl from Yorkshire who had made the fun-loving "other woman" a specialty in late silents and early talkies, or the "world's richest girl" Doris Duke, who had a healthy contempt for entrenched society. Then again, and frequently for a time, it was an amusing new friend, Speed Lamkin, a Southern writer brought to her house by Cobina Wright. Lamkin filled Marion's parlor and swimming pool with lively male companions who could make her laugh. And there was, of course, handsome sister Rose, whose sudden outbursts of ill temper remained a disruptive element in Marion's life until the end despite Rose's close affection for her sister. Rose's daughter Pat and nephew Charlie were in and out of the Beverly house almost daily.

These loyal friends and family remained steadfast, but they hardly composed a crowd even if they all attended the same dinner party, which they did not. Marion, who had so loved people and parties and who had given so much of herself—in energy, loyalty and enthusiasm, not to mention her charities—to her home community of Hollywood, was to become a recluse. Death had set her free, but a guard stood at her threshold—the conditioning of nearly three and a half decades.

Few members of the film colony made any special effort to contact her. Although she had sponsored, through a word to Hearst or to some other film executive, careers as diverse as those of Louella Parsons and Sonja Henie, she rarely had gone to others' homes. People had come to hers or to Hearst's, and Marion was not known or thought of as a guest but as a hostess. Perhaps there had been a certain *cachet* to visiting the castle when Hearst and Marion were entertaining trainloads of guests every weekend, and there may have been more than a few patronizing sightseers on the guest list like Cecil Beaton who would consider its staggering pack rat display of European plunder a high watermark in tastelessness. But Hollywood is a heartless community—unavoidably no doubt because it is made up of so many ego-driven souls—and Marion Davies bereft was not a very gay prospect. She soon would be out of vogue, moving into Hollywood legend along with the dead Hearst. It would be hard to fight, the social ostracism of belonging to a golden past.

III

Marion Cecilia Douras was born at six on a drizzly Sunday morning in her mother's bedroom in Brooklyn, January 3, 1897. The Cubans' struggle for independence from the despotic Spanish colonial government was just beginning, the sinking of the *Maine* and our involvement seventeen months away. Young publisher William Randolph Hearst's brash *Morning Journal,* which he had bought when it was failing and had built into something astonishingly new—a newspaper with much of the excitement of an accident happening right before the reader's eyes—was clamoring already for some American action against the Spanish atrocities. But a more personal drama got the headlines on that particular Sunday. Novelist Stephen Crane, whose *Red Badge of Courage* had been widely published and serialized, was feared lost at sea between Jacksonville and Havana. Attempting to see real war finally at first hand, Crane had boarded a converted tug, the *Commodore,* and it had gone down in heavy seas.

It is unlikely that Bernard J. Douras, whose interest in literature and current history was confined to what he read in the papers, caught up with the Crane saga until the next day, when Crane and other survivors turned up at Daytona. A husband whose straying from home had begun to alienate him from his family, Douras was taking all the precautions he could afford to ensure his wife's survival. "Mama Rose," as his small, peasant-bodied spouse was known to family and friends, had the services

of both the neighborhood midwife and the family doctor, Dr.
E. D. Ferris. Marion was the Dourases' fifth and last child.

At forty-three, "Papa Ben" Douras was only middlingly successful as a Brooklyn lawyer. Little is known of his background
except that his origins were French or Irish, depending upon
which of Marion's stories is to be believed, and he was a graduate
of Columbia University (class of 1878). Marion was to supply
so many versions of his background that Charlie Lederer suggested that Douras was descended from a soldier with the Spanish Armada, who fell off the boat into the Irish Sea. He had met
Rose Reilly in his late twenties and had married her before the
Charles A. Reillys, a couple forever embattled during their years
together, could look into his credentials (they separated soon
after their daughter's marriage). What appeared to be authentic
biographical details were supplied by Marion a dozen years after
his death. Then she said that he was born in New York City on
April 14, 1853, the son of Daniel and Catherine (McCann)
Douras, natives of Ireland. But as late as March 1951, Marion
was utilizing the free space accorded her in the Hearst newspapers to "clarify" her father's murky ancestry in what was also
assumed to be bonafide biographical material:

> The *Bon Homme Richard,* the famous ship of John Paul
> Jones, was originally named the *Duc de Douras* after the
> family of Marion Davies, which had figured for centuries
> in the history of France. It was later changed to the *Bon
> Homme Richard* after the fictional creation of Benjamin
> Franklin.
>
> Some time ago, Marion Davies received a letter from
> Victor Hugo-Douras, a cousin who was secretary of the
> French Embassy in Washington. This letter told her that the
> Douras chateau in Bordeaux was unoccupied. He told Mar-
> ion that if she claimed and restored it, she would be entitled
> to the title that went with the castle.
>
> Marion loves America far too much to think of living
> in France. But she still looks forward to visiting this chateau
> when she goes to Europe again. Tennessee Williams said
> after leaving her house after dinner: "She makes up for the
> rest of Hollywood."

This foolish invention appeared in a full page article intended to keep Marion's name and legend alive at a moment
some months before Hearst's death when she felt that Hollywood

and her public had forgotten her. It was Hearst's way of humoring her, but the only honest element in these paragraphs is the *non sequitur* of playwright Williams, who had been won over—ironically—by her lack of pretension. She shared Becky Sharp's practicality, if not her cynicism, and, remarkably like Thackeray's heroine, "curious it is, that as she advanced in life this young lady's ancestors increased in rank and splendour."

Marion's background was the one area where she would lie shamelessly, perhaps because she had heard too often how Hearst had lifted the entire Douras family out of middle-class obscurity once he had met her. He had achieved this practically overnight, and Marion tried to forget that she had been born in Brooklyn's Eighth Ward, a neighborhood bordered by the much more desirable Prospect Park section on one side and piers and warehouses along with waterfront saloons on the other, these being only a block away from their narrow four-story brick house on 59th Street.

Marion took after her father in her sensitivity about her past and in her preoccupation with "appearances." When she was a woman and a part of Hearst's world, she would accept almost any evasion or "covering story" from Hearst (from whom they spilled as naturally as breath) if anyone in her family or she herself got into trouble so that, whatever it was, it would come out "looking right." This habit has created obvious difficulties for her biographer and scrupulous care has been taken to avoid printing invention as fact. As for Papa Ben, in those early days he disguised his mediocrity at law by wearing expensive, carefully cut clothes and a derby hat, which gave him considerable dignity, but made him appear older than his years—a disadvantage in his womanizing since he was expected to spend money that properly should have gone toward the maintenance of a wife and five children (one son, Charles, and three daughters besides Marion).

Marion's fertile memory insisted that the Douras home was not next to the waterfront but in the exclusive Prospect Park section. She also said that their move into Manhattan was necessitated by a fire which consumed their house and which, she said, had been set by her brother Charles, who was playing with matches.

One thing that is certain is that the Douras household was a matriarchy. Mama Rose was much like the woman Marion came to be—willful and insecure, and her children became specialists in reading her moods. A solid, large-bosomed woman no more

than five feet two inches tall, she suggested strength to her brood
of five children whose father had become a visitor. Her insecurity doubtless came from feeling unloved after Papa Ben made
it evident that motherhood had put her on a pedestal in his mind,
where she permanently would remain.

According to Anita Loos, the Dourases were straight out of a
novel by Colette. Mama Rose was determined that her daughters
would be schooled in the ways to please a man, as well as the
perils of romantic love. The latter was to be avoided as a trap for
the simple-minded—girls behind Woolworth counters who had
no better prospects. When Marion won the love and devotion of a
man three times her age (at eighteen), Mama Rose felt that her
precepts had been justified. When Marion owned five homes, one
of them having one hundred and ten rooms staffed by thirty-two
servants, Mama Rose attempted to retrieve some of her early
Brooklyn life-style—sewing machines to do patchwork quilts, occasional hours in the kitchen cooking up favorite recipes—but
the effort was overwhelmed by a tidal wave of heirlooms, art
treasures, and furnishings of an elegance beyond her wildest
imaginings. She retreated into a silence, which had become her
chief defense against Papa Ben's philandering back East, and
some of Marion's friends mistook her for one of the housemaids.

Edith Wharton and Henry James were writing about the
privileged classes of New York City from opposite sides of the
Atlantic, but they both agreed that it was not only an age of innocence and smug complacency, but a time of cold, calculating
social climbing. With the quiet prodding of Mama Rose, the two
eldest daughters, Reine and Ethel, abandoned the middle-class
neighborhood that had been their retreat from frequent tours of
the vaudeville circuits and with their mother took a small house
south of Gramercy Park. Papa Ben remained behind in Brooklyn,
wanting neither to give up his small clientele nor to live in tighter
quarters with Mama Rose. Marion and her sister Rose would
return to their father and Brooklyn for their public school education, although Marion attempted to make a joke of her Brooklyn
origins ("Showgirls always come from Brooklyn," she was to
say). While she rarely referred to Brooklyn as anything but her
birthplace, public school records show that she attended Brooklyn schools, except for an interval when she was in Chicago,
through her first year of high school.

Gramercy Park was fashionable and relatively safe. The

green square itself was surrounded by a high iron fence and locked to all but those who lived nearby—an attractive island of trees, sheltering benches, and concrete walks where babies could be sunned without fear of violence. Papa Ben had expressed some concern about the family of women living in Manhattan, and likely that was why the younger children were turned over to him at school age. Holdups and gang fights had become epidemic in New York by 1900 and there were streets in lower New York where men walked in pairs only and "decent" women not at all.

This initial step away from their middle-class life in Brooklyn was entirely engineered by the Douras women, the rent shared by Reine and Ethel. Ethel had become established as a music hall singer with a kidding sense of humor on the broad side, while Reine was a brunette with more delicate features equally at home in soubrette roles in musicals, operettas, or in vaudeville. Both of them toured on the Keith-Orpheum circuit at various times, and each of them achieved some fame professionally. The sisters had changed their surname to Davies after Ethel had seen the name on a billboard advertising a real estate firm in Queens.

The distaff Dourases' home just south of the Park was in a block that was predominantly upper middle-class, but it was Manhattan where Mama Rose conceivably could help launch her girls into successful liaisons; social mobility through show business careers was common in the early 1900s. There were dozens of examples to encourage the Dourases—Fanny Ward was on her way into the British aristocracy and, in 1903, showgirl Millicent Willson would marry Hearst. Their home south of Gramercy Park would be symbolic of the Dourases' social position throughout the years of their increasing affluence. The homes of the established rich were all *north* of the Park. The Douras women always would be within walking distance of genuine society and sometimes sitting across the table from it, but never members of it. When Marion became Hearst's consort in 1916, one of the penalties exacted by society for such a relationship would be that they would have to remain outside it.

Beginning with her fifth year of life, Marion and sister Rose were shuttled back and forth between the Bedford-Stuyvesant section of Brooklyn, where Papa Ben had settled, and Gramercy Park. Bedford-Stuyvesant was then an upper-middle-class area of rows of Victorian houses. It was socially as proper as the neighborhood where his family had moved, but it was not Manhattan and it only suited Mama Rose as a safer place for the girls to go to school.

The personal fortunes of Bernard Douras were not advanced appreciably by having less family to take care of. They would not be until he became a magistrate through the courtesy of Hearst in 1918. There were his several girlfriends to look after, usually one at a time, and the temptation to spend his time with political cronies in the Tammany machine, drinking and playing poker, was irresistible. As his earnings increased at his law office, so did his losses. And when one of his clients paid a bill, it was usually an event to celebrate. Actress Marie Glendinning, known on the stage as Mary Ashley and one of Reine's closest friends in the theater, recalled one such occasion. Douras came calling on his family in Gramercy Park one night so very drunk that Mama Rose told him to "Please get out of my sight." When he waved a huge roll of bills—some $1500 or so—it gave her a start, but she insisted upon his temporary banishment.

To Marie, who was a house-guest, and Reine, Mama Rose's outburst was more extraordinary than Papa Ben's inebriation. Mama Rose was usually silent around her husband since their move from Brooklyn. Reine winked at Marie and took her father's arm. "Don't worry about Mama Rose," she told him. "We'll help you to the spare bedroom," and the two ladies gave him a hand in getting into bed. By the time they got his shoes off, he had passed out.

"Come on," Reine told Marie. "We'll roll him for a few bills for Mama Rose," and she proceeded to remove about $250 from her father's pocket. Then she went to her mother's room and said, "Papa Ben wanted you to have this."

On the following morning, Papa Ben came down to the dining room in a rage. "Some low member of my own family rolled me last night," he announced in incredulous tones, "for *two hundred and fifty dollars!*" Both Reine and Marie were shocked to learn that Papa Ben had known the contents of his pockets down to the last dollar. Mama Rose was aggrieved to discover that her husband had not made her a gift of the money—a typical Douras roundelay of chagrin and disenchantment.

A family tragedy reconciled the family briefly, but it did not last. The drowning of their only son, Charles, happened in the boy's fifteenth year while he was boating with a friend near Saratoga Springs. Charles was on summer vacation visiting his grandfather Reilly at the time. Repeating a family account of his sudden death, Marion said that his body was found "with grass in his mouth and mud in his hands" after three weeks of poling the lake near the Reilly home. Mama Rose often had called her son "a little horse" because he loved to chew on grass. Her silences as her marriage deteriorated may have been accentuated by her inability to convey in any meaningful way a feeling of love for her children. Sentiment embarrassed her and this was to bewilder little Marion, who was from infancy full of love and a need to be cuddled, touched, and reassured. After Charles's death, Mama Rose tried to express a mother's sorrow by surrounding herself with her lost son's photographs.

To Papa Ben, the boy's death was a blow from which he never fully recovered. The father had counted heavily upon his son's companionship. With that prospect gone, his visits to the family in Manhattan declined. When Marion and Rose were through with public school, he would give up maintaining a house altogether and move into a Bronx flat.

Marion could not recall her brother in life, but she was told by Mama Rose that as a small child she had been lifted up to look at him in his coffin and she had asked, "Sleep?" Later, both she and Rose would acquire Charles's stammer as something that would please Mama Rose. Possibly it did, but Marion's own insecurity, her never knowing whether her mother was even listening to her complaints, reinforced it. "Your brother Charles loved you and Rose," Mama Rose had told her daughters, "and he would haul you around in his wagon and tell everybody, 'D-d-d-on't t-t-touch m-my ba-ba-babies.'"

When this tragedy and its sorrow had passed, life became far more congenial for the Dourases. Throughout the early years of the new century, Reine had had a succession of suitors, few of whom measured up to the kind of husband and protector she and the Douras family needed. Getting her married properly had become a family concern. In addition to wealth, her future husband had to have some tolerance for living the sort of family dormitory life the Dourases seemed to enjoy. Marion was to call the brawling, tightly knit clan the "Sanger Circus," after a family of vaudeville acrobats. Reine finally accepted George Lederer, a major theatrical producer who had done one great success, *Belle of New York,* and was soon to do another, *Pink Lady,* which featured a song destined to become a popular standard, *Beautiful*

Lady. Lederer also had leases on two Chicago legitimate theaters, and his real estate holdings were to expand right after his marriage (his second). The Lederers soon became the parents of a boy whom they named Charles after Reine's brother. Reine gave up her career during her pregnancy and, following Charles's birth, they went to live in Chicago with two sons by Lederer's first marriage, Maitland and George, Jr.

If Reine Lederer's marriage was in the Colette tradition as planned by Mama Rose, it differed in one significant respect. The Dourases, despite their many battles, were as clannish as the Forsytes. Even though George Lederer would be divorced from Reine in 1912, he would continue to figure in her professional life and he would be buried at sister-in-law Marion's expense and in the Douras mausoleum at Hollywood Memorial Park. Papa Ben had regretted the abandonment of the perfectly euphonious name of Douras when his daughters went into show business one after the other, but he had the satisfaction of seeing Mama Rose laid to rest under the granite inscription "Douras" before he joined her there, as well as assurances from Marion that she never would legally abandon her baptismal name and that all the family would be buried together. "Family" to the Dourases apparently meant anyone who had married into it, including his progeny. (Lederer's son Maitland was to die in his thirties from a war-induced illness and wind up in the Douras tomb; likewise, two of sister Rose's husbands.)

While Ethel and Mama Rose managed the rent on the Gramercy house, sometimes with the help of Grandmother Reilly, who lived across the river in New Jersey, it soon became clear that Reine was living far more comfortably than they could manage in Manhattan even with the help of a fulltime housekeeper. Grandmother Reilly, who made her own living and a prosperous one as a slum landlord in Manhattan (crossing the river by ferry with a "boodle-bag" hidden beneath her skirts to collect her rents), had a reputation for being miserly. It was a strain on Ethel and Mama Rose managing things by themselves and Reine saw no reason why they should when she was living in an enormous apartment on Chicago's "Gold Coast."

Within a few months of Reine's departure for Chicago, Mama Rose, Ethel, and little Rose were on their way to join her. Rose was an object of Mama Rose's special concern ever since she had suffered a knee injury as a toddler. This injury had been inflicted upon her by a demented nurse they had employed when first in the Gramercy house. The woman would become enraged whenever little Rose declined to obey her, and she would pick up the child by the heels and swing her round and round her head. Why the nurse wasn't discharged at once must remain something of a mystery.

Having servants in the household from childhood on made it relatively easy for Marion to adapt years later when there would be a staff of thirty or more for her to supervise. Marion had been left behind in the care of the housekeeper, Emma Mowrer. Papa Ben had agreed to keep an eye on her as well as the Gramercy house. Marion was mischievous and she already was making Mama Rose extremely nervous. Her mother was unwilling to run the risk of allowing her wildness to come to full blossom in what they considered to be a wild city. It was a mistake. Despite her rascalities and her tomboy predilections, she was still the baby of the family and she sorely missed her mother, even though it is doubtful that Mama Rose missed her. Marion had got used to sleeping at least part of every night with Mama Rose. She would crawl in and put her arms around her mother's neck, earning for herself the sobriquet of "Mama's suckling pig." But it is hard to avoid seeing in Mama Rose's behavior a strong element of disinterest in her children. She had turned over Marion to Papa Ben because her daughter was a nuisance—in the way most precocious children are. She had abandoned her, and Marion was never able to forget it, although she would spend years forgiving it—it was just about the sum of her relationship with her mother.

Under scant supervision, young Marion rebelled and ran riot. She would sneak out of the house and join the "Second Avenue Gang," some juvenile ruffians who roamed the avenues, spilling garbage cans and stealing fruit from stores. Marion was very proud of winning acceptance from that thieving group and joined them in a raid upon a fruit and vegetable market. One of the several parts she would play in her single appearance for Flo Ziegfeld in the *Follies* would be "Miss Chief" on Fifth Avenue, and mischief was in her nature at least until she was forty years old.

When the Second Avenue Gang discovered once that their haul was nearly rotten, they hurried north of Gramercy Park and began tossing the bad fruit at the doorways of the rich. Perhaps Marion was embellishing the tale when she spoke of tossing spoiled fruit against Hearst's door (at 123 Lexington Avenue),

but it is possibly true since he lived part of the time in an impressive marble townhouse in the Gramercy section, which he
had shared originally with his most important editorial deputy,
Arthur Brisbane, before it became his first home with Millicent.
She was carrying their second child.

The fun of the Second Avenue Gang was spoiled by the
arrival of a policeman who noticed Marion's better-made clothes
and took her home. In a few days, she was on her way to Chicago, where she would remain for nearly all of the next two years.

All of this happened in 1907 when Marion was ten years
old and she was very much aware of her reputation for upsetting
the family. It was an unpermissive era and Marion's backside
had stung from Papa Ben's razor strop more than once. Her
teachers found her bright, but poor in deportment. At a time
when Sunday comics were a major amusement, she identified—
so she said—with "The Katzenjammer Kids," which featured two
little boys of fiendish inventiveness. During her first week in
Chicago, she was sent to a local florist by Reine for some decorative greenery and she insisted to the embarrassed clerk she
wanted "maidenhead ferns."

Most of Marion's memories of Chicago were fond ones. She
recalled the wind "howling in" from the lake, but she said she
didn't mind it because she was "tough, in perfect health." She
liked the public way everyone lived in what Edna Ferber described as "glass carbuncles known to Chicagoans as sun parlors." Later at San Simeon, she would spend considerable time
watching arriving and departing guests from her special balcony
overlooking the Esplanade in front of the castle.

While Marion was always fond of Papa Ben, he was missing
during the critical years of her growing up. The Dourases would
be reunited only in the mausoleum built by Marion in Hollywood
in 1928; alive, however, tempers always flared. Mama Rose said
she didn't care for Chicago, but it seems likely that she disliked
being so far from the battleground of New York. Her silent mar-
tyrdom didn't mean very much when her tormentor was eight
hundred miles away. Of them all, only Marion and Ethel seemed
to have what Marion called a "sunny" disposition, and Ethel was
shortly to lose hers for a time following a tragic love affair.

After one of Reine's frequent dinner parties, Marion, Rose,
and their half-cousin Maitland would take the roses from the
table before the maid got to them and peddle them on Chicago's

streets for candy and movie money. Occasionally, they would go up to the box office of one of Lederer's theaters (the Colonial was their favorite) and brazenly inform the cashier that they were "the Lederer children."

Perhaps the marriage was in trouble over Lederer's friendships with other actresses, an occupational hazard for a producer, but midway during her stay in Chicago, Reine decided to return to the stage. Her comeback appearance was at one of the larger revue houses on the Chicago loop.

Marion was taken to the premiere performance. It was not her first visit to a music hall, but it was her very first glimpse of a show from the wings. Irrepressible child that she was, the excitement of the finale with her sister in a spotlight singing a reprise of her big number moved Marion to break from Mama Rose's grip and run on stage just as the curtain was coming down. She stood in front of it and started bowing. Then someone tried to pull her back with a stage hook, but to no avail. She stood right near the orchestra and kept bowing to the audience. While everyone backstage was trying to catch her, she was so delighted with the footlights and the audience that she kept bowing and smiling. The laughter from that Chicago audience was Marion's first taste of an audience response and she loved it.

Mama Rose's nerves were doubtless rubbed raw by her daughters' bravado. In another of Reine's stage appearances, she was required to appear on horseback (she was an excellent horsewoman) during a song number about "sending a post card." Reine and the horse were to move slowly on a treadmill while thousands of post cards rained down. During one performance, the horse slid on the slippery cards and fell; both the animal and Reine escaped serious injury. Around the same time, Marion had led Rose and Maitland in a scheme to steal their way into one of Lederer's theaters (after becoming absolute pests at the box office), and they all had nearly suffocated under a tarpaulin in the lobby where they had concealed themselves until intermission. Then back East at her grandmother's home in Upper Montclair, New Jersey, Marion had taken a playmate, a neighborhood girl by the name of Mary O'Shea, to play in the railroad freightyard, the sort of tragic playground favored by Marion. A freightcar backed toward them and severed a number of the O'Shea girl's toes. Grandmother Reilly shut her in a closet without any dinner, a frequent punishment when in the Reilly home, and Mama Rose soon became afraid to let Marion out of her sight.

Beyond her behavior, Marion had another problem. Whether or not she initially derived the habit from listening to her late brother Charles, she still stammered badly. This impediment, which everyone was to find so disarming when she became a showgirl, was never to leave her. Some of her later reminiscences of her early years would indicate that Mama Rose's withdrawal, brought about by her difficulties with her husband, was taken by young Marion as some failure in herself. "I never considered myself much," she recalled. "Nothing special. I guess I wanted to be liked, but whether I was or not, that's a different story."

Her stammer would plague her in school. She was no scholar and she knew it, but when she was called upon to recite, there were always a few other children who would laugh. Her quick mind and ability to assimilate movie production management and even publishing skills in later years suggest that, like so many children with speech problems, she was handled badly by her teachers. Speech therapy classes were relatively unknown in public schools at the time. As compensation perhaps, she excelled in athletics and played basketball well enough to become a member of a championship team at Public School 93 in Brooklyn. But a girl athlete, a tomboy, was not especially admired around the Douras household. So far as Mama Rose could see, such prowess would not take her very far into a secure future. The problem was discussed with their priest—the Dourases were nominal Catholics—and his suggestion was predictable: "Send her to a convent." It did seem a neat way of making her more feminine, if not docile.

It was the fall of 1910 when Marion began boarding at the Convent of the Sacred Heart near Hastings, New York, where she would remain until she was sixteen. As a young film actress, Marion would tell interviewers that she had been taken abroad by her mother at the age of eight and placed in a convent school near Paris. Her preoccupation with France, even though in fantasy, is of some interest. Her father's lack of any known family background disturbed Marion most of her life. Rather than discussing the Reillys, the grandparents she knew well, she nearly always would invent stories about the Dourases, about whom she knew nothing. In one instance when she asserted that her father was French, she would attempt to give this fact some dimension and significance by telling a writer that Bernard Douras was descended from the Emperor Charlemagne.

Marion was to spend less than three years with the sisters

of the Sacred Heart. Her instincts were far too pagan for daily mass to overcome, but what religion she retained as a woman was instilled in her there. More than just the faith, she was given a discipline she sorely needed. Knowing how to make a bed properly and keeping the uniform she wore (a skirt and middy blouse) presentable might seem prosaic equipment for the long career she was to have as an actress and a companion, but Marion gave the nuns much credit for bringing her down to earth and setting a pattern for some decorum in her life. The sisters had done what Mama Rose had been unable to do and Papa Ben was never around to manage: they had partially civilized the wild child that Marion had been since she was old enough to walk. But they wisely had not broken her spirit, and that adventurous child so feared by Mama Rose (and later by Hearst) was always threatening to reappear and on a number of notable occasions would do so.

As for the church itself, she said that the routine of her family was to take Communion on Sunday and go to confession on Saturday night. Among New Yorker-Catholics involved in show business, it is their custom to go to midnight mass after the evening performance or, when not working, after a Saturday night party. This must have been a tradition of the Dourases. But it was not to last long for Marion. Her attendance in the confessional booth was terminated when an angry priest told her, "I've heard your voice before. I'm tired of you. Don't come back again." She was dismissed because of "too many white and black lies." Marion said she could never think of any mortal sins and had to fabricate a few tales to tell the priest.

While basking in the prosperity brought about by Reine's marriage, Marion and Rose were enrolled in Theodore Kosloff's ballet school in Manhattan. Neither of them possessed any great natural ability, but Kosloff could see at once that Marion had considerable presence upon the stage. Although Rose was determined not to be outdone by her younger sister and finally achieved a certain facility on her toes, she was far more interested in boys than in any stage success. But to Marion, who was two years younger, boys were still simply bullies who sometimes yanked her long golden curls or gave her a frightening shove forward when she was roller skating on their block.

Reine and her friend Marie began keeping a hopeful watch on Marion's development at the ballet school. It was Reine who was putting up the money, persuaded that Marion would learn something invaluable in those classes—how to curb her instinct for upstaging everyone in sight and how to move gracefully whether upon a stage, on the street, or in the parlor. Her eventual success as a ballerina was not regarded as a serious possibility. With her curling blond hair and those incredibly blue eyes that gave her the look of an expensive china doll, Reine was certain that Marion would attract either a producer who would make her a "headliner" or a wealthy patron. Years later, Reine was living in Hollywood at Marion's invitation and sometimes would embrace her younger sister as if to say, "You made it, honey. You made it." But without Reine's help and encouragement, she would not have made it. It was a Douras family trait to look out for one another.

During her boarding school days at Hastings, Marion would attend the Kosloff school on Saturdays when she came down on the train for a weekend at home. Then she would fall into her old pattern of following Mama Rose around. Marion always had liked to have her head rubbed. Perhaps intimate moments like these served to lessen Mama Rose's sense of guilt over having sent her daughter away. But it was only a partial intimacy. Marion was to say that she would have to tell her mother, "Hey! You didn't hit the right spot." And Mama Rose would remain silent and then Marion would ask, "Did you hear me, mother?" and her mother would ask Marion to repeat the question. Mama Rose's mind was usually off somewhere, out of touch. Later Marion came to see that Mama Rose simply had no great interest in her children—a feeling she would assume herself toward the children of others, excepting her sisters', and often prompting her to make elaborate gestures by way of compensating for this "lack" in herself.

IV

Marion saw her first movies in Chicago. They were called "photoplays" by the Edison Company, the firm founded by Thomas Alva Edison, who had invented the American version of motion pictures (a contemporaneous development had occurred in France), and the medium had moved beyond the nickelodeon stage to a serious form of mass entertainment by 1909. Reine's producer husband was watching them with great interest, although Edison was attempting to keep all movies—and their profits—under his control through the patents company established by him and all film players anonymous to keep their salaries low. Sarah Bernhardt's attempt at immortalizing herself in the French-made film of her *Queen Elizabeth* had yet to be seen by important stage producers David Belasco, Charles Dillingham, Charles Frohman, Marion's brother-in-law George Lederer and Joe Schenck, who would inaugurate the star system in American films. So without the lure of stardom, attractive young ladies with show business aspirations were still being magnetized by Broadway.

Ziegfeld had opened his first edition of the *Follies* by the time of the Dourases' return to New York. Lederer competed nicely with his star Hazel Dawn in *The Pink Lady*, and with all the talk of this and other revues and musicals at the dinner table at Reine's, where they were all living except for Papa Ben, Marion became completely stage-struck. Before she could complete her third year with the nuns, she dropped out of school. She told her mother that she had become too self-conscious of her stammer but soon she was attending Kosloff's every day, so it would seem that regular school bored her and neither Reine nor Mama Rose saw any point in wasting more money on a conventional education. It was an indulgent family and Mama Rose thought it best to humor Marion in this. She obviously was upset whenever she had to recite in class, and the family sensed that this contributed to her stammer. Although Marion had shown little interest in dancing as a small child, it was her mother's desperate hope that she might survive long enough as a dancer to reach the back row of a stage chorus line. A teacher friend was asked to drop by Reine's apartment in New York—Reine had left Lederer in 1912 while carrying her second child, although they were still in touch almost daily—and Marion was tutored in vital subjects. Her sketchy education, with Hearst later stepping in as an informal director of studies, was extremely successful. Marion became one of the most articulate leading ladies on the screen—her stammer and the colorful Elizabethan idioms notwithstanding. She knew something about most of the classics and, while she remained politically naive to the end, she was never the "dumb blond" she so often called herself.

Then for a year or so, beginning in the summer of 1912, Marion attended Ned Wayburn's tap-dancing classes. At Wayburn's, the pupils were required to learn "acrobatic dancing" as well, since many vaudeville houses (usually second-rate) featured dancers who could do the "split" (sliding slowly down with the legs horizontal at six and twelve o'clock in relation to the torso and head) and the backbend (in which the spine is arched and the hands and feet are touching the stage). "Double-jointed" young women were considered to be especially fortunate since they could contort their bodies into these positions without risk to the anatomy. Marion herself was said to have been double-jointed according to at least one informant, although this phenomenon, if true, added nothing of any value to her abilities as a performer in the *Follies* or upon the screen.

Marion liked the rhythms of tap-dancing and preferred it to ballet. She attributed her failure to make a professional success of her dancing to her lack of concentration. But she was not about to attempt the rigorous daily practice required because she said it was hard on the system. She believed that was what had killed Marilyn Miller.

While Marion was studying at the Wayburn School, she took time off for a few appearances in the "pony" line of small-time revues and one major musical, a version of Maeterlinck's *The Bluebird*. Her stage career had begun as a lark, which was Marion's phrase for it, but it was certainly a predictable lark. She and Rose had asked Marie Glendinning, who was already a leading actress with many contacts on Broadway, if there was a chance for them on the stage. Marie then contacted an agent, Lee Herrick, and it was all accomplished in one afternoon with sister Reine encouraging the venture in the background.

Marie had established herself as a favorite in New York's theatrical set and she was able to advise Marion about future show possibilities for several years. She was droll and had the ability, which Marion shared, to laugh at herself and her weaknesses, which included men and scotch. A native of a little village on the Thames, her British accent was no small advantage and stamped her at once as a refined type in an era when "class" was very much on producers' minds. Offstage, she was often an outrageous flirt, her favorite word was "naughty," and her capacity for fun infinite. Nearly half a century later, as Marion, who was twelve years her junior, lay dying in a Hollywood hospital, Marie would slip her a tiny bottle of gin, telling her, "I don't think it will matter if you're just a little naughty." Marion would laugh, possibly for the last time, gratefully accepting the gift.

During Marion's brief appearance in *The Bluebird*, sister Rose fell hard for a young man (as she was to do at least a dozen times during her lifetime) and ran off and got married. Marion was not surprised and not present, since this was the beginning of a secrecy in Rose about her male friends that seemed to stem from jealousy. The sisters were no longer confidantes where men were concerned. Within weeks, the marriage was annulled when Rose decided that she could not bear her young husband's presence on an everlasting basis.

Marion had made her "pony" appearances significant stepping stones upward because of her stunning blond beauty. Although pony girls were traditionally only interludes in a production, performing youthful "toe-dances" either in the background or in front of the curtain during a scene change, Marion was noticed and she began to get constant employment.

Mama Rose was quietly pleased, and Marion got warm support from both Reine and Ethel. Sister Ethel was Marion's favorite from her earliest years. She remained more in the background of Marion's life than Reine or even Rose, but within the intimate family group, Ethel was full of a bawdy humor very much like her baby sister's.

In 1913, Reine had become the mother of a girl, whom they named "Pepi." Marion was enchanted with the baby and the child would spend many of her growing-up years with her aunt, moving from Reine's apartment to Marion's townhouse on Riverside Drive and then to California. Pepi's suicide slightly more than twenty years later would be the most distressing incident in Marion's life until the death of Hearst.

Marion made her debut on Broadway with Fred Stone in *Chin, Chin* (*The Bluebird* having folded on the road), and in that summer of 1914, she suddenly emerged from being a tomboyish loner into the frenetic social life of a popular New York chorine. She discovered finally in her eighteenth year that she loved meeting new people despite her innate shyness, and she observed that no one noticed her stammer except occasionally to comment on how charming it was.

Throughout 1915 Marion was busier than either of her elder sisters as she moved from one musical production to the next. She was not terribly ambitious, but she was suddenly very popular.

The transition from pony girl to chorine had happened abruptly. The director on one of the revues had glanced in her direction and his eyes had met head on with that wide-eyed stare, which Hearst was later to describe as like a baby's but which was too frankly challenging to be that innocent. She was tall for that era—five feet five and a half, as tall as she ever would be, and she deprecated her silhouette by saying that she had "toothpick knees," but she was a willowy blond half a dozen years before the slender figure became fashion's ideal. At eighteen, she began to win a certain fame as a first-line chorus girl. She had to turn down at least two shows because she was engaged in another. The name *Marion Davies* began to mean something beyond the fact that she was Reine and Ethel Davies' youngest sister.

She had become by now a peculiar amalgam of insecurity and brashness. As the baby of the family, she still crept into Mama Rose's arms whenever she was blue. She seemed to take criticism with a kind of Brooklyn kid toughness, but she then would rush home and burst into tears. The language used by Mama Rose in her quarrels with Papa Ben and the showgirl vernacular of her elder sisters colored her vocabulary so that she was forever after expected to talk like a sailor unless she was in the presence of someone whom she either honored as an illustrious person or as a stranger. In the presence of strangers she could be reticent and, when engaged with them in conversation, that delightfully shy creature who stammered.

Marion had few pretensions then beyond what Mama Rose had told her was worthwhile—the attentions of a gentleman of means. She placed love and infatuation rather far down on her scale of values, ruling out nearly all the younger men who crowded around the stage door. She had no social ambitions and no very strong drive to succeed as an actress at that early date. She was meeting eligible older men almost every evening and her social circles became more exclusive as her name became better known on Broadway. First, there was Reine's and Marie Glendinning's crowd; then Elsie Janis's; and finally the ultimate salon where the theatrical set met the literati—Frank Crowninshield's.

She was indifferent to the headlines even in the blatant Hearst papers, and salon talk about the war then raging in Europe bored her. Marion always would retain a deafness to conversations dealing with war, inflation, economic depression, or politics. She would get quickly restless with anyone obsessed by diseases or personal health. She was insular and unprovincial at one and the same time. She was broadminded about people and narrow about issues. She could have as easily have supported a Eugene Debs as she would a Warren Harding, depending entirely upon the political views of her companion.

The only small trouble clouding her horizon in those carefree days was sister Rose. Rose resented the special attention being paid Marion despite the fact that she had lost much time and ground by abandoning the stage during the months of her abortive marriage. Inseparable companions during their Chicago days, Rose returned from her elopement and marriage to find Marion being given a contract to appear in Fred Stone's revue. She thought that she had an ally in Mama Rose when their mother burst into tears upon seeing that contract, which their mother was required to sign as Marion was a minor, but Mama Rose signed it even though she told Marion that she was going to frame it as a symbol of her broken heart—a synthetic gesture, according to Marion, that stemmed purely from Mama Rose's Victorian childhood. Rose would return to the stage for a number of other appearances, but she never was able to catch up with Marion's success.

There had been an intense rivalry between Rose and Marion from their earliest childhood. As beautiful small children, they had shared compliments, but when they were in their teens, something a little forbidding crept into Rose's beauty. Rose had then—and would continue to have until her death in her late sixties—the sort of remote handsomeness usually found in highly inbred families such as the Windsors and the Hapsburgs (one of Rose's suitors in her Hollywood days would be Prince David M'Divani). Imagined slights would be numerous in Rose's life and she early had all the signs of being a prima donna without the talent needed to give it license. But she also had the Douras capacity for enjoying life, and when she was not in a pique, she could be a delightful companion.

During one of those prewar summers, Marion had her first and only crush on a boy her own age. They met at the lake near Saratoga near the Reilly place and the young man allowed Marion to towel off his feet when he came dripping from the lake, an act of worship which sent Marion into raptures and the boy's companions into fits of laughter. There is something in this well-lost first love of Marion's that tells much about her character. Despite her eventual success as a showgirl and then as a film

star, she never would believe that she had any exceptional talent
or beauty. Even in retirement when the contrived stories of her
"great failure" began to circulate following the release of the
movie *Citizen Kane,* Marion refused to challenge them and would
tell her friends, "Well, they're right. I was lousy in some of those
epics." She was as near to being self-effacing as any actress who
ever lived despite her eventual critical success and despite
Hearst's successful effort to make her the queen of Hollywood
society, if not of films. Her childlike wish to be liked was to
make her terribly concerned about other people's comfort and enjoyment. This lack of vanity would render her incapable of ever
becoming a fashion leader when great wealth was hers (in her
days in Hollywood, she would say, "Leave that to Lilyan," meaning Lilyan Tashman, who had been in the *Follies* with her and
had become the best-dressed woman in Hollywood) and unable
ever to lose her stammer, and it would give her words the ring
of absolute sincerity whenever she was to ask a guest, "Are ya-
ya-you all right? Ca-ca-can I g-g-get you anything?" While with
Hearst she could be less solicitous, when they first met her lack
of an actress's vanity was one of her most appealing qualities.

Why was her ego so insufficient? None of her closest friends
seems to know. It was apparent as early as her first meeting with
Marie Glendinning. It may have been that, when Papa Ben
abandoned Mama Rose and the family, Marion sensed that she
was somehow to blame. Possibly she overheard her grown-up
sisters discussing the rupture between the parents and learned
that her father was being unfaithful. While infidelity may not be
fully comprehended by a child, it can be assumed that the child
believes that she is being rejected along with the mother.

V

Mama Rose did her best to chaperone her handsomest daughter,
but it was a losing battle. There were places to which Marion
was invited where mothers were as welcome as an atheist at an
ecumenical convention. Marion was having the time of her life
and making money at it (handing her weekly salary to Mama
Rose became a silent form of absolution for any misdeeds).
Looking back upon those early years, she was to say, "I had more

fun on the stage." The theater exhilarated her. It had glamour and excitement and she had no responsibilities.

The chorus line was well down the scale from the featured showgirls, and the chorines were compelled to perform certain menial tasks for such popular beauties as Ina Claire, Gladys Glad, Peggy Hopkins (later Joyce), and Lilyan Tashman—fetching coffee or running to a nearby cobbler with shoes to be repaired. They were also forbidden to watch the stage from the wings, an edict that would get Marion into trouble during her *Follies* days.

Mama Rose would sit in a corner of the dressing room used by the chorus girls and manage to make herself a kind of house mother to that spirited sorority by mothering them all. It was eccentric even in that day for a girl in the chorus to have an omnipresent stage mother, but her producers, including Charles Dillingham and Flo Ziegfeld, humored both of them in their mother-and-daughter act backstage and Mama Rose's extraordinary quietness (not to forget her sherry tippling, rendering her human and fallible) helped take the edge off her presence. While there was some doubt about her finding reassurance there, Marion counted heavily upon her mother's being nearby with her solid breast to lean against when she was melancholy. Throughout her life, Marion was easily moved into a state of sadness that often seemed inexplicable, and those who knew her well realized that her gaiety and laughter frequently masked these unfocused "blues." When the youngest of the Dourases got them—even as a working chorine—she continued to crawl into bed with Mama Rose. When this was no longer possible, she sought the same soothing feeling through drink.

The effect of all this mothering as Marion became a young chorine in demand was to make her seem innocent, in a refreshing way, especially when among other showgirls in a drawing room such as Elsie Janis's. Miss Janis, too, lived with her mother, who was a fixture at all of her parties. Her drawing room would be filled several times a month with actors and writers, an increasing number of them involved in movie work. Miss Janis herself was a major Broadway musical comedy star, terribly patriotic, a kind of female equivalent of George M. Cohan. She worked very hard at her profession of being a top theatrical talent, and went out of her way to advance others whom she considered worthy. Marion was one of them, and Miss Janis told many of her friends that Marion Davies was the most beautiful blonde in Manhattan.

It was in Miss Janis's apartment that Marion was first seen with Paul Block in 1914. Block owned a string of newspapers, the most important being the *Toledo Blade* and the *Brooklyn Eagle*. He was a close colleague of Hearst's, and in 1927 they would buy a Pittsburgh daily together in order to form a solid front against the competition there. Only slightly younger than Hearst and not so physically huge, he was married but maintained a bachelor apartment where he entertained. Both Block and Hearst were captivated by actresses, showgirls in particular. They were the sort of millionaires Hollywood was to reduce to banal caricature in a thousand "backstage" films, always much older than the run-of-the-mill stage door johnnies and sending floral and jeweled tributes in overwhelming quantity.

And it was a confused era for America. The country had awakened from its complacency at the turn of the century as Europe became an enormous battlefield that August. Hearst and many others spoke of President Wilson as a "traitor," and it was principally to these critics that Wilson addressed his frequent remarks about America's "non-involvement" in the European conflict. Wilson knew, of course, that America was involved, increasingly so, in what was happening in Europe, but the pressures against our sending American troops, chief among them that faction of the press represented by Hearst, kept the President from committing our armies until the last possible moment.

Although Elsie Janis would use the American flag as her personal banner in the years just ahead, her parties were crowded with lovely young ladies whose heads were filled with little plots on how to get a part or a wealthy industrialist, rather than whether the young men their own age were going to march onto troop ships in the morning. Both Hearst and Block knew this, and the Janis parties, more than most, composed an island removed from the cares of the world outside; for Hearst, it was an early equivalent of what San Simeon was to represent in another half dozen years or less—*escape*. And it was this insular quality of showgirls, as well as their beauty, that appealed to both publishers, as it did to many other millionaires from Samuel Insull to Colonel "Bertie" McCormick. They made ideal wives, for they usually refused to even think about political matters or famine or wars. Just being around them gave these mighty gentlemen's brains a vacation.

In Marion's case, her failure to take any interest in world affairs was compensated for in a number of delightful ways. She looked younger than her years and her stammer made her seem to be the perfect damsel in distress. There was a strong ambivalence in Marion regarding wealth. She never had been truly deprived as a child, but she was now being exposed to the parlors of the rich and her goals had been raised accordingly. Unconsciously, the years of prodding by Mama Rose to seek physical comfort and status rather than love had turned her into a "gold digger," but not an obvious one. She was much admired in the salons where she was partying and Block was only one of many men attracted to her. He had made the right overtures and there had been numerous quiet dinners. She had visited his "bachelor apartment," but, deciding that she wanted marriage and not a "relationship" (Block still had his wife), she probably realized that she had gone about as far with Block as she should go. Marion had begun to feel that Mama Rose's philosophy had its limitations.

Occasionally, she would turn up in Frank Crowninshield's drawing room, where the conversation was brighter and more involved with the world's political breakdown as armies slammed across borders in a dozen places. Usually she entered Crowninshield's on the arm of Paul Block. Crowninshield had introduced his *Vanity Fair* Magazine in 1914 as a continuing monthly commentary on America's culture, its preoccupation with the very rich, and its fads. His world embraced nearly all New Yorkers of any consequence and his parties reflected the biases of his magazine. Block was a more frequent guest than Hearst, possibly because his opinions about the war were not so unpopular, and there were writers Anita Loos, Dorothy Parker, and Robert Benchley, and actresses, including Marion's new friends the Talmadge sisters, Norma, Constance, and Natalie.

Unlike Millicent Hearst, who had become a leader of New York society in the ten years or so of her marriage, Marion was not interested in the social possibilities of a permanent liaison with a millionaire. She never would utilize such opportunities in the years ahead, although there would be many of them. Mama Rose's silences in those several mansions of Marion's in California might have been due to her profound regret that her daughter failed to (1) become Mrs. Hearst, and (2) become a

society figure to reckon with instead of the gayest hostess in
town. In many ways, Marion was a sensualist. She responded
with naive delight to the tactile experience of rubbing rich
wools, silks, and satins. And, too, there was something in her
that made her feel at home with servants. Perhaps there were
domestics among her Irish forebears; likely as not there were.
One of her friends suggested that she came from a long line of
scrubwomen and coachmen. From the first, she had an intuitive
sense that informed her how far she might go in making household staff feel like "family," and she never felt their presence
an intrusion. In the years ahead, she got to know a good many
servants as friends and, in her years of bereavement, she was
to spend much of her time with them. Only one of her staff
ever spoke of her "pulling rank" on them and putting them "in
their place," and that was when she had been drinking too
much and the employee was attempting to curb her.

With this early preference for well-staffed households, Marion knew that she could not settle for a salaried husband or
lover. It made her wary of anyone under forty. Even if a young
man qualified because of wealth, she would dismiss him out-of-
hand because of his youth. Such a case was Angier Duke, who
was Doris Duke's cousin and who used to be a stage-door johnny
hanging around Marion. She considered college boys from Ivy
League schools to be especially obnoxious. Of them all, she disliked Yale boys the least and this because of an out-of-town
tryout fracas involving Yale students, which sparked Marion's
temporary admiration. She was appearing in a revue starring
Gaby Deslys and they opened in New Haven. The "Yalies" took
a dislike to the play and brought to a post-premiere performance
rotten tomatoes, eggs and other decaying matter. They threw it
at the stage while Gaby Deslys was up front and she took the
brunt of it. She ran offstage weeping with tomato running down
her face. The pony girls, of which Marion was one, were screaming. It must have been pandemonium, and it got worse before
it was brought under control with the Yale boys removing seats
and throwing them into a pile. A firehose finally flushed them
out into the lobby and outside. One of these Yale undergradu-
ates was John W. Hanes, who came backstage, smitten with
Marion, but got a quick brush-off. "We left the stage door . . .
with our noses up in the air," she said, ignoring all the apolo-
getic Yalies. Later, a Wall Street banker and White House
aide, John Hanes would be called in to help the "Committee,"

a group of key Hearst executives who attempted to bring order out of the chaos that followed the discovery that forty years of Hearst's reckless buying sprees had undermined his publishing empire.

Despite their separate domiciles, the Dourases were agreed about one thing—their daughters' futures. It seems evident that they had carefully groomed their four daughters, all known publicly now as "Davies," to be kept or married by men of substantial means. Even Ethel was no exception. Less beautiful than her three sisters although she bore a strong resemblance to Marion, men found her personality magnetic. But she was destined to have no more luck with them than would her sister Rose. Ethel was to get involved with a wealthy Chicago manufacturer who would be stricken with a fatal heart attack when his wife denied him a divorce—clearly a man with none of Hearst's stamina.

Mama Rose's "heartbreak" over her youngest daughter going into show business was as much a part of the family theatrics as Papa Ben's "approval" of Hearst as Marion's companion when Marion brought her new friend home to meet her father—in Papa Ben's bachelor flat in the Bronx. But there were bounds to Mama Rose's ambitions and there would come a time when Hearst's largesse would embarrass her. Precious stone-encrusted bracelets or strings of matched pearls on her birthday or at Christmas would provoke her to say, "It's simply too beautiful for me. I'm just plain old Mama Rose. I can't wear anything like that." Her silent vigils, usually from a corner, were to become a slight embarrassment to her daughters, but not especially to Hearst, who knew and appreciated an eccentric when he saw one.

At eighteen, Marion did not yet consider herself a woman, but she knew that she was free. Mama Rose felt helpless to restrain her, and she was more than a little pleased that her daughter was considered so attractive. Standards of beauty had changed when war came to Europe. Already in America women were being hired in defense plants and volunteering for war work. Less restricting clothing was essential. The bustle was out for good as well as the swollen, corset-induced bustline. Marion was in the vanguard of a new kind of young woman, soon to be emancipated from more than her bustle. She radiated vitality and wholesome good cheer along with a latent (later realized) flair for parody and comedy that would keep her working for the next twenty-two years. To Marie Glendinning, she was "a fairy-like creature," and a little later Frances Marion would liken her to "a beautiful blue butterfly with dew on its wings," the blue referring to her enormous eyes, which she often matched with gowns and hats of the same hue. To nearly everyone who met her, she seemed as effervescent as champagne and it would seem completely in key with her personality when she developed such a taste for that beverage.

As she moved ahead from one revue to another in 1915, her only non-party nights were those when she made excuses and stayed home to bring Mama Rose up to date on her conquests. She showed up frequently at parties where theatrical folk such as Douglas Fairbanks, the Barrymores, Anita Loos, and Walter Pidgeon mingled with publishing tycoons Hearst and Condé Nast. If she came as Paul Block's date, he did not seem to mind her flirtatiousness. She was usually surrounded by admiring men telling their favorite jokes with Marion urging them up to the punchline with little bursts of throaty laughter. Her stammer made everyone want to protect her from possible ridicule. This effort was invariably successful, although there was one professional instance when no one could save her. In an early revue, she was given one line to speak: "And I'm the Spirit of Spring." She had agreed to make the effort because the costume for the part was, in her own words, "absolutely gorgeous," blue tulle with sequins catching the lights.

Marion hurried home to Mama Rose. She was terrified of making a fool of herself, with good cause. "I don't think I can say that line because I stutter," she told her mother. Mama Rose corrected her. "You *stammer.*" "The same thing," Marion said, and on opening night she took a glass of champagne to find the strength to deliver those six words to a sold-out house. When her music cue came, she moved quickly to the scenic staircase, looking magnificent as she slowly descended to stage level. Then she began to speak for the first time on any stage. "And I . . . I . . . I . . . I . . ." The roaring laughter of the audience was terrifying to her, the premature curtain an act of mercy.

Hearst was in the audience. He was following Marion's career with more than casual interest by this time. Quite often he was drawn to protect or shield someone with an affliction or weakness. Anyone who developed a chronic ailment while in his employ was guaranteed a lifetime sinecure; alcoholics were tolerated and seldom fired. And, of course, he had had a problem with his own voice since manhood, doomed as he was to an alto range.

It was during the run of the revue *Stop! Look! Listen!* that the affair with Hearst was begun, and not, as generally believed, during the *Follies,* by which time he already was known as Marion's steady beau. Charles Dillingham produced the show and Irving Berlin supplied the music, one of his earliest—and not very memorable—scores. One of its stars was Eileen Percy, whom Dillingham had seen on a recent magazine cover by James Montgomery Flagg. Joining her in a big production number appropriately called "The Girl on the Magazine Cover" were three other showgirls: Pickles St. Clair, Justine Johnstone, and Marion.

Miss Percy and Marion became friends backstage, with Pickles joining them frequently at parties around New York. Miss Percy was to win a more rapid fame than either of her two friends, chiefly as Douglas Fairbanks's leading lady on the stage, and she would leave for California and the movies within less than two years. Her first film would be with Mr. Fairbanks—*Wild and Woolly*—written by Anita Loos and directed by John Emerson, its title expressing succinctly Miss Percy's feelings about the western half of the continent.

In later years, Marion chose to forget that she was featured in a revue as early as 1915, since it would have made her only fifteen years old by her calculations, but to a greater extent out of deference to Hearst. Their friendship was supposed to be secret that year of their meeting—his wife Millicent was expecting, and they were hoping for a girl—and so Marion went on record as saying that they met during her stint in the *Follies.* This was widely believed to be the *Follies* edition of 1917, but careful research shows that Marion was in the 1916 edition.

Hearst would sit in the second row of the orchestra section with his publishing crony Paul Block nearly every night of the run of *Stop! Look! Listen!* It was not a very good show, but he was fascinated by two of its cast: Marion and Justine Johnstone. He knew that Marion was considered to be Block's girlfriend, so he made no overt show of his interest in her. Instead, he sent a note backstage asking Miss Johnstone, who was soon to win considerable celebrity as the most beautiful showgirl in New York, to have dinner with him. Miss Johnstone, who kept abreast of the news and political figures in the country, turned to Marion and said, "I can't go out with Hearst. Why don't you go?"

The dinner must have gone very well. During the following week, they met again at a party. Marion had entered the room on Paul Block's arm, but that did not seem to bother Hearst very much. He stood a little distance from her early in the evening and watched her do what she did best: she had a clear vocation for making people feel good. Hearst's personality was quite the opposite; most people viewed him with apprehension, if not alarm. His reputation as a man with a lust for power, the dimensions of his wealth, and his physical size were often overwhelming. He was roughly the shape of a huge bear, with sloping shoulders and suits which one friend said he had sent out to get rumpled. As Marion was preparing to leave the party, Hearst followed her into the bedroom where she had left her wrap. "I'd like to see you soon," he told her, and then handed her a glittering object, folding her fingers back over it.

There was an odd sort of command in his voice even though his remark had been one of a hopeful suitor. Hearst was then fifty-two years old, married to Millicent for twelve years, and, for the first time in his life, feeling impotent as a political force in the country. The Democrats wanted no part of his pro-German and anti-British sentiments, and the Republicans were giving him the cold shoulder as conservatism, which he actually abhorred, was being pitted against intervention in a world war, which he considered potentially disastrous. He no longer needed the façade of a "happy" marriage with his political fortunes in steep decline. Although he had to remain near his family hearth as dutiful father and husband for some months, he was ripe for an affair.

Like a number of other rich Americans born in the nineteenth century, Hearst was the son of a man who had fought his way up from near-poverty to immense wealth. George Hearst had won and lost a couple of fortunes, but finally he had been lucky or astute enough to be holding the deed to one of the richest silver mines on the Comstock. He began buying land in California and Mexico, along with mines in Montana. Soon he was a millionaire several times over. His wife, Phoebe, came from a family already established in San Francisco society. She endured his rough exterior and saw that their home was elegant and well-staffed. Young Willie Hearst grew up in several town houses in San Francisco where the gardens were the pride of the neighborhood. There was

no battle between the parents over who would see to Willie's upbringing. It was simply turned over to Phoebe, George conceding
that her manners were more refined than his own, her love of
beauty somehow appropriate to their son's nature. The boy seemed
to have inherited his mother's taste for beautiful surroundings
and his father's drive for power. George Hearst was sent to Washington as a senator in the 1880s when Willie was in his teens. It
was about this time that the youth began spending much of his
allowance on young ladies. His father encouraged it since the ex-
penditures served to allay his concern over his son's manliness;
mother Phoebe allowed it because she already had been accused
by others of having raised a "mama's boy."

Marion was used to getting trinkets from male admirers,
but she sensed that this was something more. She glanced
sharply at Block when she rejoined him in the vestibule, wondering if some agreement about her had been made between
the men during her brief absence. She was afraid to open her
hand in the car while going back to her West Side flat for fear
of Block asking what she had there.

Marion was ready to abandon Block but she wanted to be
ladylike about it. He was the right age but certainly the wrong
man. With some success, she tried to convince herself that entan-
glements with young men her own age (she would soon turn
nineteen) were a waste of time. She would attempt to compensate for this practical outlook in the years to come by throwing
together couples she believed were compatible and mooning like
a young girl over romantic attachments. All of that sentiment
would smack more of a sense of failure and lost opportunities
to her friends than it would of hypocrisy.

The gift was a Tiffany watch, Marion noticed, as she studied it alone in her room at home. It was far more expensive
than anything Block ever had given her. Block had been generous—there was extensive evidence of that. His money compensated for his physical unattractiveness. Shortly after her
Broadway debut, sixteen-year-old Dorothy Mackaill accepted a
dinner invitation from Block. She had just arrived from England and had been thrust at once into the front line of Ziegfeld's chorus on the Amsterdam Roof. The following night, she
received two dozen red roses with a one hundred dollar bill
tucked in the center. Miss Mackaill panicked and never went
out with him again, but obviously Marion had accepted such
tokens as "thank-you's" for her company, knowing that her ac-

ceptance meant there would be more companionship expected.
And Hearst's interest in her did not abruptly terminate her relationship with Block. Before she had a chance to see Hearst again
to thank him, she was taken to Boston for the out-of-town opening of *Stop! Look! Listen!* She and Pickles St. Clair were swinging down a Boston street, screaming and laughing, and when
they got to the hotel, Marion discovered that the watch had
fallen from her wrist into a snowdrift. She and Pickles spent
an hour or more in the cold sifting through mounds of snow.
Pickles, believing the matter would be of small consequence to
Hearst, told Marion to call him up.

Since Marion had not yet thanked Hearst for the gift, she
couldn't bring herself to phone him about her loss. But Pickles
insisted that if Marion did not, then she was going to call.
Within twenty-four hours, Marion had another watch (not quite
as elegant as the first) by special messenger.

With the European war going so badly for the Allies, and
Hearst persisting in his admiration for the Germans and advo-
cating America's nonintervention, he became an embarrassment
to nearly all of his friends. In late 1915, Hearst was one of
the few Americans to visit Germany, where he bathed in the
carbon dioxide waters at Bad Nauheim, said to be good for the
heart, as he had developed a slight murmur. When he returned,
Millicent gave birth to twin sons, Elbert (who later changed his
name to David) and Randolph. The unexpected arrival of *two*
more sons, bringing his brood to five, appeared to have forced
Hearst into a reevaluation of his life with Millicent. It was
immediately after this that he took Marion to dinner during the
run of her revue.

Marion was the ideal companion to a Hearst fleeing from
the ignominy of a public aroused by his continuing interest in
Germany, and from a family situation that threatened to trap
him against his will. Like many showgirls, she was just not
interested in politics, and—to her mind—wars were politics. It
was all a great mystery, like death itself, which it was better
not to dwell upon. Likewise, she had no interest in a possible
family. She did not sit and rattle on with him about how many
children she planned to have when she left show business.

Since they had just met when it was being finished, the
exquisite Gothic chapel Hearst had built into his new *American*
headquarters building late in 1915 was not intended for her use.
But within months she was told that she could make use of it

for worship any time she chose. It was only a short distance
from there to the studio apartment he maintained for their
rendezvous in the Beaux Arts building. The chapel took up two
stories in a corner of his proposed skyscraper at Columbus Circle, a project later scaled down by the steel shortage caused by
the first World War. It was torn down in 1966.

Marion rarely, if ever, used the chapel. By the time Easter
came around in 1916, Mama Rose wanted to get Marion away
from what she considered a bad situation. Hearst was not only
married, but there was a great splash in the newspapers over
his large family of sons. She decided to take her showgirl daughter with her to Florida for the holidays.

A visit during that Easter of 1916 to one of the most perfect palazzos in America gave Marion her first real taste of the
splendor that money could buy. Rather than turning her attention away from Hearst, it probably intensified it. The palazzo
was owned by James Deering, of the farm equipment family,
who was an old family friend of Mama Rose's and Reine's.
Deering, a man in his late fifties, had moved into his massive
white coral mansion only that winter. Vizcaya, as it was named,
was the passion of his life; it was over two years in the building
and twenty-five years in the collecting of its French, Italian,
Spanish, and early American furnishings, decor, and works of
art.

Like Hearst and George W. Vanderbilt (*Biltmore House in
Asheville*), Deering was not an important collector on the level
of Mellon, Kress, or Widener. His conversion of a thirty-acre
mangrove swamp into one of America's showplace homes was
an act of enormous pride and a unique achievement in personal
comfort. He was not so much interested in owning masterpieces
as he was in creating one, as Vanderbilt had done and Hearst
was about to do. His home would be his monument, and—while
he lived—his joy.

Mama Rose called nineteen-year-old Marion "my baby" in
Deering's presence, and he set her up for that week in "The
Little Princess's Room" on the second floor. Architect-designer
Paul Chalfin had done the suite in black marble with pink satin
draperies and a bedspread of pink ostrich feathers. Although
Mama Rose had known Deering for several years after having
met him through her father at Saratoga Springs and she knew
that he had an eye for young ladies, she pretended to be un-

aware during her visit at Vizcaya that her most attractive daughter was anything but an incidental guest brought along at her own request. Reine knew Deering socially from her Chicago days. Marion would invent a romance between Mama Rose and Jim Deering, as unlikely a duo as one could imagine. Marion was to say that Mama Rose refused to leave Papa Ben even though Deering proposed to her many times, wholly forgetting that her father already had moved out of their home.

Like its later western architectural cousin, San Simeon, Vizcaya had been fitted around its antique archways, ceilings, walls and fireplaces. Its very perfection probably troubled Marion, since she said that she was afraid of scuffing floors and soiling relics. For her, it had the feeling of a museum. Whether Deering was moved by Marion's presence to indicate that he might be interested in her can only be surmised. He certainly knew of her friendship with Hearst since he was on the closest of terms with Mama Rose and she must have confided to him some of her anxieties about that relationship. A curious memory of that visit surfaced in Marion's mind over thirteen years later and indicates that Deering was fixed in the same compartment as Hearst in her mind. Minutes after Hearst had left a party gathering in the Assembly Room of the castle, the phone rang. Marion answered it, hung up with a sigh, and then, as she walked toward their private elevator, she turned to tell her guests (among them Frances Marion, who remembered), "The Little Princess has to go up to her tower now." A summons from Hearst often made her sniff with annoyance. He was breaking up the party just as Deering did unfailingly on her first visit to his home.

She found Vizcaya far too stuffy after her high life in New York. The Great Boom had not yet hit Miami under the inspired management of George Merrick, and for any excitement outside the mansion walls one had to go to Palm Beach. Deering had activities programmed inside his estate, with everything, including breakfast, taken at a certain hour. As a foretaste of what was to come in the years ahead as other millionaires settled in the neighborhood, Deering had installed a large land-locked boat carved of marble to adorn his front lawn.

Deering was also something of a snob. Even those in the social register were not invited to Vizcaya unless they were his cronies or their families. He did not have teas or other gatherings of fashionable acquaintances. Marion soon realized this and saw that she was going to have to seek her own amusement. Even as early as that, she needed lively people around herself and, so far as she could see, the Dourases were the only guests at the villa that Easter. Two or three times, she climbed over the wall surrounding the estate and made her own way to Palm Beach. The third time she got caught. She went to the resort, attracted by tales of secret sin among the rich, who had been drawn there at the turn of the century by Henry Flagler and his hotels, the Royal Poinciana and the Breakers. Mrs. Jules Widener recognized her background immediately. "You're from the New York stage, aren't you?" she asked Marion. Marion was impressed to be meeting a member of one of Philadelphia's oldest and richest families, and Ella Widener was just as pleased to be able to indoctrinate a charming young girl in the amusements of the rich. Mrs. Widener loved to gamble and it was not unusual for her to drop ten or twenty thousand dollars in a night. She haunted the gambling casinos and was often seen there in the early morning hours, having breakfast of champagne with ham and eggs. She was also curious about Jim Deering, who never appeared in any of the gay places of Palm Beach. She told Marion that she would like to meet Deering, but Marion demurred, telling her that he was such an old fogey, she would not be happy with him. When Mrs. Widener persisted, Marion agreed that the Wideners could come to Sunday evening supper.

Then Marion returned to Vizcaya and forgot all about the casual invitation she had extended. Sunday evening came, and Jim Deering unbent a little and invited a few other early Miami settlers in for sandwiches and ice cream. Marion remembered that they were mostly old and stiff in manner. Suddenly, the butler walked in and whispered noisily to Deering that the Wideners were in the hall. Deering wanted to know by whose invitation, and when they seemed to have invited themselves (as Marion was too frightened to speak up), Deering asked the butler to tell them that he was not at home.

On another occasion when Marion "broke jail" at Vizcaya, she went to stay at a theatrical hotel in Palm Beach where she shared a bath with Ann Pennington, whom she soon would join as a *Follies* showgirl. The hotel stood at the edge of a country club with a pool where young ladies of the theater mingled with the daughters of the rich.

There were bicycles for hire at the club, and one day Marion was invited by Gene Buck, a song-writer for Flo Ziegfeld,

to go off on an excursion along the shoreline. Buck must have
had some assurances from Marion that she was temporarily
free of any romantic entanglement that might embarrass him,
since the Hearsts had come to Palm Beach with their newly
born sons. But he could not contend with the "accident" of
bumping into Hearst almost immediately. Buck spotted a maroon
limousine coming down the hill in their direction and said, "That
looks like Hearst's Caddy."

Marion swerved her bike wildly into the curb and spilled,
lying for a few moments with her feet in the air, her bloomers exposed along with some leg and ankle. Before Buck could
reach her, the Hearst vehicle passed her, slowed, and stopped.

Hearst leaped out of the back seat and rushed over to her.
He pretended not to recognize her and Marion was bewildered
until she saw a dignified woman in a large white hat with veil
in the back seat looking in her direction. It was, of course,
Millicent. "May I help with this accident?" Hearst asked, while
Buck played along with the charade for Millicent's sake.

The rivals met, Marion working desperately hard at her
role of stranger and Millicent coolly appraising her. "We'll have
a doctor take a look at you," said Hearst, asking his chauffeur
to stow Marion's bike in the trunk and nodding a good-bye to
Buck.

Millicent was older than Marion by fifteen years, far more
worldly, and she would have no part of the role of the martyred
wife. She even retained a sense of humor about her rival. Once
when Charlie Chaplin was having lunch at the Hearst apartments in the Clarendon, he told Hearst, "the first time I saw
you was at the Beaux Arts Restaurant, sitting with two ladies.
You were pointed out to me by a friend." Then Chaplin began
to falter. "Well, if it wasn't you, it was someone very much like
you. . . ." And Hearst said with what Chaplin described as a
twinkle, "It's very convenient to have a double." At this point,
Millicent had graciously terminated the discussion by saying,
"Yes. It's very convenient."

That evening, Marion had recovered from her spill on the
bicycle and was seated at a casino roulette table with Ella Widener. A casino staff member appeared at Marion's elbow and
handed her a thick envelope. When she looked puzzled, the man
made a gesture toward some red portiere drapes hanging on
either side of an alcove. Standing in the unlighted alcove was
Hearst, who nodded to her encouragingly. The envelope con-

tained a thousand dollars. Ella Widener saw it and asked, "What have you got there?" Before Marion could answer, Mrs. Widener had taken the whole amount and, reckless as usual, had put it on one number. She lost, and the money was gone. When Marion looked again toward the alcove, Hearst was gone, too.

When she returned to Vizcaya, there were frequent phone calls from a "Carl Fisher" to Marion. Jim Deering teased her about it, and Marion—as she was inclined to do when really cornered—lied and claimed that she was as mystified by the calls as anyone. But there was no doubt in anyone's mind that the caller was Hearst.

It is quite likely, too, that she must have known that Hearst was going to be in Palm Beach, but she must have believed that meetings would be next to impossible because of Millicent's presence. She did not yet appreciate the depths of Hearst's determination. The "Carl Fisher" phone calls suggest that meetings were planned and accomplished in Florida.

VI

Hearst's fascination with showgirls was different from Block's. He was not seeking a temporary companion. There were at least two cogent, if not laudable, reasons for this. His ambitions for high public office were still shelved for lack of opportunity, so the need for a façade of an untroubled domestic life was unnecessary for the moment. And he had long known one thing about Millicent. The ex-showgirl had gone social with a vengeance and had become involved with proper New York society to the exclusion of all else but the upbringing of their sons, which was largely in her hands. Much of their early compatibility was gone.

Marion was unconventional from childhood and this was to become a kind of bohemianism when she reached maturity. It appealed to a similar quality in Hearst, who wanted to experience all of life and not just what was permissible, and who cared nothing for what others thought of him. As a young man, he would walk down the street eating from a bag of candy and munching on some fruit from the other hand, giving the candy to the first group of children he came across. He wore a Western Stetson everywhere in New York, including to all of the new musicals, where he could be expected to turn up on opening night. When he attended a show with Millicent, it was usually a special occasion, such as the opening of the Metropolitan Opera season, and it was Millicent and not Marion whose pearls broke during one of those opening nights (Marion never attended an opera in her life) and who said, "Geez, me beads" in New York accents that were to vanish completely from her speech in the years to come. Millicent did not have as much education as Marion, but she had the will to become a lady of consequence in New York society, nearly as much ambition in this direction as her husband had in politics.

Hearst gravitated to girlfriends who were "unfinished" with the exception of Katherine "Pussy" Soule, daughter of Senator Frank Soule, on whom Hearst had a boyhood crush back in San Francisco, and Sybil Sanderson, with whom he was even more infatuated when he was in his teens and who went on to become a popular operatic singer in Paris and a favorite of composer Massenet. His mother, Phoebe, terminated his affair with Miss Sanderson because of the extreme youth of her son, who was still "Billy Buster" to her. Another liaison that was nipped in the bud by Phoebe was with Eleanor Calhoun, who spoiled herself in Phoebe's eyes by declaring her intention to pursue a career upon the stage. This would have been fine with her son, Willie, but Phoebe still looked upon the theater as harboring only loose women. To the end of her life, her son was "Sonny" or "Billy Buster," her fair-haired, spoiled darling, whom she surrounded with beautiful things.

Following these boyhood and adolescent romances, Hearst became seriously involved with Tessie Powers, a waitress in Cambridge where he was an undergraduate at Harvard University. They had met when she began serving his table about a year or so before his expulsion from college. He had been accused as the culprit when gifts were sent to each of his professors, carefully wrapped chamber pots with the teacher's name inscribed on the inside bottom. Tessie was about all he could salvage when he was thrown out of school.

Gossip about his young mistress spread out from San Francisco; Sausalito, where the Hearst family maintained a home and yacht; and later New York—but Hearst flaunted her in the face of society and everyone else. It was a foretaste of the very open mode of living with a young woman outside the bonds of matrimony that he later would assume with Marion. Following an excursion to Europe and Egypt with her lover (she got camel-sick going out to the pyramids), Tessie was secretly persuaded by mother Phoebe to get out of her son's life, and it is said that some thousands of dollars helped ease Tessie back to a more comfortable obscurity. It must have occurred to Phoebe then that she had intruded into an area of her son's life where she no longer belonged, for he never consulted her again and did not ask her opinion of Millicent Willson until the marriage plans were a *fait accompli*.

Although Millicent and her sister Anita were born into show business—her father, who was known on the stage as George Leslie, was a famed clog-dancer of the nineties—her ambitions were solidly set upon a good marriage. For Hearst, settling down with a young woman who aspired to a life of taste and high principles (Millicent would turn her back on show business as soon as the engagement was announced) would put to rest the rumor that he was a millionaire voluptuary—until he met Marion.

When Hearst met Millicent Willson, she was dancing with her sister in a stage group called "The Merry Maidens" in *The Girl from Paris*. He immediately took into his circle her entire family—easy only for a man of Hearst's growing imperviousness to what was said about him. The Willsons were taken to Europe by Hearst in 1900 and, following that excursion, he would escort both sisters, Millicent and Anita, to affairs around New York. Frequently the girls were seen in Hearst's newspaper plant at the *Herald* after a midnight supper, where he would work over the front page. He was his own best editorial writer and he pored over every column, making the meaning clear to the least literate of his readers.

Hearst had been seeing Millicent for six years, almost always chaperoned, when they were married on April 28, 1903. It could not be said to have been an impulsive act, and it was, in the end, an irrevocable one. Millicent was then twenty-two years old and Hearst was a day less than forty. Within a few short years, she would be as impeccable in her social life as was her mother-in-law. Phoebe finally would see in Millicent her own likeness when her daughter-in-law joined her among the symbols in Hearst's life.

For several years there was a surface happiness to the marriage. Hearst then lived a life of respectability or, if not, knowledge of his lapses was kept within the family. When he had proved his manhood in 1904 with the birth of their first son, George, there was rejoicing on all sides, his reputation as a mama's boy dominated by Phoebe Hearst scuttled forever.

The Millicent Hearst who began to dominate the society pages of New York's newspapers was not the amusing companion Hearst had known as one of the dancing Willson sisters. She got involved in benefit teas and became a sponsor at the Metropolitan Opera. The pleasure Hearst had enjoyed in presenting his outsider wife to the Belmonts, the Vanderbilts, and the Rockefellers was killed when he saw that Millicent was very much on the inside. She no longer joined him on midnight look-sees into what the next morning paper would consist of (there were the boys to look after), and she enjoyed the rounds of benefits, teas, and callers. Sadly, for Hearst, it seemed to be all she wanted from life.

If Hearst recognized any society as such, it was that of the amusing and successful, those who had wit and had made it—statesmen, film people, fellow publishers. The "right people" whom he saw with Millicent were often described by him as "asses and stuffed shirts."

The names appearing on the society page of the newspapers were all in "Mrs. Astor's territory" to Marion. She rarely read such columns and only knew their names from Mama Rose, who did. She was always one of the crowd, never terribly interested in dressing fashionably or going with the Fifth Avenue and Long Island set. It was to be the phenomenon of her unique position as Maid Marion, a latter-day Guinevere, in the astonishing settings of San Simeon here and St. Donat's abroad, that would pique the curiosity of the great and near-great of the world so that George Bernard Shaw, Winston Churchill, Calvin Coolidge, the Mountbattens, not to mention a host of film superstars and studio chiefs, went out of their way to see her by Hearst's side. If Marion had been a dull beauty with only her looks to attract, interest would have died quickly. But her laughter was frequent and contagious, and her gaiety enlivened any gathering. Marion was fun to be with, so there was an added inducement to all of these people to visit Hearst's curious, inhabited monument.

Hearst always had preferred young women for whom the most prized gift he could give them would be himself, or that part of himself he allowed them to share. It was a gift that had failed with his first sustained love, Tessie Powers, but it was one around which Millicent had structured a new life. The trouble would be that with Marion, he would have to give more of himself than he had planned to, but less than she demanded. It was a struggle that would last until he died.

But Marion gave nearly as much in return. Hearst's social handicaps were minimized when he was with her. His biographer, W. A. Swanberg, believed that he was

> always "Mr. Hearst," never becoming "Willie" or "Bill." There was something strange about Hearst that would grow stranger with the years—a built-in failure of communication, an aloofness of temperament, an air of secrecy and loneliness, an inability to unbend into the true, easy spontaneity and exchange of confidences that bring men together. The victim of an abnormal childhood, he was hedged in by inhibitions. Now and then he would seem close to breaking through, only to recede again, like a turtle withdrawing into its shell. His men respected him, admired him, were even enthusiastic about him; but it is doubtful that any of them understood him.

Yes, but it is leaving out much to fail to state just how far out of his shell Marion was to take him. The world figures whom Hearst and Marion met, often on an intimate basis, sometimes would find Hearst inscrutable behind his uneasy, high-pitched laughter, but he was giving far more of himself than he ever had given before.

Hearst was both reserved and an eccentric individualist— qualities that would make communication difficult if he had not seen the possibilities in using Marion as his intermediary and the isolation of his several villas and castles as his working places. His executives were usually *summoned* to these home-headquarters, an action that had its own built-in advantages. Like his fictional counterpart Charles Foster Kane, he created and was master of his own world. In an almost tribal sense, Hearst was treated in his publishing empire as "the Chief" and was so named by his staff. His shrewd abilities in building circulation and establishing the daily newspaper as something to startle its readers daily were seldom challenged.

At Marion's touch, barriers fell between newly met friends. She seemed to be saying to one and all, "We're all human, aren't

we? And we all get afraid and lose our way." She did not seem
especially religious, but she communicated a feeling that everyone should cheer up a little and the resultant glow would light
up this darkness through which most of us move. Some powerful men resort to chill, impeccable manners to get them through
encounters with those who are outside their family or daily
associates. Others break out the whiskey and hope for the best.
Hearst relied upon Marion and she rarely let him down. He was
eternally grateful, and it more than compensated for any of
her weaknesses.

Even her chief weakness—alcohol—did not offend or cause
an inordinate amount of gossip. Her close friends knew that she
had no tolerance at all for liquor, but they knew that she had
no plans to ever stop drinking. Rightly or wrongly, they, and
Hearst, accepted this as her defense against the bourgeois attitudes toward mistresses that prevailed in America until her
death. She did not live quite long enough to see these prejudices
challenged, although there were portents of moral revolution
already in that year (1961).

Hearst was a man who was generous to a fault—and, he
would have said, to every man—but he was not always just (as
one of his staff pointed out), driven as he was by those desperations of a son who has cut himself off from the strong will
and protection of his mother. This included Marion. But she
rarely allowed him to get by with some imperious move or gesture. She would yell, throw things, and this quietly amused
Hearst.

Marion felt from the beginning that his love for her was
such that she could challenge him more vigorously than anyone
else. Sometimes she would take advantage of this. She saw that
those glacially blue eyes of his thawed whenever he looked at her.
His love letters to her were filled with professions of his devotion
but read very much like a man whistling in the dark, for he was
convinced that he could never possess her completely. She played
upon this insecurity and continued seeing other men. He sent her
a diamond bracelet with a note saying, "I saw it in the window
and it said 'Send me to Marion. I've heard a lot about her and I
must see her.'" The note was written in pencil and a few days
later, a chastened Marion said it was the sweetest communication she ever had received and could she have the pencil he had
used? Hearst discovered that he had thrown it out, but he sal-
vaged some shavings from the sharpener which he swore were

from the same pencil. Marion slipped the shavings into the envelope with the note and kept it all of her life. Such trifles began to accumulate and Marion's sentimentality was enough like Hearst's so that she treasured the shavings more than the bracelet. Years later when they were moving her things to another, grander house, they rediscovered the curious memento and laughed at their own foolishness.

It was probably unnecessary, but Reine Davies Lederer, with the help of Marie Glendinning, was doing what she could to keep Marion's relationship with Hearst from foundering through possible indiscretions of the past. Whenever Marion was out of town with a show, she had written notes to Paul Block, many of them tender enough to sustain his interest and allegiance in her absence. She was addicted to sending off short notes to people saying such things as "You're so nice!" To Block, she probably went further than that. There were also photographs with affectionate inscriptions. Since Block and Hearst were close friends, it was conceivable, and even a clear danger, that Block would scoff at Hearst's assertion that he had fallen deeply in love—for he had—and show him his collection of Marion's letters to him dating back only to a few months earlier. Reine was afraid that all would be lost with Hearst if Block suddenly should decide not to be so generous with his friend.

Marion's affair with Hearst was in its most vulnerable stage. In her mind, she was willing to give up her other admirers, but she was not yet very strongly motivated to do so. A man, even a multimillionaire thirty-four years her senior, might qualify a little too definitely as the older man she was seeking. By the time she was thirty, she reasoned, he would be ready for retirement. From Hearst's point-of-view, there was no other woman possible for him, including his wife, after he fell in love with her. His closest friends all affirm that this "older man" was like a schoolboy suffering the pangs of a first schoolyard crush.

Reine and Marie Glendinning thought that recovery of Marion's letters and photos was an urgent matter and, impulsive as usual, decided to accomplish it themselves. They caught a taxi to Block's "bachelor" apartment, found him at home, and charmed their way into his living room.

After accepting drinks from the publisher, Marie asked "Where's the *loo*?" a euphemism for bathroom which Marion would appropriate and use through much of her lifetime. While

Reine told Block what a handsome creature he was—and there was considerable need for her to exaggerate—Marie rummaged through the adjoining master bedroom, found the letters and photos and concealed them in her girdle.

As the ladies were leaving, Block was distressed over having had such little luck with Reine during Marie's absence, so he casually suggested that Marie "drop around some time again" when she was not in such a rush. "I can hardly wait," Marie told him with an equivocal wink designed to give Block something to think about for a few minutes. Once on the street, Reine and Marie embraced each other, laughing as Marie patted her stomach in triumph. Block was a reasonable gentleman and they might have had as much luck if they simply had asked him for the incriminating material, but this adventure had been more exciting. In any case, Marion's reputation was intact.

VII

Marion's career as a showgirl was going very well before Hearst came into her life, and for nearly a year afterward, his influence was not needed to help her rise in the theater. In April 1916, a call came from Florenz Ziegfeld's casting director. Perhaps Ziegfeld, too, had witnessed or had heard about Marion's disastrous first attempt at a speaking part as the "Spirit of Spring," but he knew talent when he saw it, and her face and figure were perfect examples of the sort of talent he merchandised better than anyone alive. The voice could be fixed up later, although Ziegfeld had no plans for her to do anything other than carry a plumed and sequined headdress and costume.

The Ziegfeld Follies of 1916 was to open in early June. By the middle of May, Marion was not only in the chorus of one number, but billed as "Miss Chief" in an amusing take-off on Fifth Avenue snobbery narrated and sung by the great Bert Williams, black minstrel extraordinary. Then at her friend Gene Buck's suggestion, she was given the part of Jane Seymour in a spoof of Shakespeare's *Henry VIII*. Buck's Gilbert and Sullivan–type song for the occasion was "Six Little Wives of the King Are We," and Marion was given the closing line, which was "He sure was a helluva king."

Flo Ziegfeld had taken a special interest in her and even had given her a five-dollar-a-week raise as encouragement to remain with his company. The figure is Marion's recollection, but it may have been more. It was her habit in later years to lend her stage years an aura of deprivation while describing her movie period as a time of a bewildering flood of riches. Reassured about her stage abilities, she neither flubbed a line nor stammered during her Ziegfeld days.

By the time of the opening of *The Ziegfeld Follies of 1916,* Hearst was taking Marion to dinner every night after the show. While no mention of her performance appeared in any of the reviews, she became known in show business circles both as one of Ziegfeld's beauties in that unusual temple he had erected to the female stunner and as the girlfriend of one of New York's most powerful men at about the same time. The famous unsmiling Dolores and Marion made a striking combination—Marion all bright eyes and dazzling sunshine and Dolores as dolorous as her name.

Hearst began appearing in the second row front, and Block no longer sat at his side. He left that vacant for his famed Stetson. An old family friend of Hearst's said that Marion "crawled up in his lap, ruffled his hair, and called him daddy." She did not take the romance very seriously. Mama Rose was distressed over the number of gifts pouring in between Christmas and just before Easter. She might have been reassured if Marion had told her that she was in love with Hearst, but she was not—that would come later.

She may have been interested only in wealthy older men, but Marion did not need money to find fulfillment in life, and when it began to come in large amounts she invariably spent most of it on others.

When she began to love Hearst around 1917, she saw him as a husband and not as a money-fount or a "sugar daddy." More than anything, realization of this—her disinterest in "taking him" for his money—undoubtedly deepened Hearst's affection for her. His final decision not to marry her after several, possibly purposely self-defeating, attempts to get a divorce, placed him in a position of having to spend years attempting to compensate her, this woman who loved him not for his name, not for his wealth, but simply for himself, funny voice and all.

Marion was far more a homemaker than any of her sisters. Before her trip to Florida, she had gone out of town with a show and, somewhere in New England, a young college boy had got a

crush on her and after several dates proposed. They were going
to elope, since he was uncertain about his family's attitude toward having a showgirl in the family. All of these plans were
made hurriedly during an after-the-show tour of the local bars,
but in the sober morning, Marion remembered and hoped and
waited, vainly as it turned out.

It is hard to sustain any spontaneity in the performance of
a long-running revue. In the case of the *Follies,* Ziegfeld set a
cut-off point for each of his "editions," which was both wise and
merciful as it kept his stable of performers fresh. And Marion's
bright presence helped. She was bouncy and resourceful and she
was vastly popular backstage with everyone except comedian
W. C. Fields, an irascible misanthrope in his stage image and not
too different off-stage.

The Fields contretemps had occurred because of Marion's
innate curiosity. There were signs posted backstage: "Do Not
Talk to the Principals." Such a prohibition sparked Marion's old
rebelliousness. She was not only perverse on occasion but inquisi-
tive to the point of recklessness. Signs that read "Do Not Enter"
were signals to her to peek through doorways. It bothered her
that she was in the same show as Ina Claire, Fannie Brice, and
Fields but never got close enough to any of them to even introduce herself, much less discuss their art (and comedy—high or
low—was for Marion the supreme theatrical art). She *had* to
know why the audience laughed each night at an absolutely
silent part of Fields's act. She crept into the wings where Fields
immediately spotted her. His performance, what she saw of it,
disappointed her. "He was doing something stupid with a golf
ball," she remembered. As Fields left the stage, he was in a fury.
"Where's that dirty jerk blonde that was in the wings?" he asked.
"Tell her I'm going to have her fired, whoever she is!" Then Marion, who had ducked into a smelly prop trunk, heard Fields say,
"Let me spot her. I'll have that dirty bitch fired." From that time
on, Marion managed to lose herself in the crowd of crew and cast
backstage whenever Fields was nearby. Later she learned that
Flo Ziegfeld had warned Fields to "leave the kid alone." Eight
years later, she would have Fields hired as comic relief in her
film, *Janice Meredith.*

Hearst had taken a studio apartment in the Beaux Arts
Hotel in the West Forties and given Marion a key. She was invited to go there whenever she wanted to get away from her

family. Marion never in her life craved solitude and she only used the studio apartment for meetings with Hearst and her Tuesday evening "cat nights," when her girl-friends Norma and Connie Talmadge and Anita Loos would join her there for a few hours of clowning, gossip, and cocktails—an institution honored by Norma's husband Joe Schenck, Anita Loos's John Emerson, and by whomever Connie Talmadge was dating at the moment.

Her girlfriends at that point were nearly all from the theater or films. She readily adopted many of their tastes as well as all of their backstage lingo and she could crack wise or be softly beautiful with the transition being nearly invisible. Her career as a showgirl was clearly an integral part of their relationship. Hearst never seemed to tire of seeing Marion on the stage, as he never would tire of seeing her films run off. He was there nearly every night of the run of the *Follies of 1916*, and, as one observer remarked, he seemed to "possess her with his eyes."

If Mama Rose had lost most of her control over Marion's nights out, she still had a hand in matters backstage. She was shocked when she saw that Marion's "Jane Seymour" costume was split to the thigh along its sable-trimmed skirt. She went to Ziegfeld at once and said that she had looked at the other girls and Marion was the only one with a costume that was split. Ziegfeld smiled indulgently and explained to Mama Rose that this was because Marion had the finest legs. "Well," said Mama Rose, "we're not selling any flesh in this show," and the dress was "repaired."

Mama Rose's concern for Marion's public modesty soon would be taken over by Hearst when he began to guide her career. They were both Victorian in origin and he was, where Marion was concerned, often Victorian in outlook. His clucking tongue as he disapproved of a proposed custard pie in Marion's face for a screen comedy or her skirt being torn off "accidentally" would make him a hero forever in Mama Rose's eyes.

Marion's own first appraisal of Hearst and his intentions was untarnished by any trace of hypocrisy. She frankly admitted to having responded to his first overtures with the attitude of a "gold digger," the young lady from show business, for the most part, who was given trinkets from Tiffany's as well as an occasional checking account or apartment by "sugar daddies," much older men who sweetened their images through big spending. The most celebrated of these was "Daddy" Browning, who

launched fifteen-year-old Frances "Peaches" Browning into the
sweet life by marrying her. But Marion was no "Peaches" and
Hearst was far from being a "Daddy" Browning, who sought to
legitimatize his affair with a very young girl after the tabloids
began crucifying him. There was considerable dignity projected
by Hearst even with Marion by his side. And this quality was contagious. She could be exuberant and the liveliest girl at the party,
but she was nearly always a lady by Hearst's side. The surprising
thing did not turn out to be that Marion would fit in with even
the most exalted company but that she so clearly was not there
for the sake of the wealth and power but out of a love, the depths
of which surprised even her.

The other girls in the *Follies* warned Marion that Hearst
had a reputation as a wolf, but she must have known otherwise
after six months or more of being his constant companion
around New York. She told the chorines that he wouldn't hurt a
fly. There was always a certain literal-mindedness in Marion and
she associated the word "wolf" with animals who prowled at
night, baying at the moon. What these ladies of the chorus probably meant was that he had seen a number of them on occasions
prior to his meeting Marion and that his intentions were not hon-
orable in the Victorian sense of the word. All of the many
flowers, silver trinkets, and other tokens of his interest alerted
the veteran chorines to tell her to look out.

But he was beginning to give her career a boost by the fall
of 1916. She received word from Hearst's city editor Victor Watson on the *American* that they would like to feature her in the
Sunday supplement and Watson set up an appointment for her
at Campbell's Photography Studio. Mama Rose went along, per-
suading the wardrobe mistress on the *Follies* to let them borrow
some costumes from the show. Justine Johnstone's beauty already had been much publicized, as well as Lilyan Tashman and
other Ziegfeld girls, so now Marion would be elevated through
publicity to their ranks. This gesture by Hearst made her contribution to the *Follies* seem to be more than it really was and gave
her a lasting place in theatrical histories and chronicles dealing
with the Ziegfeld era. Her portrait was destined to be displayed
alongside Billie Burke's and Ann Pennington's *and* a bust of
W. C. Fields in the new Ziegfeld Theatre lobby, a film house that
opened in New York City in the 1960s.

When Marion left her dressing cubicle at the photographer's

she saw Hearst sitting near the camera. She said that she panicked and ran back inside. That first year of her association with
Hearst was marked by such unpredictable flights and they must
have been disturbing to him. Her "timidity" after accepting
Hearst's gold watch, silver cases, bracelets, and other gifts as
well as the use of his studio apartment would seem to be false,
but it should be remembered that Mama Rose was at her elbow
through much of this early stage of Hearst's courtship. Marion
wanted her behavior to seem innocent to her mother because
they both pretended that it was. Like Gigi, Marion was having
innocence pumped into her like vitamin shots by her mother
after every bedroom encounter with Hearst.

The Campbell photo of Marion in a picture hat of the period
took up a full page in the *American Weekly,* and the caption
read: "Marion Davies, the Type of Chorus Girl Who Marries Cap-
tains of Industry and Coronets." The headline over the photo
must have been written by a Hearst editor (Watson, perhaps)
secure enough in his job to risk a sly reference to his employer:
"FOR EVERY MAN THERE'S 'ONE DANGEROUS GIRL.' "

When she wasn't getting flowers or Tiffany trinkets, she
would find notes or poetry on her dressing table. In her tape-
recorded memoirs, she recalls that the hand-written verses would
come by messenger and seem to be original. Certainly there were
touches here and there that could only have been inspired by
Marion's own character and affairs. No one can document
whether or not they were conceived by Hearst but some of them
were preserved by Marion and appear to be in Hearst's handwrit-
ing. One of the quaintest and most light-hearted, dating from the
Follies period, follows:

The Cynic's Love Song
I had a little lady love whose name was May
Her eyes were bright, her teeth were white, her smile
    was sweet and gay.
She smiled at me and I was hers forever and for aye,
But she smiled at many others in the self-same
    way. . . .

I had another lady love whose name was Ruth.
She told me all her secrets with the innocence of
    youth.
She said I was her only love but when I hired a
    sleuth,

I found she'd told me everything except the
truth. . . .

I love a girl named Marion, she holds me in the
thrall
Of her blue eyes and golden hair and figure lithe and
tall.
She loves me too, she tells me so—Alas that isn't all.
She likewise loves Flo, Charlie, Henry, Nealie, Joe,
and Paul.

Since "Flo" could only refer to Ziegfeld and "Paul" probably
to Paul Block, Hearst saw them as rivals. It is well-known that
Ziegfeld dated several of his showgirls, but this doggerel is the
only documentation extant that would link him with Marion. The
line about hiring a "sleuth" was not to be without its special irony
for Marion in a few years. Hearst was addicted to the use of
private detectives to keep him posted on his associates as well as
his enemies.

There was enough publicity steam engendered by the Hearst
press by February 1917 to liberate her from the ranks of the
Ziegfeld line. She was given the part of Jane Packard, a debutante of sorts, in *Oh Boy*, a hugely successful musical comedy by
Guy Bolton and P. G. Wodehouse with a score by Jerome Kern.
It ran for months at the Princess Theatre, the best in a series of
musicals that had been launched with *Very Good, Eddie*, in which
Marion had a small role. *The New York Times* said, "Then there
is that old reliable Hal Forde, to say nothing of Justine Johnstone, who gets in on her looks, and Marion Davies, who adds a
bit of a voice to those credentials."

When President Wilson, with much anguish and hesitation,
declared war on Germany in April 1917, Hearst found himself in
bad odor with practically everyone in the country. Pacifists and
dissenters were not easily tolerated then. If they weren't threatened or beaten up, great pressure was put upon them to recant.
Hearst could not be called a pacifist after his saber-rattling, atroc-
ity-shouting reputation from the Spanish-American War. He was
simply thought to be for the wrong side. His passionate dislike of
the British was well-known and unrelenting (and it would not
subside until the late twenties when he would buy a castle in
Wales and begin to spend vacations there with Marion), and his
long-held conviction that the Germans were superior in every

way and would surely win the European war, which he had insisted was not *our* war, now made him the most hated man in
the country, burned in effigy, his newspapers destroyed by the
bundle by mobs. Hearst newsboys, fearful of being manhandled,
had to be given American flags to wear on their jackets as evidence of their patriotism.

His nineteenth-century Kiplingesque view of war as a solution for differences between nations was unchanging throughout
his lifetime. The slaughter on the battlefield, so enormous in that
war (and still only a pale foretaste of what was to come little
more than twenty years later in battle, in the cities and in the
death camps) never would move him to anything beyond a feeling of excitement. In 1920, Marion received a poem curiously
devoid of any acknowledgement that there was any true horror
in war:

> The Bungalow is on the bum,
>   the studio is stupid.
> For life is slow unless there's some
>   companionship with Cupid.
>
> Mars is all right to strive and fight
>   and from our foes to screen us
> But there are times when thoughts and rhymes
>   turn longingly to Venus.
>
> So while I write with much delight
>   of armies and of navies
> The sweetest thing of which I sing
> The Muse to whom my soul I fling
> The idol to whose feet I cling
>   is lovely MARION DAVIES.

Hearst hastily left Marion and New York that first summer
of the war and fled with his family to California and the ranch at
San Simeon. Large tents had been erected there on the hillside
where eventually his castle would be built. The tents were a custom of the family for some years, beginning in the days when
Hearst brought friends down from Sausalito by yacht. He liked to
think this was a way of "roughing it," although the mode was
more an Americanized version of a sheik or a pasha's desert camp
with food out of season served in a round of picnics, amateur
movies, or live entertainment. There were occasions when he

tested his family's and friends' endurance through long rides
deep into the mountains surrounding the campsite, but the des-
tination often was one of several comfortable old ranch houses
on the vast property, where a warm bath awaited the victims of
these spartan urges. Still, the ride seemed nearly unendurable to
many, including Marion, who was afraid of getting astride a
horse and considered such compulsory recreation a kind of
torture.

He commissioned a tiny lady by the name of Julia Morgan,
graduate of the Architectural School of the Beaux Arts in Paris,
to design a castle with twin towers, and he permitted himself to
drift away from thoughts of war and his own ignominy into an
altogether private world, which would become his permanent retreat from an unsympathetic public.

There was something childlike in Hearst's cyclic swings
away from and toward the "people." After a summer of recovering from their "treachery," he again came East to see if he had a
chance in the upcoming New York City mayoralty election. Boss
Charles Murphy of the powerful Tammany machine believed
that Hearst would have a chance with *the pro-German elements*
on New York's East Side! With the entire country geared to all-
out war against Germany since April, this was political cynicism
of the deepest dye imaginable. "Big Tom" Foley, also of Tammany Hall, allied himself with young Alfred E. Smith to block
Hearst's candidacy.

Throughout these maneuverings, Marion was living quietly
in Reine's old apartment at the Cleburne on West 105th Street.
Her meetings with Hearst at his studio apartment in the Beaux
Arts seemed to have been terminated for reasons of political necessity. Marion demonstrated her distaste for such treatment by
promptly resuming her friendships with Paul Block and other old
beaux. She felt much more strongly about Hearst now; if his
glacially blue eyes thawed whenever they looked at her, she was
beginning to feel stirrings of an equally deep attraction to him.
By the 1920s when she was a star, her fame and her talents
could have liberated her at any time, but she was much too emotionally involved to walk away. By then, Hearst was giving Marion his complete devotion. She was something that had become a
part of him, like his castle complex, and everyone, including
Millicent and his sons, had to accept this reality or face a sudden
Hearstian storm that could be terrifying. If she had been less flirtatious and never got involved with other men, she would not

have been the Marion for whom Hearst would do everything short of dying. And if she had been a great beauty obsessed with her appearance, she would not have become Hearst's casual, vulnerable darling who dressed out of fashion, spoiled her nails with nicotine and over-drank.

While Marion displayed some of her old rebelliousness in dealing with this early encounter with Hearst's political needs, she knew that Al Smith was going around New York loudly impugning Hearst's moral character for "taking up with blond actresses." Smith and Foley succeeded in forcing him to withdraw from the race, but they could not prevent the emergence of Hearst's own hand-picked candidate, Brooklyn County Judge John F. Hylan, as the alternative and—after a massive publicity campaign in the Hearst press—the winner. But again, Hearst was defiled publicly in the opposition camp. He was attacked as the most heinous of the triumvirate of "Hearst, Hylan, and the Hohenzollerns." Hylan was not without his virtues. He was a solid red-haired Irishman of unchallengeable morality, refusing to believe the rumors of Hearst's philandering even when Marion was clinging to his sponsor's arm. He appointed Millicent Hearst as chairman of the women's division of the Mayor's Committee on National Defense. It was Millicent's job to instruct housewives in how to keep the home fires glowing with a minimum waste of coal. Her husband's prodigal spending was not yet generally known to the public.

Marion was too involved with her stage career even to think about the war, and, reassured by her old boyfriends, she tried not to feel too hurt by Hearst's offhand way of picking up their romance when it seemed safe to do so. In the years ahead, she would get used to his going to Millicent's side whenever it was politic or necessary to do so, and she would fill his absences with acting chores or, if his absence seemed too uncalled for or prolonged, with small affairs with attractive Hollywood males, which would drive Hearst wild and back to her side.

Her failure to recall "one thing" about the war *is* mystifying when she was so much in Hearst's company and must have seen his newspapers once in a while—papers that were harvesting a fortune out of this world tragedy. She explained that she was working too hard on the stage to pay any attention. She only recalled one matinee when some West Point cadets got up on the stage after the show and danced with the showgirls. Since she was not interested in men of her own age, doubtless she did not miss that generation of males gone from the streets and missing from audiences—a generation gone to France throughout those first years of her affair with Hearst. She was barely twenty at this point, but it would be a problem of Marion's throughout her life that she rarely could connect with outside events. She would worry about the welfare of others, especially the children of the poor, or she might shudder about an especially grisly murder and pull her head underneath the bedclothes, and she would make bandages for the wounded during World War II and permit the grounds of her Children's Clinic to be used by the State Guard; but very little exterior to her stage world, the Hollywood that became her personal playground, or the lavish retreats she shared with Hearst, ever touched her. She had her own small desperations simply coping with the day-to-day strain of living with a man who liked to toy with history but yet chose to believe that he was her "Pops," her lovesick swain. This required a brand of bravery not so terribly different from the battlefield kind, and only Hearst ever acknowledged her courage. But that was enough.

Her nephew Charlie, who was a youngster when America entered the war, was to recall far more about it. He remembered that there was much discussion at the Douras dinner table about German atrocities. Sometime in 1917, Reine decided that he had to be circumcised. Charlie remembered following "a nice man down a corridor and then waking up with a terrible pain"—in his genitals. He thought the Germans had got him. About eighteen months later, his half-brother Maitland returned from the war and Mama Rose had a great gathering of the clan at dinner, during which there was much discussion about a family friend, Herbie Winslow, being wounded. Charlie rather indignantly told the family that he didn't know why they were talking about Herbie Winslow so much when, as he told them, "I was wounded in the war, too." Then young Charlie unbuttoned his fly and showed Mama Rose at the table. "There was shock all around," recalled Charlie, "and then I found myself being examined by a psychologist to see if I was a pervert."

IX

In October 1917, Marion was given a small part in a lavish musical drama set in the Orient, *Chu, Chin, Chow.* It was her fourth

Broadway appearance in less than a year, and as a celebrated showgirl, she was one of dozens of attractions in the spectacle. Adapted from the story of Ali Baba and the forty thieves, it was remarkably like the successful musical of the 1950s, *Kismet,* written by her nephew Charlie and financed in part by her.

Throughout much of that year, Marion's affair with Hearst had become far too discreet to please her, and she was becoming far less adoring, referring to him as "Droopy Drawers" and "the Old Man" to girlfriends Connie Talmadge (then entering films) and Anita Loos, who was doing well as a script-writer. She understood his motives, but she never ceased complaining about the secrecy, a policy for managing this delicate matter urged upon Hearst by his advisors. By this time, it was understood by everyone in the Hearst organization that Marion was the Chief's protégée. Funds to elevate her style of living came through a Hearst agent; she now had a chauffeured limousine, which she said she needed because of Mama Rose's arthritis, and an elaborate wardrobe. She attended the Sargent School, where she took drawing lessons, and the Empire School of Acting, where her classmates, she said, were Katharine Hepburn and Rosamund Pinchot. A special switchboard operator in the Hearst building always knew where one could reach the other. Marion never gave a moment's thought to any of this expense, and as the expenses mounted, no one ever saw her hesitate because of the cost of something. Hearst's profligacy seemed to be contagious—she caught it almost from the very beginning. But she still didn't connect huge expenses with money or bank accounts. Affecting the manner of a good-time blonde, she was quietly parlaying her small fortune from Hearst into such wealth that by the mid-twenties she would be one of the richest film stars in Hollywood history.

Hearst did not yet grasp what acumen she had for real estate and other business ventures. He wired her from the Park Hotel, a mineral spa in Mt. Clemons, Michigan, telling her to develop her talents and be a great little girl. At this time, in 1917 and 1918, he was signing all of his wires and letters "Daddy." Hearst had gone to the Michigan resort to take the waters for his circulatory problem. He followed the wire with a book by Lucien Hubbard, "Little Journeys," which his best friend Orrin Peck suggested that she read in small doses. There was to be a whole parade of volumes sent through the mails and by messenger to Marion over the years, and she dutifully would read them all.

While Marion's assertion that Katharine Hepburn was a fel-

low-pupil at the Empire School cannot bear very close scrutiny
(Miss Hepburn could not have been more than ten years of
age at the time), Rosamund Pinchot, the daughter of one of the
first great conservationists in America, apparently was in several
of Marion's classes. A queer young woman, brooding and easily
turned to melancholy (she was to die a suicide after some success
as an actress), Rosie was called upon one rainy day to recite
Juliet's speech beginning: "Thou knowest the mask of night is all
my face . . ." When she rattled through the lines, letter-perfect
but with little feeling, Professor Currie, who headed the elocution
department, plainly showed his disappointment. While the next
girl went through her recitation, Rosie sneaked out of the window
and sat on the outside ledge, several stories up. In a few minutes,
the bell rang dismissing classes for the day. Marion and some
friends saw Rosie on the ledge from the street below and went to
find a janitor who could unlock the building and persuade her
back inside. This kind of acute depression was something Marion
never would be able to comprehend in others. "After all," she
would say, "if you have your health, that's a blessing. Life is short
enough without going around being miserable." When as a young
woman her niece Pepi suddenly began to show some of the signs
of being another Rosie Pinchot, Marion hoped that it was just a
mood that would pass. And Pepi had inherited her aunt's talent
for concealing her melancholy so that her desperation went unnoticed by many.

Marion's teachers at the Empire School were patient with
her and often permitted her to do her recitations after class.
Alone with her teacher, her stammer would leave her, as it would
in another decade when she made her first sound film and Hearst
and her director arranged to have visitors barred until she felt at
ease in the new medium.

Study in body movement, begun at Kosloff's and continued
at the Empire School, began to free Marion from thinking about
how she moved and walked. Her self-consciousness seemed to
stem from a feeling of inadequacy, a fear that she was not as
attractive as she should be or bright enough to measure up to
Hearst's demands. If anything, this insecurity gave her a determination she probably would have lacked otherwise. Ambition
was never a motivating force in her. But she developed a strong
will to improve herself that passed for ambition and became in
time a kind of perfectionism. She was a middle-class Liza Doolittle with a taste for celebrity but none at all for high society.

Despite her progress as an actress, there was some discipline involved in attending school at twenty and often going for weeks without once seeing her lover-patron. She needed a hug and emotional reassurance, but Hearst was not yet aware of this. Sometimes she would show her contempt for her situation by not bothering to keep in touch with him at all when he was out of town, even though she was always supplied with his itinerary. He complained that he would not stay wherever he was at the time unless she wrote, that he would return to New York and spoil all of her parties or go into a nearby town and find a beautiful blond Swede and go gallivanting. In these complaints, he called himself "Desperate Desmond." He was also "Lonesome George" at a later point, then simply "G" for George. Even though many of these excursions out of town were in pursuit of better health, as he went from one spa to another, Marion felt that she was "abandoned" much too often.

Hearst's circulatory ailment was the first hint other than a slight heart murmur that he was anything but a sturdy rock of a man. It was not considered very serious then, but he was never out of a doctor's care again and he became vigilant about his health and habits. It angered him that he was more than three decades Marion's senior and at fifty-four his body was no longer altogether dependable. But he quickly made his peace with this condition and carefully paced himself so that he would be not only a fit companion for a young woman barely twenty-one but a possible candidate for the presidency of the United States. His persistence in that, amounting to arrogance in the face of the intense vilification he had received, was one of the most remarkable things about him. His faith in himself, as with certain fanatics, was absolute.

PART TWO

THE
NEW
POLLYANNA

I

Marion was more than Hearst's "girlfriend" once she had gone onto his payroll in 1917; she was his mistress. She probably was considered by his bookkeepers as "personal expense," but there could be no equivocation any longer about her status. Still, Hearst never would consider her as constantly available. Her career had then, and it would continue to have, first priority. If she was tied up with a rehearsal or a performance, that was that. Once she became a star for his film company and then its president—that situation would change. "S-s-s-school's out for the day," she would tell her director and crew whenever Hearst or she decided to go off yachting or simply to picnic on the beach.

She always had had a great deal of nervous energy and nearly all of it now was going into her work as an actress. She made no long-range plans—she never would—but she was a dynamo each day as she rushed about New York, rehearsing, performing, attending her classes, partying, and filling in the corners of her day with family concerns. Invariably, when he was in town, Hearst would meet her after each performance. If her sleep was sacrificed at times, she was physically strong and it rarely showed.

There was a casualness in Marion's attitude toward Hearst that belied her very deep feelings. To many of her friends, the thirty-four-year span of years between them seemed to suggest that she finally had a loving father who was there when she needed him. And Hearst, for his part, tried not to permit his fiercely jealous streak, his pride of possession, to be too evident in their relationship. He knew that if he did so, he would lose her before she was truly his.

Her fame as a showgirl had reached such proportions by late 1917 that the inevitable film offers began coming in, as they had to Justine Johnstone, Lilyan Tashman, Ann Pennington, Billie Burke, and all of her glamorous predecessors. She was being given featured billing in theater ads whenever she appeared. On Christmas Day, 1917, she opened in a show called

Words and Music, advertised as a "snappy revue." One reviewer wrote that it was second-rate, its satire too obvious (William Shakespeare, credited in the ads as the show's author, appeared "in person"), but it settled down for a long run. It was the kind of appearance that was becoming routine to Marion—her beauty set off by a sizable cast of comedians. No producer seemed about to give her anything more challenging, and she began seriously considering accepting one of the film offers.

Her ex-brother-in-law George Lederer was already into motion picture production, having formed a company called "George W. Lederer Filmotions, Inc.," in 1915. In July of that year, he had released a movie version of Ethel Barrymore's success, *Sunday,* with a full page ad in *The Moving Picture World,* describing the film as "an absorbing drama of the Lumber Camp and Modern Society Life. A woman's honor is saved. The Assailant pays the penalty of his baseness, falling headlong over a cliff into the waters of death." The star of that film was the former Mrs. Lederer, known professionally, of course, as Reine Davies. Reine had signed a contract to do several pictures for Lewis Selznick and his World Film Corporation, but Lederer had obtained a release to use his ex-wife's services.

Sunday had been moderately successful, and Reine made a number of other films. Much of the dinner-table talk at her apartment, where Marion lived at the time, was now concentrated on the movies and the people who made them. There was not only the lure of greater fame for the Davies girls; there was an incredible amount of money in films for the successful. Mary Pickford was now "America's Sweetheart" and the highest-salaried woman in the world. Charlie Chaplin did not trail her in earnings by much, if at all, and Douglas Fairbanks had become a millionaire. Other stars who had become America's new elite were Norma Talmadge, Harold Lloyd, Gloria Swanson, Francis X. Bushman, William S. Hart, Lillian Gish, and Tom Mix. Rin Tin Tin, a German shepherd dog brought back from the trenches in Europe, was about to make his first film, and the dog's success was so phenomenal he became known around his studio as "the mortgage lifter." A young man by the name of Darryl Zanuck soon would take over as Rin Tin Tin's chief scenarist.

Since 1913, Hearst had been producing short films, principally serials and newsreels, and Marion must have told him of her wish to enter the movies. But he was not yet ready to help her in this direction. He may have believed that she was ill-prepared for film stardom, as she was, and he was always a perfectionist. It may have been, too, that if it was his future intention to obtain a divorce from Millicent and marry Marion, the latter's obligations and duties as the new Mrs. Hearst would make a film career impossible. Some of her friends believed that her determination to enter films might have been a device to bring Hearst to a decision about her.

Whatever her motives may have been, Lederer was quick to oblige her. Marion had a face familiar to the public; she was more photogenic than Reine; and she had an old beau waiting in the wings—Paul Block—eager to supply the financing. The enthusiasm within the Douras household over getting Marion launched in films even moved Mama Rose to say, "She's a thousand times prettier than Mary Pickford," a great exaggeration, of course, although "Little Mary" was abnormally short, a defect minimized by artful camera work and her perennial role as a young girl.

Hearst could not ignore the fact that Lederer was going to use Block's money for the film. It could only have been upsetting to her principal sponsor and the man footing most of her bills. It was the first of a series of reckless gestures of independence from Marion for Hearst's benefit. Sometimes Hearst would call her "heartless," and with reason.

It was Block's newspaperman's instinct that told him that more important than having Marion move around on the screen showing off her charms would be to have a gripping story. He walked into a reporter's hangout on the West Side and offered $25 to anyone in the room who could come up with a story idea about a "white gypsy" that would not be offensive to a general audience. Clarence Lindner, who later became a crack reporter and then publisher for Hearst on *The San Francisco Examiner,* came up with a story about a very rich man whose daughter has been kidnapped and they spend years looking for her. "Suddenly," reads Mr. Lindner's scenario, "the father comes upon a gypsy camp where he sees a girl with blond hair and, upon examination, a strawberry mark is discovered on her left shoulder, there since birth." While its intentions were serious and it was even acceptable fare in that early period of feature-film production, it was a trite fiction, as awful in production as in the writing. But it was typical of the day's quickly made features, and Block had it serialized and published in over forty newspapers as an advance promotion of the film. Mama Rose contributed the title,

Runaway, Romany, and, with George Lederer doubling as producer and director, it was brought in ready for distribution by Ardsley Art Film-Pathé at a cost to Paul Block of only $23,000.

While this sounds absurdly cheap today, many feature films in 1917–18 were being made for less. Of the large-budgeted films, much of the money was going for stars' salaries since the star system had become firmly established, or, in the case of such spectacular films as D. W. Griffith's *Intolerance* (1916), for sets and costumes. In the case of *Runaway, Romany,* Marion was given a deferred fee for her appearance, to come out of future profits, with most of the budget going as salary to her three leading men, Matt Moore, Joseph Kilgour, and Pedro de Cordoba. All of the interiors were shot at the Pathé studios in New York and the exteriors in the wilds of New Jersey.

After seeing the first rushes, Block felt that it was a losing proposition and urged Lederer to cut costs wherever he could, hoping to salvage something from his investment. One of Lederer's economies was to cut the box lunches on location in half, giving each member of the cast and crew half an egg and half a sandwich, provoking Marion, who always had a good appetite, to say, "It was the most ridiculous thing I ever saw."

Hearst eagerly sought a screening of the film upon its completion. He came away from the screening room at Pathé shaking his head, and Marion ducked out of sight, fearing the worst. To her surprise (but to no one else's), Hearst was greatly impressed and excited by her appearance on the screen. Pragmatist that he was, he may have seen Marion's film possibilities as a way out of the triangular situation his love for her had created, although, if this is true, he kept her in ignorance of this. What he said was, "I'm going to make you a star, Marion," and on that day she accepted the fact of her certain stardom as she did all of Hearst's pronouncements. She was accepting, too, the likelihood of her never becoming Mrs. Hearst. She was being offered something in its place, and the glamour of it made her temporarily not only willing to accept, but anxious to do so.

Hearst's newsreels were making money, and he long ago had begun coproducing serials with Pathé, finally making his own. He had set up a corporation for the purpose of making features to star Alma Rubens, known as International Films (later Cosmopolitan Pictures). Miss Rubens was a dark-eyed brunette with patrician features. Hearst was convinced that if he starred the actress in productions with the look of quality and a strong story line, he could not lose. The films he was to make over the next several years until Miss Ruben's premature death came out slightly ahead.

With Marion, he was taking more of a chance. He could not have known then how very good she would become as an irrepressible comic leading lady of the flapper era—that came as a surprise. His motives were transparent: Marion was pliable; she could be made a star; and they could manage to spend much more time together as professional partners. If he was not about to give Marion the name of Hearst, he would make the name of Davies equally famous. Mistresses and consorts had been consigned usually to a role in the shadow of their prestigious companions. Hearst would give Marion the means to shine by herself.

In the years to come, even non-Hearst publications always would allude to Marion and Hearst as "friends"; Marion was Hearst's "companion." There was never even a line suggesting anything more until after Hearst's death when certain scandal magazines such as *Rave* and *Confidential* published their "exposés." But friends knew the depths of Hearst's passion for her; he was even blind to her loss of beauty when she became overweight. If she *lost* too much weight, then he would worry that something might be wrong with her and send her for a check-up. Marion returned this profound affection but behaved at times with less gallantry. She was, in a sense, bought and paid for, and she resented it bitterly. She was a free spirit at heart, and when his announced plans clashed with her own, she knew that she would have to give in. In return for these concessions, she was to become the first mistress in history to be advertised and promoted to fame by her "protector," as he called himself. Then, when she was accepted by the public, that was the cake-icing. She *did* shine all by herself for a very long time.

Hearst's promotion of Marion was to last twenty years, and no film star in America would ever exceed her in terms of publicity. The rub was that, as Marion became more confident in front of the cameras, she turned out to be a movie natural and she would have to fight the publicity hoopla most of her career. She would also have to fight Hearst's constant meddling, since he saw her as a lady of quality on the screen, a kind of blond Alma Rubens, while the Marion Davies who became a legitimate

star and not a phony one was impish, unpredictable, and eager
to prick pomposity wherever she found it.

By December 1917, when *Runaway, Romany* had its igno-
minious release, the American film industry had come of age. Its
maturity had been suggested as early as 1915 with D. W. Griffith's *Birth of a Nation,* but during the war other creative directors had emerged to foster a rich and exciting medium. Allan
Dwan, who first used the tracking shot in *David Harum* (1915),
was turning out a torrent of competent films. Clarence Brown,
who was to gain fame as Garbo's favorite American director, was
well on his way. Cecil B. De Mille, backed by studio head Adolph
Zukor, was discovering a golden vein, which he would tap again
and again, in *the sinful woman* with a successful blend of the
Bible, sex, and sadism. Charlie Chaplin's *Shoulder Arms* was
about to be released, and it would be discovered that the man
whose name alone would attract throngs to any moviehouse was
also a great director.

There were equally creative producers: William Fox,
Thomas Ince, Lewis Selznick, and Samuel Goldwyn. Hearst
shared their instinctive feeling for an emotional response from
the audience, a talent he had brought to his publishing career.
His contributions to films have been widely underrated by critics
unaware of both the native equipment he brought to Cosmopolitan Productions as well as the several truly distinguished films
made by that company. Not only did such films with Marion as
Show People, Little Old New York, and *Marianne* win rave reviews and earn impressive profits, but so, too, did *Gabriel Over
the White House,* starring Walter Huston, *The Big House,* one of
the first realistic prison films, *Oil for the Lamps of China* with
Pat O'Brien, and Dick Powell's *Shipmates Forever.*

When Hearst blundered, as he was to do a dozen times in
his obsessive search for legendary stardom for Marion, it was in
no small way, so it is easy for film historians to point them out.
He saw Marion as Guinevere, as the Princess Royal, as any number of golden-haired maidens, even though one of her principal
charms for him was her spontaneous guffaw at all the sober-sides
who could not laugh at themselves. And there were a few others
as reckless as Hearst with a film's budget. Director Erich von
Stroheim would shoot 200,000 feet of film in making *The Wedding March,* nearly as much in the never-released *Queen Kelly,*

and was reluctant to cut the twenty reels of his film *Greed*. Chaplin sometimes would spend a year or more in shooting a film. But these men were seeking artistic perfection. What Hearst was seeking was success for Marion, no matter what the cost.

He was also insistent upon achieving convincing realism in rendering the life of the rich or the royalty who were usually the leading characters of his early productions. John Winkler, another of Hearst's biographers, writes, "If the script called for the ladies of the ensemble to wear Irish lace, Belfast was asked to send entire bolts of its best and most costly hand-woven product." He was making costly spectaculars several years too soon, as D. W. Griffith was discovering at the same time. The public resisted paying $2 to see a Hearst film, and some financial success would come only when Marion began making a series of "program" movies early in the 1920s, first for Paramount release and then for Metro-Goldwyn-Mayer, but always under the aegis and watchful eye of Hearst. In these, the principal cost was Marion's huge and growing salary. Mary Pickford's earnings set a difficult and, at times, exorbitant standard for Hearst to follow in paying Marion for her screen work.

To most directors and screenwriters who worked for him, Hearst was an intrusive, overbearing despot. While he was no "glacier watcher," a Hollywood term of contempt for useless producers, his film staff often wished that he was. He had his piercing blue eyes on every phase of production: the direction, which would bring him into open conflict with King Vidor and other directors who had their own strong convictions about the films they were doing; the design (he frequently would use his own museum pieces as props in his quest for Belasco-like authenticity and sets would be built around them); the editing, which he often did himself; and the script, which he would rewrite on occasion, sometimes through telegrams of more than a dozen pages. He was seldom criticized for not knowing what he was doing; he knew precisely what he was doing and what effects he wanted. His difficulty lay in the fact that he treated his film activities very much as he did his castle enterprises—as a fascinating project that was, in his mind, totally fluid and changing as his visions were altered. The results were often striking, but devastating to the Hearst financial structure. Reaction to the film trade announcements about his launching a series of important features was far from skeptical. He had a reputation as an expert at pandering to public taste and for that reason alone he was considered a strong threat to the men at the top of the several major studios.

It was still an era when a leading lady could be created overnight whenever a producer or director saw something of potential in a young girl. Making her into a star meant public acceptance as well. But a great deal of this acceptance could be achieved through handling her properly: the right director, story, camerawork. Then if the public related to her screen image, she was launched. Ingénues discovered in the street or in a crowd of extras might be Marie Prevost or Gloria Swanson, depending upon that intangible "star quality" combined with the expertise of the director, crew, and writer.

There was little in the background of a showgirl to equip her for films except perhaps the poise gained from strutting across a stage before an obviously admiring audience. While the unsmiling "Dolores" and Justine Johnstone were among the most popular showgirls in town, they rarely danced, sang, or recited lines. They posed and postured and walked across the stage with plumes waving to appropriately dignified music (*A Pretty Girl Is Like a Melody* was such a Ziegfeld tune). Marion had left their ranks and had taken a small step into acting in several minuscule musical comedy roles. Her contribution to *Runaway, Romany,* was mainly looking lovely as she posed in a series of dramatic tableaux. And when she went straight from that venture into her important alliance with Hearst, she was far from being an actress. But Hearst was as determined in this as he had been in making his first newspaper, *The San Francisco Examiner,* a success. Marion's career was to be primed with lots of money and with all the available talent surrounding her that he could find.

II

In 1918, New York City was still a major film center. D. W. Griffith even brought his "stock company" back East following the production of *Broken Blossoms* and equipped a complete studio at Orienta Point just out of Mamaroneck. Adolph Zukor had built a large studio complex for his Paramount company in Astoria, Long Island. Actors, once ashamed to work in films and sneaking in the side door of the studio buildings so their stage repu-

Marion Davies

(Above) Bernard "Papa Ben" Douras with his daughter Marion at the racetrack, 1933. (At right) Mrs. Rose Douras with her daughters, Marion, at left, and little Rose, 1908.

(At left) Actress Marie Glendinning, who saw that Marion got on the stage, 1915. (Bottom left) Marion in a pensive mood, 1918. (Bottom right) Marion, at left, with sister Rose, 1910. (At right, top) Reine Davies Lederer, as she appeared on the stage, 1903. (Middle) Nephew Charlie Lederer, Reine's son, circa 1917. (Bottom) Norma, at left, and Constance Talmadge with Buster Collier at Norma's Santa Monica beach property, 1924.

MARIE GLENDINNING

CHARLES LEDERER

Marion Davies of *The Follies*, 1916 edition. She already had met Mr. Hearst, but she got this part on her own.

Again *The Follies of 1916*. Flo Ziegfeld kept her busy in three different scenes.

Marion in *The Young Diana*, 1922.

Marion as film queen Patricia Pepoire in *Show People*. This was Marion's best movie and is the most frequently revived of her films, 1928.

(At left, top) Marion enters films for her brother-in-law, George Lederer. The pearls were fake then, 1917. (Bottom) Marion in her first big film hit, *When Knighthood Was in Flower,* produced by William Randolph Hearst, who was so pleased that he allowed his name to remain in the credits. With leading man Forest Stanley, 1922. (Below) Marion is photographed by Campbell Studios for the Hearst roto Sunday section, 1919.

(At left) Marion poses with
some of her real jewelry and
inscribes it to niece Pepi
Lederer, 1918. (Above)
Another big film success,
Little Old New York, in which
Marion impersonates her own
brother through two-thirds
of the movie. The man looking
soulfully at her is her cousin
(Harrison Ford), who has to
fight to control his feelings
toward this "young man," 1923.

Marion Davies as a cover girl. (Top left) A still from *The Bride's Play*, 1922. (Bottom left) In the title role of Janice Meredith, her most spectacular film, 1924.

CHARLES LEDERER

(Top right) Marion as Yolanda, in disguise as a peasant girl, 1924. (Bottom right) Her first movie role—and her first magazine cover—in *Runaway Romany,* 1917.

Marion as Cosmopolitan Productions' major star in the latest style from Paris—short gloves with fringed cuffs—especially posed for Hearst's *New York American*, 1922.

Marion as Patricia O'Day in *Little Old New York*, the successful film that made Louis B. Mayer one of her staunchest admirers, 1923.

Marion wears Mary Pickford curls in this studio portrait, 1927.

tations would not be sullied, now frankly sought both screen work and film reputations.

Hearst rented Sulzer's Harlem River Park Casino, a former nightclub at Second Avenue and 127th Street, and began equipping it with everything needed to make feature-length films. Always an expert photographer himself, he purchased the finest camera equipment available. His custom of paying higher salaries than his competitors lured away from them a full studio crew. Marion was shocked when she learned that she was to be paid $500 a week, her last stage salary having been only $75, but then she tried to expunge her sense of guilt by telling friends that she was saving Hearst that much in rent every week. (She had overheard a conversation between the rental agent and the landlord in which the agent said that he was extracting $1000 a week from Hearst as rental for the Casino building and pocketing the $500 difference. Hearst went straight to the landlord and got the agent fired as well as a more honest lease.)

Hearst had produced two cliff-hanging serials—*The Mysteries of Myra* and *The Exploits of Elaine,* and both serials were successful, although forgotten today. Now it was his notion that Marion might become more quickly famous if the public were exposed to her in a serial rather than running the risk of failure by launching her in an expensive feature. *Beatrice Fairfax* was fed in installments into the theater circuits over a period of thirty weeks. It was the story of an adventurous young lady of wealth and social standing who gets into near-fatal mishaps mostly out of an irrepressible curiosity. But Marion was not the quick sensation as Beatrice that Pearl White, the most successful of the serial queens, had been as Pauline and the project was abandoned after several months.

Hearst then became bolder in his efforts. Perhaps it would be best, he thought, for the public to assume that she was already a star. Marion's rise to star status with all its prerogatives was achieved in a matter of weeks through extraordinary publicity in the Hearst press, huge infusions of cash into her personal bank account with unlimited charge accounts at all the best stores, and by moving her and her family (all except Papa Ben, who had no interest in sharing a place with Mama Rose) into a white marble townhouse, remodeled along palatial lines, at 331 Riverside Drive. Hearst called in an architect and had all of the rooms redone. A marble fountain with two cupids was installed in Marion's sitting room. The library was paneled in

expensive imported woods, and the shelves filled with rare editions bound in calf and morocco. Marion told a visiting fan
magazine reporter, "I-I'll r-read all of these when I'm an old
w-woman," and reached up to take down a French novel that was
inlaid with mother-of-pearl. "Now h-here's a pretty book," she
said. She stressed that she *did* read. "Plays—and things I think
would film . . . ." suggesting that she probably was guilty of poor
judgment in choosing some of her failures. She said that the
public responded best to "snappy stuff." "All my first pictures—
well, they didn't please me particularly; but in a way they were
good for me, too. I had to learn more." Marion told the reporter
that she wanted to do the heroines of Galsworthy sometime, "the
fragile, sensitive, restless children with whom the Englishman
loves to illuminate his pages." It would be the film-goer's loss that
she never would, but specialized instead for too long a time in
the works of Robert W. Chambers.

Despite her elegant surroundings and the maids coming and
going, Marion impressed all of her guests as having no false
ideas of her own importance. But she did project a sense of being
in command of her situation. She knew what to say to her fans
when they wrote to her, although there was not yet any great
flood of fan mail reaching her. She had been a movie fan herself
since her early teens and knew the illusions they wanted played
out in the movie houses. And she instinctively knew how to dress
for interviews. Then she played her role as star, and when she
received at home she usually wore the daintiest things in her
growing wardrobe—pink or white negligees, delicately sheer, if
the reporter were a woman; sheer silk blouses under a tailored
suit if it were a man. Diamonds glittered under the crystal chandeliers on her hands and wrists; a brooch was at her throat; one
or two perfect pearls pinned back her blonde hair, which was
baby-fine but teased by a hair-dresser into looking luxuriant. Her
beauty was the most impressive thing about her but not too far
above her practicality. "She is not the wittiest woman in the
world, perhaps, nor the wisest," the *Photoplay* Magazine interviewer concluded. "No Venus can double as Minerva—but this
is a perfect pantheon of common sense."

She felt that she had to be practical, if nothing else. Hearst
was carefully leading her by the hand toward greater fame than
either of her celebrated sisters had ever enjoyed. The rebel that
she had been as a child had to be contained while he manipulated her this way and that, and at times it was a sobering

realization to her that she was being exposed to hordes of photographers, personal appearances beyond number, and lessons in a variety of subjects she could readily have left alone had he not taken over her career. Sometimes she would say to herself, "This is all too much." When it *did* become too much, she would put her head in Mama Rose's lap or, if that was not possible, then she would retire for a few pink ladies.

And so her early days of carefully engineered stardom went that way—all out of love and devotion, of course, with Marion herself as flawless as any other part of the project except in the acting department, but she was trying to catch up on that and she would do so. All of her innate cunning and keen perceptions were called into play, and she tried to subdue the mischievous side of her nature through all those beginning years. With the weight of entire film productions on her shoulders, some of the fun would have to go.

But not all. Anita Loos recalls that there were considerable "monkey-shines" going on during the filming of *Getting Mary Married* (1919). Hearst's departure from New York on a business trip would be the signal that would send Marion, writer Loos, and anyone else who looked to be slightly zany off on a three-day binge of hilarity and "high-jinks," burning up $10,000 to $15,000 of Hearst's money in the process since all film shot then was highly dubious material. Marion would pretend to be ready to do a scene and emerge from the proper door with her costume bursting from a sudden "pregnancy." She was not above blacking out one of her teeth during an intimate love scene in closeup so that her smile would devastate her screen lover. Hearst always had his spies around and he inevitably found out what was going on in his absence, but he rarely complained. In time, Marion would see how desperate he was for ready cash, when the studio payroll could not be met on schedule, and she would feel a profound shame over her own contribution to this embarrassment. But she was never cured of her need to clown her way through her career, and as she became more famous her need for a few laughs on the set increased.

Her family fell into their role as succor and emotional security for Marion with equal ease. Each of the female Dourases was given an allowance to furnish her own room in any way she wished. There was no neat way of determining then or in the future how much of Marion's salary or how much of Hearst's generosity was tapped by her family in immersing themselves in

their new life of luxury. Eventually, they became principally
Marion's charge, but even then there were homes purchased by
Hearst for one Douras or another. There was only one of them
who would feel embarrassed by these subsidies, Charlie Lederer,
but that was later and now he was sent off to military school
in Poughkeepsie. Charlie's sister Pepi was fond of Aunt Marion
reading to her from "Father Goose," which was soon dog-eared
and the most-read book in the house. She was six years old and
her chief diversion was beating up the other kids in the neighborhood, especially boys. She would come home all bruised and
dirty and then tell her aunt, "Well, I saw him," and when Marion
asked her who *he* was, she would say, "Why, the little boy who
made a face at me the other day when he was with his nurse.
I saw him today without his nurse." Papa Ben made a pretense
of keeping himself afloat through his own industry. He looked
upon Marion as the one successful accomplishment of his life,
and he got on extremely well with Hearst. The two men exchanged jokes and, less often, opinions on world affairs and politics. In a small way, Papa Ben was a collector, too. He had a
fine collection of silver and gold pocket watches. But Marion was
shocked to see how Hearst towered above her father. She observed that it was not just an aura of wealth and power he
projected; it was his physical size that dominated and attracted
respectful glances. Douras, of course, had his own distinct
image. Lately, he had taken to wearing spats. Hearst saw Papa
Ben as "a proud man." He was soon to learn that the peacock
façade covered a considerable amount of disappointment and
unhappiness, and he would take steps to give Marion's father a
legitimate reason for his pride by having Mayor Hylan appoint
him a municipal magistrate at a salary of $8000 a year. Later,
he would persuade Douras to move into a townhouse adjacent to
the one the family occupied on Riverside Drive. Marion told her
friends that the building was purchased as office space for her
father, but those who knew the family well realized that Papa
Ben was making it his home, too. He would hold the job of
magistrate until 1930, which was his seventy-fifth year and way
beyond the retirement age required by law, but Papa Ben had
taken ten years away from his age when he was first asked to
give it for the city records—a family habit which served him as
well as it would Marion at that future time when she dropped
three years from her age. Upon his resignation, he would make
a plea for pensions for magistrates, contending that they should

receive the same recognition as other judges. It is unlikely that Douras had any personal benefit in mind since his daughter Marion was by then a multimillionairess with five homes, and he would live in one of them until his death.

In the winter of 1918–19, Hearst felt that she was ready for her first feature production. All of the facilities of the Harlem studio were put at her disposal when shooting began on a romantic story of American family life entitled *Cecilia of the Pink Roses*. Julius Steeger, an expensive and capable director, led her through the uncomplicated paces and, when it opened in New York in June 1919, Hearst arranged for thousands of real pink roses to frame the motion picture screen, their fragrance wafted over the audience by huge fans. The *New York American* film critic wrote that "there were few dry eyes at the Rivoli Theater yesterday when the vision of Marion Davies faded on the screen." The word "masterpiece" was used, as it would be again and again until readers of Hearst publications began to have doubts and "masterpiece" entered the realm of the questionable, like the later "stupendous" and "colossal." Still, Hearst's company, with several Alma Rubens dramas in release, and now Marion's, was not looked upon by other film men as a rich man's toy, but as a firm that was making good films with solid production values.

Adolph Zukor was one of the first studio heads to see that audiences were responding to Marion as a star, and she was no longer simply a producer's girlfriend who was being forced upon the movie-going public. A deal was worked out immediately whereby Paramount would distribute Hearst's Cosmopolitan films, an agreement that survived from 1919 through 1922. Paramount had become a major rival to First National Pictures (a producing, distributing, and exhibiting combine begun by a syndicate of theater owners). Zukor (with Paramount) soon would enter the exhibiting end by building what he insisted had to be "the most beautiful theater in each major city." He was a man in pursuit of ideals of beauty as he conceived them to be found in tons of marble statuary, Grecian urns, and acres of red plush velvet. There were the classical palaces of terra-cotta with strong Renaissance touches designed by Thomas W. Lamb and the "open sky with clouds and stars" of John Eberson with their reproductions of the interiors of Spanish courtyards, Egyptian temples, and Persian courts. Paramount Theaters designed by these men and others of similar bent rose across the country, as well as hundreds of others in the Loew, Fox, and Balaban & Katz movie-house chains. The Wurlitzer Company had a tremendous backlog of orders for giant pipe organs. Symphony orchestras were regularly employed at the larger theaters, always with fifty or more men and a conductor of some musical standing. Many of the lobbies rivaled Versailles in dimension and quantity of crystal chandeliers, if not in aesthetic satisfaction; but even aesthetically, there was something to be said for their brave mixture of Moorish, French Empire, and what came to be known as "pristine Loew's." For the price of a ticket, the *hoi polloi* could luxuriate in the splendid comfort of these rococo palaces, and when doomsday came for most of them half-way through the twentieth century, parking stations and van der Rohe slabs went up in their places—austerity supplanting Renaissance extravagance, as "purity of line" and other contemporary excesses began scrubbing out and destroying the enriching corners of the average man's world.

Hearst's choice of director for Marion was almost always the result of much consideration for their suitability to the script. During the next twenty years, he managed to employ many of the most gifted in American films. He was equally determined to make her films both literate and, on occasion, scholarly, so the most expensive writing talent was hired, that chore frequently falling to Frances Marion.

Allan Dwan had come into prominence in 1914 as a director of features with a production of *Richelieu,* made for Universal and featuring an actor of great promise, Lon Chaney. His first film with Marion, *Getting Mary Married,* had made a modest amount of money for Cosmopolitan Pictures, chiefly because the film audience reacted positively to Marion's flair for comedy, a facet of her own personality that had been kept a secret in *Runaway, Romany,* and *Cecilia of the Pink Roses.* To his dismay, he found on his second assignment that Hearst had chosen *The Dark Star;* it was the first of many Robert W. Chambers novels that he would purchase as properties for Marion, some creaky rubbish about a fabulous jewel. Dwan's observations of Marion at work in those first days are of some interest. He was to say that "Marion Davies was lots of fun. She stuttered and stammered and it was a little difficult for her to speak at times, but she was fine. As an actress, I can only say that she was very pretty, but no great shakes—never tried to be—and nobody ever tried to make her very much of an actress. But she had a sense of humor and if you gave her anything funny to do, she'd do it funny. She had a great smile. Half the time they didn't pick stories for her with enough humor in them. He [Hearst] was involved in the sense that he was very interested in her and he'd come around and see how things were going, invite us all to lunch and take too much time—the whole afternoon would be gone before we'd get back to work—which didn't bother him much. . . ."

Dwan's opinion of Marion's abilities and the depth of Hearst's interest was a fairly common one in Hollywood in those early years and closely approximates that of King Vidor in his memoir *A Tree Is a Tree*. They believed then that her career was an indulgence rather than a necessity, and such views became key factors in the careless process by which her film reputation was destroyed following the release of *Citizen Kane*. In Vidor's case, his book was published in 1959 and he was speaking at a time when Marion's career already was in ruins as a result of film invention being taken for fact—a near classic example. His comments in her defense may seem patronizing in retrospect, but several of Marion's films have now been revived and Vidor's own film with her, *Show People*, is fast becoming the most popular of all the Vidor silents.

In the early years part of the criticism was justified. Hearst was impatient to get Marion established; in his mind's eye, she was already a queen in an industry fostering royalty almost overnight. The secret of their affair was out (he now permitted photographs to be taken of them together), and he was determined that the woman everyone said was either his "friend" or his mistress was not just a showgirl, a glorified chorine. Perhaps it was for Millicent's sake as well as his own. Millicent might understand his permanent affection for a leading actress of the day, Millicent's friends as well, but a simple-minded blonde lady of the chorus would never be an acceptable cause for rearranging their lives.

Most of Hearst's real estate projects and newspaper work that year kept him in the West, and he had left the management of the movie company in Marion's hands. Within another year, she would be made its president. There were daily letters and telegrams dispatched to her, filled with suggestions about the movies their studio was making at the time. She had the help of sister Rose's husband, George Van Cleve, who had been made an executive at Cosmopolitan-International Pictures and who had become a permanent resident of the Riverside Drive townhouse. The Van Cleves recently had become the parents of a baby girl, named Patricia. Sister Reine was finding steady employment as a supporting actress at Hearst's studio. In those days of frantic activity, Marion's loneliness was nearly always succored by large doses of family. She broke completely with Paul Block, who had been of late, she insisted, only a professional associate. Once in California, another kind of pattern would be established, allowing her a modicum of freedom, enough to permit her to pretend to her friends that she was not owned body and soul by Hearst, but it would be a freedom under the surveillance of Hearst's hirelings. Even in the wake of Hearst's death, she would not feel truly free. His domination could not be broken by his mortality.

It was not Trilby and Svengali. Dutifully following Mama Rose's precepts, she had captured a millionaire. But the tables had turned and soon she was his slightly rebellious captive. Her defenses against this wholesale takeover of her person and personality were highly visible. She remained flirtatious (but the male objects of these small encounters were always carefully watched by Hearst), voluble about her own family and its welfare, and the possessor of a rich trove of words not usually heard very much outside of the Navy, card parlors, and chorines' dressing rooms. When she eventually began having a series of small affairs, almost always with already-married leading men, she was not seeking a break-up with Hearst; she was showing her resentment over one of his trips to Millicent's side. If he tried not to show his intense jealousy, then she would think that he no longer cared what she did and she would go off, as one of her friends put it, "on a bat" with her gin or scotch or "mimosas" or whatever she had a taste for at the time. There are some former co-workers on her films who believe, too, that all of her clowning on the set was her way of showing Hearst that she knew that she was being exploited, that he was using her for leverage in getting his films distributed, in keeping his whole film operation from collapsing.

In July 1919, Marion was finishing *The Cinema Murder* and director George Baker was disagreeing with Hearst's concept of the film. All of his complaints were addressed to Marion since Hearst was out of town. Baker threatened to leave before the film was completed, and there were other problems plaguing the production. Studio manager Zittell was going off on an extended summer vacation while production was moving ahead full blast, and Hearst wrote Marion asking her to consider promoting her brother-in-law George Van Cleve to take his place. Although his background was in advertising, Van Cleve was elevated to studio manager. Then leading man Conway Tearle, who had a classic profile and considerable fame as a Shakespearean actor, let it be known that he had agreed only to a certain number of weeks in which to complete the movie, and he balked on retakes. Hearst told Marion that he would fire Tearle and "retake the whole picture later," a threat provoked by Hearst's feeling that he was being intimidated by Tearle's reputation. Such a threat was not to be taken lightly since those close to Hearst knew that it could be carried out as casually as anyone else might order a second cup of coffee.

Marion's own letters to Hearst were not nearly as sentimental as his although they were sometimes signed "Sorrowful Sophie," to show that he was missed. But she surrounded herself with friends and family to curb her loneliness. She never could bear to be alone. Much later, when most of her friends drifted away, she relied upon one or two companion-nurses to keep the blues away. And it was difficult for anyone with Marion's love of parties to be sorrowful in New York City at the time. The Volstead Act (Prohibition) was due to become the law of the land in January 1920, and Manhattan was awash in "one last fling." The Davies girls' capacity for a good time was boundless, and their capacity for alcohol was becoming equally exceptional. Marion was just beginning to acquire a taste for gin after one unhappy episode in her teens when she thought it had "poisoned" her. Sister Rose had begun using scotch as a refuge from the routine of daily life. So with Mama Rose's sherry tippling, the Douras household on the Drive kept the liquor store on nearby Broadway busy with deliveries.

But Marion's dissipations did not yet show in her twenty-fourth year. In photos taken that year, she is deceptively docile in appearance and a childlike innocence shines from her eyes. Only her generous mouth—without that foolish pout which Mae Murray was making popular—in those poses where she is smiling, suggests that she is a woman who enjoys giving herself to a man—a faintly wicked smile. She would have it throughout her career, and it was undeniably attractive, as a tasteful suggestion of sexuality always is. The woman within that attractive exterior was driven to indulge herself in fancied infatuations, parties that would begin to pall before the night was out, and other excesses in her strenuous pursuit of pleasure. She was like Hearst in her conviction that material pleasures should be pursued for no one really could guarantee any joy in the hereafter. In fact, she shared Hearst's doubts about an eternity, and when really troubled about it, she attempted to salvage some reassurance from the Catholic dogma that was to be her resource in any prolonged crisis in the future. But she considered herself one of the Church's "black sheep," and indeed could not later manage to get even Mama Rose buried in a Catholic cemetery when it was learned that she intended to reserve a space for herself in the same plot.

Hearst's own attitude toward liquor and other possibly dangerous distractions was one of tolerance, at least until their San Simeon days when he would attempt—vainly—to police the alcoholic consumption and the behavior of his mistress and their guests. Marion's own family would be tolerated without comment and almost without exception. Hearst and the Douras clan had come to an understanding that would last until his death; in American annals, it was probably unique. Marion was as much the royal consort as anyone ever would be in the United States, and the Dourases were to enjoy the same largesse and status-by-relation as had the family of the Marquise de Pompadour from Louis XV. On Hearst's side, from the moment of their meeting his earlier philandering had ceased and he was in love with Marion until the end of his life. But on quite a different level, Millicent was kept content. Perhaps both she and Hearst sensed that their earlier love had burned itself out. If he had committed himself by marriage or—in the case of Marion—by pledges of devotion which he claimed were eternal (and apparently were), then he would reconstruct his life-style so that each woman had her place, rather like the way he fitted his castles around the historic rooms with which he had fallen in love. This adaptability was to be put to a severe test within a year, however.

But Marion was not to be easily fitted into place. She had enjoyed her earlier bedroom encounters with Hearst, and when they became less frequent as he moved into his sixties, delicate decisions had to be made. She had to be allowed an occasional truancy from fidelity as a diversion or as an anodyne against boredom, but it meant much less to Marion than to the average actress. Even her occasional professions of love to a temporary lover could not be taken seriously and the man involved sensed this. Sex was just another form of pleasure to her and less exhilarating than a fast Charleston or even a particularly gamey joke. If she had been truly involved in sex with a succession of partners, Hearst probably could not have abided it. Sometimes she would make it a point to inform a temporary lover that their affair must remain secret, but *her* secret was always that she knew that she was being watched. She was not promiscuous, but she frankly enjoyed human contact—in the bedroom and in the parlor—and by the time she reached the peak of her stardom in 1927, Hearst would be in his sixty-fifth year.

III

In the summer of 1920, Hearst was involved at the Republican convention in getting Senator Hiram Johnson of California the nomination. But his political albatross was still pendant and his man lost to Warren Harding of Ohio. Harding would have accepted Johnson as his running-mate and told Hearst so, but Senator Johnson was not interested in second place on the ballot. Harding finally was teamed with Calvin Coolidge, and Hearst was again out in the political cold. If the convention had heeded Hearst's compromise suggestion, Hiram Johnson would have become President in 1923 and forty years later the United States would have had three Johnsons in the highest office of the land.

Hearst angrily tried to rally his readers to form a third party with Johnson, but got nowhere. Then, in another of his wild and seemingly plotless political swings, he was off to San Francisco and the Democratic convention, where he personally received one vote on the first ballot. He had garnered 263 votes in the 1904 Democratic convention, a frightening number to his enemies, but sixteen years had seen him slowly becoming a known quantity to many—a man with a lust for political power but with little redeeming interest in the public at large. This impression of Hearst was unfair; there were countless humane causes advanced in the columns of his newspapers, but he lacked an ability to relate to the constituency to such a degree that much of the good he performed, like Caesar's, would be buried with him. His "grass roots" grew about his castles and villas, and he was not slow in getting the message that the delegates of both parties simply didn't want him.

At San Simeon, construction was going on under Julia Morgan's supervision, and the three guest houses were well along. Hearst's boyhood friend, Orrin Peck, an artist frequently down on his luck, came to the mountain to help in any way he could. He was assigned the landscape design and execution. Peck was perhaps the only man Hearst ever took into his confidence concerning his love life, and he had known of all of Hearst's travails with Tessie Powers, Millicent, and finally Marion. They talked of Marion's future in films and of Hearst's fear that she might fall in love with someone else in New York during one of his many absences. "Marion is a popular young lady," Hearst told Peck. "She's going to tire of staying home with her family even though she loves them dearly." "Then you must bring her to California," Peck told Hearst, and Hearst conceded that the future of motion pictures was probably in the West. It did not seem to bother him much that he just had spent over a million dollars redecorating and remodeling her Riverside Drive home.

Hearst sent Marion clippings from California newspapers marking some important items, telling her that she should read up on California news before coming out so as to be familiar with the leading topic of interest, which was *girls*. He asked her to note the verse he enclosed on "Blondes" and the one on "The Forgetful Maiden."

Edna Ferber observed that Hollywood had a crude lavishness about it in 1920. "It wasn't American," she wrote, "it had no virility, it sprang from almost pure vulgarity. There was about it none of the lusty native quality of the old gold-rush camp days. . . . I discovered that when I walked in the deserted sunny town, people peered from windows at some strange animal loose in the streets. I learned that no one walked in Hollywood. . . . The sun came up, day after day, day after day. None of the clouds, none of the storms, none of the summer caprices of the temperate climate to which I was accustomed. It was like seeing someone in red satin daily. What a grateful change to see them in clean gray gingham for a change." Miss Ferber complained, too, that the roses had no scent at all, "like ghosts" and "the whole city appeared ghostlike."

But if it lacked the gutsy American spirit so appealing to Edna Ferber, whose career had been built upon a series of books on nineteenth- and early twentieth-century America, (*So Big, Showboat, Cimarron,* and *Come and Get It*) Hollywood was instantly attractive to Marion. The air was relatively pure and the days endlessly sunny. She thought the place might be good for Mama Rose's arthritis. And, of course, Millicent Hearst was over three thousand miles away. Hotel living was far more austere than her marble townhouse, but she was too excited to mind. She came out with sisters Rose and Ethel and Mama Rose, staying first at the old Hollywood Hotel. It was the social hub of the film community and nearly all the stars who weren't living in their own homes in the Hollywood hills or in nearby Beverly Hills would stay there.

Hearst seemed ill at ease for some reason. He owned a major newspaper in Los Angeles, the *Examiner* (and he soon would add a second, the *Herald*), and Millicent had come West numerous times and knew all of his key executives. He now found it difficult to introduce these men to Marion, although he would overcome this embarrassment and take her on a tour of the newspaper offices. She finally met Orrin Peck, who came down from San Simeon for the occasion, and Hearst escorted her to dinner with other stars and movie people. She got in touch with her old friend Eileen Percy, who was by now established as a leading lady in films, and they spent several evenings catching up on the changes in their lives. But that was about the sum of her days in California and when she complained of being neglected after a month of this selective socializing, Hearst took her up to an inn at Santa Maria for a quiet weekend alone together.

It was during those four days at Santa Maria that their feelings for each other crystalized. If a honeymoon was denied them, this was its closest substitute. At fifty-eight, he had the ardor of a young man and the sentiments of a youth of the Victorian era. There at the inn, he made his love for her abundantly clear. He declared once again that they would settle on his enchanted hill, which was just to the north of where they were staying. She didn't ask about the ring. She was willing to continue trying his alternative to marriage, which was first of all her career and then his showering upon her everything his spendthrift genius could suggest as well as making his devotion to her a constant in her life. To give their alliance some sense of permanence, he pointed out the place where his castle would rise. She would be its chatelaine and, at that moment, she chose not to ask what would happen if Millicent should suddenly appear. By this time, treasures and rare furnishings were beginning to fill a warehouse he had constructed next to Sebastian's General Store at the bottom of the hill adjacent to his private wharf. The treasures meant much less to her than they did to Hearst, but he appeared to be implying that she was the inspiration for all that acquisitiveness, its focus.

Their future together seemed less remote upon their return to Hollywood. But her days in the film colony were terminated abruptly following an evening when Hearst called on her and found her in the hotel lobby surrounded by handsome young men. He turned pale and nearly lost control. The young men, nearly all of them film players, looked at Hearst with the enormous respect due a man of great power and influence, nodded a polite greeting to him, and drifted away. Marion displayed some anger, asking him why he drove "those nice boys away." It was her nature to be flirtatious; if she had been retiring, Hearst never would have been captivated by her in the first place. She was a strange mixture of shyness and open friendliness, not too uncommon among show people, and she believed now that she had done nothing to provoke this wrathful mood in Hearst. What harm was there in a mild flirtation, especially with a small crowd?

Her answer came in the morning. With his usual dispatch, Hearst rented a spacious estate for Marion on the outskirts of Santa Barbara, one hundred miles north of Los Angeles. Known as La Paz Ranch, it had a large lemon grove, a fine view of the hills, and an elegant old Spanish Colonial ranch house. Marion would be nicely out of reach of the Hollywood predators there, but not especially happy. She was getting used to an element in her life that went along with her role as cherished possession— being ruled absolutely by Hearst. She shrugged and accepted this without complaint even though she often "boiled over," as she put it, giving him a tongue-lashing over other matters that probably stemmed from her old resentment at having been bought and knowing that she was too much in love with him ever to break free.

There is some evidence that Hearst considered building studio facilities in Santa Barbara. It would make a Hearstian kind of sense. It was remote from Hollywood's illusions, snares, and bitchery; it was over a third of the way along the road to San Simeon from Los Angeles; it had the same sunny climate, barring an occasional fog; and it would be a studio world of his own devising—probably its greatest attraction for him. But it was a long way for Marion's leading men to commute. They would have to live in the community during production, making the probability of Marion becoming over-friendly with them all the stronger. It was simply another of Hearst's plans carried out to the smallest detail that could not work out.

She was alone at the lemon ranch much of the time, and Eileen Percy came up for visits whenever she was free. During one of them, Hearst came down from San Francisco for the weekend and took them over to his mountain, where they stayed in elegantly furnished tents and ate out-of-season foods from a chuck wagon manned by one of Hearst's chefs.

It was a mystery to Hearst as to where she went, but Marion began disappearing from the lemon ranch, sometimes for an entire day, and he could not reach her by phone. In one of his frequent telegrams, his constant resource when she was not at home, Hearst mentions that he would try her the next day "at the studio." Some temporary facilities had been set up in downtown Santa Barbara, where their film plans were carried on, but it was mostly a paper operation for production correspondence and property acquisition, and no actual filming was ever done there.

The year 1920 saw Hearst become increasingly enthusiastic about the movies. This enthusiasm was channeled in specific directions: there was a property he had worked up in scenario form entitled *Mother Maginn* as well as one called *Joss*, which he said would make a powerful and picturesque movie. They also had begun thinking about a film of *The Young Diana*, which would be in the planning stages for over a year and eventually would be filmed—back in New York. Screenwriter Frances Marion was invited to come up and discuss film possibilities with them. Frances first had met Marion back in New York through Elsie Janis. Miss Janis told her that she wanted her to meet the most beautiful showgirl in New York. When Frances saw her, she was struck by her blond beauty "set off by the blue in her eyes and in her costume. I could only think of *Blue Bells*, Frances recalled.

Frances Marion had started her writing career as a very young woman back in her native San Francisco, where she had gone to work for Hearst on the *Examiner*. One day, Hearst came into the newsroom where she was working as a cub reporter and found her sitting on a desk.

"Get off that desk!" Hearst ordered, sensing a breach of discipline.

"No, I won't," she told him. Then Hearst said that she was fired, and the rebellious young reporter told her fellow reporters that she was going to join the Salvation Army.

In 1919, when Frances had become the highest-paid lady screenwriter in films, Hearst approached her to do a script for him. She set the price so high—$2000 weekly—she didn't expect to get it, but she would have the satisfaction of letting him know what his ex-girl reporter was worth on the marketplace. Hearst met her terms, and she wrote *The Cinema Murder*, which made a little money for Cosmopolitan Pictures, and *The Restless Sex*, which earned back its cost.

But in Santa Barbara, Frances decided to be candid with Hearst, since he spoke of nothing but, as the screen writer put it, "big period epics with overstuffed costumes and overstuffed emotions." Then she told him tersely, "I'm not going to write for you now, W.R. I'm busy on something else." The implication was strong that she no longer wanted to be a party to Hearst's willful insistence upon Marion's absolute and incredible purity on the screen.

Hearst was indignant. Frances thought he was on the verge of throwing a fit of some kind. She quickly explained that she knew how much Hearst thought of Marion, but that "love can destroy as well as help, and love in this case is very harmful to Marion's career." When she saw Hearst beginning to look choleric again, she gently moderated her tone. "W.R.," she said, "why do we all love her? Because she makes us laugh. She is neither Little Miss Pollyanna nor Snow White. Let her have the thoughts and emotions of a grown woman. Let her have children —Marion loves children. Let her have a man and lose him."

Hearst may have observed in all of this that Marion's life, including possible motherhood, was being lived much of the time vicariously, upon the screen. But probably he did not, blind as he was where Marion was concerned. He smiled at Frances with the distant eyes of a prophet and said, "I see the opening of the picture as showing Marion walking through a field of wheat wearing a sunbonnet." And Frances Marion felt that it was a lost cause.

To say that these suggestions from a trusted friend came as a shock to Hearst would be understating its effect. He had always regarded her as a sage in movie matters and often phoned her to get an opinion on film material. Marion adored her and the feeling was returned. Frances Marion understood Hearst's commitment to Marion better than most, since she had done for cowboy actor Fred Thompson what Hearst was doing for Marion. She had fallen in love with the cowboy and had written for him a rip-roaring western script and persuaded a producer to do it. Fred Thompson was, in fact, her husband at the time of her journey to Santa Barbara and had accompanied her there.

After their guests' departure, Hearst attempted to dispel the gloom by telling Marion that she was not to be discouraged by such stubborn wrong-headedness as she had just witnessed. Marion was aware that Hearst was doing everything possible to make her something more than a successful mannequin posturing upon the screen, which was what she understood Frances Marion to have meant. It had not yet occurred to her that her off-screen clowning might be a clue to the direction her career should follow, but something of Frances's cool logic had struck a responsive chord. She told Hearst that she hated a proposed film idea based on a character called "Gwendolyn"—another costume affair—a rare instance of her disagreement with him over film matters. And only after her career was done with would she see, in hindsight, something else that Frances Marion had touched upon, that her most successful films, her comedies, had been such hits because she had carried her predisposition for a good time right to the cameras; they had recorded a very natural gift of hers for laughing at life and infectiously getting an audience to laugh along with her.

Marion soon grew weary of her isolation. The ranch was too remote from everyone, especially the new friends she had made in town. She needed a little activity around to wind her up or she would run down like a mechanical toy. And so she moved to nearby Montecito into something known as "Mon Desir" Bungalow, one of a group of luxury cottages on Ocean View Avenue. Hearst went back to San Simeon to follow progress on the castle, keeping in touch with her by phone and telegram. She remained in Montecito less than two weeks. When Hearst phoned one day to say that he was going to Los Angeles, she said that she would meet him there, that she had something to discuss with him. When Hearst arrived, Marion was surrounded by her luggage. She told him that she had decided to go back East. Hearst put her on the train, smiling sickly and terrified of the possibility of losing her. That night, after leaving her on the train, he wrote her that he felt as though someone had kicked the bottom out of the universe, that everything looked the same, the sunlight and flowers, but there wasn't any Marion to make them delightful. "Delightful" was a word Hearst often used in describing her. He once defined the word for a friend as meaning "effortless charm," and he may have been thinking of Marion as opposed to Millicent.

The drive north to San Simeon made Hearst melancholy as his car passed through Santa Barbara and he recalled the times he had gone that way with Marion. He forgot that she was not there and turned to say something to her, and the bottom fell out of his universe again. He told her he didn't understand how it all had happened, that she had just gone off and left him, and he supposed that the next time he saw her she would be "Mrs. Deering" or something and she would be saying, "Haven't I met you somewhere before?" He asked her to write him and tell him a story and he would try to believe it and be happy. The phrasing was in Hearst's usual deliberate bright tone that often was a signal of his desperation.

Back in New York in the Riverside Drive mansion where Mama Rose and the others regrouped themselves around her—a retinue she would never be without—Marion remained in her own melancholy mood for days. Her brooding silence was so much like that of Mama Rose, her family may have feared that she had suffered some bitter emotional experience in the West that had unhinged her, but they were all afraid to ask what it might be. She said little to anyone about her film career, about Hearst. She had good reasons for despairing. Her successes had been small ones; Mary Pickford's popularity was such that her visit to godless Russia incited a crowd of worshiping fans to an idolatry approaching that once accorded the Virgin Mary. Some reviewers had pointed out unkindly that Marion was not yet an actress. When in April 1920 she returned to the stage as a featured performer in Ed Wynn's *Carnival,* the press, including Hearst's *American,* failed to mention her at all in their reviews. Her role as one of four beauties intended mainly as foils for the comedy was a step backward for her, but she had insisted upon doing it. When Hearst suggested to her that this omission on the part of the reviewers was actually an act of kindness since the part was so unsuitable, her personal crisis reached the breaking point. She told Hearst that she wanted something more out of life than she was getting. She said that she was not happy with the bargain she had made.

Hearst was in the East to follow the election. Warren Harding had won the presidency by a landslide Republican vote that turned Democrats out of office all across the country, including Governor Al Smith, Hearst's nemesis in Albany. Woodrow Wilson and his League of Nations had been repudiated by a nation misled by such as Hearst. He had been staying at the Clarendon, and, as usual, he was seen frequently in Millicent's company at social events. But following the confrontation with Marion, he told Millicent that he wanted a divorce, that, as she well knew, he was in love with Marion. Millicent refused even to consider it, but, according to her friend Elsa Maxwell, she showed no anger to Hearst. She simply went to Tiffany's the next day and bought a necklace of matched pearls costing a small fortune, telling the jewelry firm to "send the bill to my husband's office."

After several further attempts, including hiring a detective to follow Millicent in Palm Beach in the hope of catching her in an adulterous situation, Hearst abandoned any effort in that direction. The marriage would continue in name only—a charade for the sake of the boys. Millicent might not truly have a husband, but she would have his presence at important affairs and the power of a name that had figured prominently in American history for decades. Until her late eighties and long after Hearst's death, Millicent was to tell anyone who would listen what a great man "W.R." was. And there is a strong possibility that she knew that Hearst and Marion had had a showdown about their triangular situation and Marion had demanded that he approach her about the divorce—a performance by Hearst that once played out could be forgotten. The performance itself appeared to satisfy Marion that he had made an effort to be free, while the marriage returned to its functional, loveless state.

Still, Marion was shaken. It was a critical time in her life. Even her family was no longer the sprawling "Sanger Circus" it once was and in which she could recover her girlhood and heal her wounds. Reine had taken a house in Freeport, Long Island, near the Lights Club, a kind of country club for vaudevillians. She had moved Marion's favorites, Charlie and Pepi, there with a Negro housekeeper to look after them whenever she was in town.

Marion attempted to lessen some of her distress by spending long hours at Hearst's film studio in Harlem. The movie was another program feature, *Buried Treasure*, but she was relieved just to be working. In an effort to shake her out of her mood, Hearst hired a five-piece string orchestra to play between takes. These musicians became known as "the Marion Davies Orchestra" and became a fixture on all of her productions. They would play all of the latest song hits as well as old favorites such as *The Blue Danube Waltz* and *Alexander's Ragtime Band.* Marion then had a personal press agent, Rose Shulsinger, who was the first in a long line of well-paid staff who became a second family to her, and—toward the end of her life—excepting nephew Charlie, the family upon whom she would depend.

The films continued to be forgettable ones, but they were being made quickly on modest budgets. *Enchantment* was Marion's bid to rival Swanson. She was out of her element in such arch romantic nonsense, but some film audiences were taken in by the trappings of glamour.

Hearst's "perfectionism," which others saw as an absurd recklessness with a film budget, would become legendary with the years. In *The Young Diana,* Marion was often overwhelmed by the trappings—the massive scenery and the heavy costumes —but she was called upon to show such emotions as joy, fear, and disdain. The ex-Ziegfeld girl, used to posturing and strutting about, was not up to the demands of the role. This lack was only temporary. With the right director and with some elements of comedy injected into the script, critics began to see that she was something more than a clotheshorse. She would be, by 1922, a skillful professional film actress, but the often needless retakes demanded by Hearst would continue to give her productions a deserved reputation for extravagance and waste. The money squandered in such fashion eventually would take some of the luster from her screen image and spawn any number of false tales, focusing on her alleged shortcomings as an actress.

In the fall of 1921, Hearst and Marion invited sister Ethel (who still had a streak of sadness in her over her dead lover, although her humor was bawdy and Hearst enjoyed her company), set designer Joseph Urban, his daughter Gretl, director William LeBaron, scenarist Luther Reed, and Mama Rose on a cruise out of New York harbor on the Hearst yacht, *Oneida.* The invitation was for a sail and a screening in the yacht's projection room of Marion's latest film, *Enchantment,* then about to go into release.

On an impulse, Hearst said that, if all were willing, they

would continue on to Mexico, where he soon was expected on business. "None of us were equipped for such an extended journey," Gretl Urban later wrote, "so Mr. Hearst dispensed cash largesse to one and all for necessary supplements of clothing, etc." The *Oneida* dropped anchor in Baltimore port where the party went ashore and bought clothing. Once in Mexico, they set out in a private train Hearst had hired for a six week tour there. It was his particular pleasure to go out in the native villages and buy tamales and fresh fruit to serve his guests with their morning coffee in the train's dining room. Hearst set up a temporary office in his compartment and worked over his newspapers and film productions while the other guests enjoyed the scenery. He was the perfect host, seeing to his guests' every need. It was a side of Hearst which Marion, Mama Rose, and Ethel had become used to by this time, but it surprised Gretl Urban, who had heard stories about his wickedness and selfishness. She wrote Hearst's biographer Swanberg, "I shall cherish his wonderful kindness forever."

Hearst owned millions of acres of ranch land in Campeche, in Chihuahua, and on the Isthmus of Tehuantepec in Veracruz —land inherited from his father, who had got it for practically nothing. Though the ranch had been under attack earlier in the century by brigands under Pancho Villa who even had killed one of Hearst's ranch hands, all was relatively peaceful during their visit, which Hearst attributed to the pacifying methods of President Álvaro Obregón. He and Marion had a private interview with the Mexican President, the first recorded instance in which Marion was Hearst's companion on a state visit. Hearst was never to be intimidated by convention. He was also a rarity among men, almost wholly free of self-doubt. It was a resource nearly large enough for himself *and* his lady-love.

IV

Marion's affair with Hearst suffered a temporary set-back in the years 1921 and 1922. His confidante in matters of the heart, Orrin Peck, died unexpectedly—of a heart attack—early in 1921. Then Hearst attempted to buy peace with Millicent by taking her and their three eldest boys to Europe in the late spring of

1922. She had complained bitterly about his Mexican trip with Marion the previous fall. They took with them Mr. and Mrs. Guy Barham of Los Angeles. Barham was publisher of Hearst's latest acquisition, the *Los Angeles Herald.*

With Hearst's divorce now increasingly remote, Marion had accepted the role of mistress, but with one clear reservation: she was to be treated with the same dignity and respect he accorded Millicent. Although sometimes in the future she would make it difficult for Hearst to keep her image dignified, he was to keep that promise. As a first step toward that end, immediately upon his return to America, he would commission Victor Herbert to write a *Marion Davies March,* to be played at theaters where *When Knighthood Was in Flower* was to be shown. Just in case Marion believed that Millicent's status as a multimillionaire's wife gave her a dignity she herself lacked, Hearst gave Marion the deed to some Manhattan real estate in addition to her family's two homes. It was the beginning of Marion's huge holdings from New York to California (with that vast acreage to come in Mexico as well as such well-known structures as the Marion Davies Building and the Douras Building, both in New York City, the famed Desert Inn in Palm Springs, and her fifty-five-bathroom beach villa in Santa Monica known as "Ocean House").

Marion accepted these gifts, the jewelry, and the subsidies to the Dourases with an uncertain gratitude (Hearst never would know just how grateful she would be for anything he gave her) and never with any sense that she was being spoiled or overcompensated for what she was giving him. Money had meant little to her when she was growing up and Hearst had taught her to be even more careless about it as an adult. The difference between them was that there was a limit to Marion's acquisitiveness—she cared little for expensive clothes, for example. But she did care about his attentions. As Millicent's rival, she demanded more than equal time and she usually knew how to get it. Neglect was something she could not abide. Whenever she thought she was being slighted, she would become uncertain of her role in his life, and uncertainty filled her first with rage, then fear.

His mother Phoebe had instilled in him a firm sense of loyalty and conscience. Hearst had them despite the singular way in which he applied them in manhood (not to his family;

another ethic, responsibility, moved him there) and now his deepest loyalty and his troubled conscience began working almost as soon as he and Millicent and the boys were off the boat in England, prodding him into sending a wire, knowing that he would be in for all sorts of complications. The telegram beseeched Marion to come at once, and he said that life was not worth living without her. But Marion was not so easily appeased, and she was still smarting from having been shoved to the background again. Before he left New York, she had thrown things at him—an ashtray and her slippers—because his reasoning had seemed so specious to her. He *owed* this trip to Millicent, he guessed, and Marion wanted to know why—when he was seeing to it that his wife and the boys lived better than anyone in the country and Millicent knew about them, why he owed her a trip to anywhere. She wired back, "What will you do with the Black Widow?" Hearst reassured her, cabling back word that Millicent was busy with the boys and that he was away from all of them during the day, involved as he was with his British publishing affairs.

Marion sailed for England in late May 1922, her first trip to Europe. The Hearsts were staying at the Savoy; Marion went into an elegant suite halfway across the city, accommodations arranged by Hearst's British representative J. Y. McPeake. On several evenings, McPeake turned out to be Hearst's proxy escort as well, taking Marion to dinner, attempting to break through his British gravity and lighten her mood and the situation, and failing.

Then the entire expedition went to pieces when publisher Guy Barham was stricken with some abdominal flare-up and, within hours, died following an emergency operation. Hearst and Millicent were together at the hospital; Marion fretted through the crisis back in her suite. It was the sharpest example she was ever to have of the backstairs aspect of her life with Hearst, an aspect he had gone to some pains to spare her from nearly always.

Hearst, of course, knew that Marion felt wretched. He had let her down, broken her heart ("heartbroken" was one of his favorite words), let her sit for hours in a city she didn't know, *wouldn't* know, and then, on that trip, sent around a white-haired executive with pince-nez glasses and the manner of a professor to take her to dinner, to the theater. And now he was sharing a sudden tragedy *with Millicent*. Marion could not have been more out of it all if she had been in Nome, Alaska.

Hearst moved swiftly to avert another showdown with her. Millicent he could control; Marion was unpredictable, and her flashing anger could hurt him. He was a vulnerable, oversensitive "swain" in her presence, open to a wound even by an inflection of a word (if Marion called him a "bastard" with a laugh in her voice, everything was fine, but if she shouted it in anger, it would upset him for days). He knew that he never should have sent for her, that he had put her in an intolerable situation. Seizing upon the death of Guy Barham as his pretext for leaving, he told Millicent that he had to rush to Los Angeles since Barham's sudden passing had left his *Herald* without a publisher. Leaving his wife and sons in England, Hearst sailed for home with Marion—in a suite separate from hers—aboard the Olympic.

The sadly terminated European trip made one thing abundantly clear to Marion's friends. She had come to love Hearst. Everyone close to her had believed that the clandestine journey could come to no good end. After at least three years of moving freely around New York as Hearst's "friend," she hadn't needed it. But she had insisted on going because Hearst wanted her there. Knowing Millicent would have all of his important time and that she would get the leavings, she had put her pride— that Douras pride in which feathers were easily ruffled—to one side, and accommodated him.

When she came home in late June, Reine gave a garden party in her Freeport home to celebrate her return. Among the guests were Constance Talmadge, the Leo Carillos, the Victor Moores, the elder Dourases, who arrived separately, and two neighbors, Mr. and Mrs. Oscar Hirsch.

Hirsch got progressively drunker on Reine's scotch. It was good scotch, since Reine's bootlegger was one who serviced the Mayfair Club, a speakeasy in Manhattan. It was not inferior alcohol, which so often inflamed minds and sent drinkers berserk in the twenties, but Hirsch apparently had no capacity for it. He and his wife got into an argument over a pistol he was carrying. Hirsch was shot, suffering a superficial neck injury. A scandal, of course.

The police arrived, and the tabloids, including Hearst's *Mirror*, reported the incident the next morning. The *Mirror* failed to mention that the party was in Marion's honor. Following instructions from a worried Hearst, Marion's lawyers phoned the local press to inform them that she was not present—a probable falsehood for two reasons. Constance Talmadge, who was among the guests, was Marion's friend and usually saw Reine only in Marion's company; and Marion was never the kind of sister who would fail to show up at a party given to celebrate her return.

Already Hearst was attempting to keep Marion's name free of any taint of the reckless disregard for morality that had precipitated the scandals in Hollywood. It had contributed to his decision to keep his film production in the East, although with Paramount about to move from Astoria to huge facilities in the heart of Hollywood, he and D. W. Griffith (with his productions still being done in Mamaroneck) were about the only major producers left in New York. It was among the many paradoxes in his nature that Hearst could imagine that he could squire Marion publicly around the city as his mistress but keep her screen image virginal.

But Hearst was not alone in his concern. Nearly every film producer was alarmed by a series of real-life shockers in the Western film colony. They did not seem to realize that they themselves had elevated to sudden wealth and prominence bus boys, housemaids, and dime-store clerks for only one reason: they were physically attractive and photogenic. Thousands of dollars had been thrust into their hands, palatial villas bought or rented, and gold-plated Pierce-Arrows or Hispano-Suizas parked in their garages. But they were often bored and boring types with small education, no background in the amenities of life. Like children, they filled their leisure time with games, but since they were adults, many of the games were sexual. And when the activity in the bedroom palled, oceans of bootleg alcohol were consumed, and when that began to lose its kick, a number of them turned to cocaine, heroin, and other drugs. Famed comedian Fatty Arbuckle had been tried for manslaughter, following the party death in a San Francisco hotel room of a young demimondaine with whom he and others in his party had had intercourse. Arbuckle was acquitted of having caused Virginia Rappe's death from a ruptured bladder (she had previously suffered from bladder difficulty and had been under a doctor's care), but his screen reputation was destroyed overnight. Then that February, director William Desmond Taylor was found murdered in his study and both star Mary Miles Minter

and comedienne Mabel Normand, who had the same bubbling
spirit Marion later would display in films, were summoned to
testify: Drug-taking was among the matters investigated at
the inquest. Olive Thomas, an actress married to Jack Pickford,
Mary's brother, would kill herself in Paris with an overdose of
drugs to which she was addicted. Wallace Reid would get so
involved with heroin, he would be unable to fulfill his commit-
ments as an actor.

The Hays Office was the result, the producers' answer to
Babylon. Will Hays was appointed to oversee the content of
films, purging them of the prurient and salacious, and his office
helped the producers draft new contracts with stars with clauses
relating to their behavior, allowing the film companies to drop
anyone who committed breaches of public decency.

Later, in Hollywood, Hearst was to tell Marion that the
only intelligent attitude toward scandal was to ignore it. It was
his habit to call unfavorable publicity slanderous, while his
advice was to never sue. "You only enlarge the thing and keep
it alive." But in June of 1922, he was hysterical over Marion's
bad publicity. He ordered Marion to have her lawyers launch a
suit against the *Daily News*, the *Herald*, and the *New York Telegram* for persisting in their attack upon her reputation—they
all had kept the story going for a couple of days by printing
Marion's denial that she had attended Reine's party with headlines such as "MARION DAVIES SAYS THAT SHE WASN'T THERE."
What Reine must have thought of all this is unknown, but it
was her first brush with the paragon that Marion was becoming
under Hearst's aegis, and it was not to be confused with her
private self. Nothing came of the suit; the story died the usual
death of yesterday's news. But Hearst again began thinking of
California and of the clean, windswept hills of San Simeon
where Marion could stay between films, out of harm's way.

In their private life together, he was getting bolder. Nothing had been made of their return trip together on the *Olympic*.
Precautions had been taken for her to leave the boat separately,
but it was still a risky venture. Public opinion—and Millicent—
had been tested, and he had learned that the possibility existed
for him to live openly with Marion without fear of repercussions.

In September 1922, *When Knighthood Was in Flower* had
its opening at the Criterion Theatre on Broadway. Hearst had

remodeled the theater especially for the premiere of the film with new loges installed patterned after the royal boxes seen at the jousting tournament in the film. He had asked Marion to make a simple, gracious speech following the end of the film and the great applause he was anticipating. All through dinner, Marion was in a dither, saying that she couldn't memorize those few words, that the very thought of it was driving her crazy and she couldn't eat. When the film ended, there was polite applause in keeping with the dignity of the film, and everyone began filing out of the theater before Marion could get to her feet. Instead of being relieved, she later said that all she could think of was that she had not eaten any dinner and was too nervous to look at the picture. Her discomfiture had been heightened by the presence in their box of guests Arthur Brisbane, who as Hearst's chief editorialist and confidante spent more time in his company than she did at this point and whom she thought of as a rival for Hearst's attention and interest, and film czar Will Hays.

The success that *When Knighthood Was in Flower* became upon its release was genuine and not a result of Hearst's own papers' ballyhoo. Every newspaper in town hailed it as one of the finest spectacles yet seen upon the screen. Beyond this, they all pointed out that Marion at last had become an actress, and, something more, they all agreed that Marion's comic moments were brilliant. For a period of over ten years, Marion would receive only the most glowing notices for her acting in both the Hearst papers *and the non-Hearst press*. Her fame as a leading lady would become a highly negotiable commodity to the Hearst empire and not the reverse, as many film historians later would claim.

The *Knighthood* film is not generally available today. It should be, as it is almost completely free of the exaggerations in performance that flaw so many movies of the period. Lyn Harding's bemused Henry VIII is absolutely right and he is a fine foil for the rebelliousness of his younger sister, Mary Tudor (played by Marion). There are equally skillful performances by Ernest Glendinning (then married to the Douras family friend, Marie) as Sir Edwin Caskoden and the droll William Norris as feeble old King Louis XII. William Powell, of *The Thin Man* fame, is seen as Louis's nephew Francis, next in line to the throne and a deep-dyed villain, both lecherous and treacherous. It was Powell's first important screen role.

We first see Mary Tudor (Marion) in a barge on her way
to a tournament. Numerous closeups reveal her youthful, un-
blemished beauty as seen in the morning sunshine. One of the
jousting knights is Charles Brandon (Forrest Stanley), a handsome soldier and a commoner. Brandon wins the tournament
and Mary Tudor rewards him with a gold neck chain and a
glance that plainly shows how taken she is with his person.
Brandon returns this glance and sets the drama in motion.

The film holds up well as a distinguished historical romance. Its facts are reasonably faithful to history. (During the
filming, Hearst wanted Marion to be seen as Mary Tudor sitting
on a throne next to Louis XII. Actor Glendinning told Hearst,
"You can't do that. She's not yet queen," and took some time off
to check the public library to confirm it.) There are moments,
especially when we see sunlight striking through a leaded window pane in a castle hallway, where this production closely
resembles the much later *The Private Life of Henry VIII* with
Charles Laughton (1933). Tottering old King Louis XII, half-
blind and suffering from other ills of advanced years, provokes
nearly as much laughter as Mary Tudor's outrageous behavior
in his efforts to remain on his feet for her sake. He successfully
seeks a marriage with her, throwing into the marriage contract
an alliance favorable to his native France as well as to England.
When Mary Tudor's apartment in the castle is visited by a male
dress-goods salesman come to see how much material and which
pattern she requires for her wedding gown, there is an enormously funny scene as Mary Tudor throws the materials at him
one after the other until he is an ambulatory tent, finally collapsing under the weight of the rich fabrics. She finally agrees
to marry Louis in order to save the life of her lover, Brandon,
who has been trapped by a Tudor palace conspiracy to get him
out of the way, a plot in which Henry has had no part. Louis
climbs out of bed and swears that he is going to dance with
his young bride "if it is the last deed of the King of France," and
immediately drops dead. Mary Tudor is rescued from a perilous
future as the probable bride of Louis's nephew Francis by
Charles Brandon, who had been sent into exile by her brother
Henry (as the lesser of two evils—Brandon had been framed
and accused of murder; exile was better than death in the
Tower) and there informed by his friend-at-court Caskoden of
Mary Tudor's predicament. Safely back at the Tudor court, Mary

Tudor and Brandon are allowed to marry, and Henry VIII sagely remarks that perhaps he should have given his consent from the beginning and saved himself and others all that trouble.

The scenes at court and in the streets of London and French villages have a solid, richly detailed look, which was to become typical of Hearst's films. *Knighthood* was designed by the Viennese set designer, Josef Urban, who had come to America in 1913 and soon had established himself in the theater with five annual editions of the Ziegfeld *Follies* and a number of operas staged at the Metropolitan Opera House. "Urban" colors had become famous, especially an "Urban blue." He was described in *Photoplay* Magazine as being "a very gentle man, very tolerant, very enthusiastic about other men's enthusiasms," which made him precisely the kind of man Hearst found most congenial. Urban himself said that the movies were "the art of the Twentieth Century, and perhaps the greatest art of modern times . . . an unknown ocean stretching out before a modern Columbus." Earlier Urban had moved into Hearst's studio building near the Harlem River. An assignment almost as lavish as *Knighthood* had been the design and construction of a complete Spanish hacienda and its out-buildings—using as his blueprint several postcards Hearst had given him—for the setting for an Alma Rubens vehicle, *The World and His Wife*. The Urban-Hearst collaboration would last for nearly a decade and soon Urban's daughter Gretl would be signed on to design Marion's costumes.

The premiere of the film had been a social function almost on a par with the opening of the Metropolitan Opera. It was the prestigious kind of thing Hearst usually attended with Millicent. There would be several other films of Marion's launched in New York with equal flourish and attendance by public figures and socialites, but *Knighthood*'s premiere was the most significant of any. The film's merit justified all that expense (the film negative had come to in excess of $300,000 and an additional million or two had been spent in remodeling the Criterion Theatre and exploiting the film). Film audiences immediately became aware that Marion had an extraordinary naturalness before the camera, a touching presence in comedy-pathos, and for a long time moviegoers relaxed their resentment and defensiveness over all that publicity, which was helpful as they would be exposed to an unremitting torrent of it. It was Marion's fate as an actress that her talent and the public's response to it would not be allowed to flower naturally, but would be nearly overwhelmed and destroyed by Hearst's overeagerness.

Yet another cog was added to the publicity machinery that would spew out reams of material about Marion as Hearst sought to puff up her success in this one film into the celebrity and fame of a Norma Talmadge if not a Mary Pickford. It was a piece of luck, one of the few such pieces in Marion's long career. An obscure young film reviewer for the *New York Telegraph*, Louella O. Parsons, wrote an article reprimanding Hearst and Cosmopolitan Productions for promoting the film as a spectacle rather than as a successful vehicle for Marion. "Why don't you give Marion Davies a chance?" Louella asked in print. "She is a good actress, a beauty, and a comedy starring bet. Why talk about how much was spent on the lovely costumes and the production cost?" The comment had been the direct result of a casual friendship struck up by Louella and Marion soon after *Cecilia of the Pink Roses* was released with such flamboyant publicity. Marion had got in touch with Louella to thank her for saying something nice about this early movie. Marion's press agent, Rose Shulsinger, as protective of Marion's sensibilities as any of her growing staff, extended to Louella an invitation to lunch and then discreetly asked the columnist if she could possibly tell her employer that *Cecilia* was not as bad as Marion thought it was. Over lunch, the movie writer was struck by Marion's disarming frankness and her "confused little stammer." "She had no false illusions about herself," Louella said, "and kidded *Cecilia. . . .*"

Shortly after Louella's criticism of Hearst's handling of *Knighthood* appeared, she got another call from Marion asking if Louella could accompany her to a banquet being given by the Theatre Owners of America, where the film columnist was to make a speech. That evening, Louella's young daughter Harriet, a student at the Horace Mann High School and very much aware of Hearst's alleged malevolent influence on the country, took a call from the hotel lobby that Marion was downstairs with a "young man." It was a joke of Marion's and the "young man" was Hearst. On the way to the banquet, Hearst told Louella, "I read your editorial. It was good. You should write more things like that!" Through Louella's candor, he realized that he had allowed his pride in Marion and his taste for the spectacular to make him forget why he was spending all that money in the first place. Louella thanked him, but nothing more came of the matter until, at a later luncheon date with Marion, Louella complained about her job on *The Telegraph*. "I'm getting good and tired of things down there. I think I'll leave," she said.

"Well," Marion told her, "Mr. Hearst will be interested in hearing that. May I tell him?"

Within twenty-four hours, Hearst had extended a dinner invitation to Louella. Reminded by her daughter of all the terrible things she had heard about Hearst and his empire, she said at first that she couldn't make a change for less than $250 a week, to which he immediately agreed, and then she added that she couldn't sign any contract without seeing her lawyer. Her contract, as drawn up, was an extraordinary one, demanding all sorts of concessions. Hearst took one look and said, "I can't sign that thing." Her daughter and her friends on *The Telegraph* were relieved when Louella sent word to Hearst to forget the whole thing. But within a few weeks, thinking it was a fine joke on himself, Hearst signed the contract, telling her, "I'm disappointed in you. You forgot to ask for hairpins."

Louella's later relationship with Marion, especially after the death of Hearst, deteriorated according to Marion, but not according to daughter Harriet. Louella herself was stricken with a series of massive strokes in the late 1960s and was unable to contribute to this biography, but her daughter denies that there was any rupture between the two and attempts to bolster this opinion by saying that her mother sent an autographed first edition of Cardinal Spellman's novel *The Foundling* to Marion after Hearst's death and Marion was grateful and touched by the gesture. A gracious note of thanks might well have been the extent of Marion's reaction to the gift.

By 1925, Louella Parsons would become the film wonderland's Queen of Hearts, as quixotic and terrifying to many as Lewis Carroll's original. Her journalistic power was by then absolute, and Marion knew that it was. The one trump in Marion's hand was that with a single word of rebuke or condemnation to Hearst she could shake the foundations of Louella's supremacy, and if she really put her back into it, she could have toppled the columnist altogether. It was not in Marion's nature to be vindictive, though she was so a few times with Arthur Brisbane some years later and she would like to have been with Norma Shearer if Miss Shearer had not been married to the studio's chief of production, Irving Thalberg. But Louella was patronizing; her columns were filled with references to Marion "never looking lovelier" when Marion and her friends knew that such descriptions were used even if Marion had gained fifteen pounds and was wearing last year's slacks.

But in those first years, Louella and Marion were as close as sisters. Hearst thought that this was fine. Though her syntax was questionable, Louella was useful as his film enterprise's loudest apologist and barker.

V

With his success with *When Knighthood Was in Flower*—and it made some profit even beyond its huge cost—Hearst had succeeded in the first and most gratifying of his goals for Marion. He had surrounded her with talent, and she had measured up to the challenge. More important, the movie public had accepted her. They were filling theaters in nearly every major city in America to see her lively performance as Mary Tudor. Hearst had been so excited by the first rough cut of the film that he had had his own name added to the screen credits, "A William Randolph Hearst Production," the only occasion when he would do so. And his faith in the fil   d been vindicated. By any standard, it was a major triump   lmmaking.

For Marion, it signaled the beginning of her larger legend as a latter-day Nell Gwynn. Her photograph had been a fixture in the roto pages of the Hearst press for a long time, and there were few Americans of any sophistication at all who had not made the connection. She was rarely shown candidly; she was posed in settings comparable to Versailles. Nell Gwynn, whose elegant portrait by Sir Peter Lely was to have an honored place in Marion's home, had been a gifted comic actress, too, before she became mistress to King Charles II of England. But Marion was living in a more democratic age than Nell. She could be seen in any movie palace for 50¢ ($2 for her road-show films like *Knighthood*). To Marion's intense satisfaction, her face and her name were becoming familiar to people who had never heard (and would never hear) of Millicent Hearst. She was becoming rather fond of her own success; it nearly made up for the lack of a wedding ring. But not completely, and Marion's lack of complete fulfillment in her life was felt most keenly by Hearst. It kept him chained to his heaving publicity and production machinery for years as he attempted to achieve it for her in the hope that one more ovation at a premiere or one more Sunday supplement full page devoted to her career might turn the trick.

Hearst laughed along with the audience at Marion's comedy, but he miscalculated the components of her success in that film. He became convinced that her forte was big costume spectaculars, which would set off her beauty, as this film had done. He seemed to connect comedy with clownlike faces and later much admired Polly Moran, Marie Dressler, and Buster Keaton. He considered Charlie Chaplin to be the most gifted man in films. But a beautiful woman, in Hearst's view, was to be worshipped on the screen. Not only was she to be idealized, but, if threatened, then protected or championed by the hero through to a soft-focus romantic fadeout. "It doesn't take any beauty to get pie in the face," he once said. It was a blunder in which he would persist.

Marion's appeal as an actress—as a genuine star—was an amalgam of good will, high-spirited unpredictability, and the sensual warmth of a kitten. In her first five years of filmmaking, she had completed fourteen features. The most successful were *Getting Mary Married, Belle of New York, The Cinema Murder, The Restless Sex, Adam and Eva,* and *When Knighthood Was in Flower,* all but the last being "program pictures" made quickly on a relatively small budget. As her career moved on, there would be other successes, her entire catalog of films breaking down roughly into not quite one-half successful and the others losing small amounts in most cases or, in the case of *Cain and Mabel* (a critical failure) and *Beverly of Graustark* (a critical success), substantial losses. Contrary to nearly every recent evaluation of her work, Marion's films were neither mediocre critically nor "bombs" at the box office. Her career is roughly analogous to that of her future arch-rival on the Metro lot, Norma Shearer. Miss Shearer, who married the studio's production chief Irving Thalberg in 1927, would be in a position to be given almost any role or property she might desire. She was to become a better dramatic actress than Marion (although even this can be challenged when Marion's performance in *Quality Street* is measured against any dramatic role of Miss Shearer's), but a lesser comedienne. Miss Shearer's financial failures such as *Strange Interlude* and *Marie Antoinette* would be even larger in scope and in money lost than Marion's, but because she had come to some small prominence as an actress before she married Thalberg, there would be no aura of purchased fame hanging about her name or reputation. Marion's comic skills were taken for granted and not much discussed in favor of gossip about her off-screen role as the mistress of San Simeon and other posh residences, where she was established as the busiest and most lavish hostess in Hollywood history. Hearst and Thalberg shared a belief that quality cost money, lots of it, the difference between them being that Thalberg was more perceptive about the public's taste than Hearst. They shared a passion for anonymity in films and both men nearly always kept their names from the credits of the pictures they were responsible for. Hearst loved the theatrical and the flashy impression, castles and great houses abounding in his films, jacking up the budget of many films that were otherwise simply modest entertainments. When someone later told him that there was money in making movies, he told them, "Yes, mine." Thalberg prized quality above all else, giving his films a rich gloss that became a Metro trademark over the years. Hearst had a few skillful screenwriters who had to work over some pretty shoddy material by Robert Chambers and others; Thalberg hired the best writing talents in America (Faulkner, Fitzgerald, Dorothy Parker) and had them work and rework the finest properties available to Hollywood in such an assembly-line fashion that often he got the least out of them rather than the best. Fitzgerald in writing *The Last Tycoon* and Thalberg's own early death helped to create a legend of genius untouched by failure. Although his successes did outnumber his failures, his contribution to films was his willingness to take risks for the sake of quality. His error was in thinking that two brilliant minds could save an uncertain story.

It was clear by now that Marion was not a mistress first and a star second. For over a dozen years, from the early twenties to at least 1933, she had the fans to prove it. That massive Hearst publicity was an encumbrance rather than an asset. Her growing reputation as an actress of value contended against a surprising enemy: Hearst's obsession to see her achieve stardom on a par with Mary Pickford, Gloria Swanson, or even Norma Talmadge, who had far less talent. The public had fallen in love with Miss Pickford almost from the very beginning of her career. She could communicate with a film audience on a primitive, wordless level—the ideal silent picture star. Her fans numbered in the millions by the time of Marion's advent on the film scene and her movements were followed with fascination by readers of a growing body of fan magazines and movie columns.

Similarly, over thirty years later, another generation of fans fell instantly in love with Marilyn Monroe. Marilyn had fought for publicity, for public attention during a four-year period of relative obscurity. She was so unloved as a child, she sought the love of Everyman and she eventually got it. On the other hand, Marion got a great deal of supportive love during her childhood; she was never deprived, and she was handed the materials for stardom—a vast machinery to publicize her name, her own film corporation, and, for a variety of reasons including her own beauty and talent, the interest and services of great film distributing companies, Paramount and, later, Metro-Goldwyn-Mayer and Warner Brothers. But Marion was never to approach the kind of public adoration that came so naturally to Mary Pickford and sometimes became a frightening and uncontrollable menace to Marilyn Monroe. Marion won loyal fans who would sit in darkened movie houses waiting for that glow from her, which would light up the screen. I know this was so: as a boy in Des Moines, I was one of them. She was often a very gay lady, who somehow managed to take care of herself in all of her screen roles. Hearst could not see that the public only gave its enthusiasm to those few whom it could worship or with whom it could identify—performers who seemed to be innocent or lovable victims of life (Lillian Gish) or those who had an authentically aristocratic beauty (Norma Talmadge and then Garbo) or those who gave off so much energy and singlemindedness it substituted for beauty (Joan Crawford and later, Bette Davis). In the years just ahead, Hearst would begin to see many of Marion's strengths and weaknesses, but she was seldom allowed the freedom to continue her erratic rise as one of the screen's great comediennes. That she reached true stardom at all is the surprise, considering the burden and resentment of all that publicity. She was more unique in her screen image than many of her peers. More often than not, audiences of her day looked forward to an entertaining evening whenever they went to a Davies movie. If Hearst had allowed her great talents as a mime and comic to come to full flower in a long series of comedies as bright as her *Show People* and *The Patsy*, her screen reputation could not have been so readily damaged by the controversy surrounding *Citizen Kane*. It is only in recent years that she has been rediscovered by film audiences as delighted (and surprised) by her brilliance as were many millions in the twenties. She has become posthumously one of the few comic leading ladies of the silent screen. Her value as a screen performer, acknowledged by

Thalberg and, of course, by Hearst, is being reestablished and comment about her "small talent" today smacks of the uninformed.

If Hearst had given his filmmaking the same enormous energy and obsessive preoccupation he gave his newspapers, his movies might have been successful enough to accord him a place in film history at least on a level with Alexander Korda, a man who had similar tastes in subject matter. The concerns of the common herd were not for him, although there seems to have been a reductive element at work in his film property choices, so that in one of Marion's last movies (*Page Miss Glory*), she would be playing a scrubwoman. He was one of the very first to use technicolor, to do a musical, to insist upon historical accuracy (even though it was not an ethic of his newspaper publishing), but he is seldom cited in film histories for any of this. Part of the difficulty in getting his film career into focus is his overriding fame and notoriety as a publisher, as a political influence often assumed to have been wrongheaded when not sinister. It was his ambition to be the biggest and most influential publisher in America, if not in the world, and he had succeeded in this. He wanted to be a power in Washington where he had lived spasmodically through two terms as a congressman during the first decade of the twentieth century. He thought he should be President, but that had not worked out; the political laity distrusted a man of such wealth so lacking in the appealing magnetism—except on a personal level which didn't count for much in politics—of a Teddy Roosevelt, and the political hierarchy in both major parties, whose first loyalty often was to big business, considered him a heretic who was out to destroy the American system (no business leader could forget his newspapers' war against the railroad trusts).

These obsessions meant that he often deputized someone to run his movie business for him. Marion was nominally in charge, but she would much rather enjoy herself when she was not before the cameras than look over a budget statement. And it was not only her own films that were over-budgeted. A film starring Alma Rubens, *The Red Robe*, was considered so terrible by Hearst he felt it could not be released until it was improved. "It is an outrage," he told Marion, "to spend seven hundred thousand dollars on a picture and then neglect it the way this picture has been neglected—because *that* is what is the matter with it. The scenario is very bad. It doesn't stick to the story. The direction is atrocious. The photography in most cases is miserably poor—ten years behind the times. Poor Alma Rubens hasn't anything to do and is terribly lighted. Judels [Charles Judels, a comic character actor often used by Hearst] was paid several thousand dollars for comedy and then no comedy was written in for him. Clon's death, which was supposed to be a big dramatic climax, is a foolish fiasco—good for a laugh. The dueling is childishly poor—only good when done by doubles—like the duel on horseback. The cutting is hopeless and the titles are jokes. We have got to start in now and recut the picture entirely from the beginning. Then we have got to retake a lot of stuff and add more expense. Finally, I hope we will have a reasonably good picture—the kind that should have been made for three hundred thousand dollars. I have got to make some drastic changes and the first thing is to get some folks who will attend to business."

There is considerable bitterness in Hearst's tone in this dialogue with Marion. His critical judgment was keen; he simply did not have the time to oversee what was happening with some of his pictures. It suggests that, on this particular film, the bulk of the production was done without his presence and with little contact with him from day to day. Within a few days, he hired Dr. Daniel Carson Goodman, who was Alma Rubens's constant companion, as his studio manager because he believed that Goodman was industrious.

He had no quarrel with Marion's contributions to his films. She had given his film enterprise a stable and dependable leading lady, no small achievement when one looks back over the number of Carol Dempsters (D. W. Griffith's protegée) who had tried to win wide audience approval and had failed, or who married well and dropped out of sight, or who insulated themselves from reality through the abusive use of drugs—from Hearst's own Alma Rubens down to Marilyn Monroe.

So the plan—to keep them together through their joint endeavors in the movies—was working, but as a man of politics, Hearst relied completely upon Millicent. He not only asked Millicent to accompany him to state dinners and other political gatherings, but he discussed stratagems with her and sought her opinion. With Marion, he aired film deals and publishing and related projects *ad nauseam*. He would pore over the pages of his newspapers with her, asking what she thought of an article, an editorial, the layout of a page. She had got to know all of his executives and had taken their measure, which didn't always agree with his. The need for Millicent by his side as he sought high public office was to keep that moribund relationship alive when it was dead in nearly every other sense. When Hearst lost out in his battle for power with Al Smith, Millicent's influence in Hearst's life was substantially diminished. (Smith had refused even to consider Hearst as his running mate on the New York State Democratic ticket.) The marital relationship would atrophy during the next three decades so that by 1951, she would be burying a man whom she rarely saw, not a stranger so much as an abstraction, a force in her life she felt from a distance and through deputies.

Hearst went West to lick his wounds, leaving Marion back in New York, where she was completing *Little Old New York*. A film done in the same careful manner as nearly all of Hearst's films, it was destined to be an even bigger hit than *Knighthood*. He phoned her every day from his suite at the Palace in San Francisco, worried sick that she would not keep her part of the bargain, but run across some other younger man who would want to marry her. His fear was understandable; Marion had fame now, she had financial security. There was nothing to hold her to Hearst except her love for him, and his letters indicate that he had doubts about that. She was going out with a New York architect during his absence, according to Hearst's spies, and Hearst kiddingly told her that he would run down to Los Angeles and get himself a sweetie who was not so cold and matter-of-fact and full of business. He fretted after each phone call because of her "coolness." She would ask after his health or "his corns" and then tell him, "Well, it's getting late and I've got to get up early. Good night," and then before hanging up, she might add in an angry rush, "Don't call me so late next time." He told her that he supposed if he kicked off the covers that night he would dream of her, "that is, if I get cold enough, and I will probably think I am sitting on the top of Mont Blanc with my arms around a snow drift."

The *Little Old New York* project had begun with a phone call to Marion from screenwriter Frances Marion. In a state of high excitement, Frances had told Marion that the leading role of Pat O'Day not only called for a comedienne, but there were moving dramatic scenes which Frances was confident Marion could bring off with skilled direction. The two ladies attended a matinee that week and Marion loved it. It was a gentle reprise of Robert Fulton's efforts to get his steamboat financed, enlivened by the tale of a young Irish immigrant girl who accompanies her father and her gravely ill brother to America where, they believe, they can claim a large inheritance. When the brother dies at sea, Pat is asked to take his place as claimant, putting her hair under her cap and pretending that she is her dead brother. The two stories are intermeshed through a cousin of Pat's, a wastrel friend of Fulton's who is in line for the inheritance if the O'Day youth does not show up. Naturally, the cousin and Pat feel a strong attraction pulling them together despite the inheritance she has cheated him of and despite their supposedly being the same sex. The cousin's firm efforts to regain his sense of propriety when he finds himself gazing longingly at a "boy" are astonishingly contemporary in feeling. A very subtle homosexual tenderness runs through about a third of the film, which was released in 1923, and just about the only such "romantic comedy" ever to appear in American films. It is all made proper, of course, by the discovery of Pat's true sex, but it is fascinating to speculate upon two related elements in this film—Marion's male disguise, which would be worked into the script of more than half a dozen of her films, and the good taste shown in both the script and the performances relating to the wastrel's fight to subdue his love for his "male" cousin. Hearst's fondness for seeing Marion in male attire was well-known in the film world by this time, and he shared Marion's tolerance—common to most theater folk—of homosexuality. He was never heard to say anything demeaning of any homosexual whom he had befriended, nor did he ever make them the butt of a questionable joke.

Sidney Olcott directed the film, the most distinguished of his career, which had begun in 1907 with a one-reel *Ben Hur* (the chariot race) and would continue on a high level in 1923 with George Arliss in *The Green Goddess*. He would bring the massive production to a windup in less than three months, despite a disastrous fire at the Harlem River studio, which destroyed the elaborate nineteenth-century exterior of New York's streets designed by Josef Urban, Fulton's steamboat, and, by far the most tragic loss, Urban's library with his valuable collection of costume and architectural designs. Typically, Hearst was far more distraught over Urban's loss than his own, which not only included the set and costumes for the production, but many valuable paintings and antiques he had stored in his studio for possible movie use.

The fire caused another pinch in Hearst's financial reserves and studio personnel were told to wait a few days before cashing their pay checks.

Designer Urban had been assigned to rebuild and redecorate a moviehouse on Columbus Circle to be renamed the Cosmopolitan, after Hearst's film company. At a cost of $225,000, much of the work was completed by opening night of *Little Old New York* on August 1, 1923. But not all, unfortunately. It was to have a five tiered chandelier of glittering crystal, which was not yet in place by eight o'clock on the evening of the premiere. Notables gathered on the sidewalk and in the lobby—Mayor Hylan, Vincent Astor, Mrs. Harry Payne Whitney, and a number of film and stage stars there to see and be seen.

Urban ran about the lobby, fretting and wondering what could be done to minimize the risk to their audience. At eight-fifteen, he was able to hire some trouble-shooting mechanics who came in and tied up the fixture with block and tackle.

Hearst was not present. The Harlem studio fire, with the huge costs of completing enough of his castle at San Simeon so that it would be habitable, had forced him to scurry West, literally with hat in hand, seeking a million dollars. At San Simeon, he was having daily conferences with his architect Julia Morgan and running his farflung enterprises from one of the guest houses. He told Marion that he felt like the "May Queen," who said, "Just a few grains of corn to keep what little life there is till the coming of the morn." He referred to his revolving-door bank account as "that damned old thing." In his desperation, he had turned to Edward Hardy Clark, an aging former financial advisor to his late mother Phoebe, a man who looked like an angry teddy bear and yet strangely resembled the trustee who raises Charles Foster Kane in the movie based upon Hearst's life. Clark had agreed to secure for him a check for the million dollars he required, presumably from his inheritance, upon which Phoebe Hearst wisely had imposed restrictions. He wrote Marion that he had to remain West to "get things fixed."

Hearst's need for money at that time must have been staggering and beyond the ken of even an average millionaire. He was known as a "slow payer" to all firms with which he did business. The wonder was that they all eventually got paid, for he was in continual financial disorder. It has been said that he lived "from hand to mouth," one of his most profitable papers sending him a "life-sustaining" $25,000 each week. When pressed for cash beyond this, he would call up the publisher of one of his other newspapers and ask that funds be sent at once.

It was typical of the pattern of their lives that Marion would be enjoying one of her greatest successes while Hearst was pacing the library floor at the San Simeon guest house waiting for a million-dollar check to keep himself solvent. He kept a line open to New York so that an aide could read him the reviews of Marion's movie, all of which were raves, and then sent off a wire to Marion telling her that he knew her genius would be recognized in time and that she would reach the summit. No one else, he said, had her talent and beauty and courage and determination; difficulties didn't discourage her and success didn't spoil her.

This message may have helped to take the edge off his absence, but far more exciting to Marion was a congratulatory wire from stage producer David Belasco to which she replied, "I hope and pray that I may always be worthy of such wonderful praise from the master genius of our world!"; and a wire sent to Hearst by Flo Ziegfeld, which Hearst forwarded to Marion:

MY DEAR MR. HEARST,
    I HAD THE GREAT PLEASURE OF WITNESSING THE OPENING OF THE COSMOPOLITAN THEATRE WHICH YOU HAVE MADE ONE OF THE FINEST THEATRES IN NEW YORK JOSEPH URBAN HAS DONE HIS FINEST WORK IS THE UNANIMOUS OPINION OF LAST NIGHTS AUDIENCE THE PICTURE LITTLE OLD NEW YORK WAS EXCELLENT AND MARION DAVIES PERFORMANCE WAS PERFECTION MY WIFE [BILLIE BURKE] WAS ENTHRALLED WITH MISS DAVIES WORK ON THE SCREEN AS MARION SAYS I AM A HARD BOILED EGG I CAN FRANKLY SAY THAT YOU ARE TO BE CONGRATULATED ON THE UNQUALIFIED HIT OF EVERYTHING IN CONNECTION WITH LAST NIGHTS OPENING I WAS PROUD OF THE FACT THAT I WAS RESPONSIBLE FOR BRINGING JOSEPH URBAN TO NEW YORK AND THAT MARION DAVIES WAS ONCE A MEMBER OF MY COMPANY REGARDS AND CONGRATULATIONS TOO BAD YOU WERE NOT HERE

On the bottom of the wire, Hearst had written: "Marion is right too. He thinks he will claim some credit now.

"I told you when you once succeed everybody begins to tell how they found you. I said it is funny and isn't it *fine*. W.R."

During the premiere performance itself, Marion spent nearly all of the two hours it required for the film to unreel looking up at the Damoclean threat of the hastily hung chandelier above the audience. She recalled taking two hasty bows and then hurrying out to the sidewalk, hoping everyone would follow. They did, to her great relief. The next day, the predictable Mayor of New York was quoted in the Hearst press as having said, "This production is unquestionably the greatest screen epic I have ever looked upon, and Marion Davies is the most versatile screen star ever cast in any part. . . ." Carefully briefed in fatuity by Hearst publicists for whom this was just another Davies opening, Hylan said nothing about her projection of comic pathos, so engaging in this film; no word of the poignancy of her performance, which was so much more important than production values. He was every bit as fatuous as those critics of the 1940s and 1950s who wrote only of Hearst's overblown costume extravaganzas with Marion Davies kept from seeming "too unprofessional" by cadres of the best acting talent he could buy. By the time of the success of *Little Old New York,* Marion was the most popular and commercially successful ingredient in any of Hearst's productions. Marion was selling the tickets, not the undoubtedly skillful actors who made up her supporting casts. Her popularity as a lively leading lady had begun to equal that of Mabel Normand, whose health was failing and who had endured undeserved notoriety since the murder trial at which she testified, and it had moved beyond that of Colleen Moore at that point in her career prior to Miss Moore's making *Lilac Time.*

With this great success, Hearst no longer had to seek out a distributor. The Goldwyn Corporation under Frank Joseph Godsol, distributor of the film, was about to merge with the Metro Company, headed by Marcus Loew. Among the assets brought into the deal by Godsol was the distribution arrangement with Hearst who, with two solid hits behind him, was ranked among the most important producers in the United States. There was also a well-equipped studio in Culver City, which had once been the operational base of Thomas Ince and his Triangle Pictures. Samuel Goldwyn had been unseated from his own company in 1921 and was operating under his full "new" name—it had been "Goldfish" originally.

In Frances Marion, Hearst had found the perfect scenarist for Marion. She knew how to maneuver Marion into mischief that was never risqué. *Little Old New York* had been her third screenplay for Marion and by this time she had a keen sense of Marion's strengths as a film actress. Her success in writing material that Marion could make human and engaging is borne out in these comments by a *New York Times* reviewer, who said, "Miss Davies triumphs . . . gently appealing . . . poignant." Friends of Marion's and Hearst's from the Hollywood years just ahead would be put under a considerable strain by too frequent private showings of some of Marion's films, but there always would be a round of applause whenever the title credits of *Little Old New York* flashed on the screen. Eleanor Boardman and others were to say that it was much their favorite of Marion's films.

Hearst was more intoxicated by this success than Marion was. Perhaps part of his euphoria stemmed from his sudden release from his obsession with politics, which had been so rudely terminated by Al Smith's disavowal of him. Of course, he would return to the political arena when his bruises had healed—it was an all-too-tempting avenue to great personal power, one of the consuming passions of his life. But not for nearly a year.

Marion was privately becoming much less shy and more truly herself. Fame seemed to have liberated her. To Hearst, she seemed a bundle of contrary forces. She looked younger than ever in her designer clothes, but there was something of the hard-headed business woman about her. She was more vehement in her opinions, but often wildly foolish in these and in her choice of friends. Hearst did everything this side of divorcing Millicent to please her, but it always fell short of achieving her heartfelt gratitude. He asked, "What on earth is the matter with you?" in those early years of bafflement. He became defensive and said that he "was not going to parties" whenever he was out of New York. "Last night," he told her, "I went to a dinner at an old lady's house (she is 86 years old), as quiet a dinner as could possibly be. This old lady lived opposite us when I was a child and I used to play with her son, who is long since dead. She said she wanted to see what I looked like since I had grown up. Good Lord! I have been grown up for forty years and I am now growing sideways and every other way." Hearst had no personal vanity, and was not offended when a close friend described him as resembling the rear of an elephant whenever he walked away from somebody. He felt that the only way that he could compete with the attractive younger men gravitating toward Marion at any social function was to buy her things, to take her places in regal style, to make himself indispensable as her life-style was elevated to one of such extravagance that no ordinary leading man or man-about-town could afford to come between them. Perhaps that was why he would find Charlie Chaplin, the multimillionaire leading actor of the world, such a threat within a year.

VI

Marion was kept working before the cameras more than ten months beginning in the winter of 1923–24. Hearst saw that his "formula"—that of placing Marion in a context of history heavily romanticized and rendered "human" mainly through Marion's infectious personality—was working at the box office. His film enterprise was beginning to have the smell of success about it and all the snide comments about Marion's being pushed beyond her capacities ended in the non-Hearst press.

For four of those winter months, Marion was involved in the making of the romantic drama *Yolanda*, set in the France of Louis XI. Hearst was now expected to stun his audiences with pictorial splendor and *Yolanda* fulfilled this expectation. It opens in a huge cathedral, then moves on to the impressive castles of Charles the Bold and King Louis XI. The interiors are vast, realistic and often breathtaking in scale and beauty. Besides the castles and country roads of medieval France that seemed to be of solid stone, there were tall, storm-tossed oaks and pines surrounding them in vast meadows. The main set covered all of a city block in Hearst's Harlem studio. Marion as the Princess Mary of Burgundy continued her rise as the screen star whose trademark had become the richness of her settings and costumes. Hearst saw it as the special element he had been seeking to compete with Mary Pickford's piquant charm. He already was aware that the public responded most to her comic scenes, but these seemed to be added to *Yolanda* as a kind of after-thought. It was derring-do that he was after and it came as no surprise that Charles Major, author of *When Knighthood Was in Flower,* had supplied the story. Victor Herbert again contributed the special overture, and there was a musical score by William Frederick Peters to be played with the solemn gravity reserved for "the classics" by the ever-increasing numbers of symphony orchestras that were supplanting the old pianists and organists in key theaters. There were knights in armor, a torture chamber, duels, and a plot intent upon getting Marion married to a half-idiot (the Dauphin), with Marion escaping in disguise as the peasant "Yolanda" and finally winning out in the last reel, her true love Prince Maximilian by her side.

There was another elegant premiere when *Yolanda* opened in February 1924, at the Cosmopolitan Theatre, where it ran for three months as a road-show attraction. The New York critics were kind, Robert E. Sherwood writing in the *Herald* that Marion looked lovely and Harriette Underhill in the Tribune going much further, saying, "Marion Davies is charming as 'Yolanda.' One of the screen's most arresting actresses; whatever she does is interesting." *The New York Times* and the *Tribune*, both far removed from wanting to give Hearst any free publicity, were nearly always enthusiastic about Marion from this period on until her very last talkies in which there was a decline in quality. But unlike *Knighthood,* which had the advantage of coming first, the public did not queue up to see this even more populated and costly sequel. It simply had been budgeted too high for Hearst ever to recoup.

In Los Angeles, Hearst arranged for a spectacular opening of the film at the California Theatre in August, the time of its regular release. Crowds began gathering in the early afternoon to see what the Hearst papers promised would be the largest turnout of stars and public figures ever to attend a film premiere. When they saw that every Metro star was in attendance and many other film queens and leading men as well as literary and society figures (Elinor Glyn and Mrs. Charles Fleishman among them), there was a near riot and police barricades kept back the excited public. Marion's own entrance with Charlie Chaplin, Pola Negri, and the two Talmadge sisters, Norma and Constance, brought cheers from the crowd, and there was a noisy clamor inside the theater among the celebrities when she came down the aisle to take a quick bow after her introduction by actor Milton Sills. The Los Angeles *Examiner* covered all of this with a full page of stories describing everything from what the picture was about to what Mrs. Fleishman and the other ladies were wearing.

Much of this furor was carefully engineered by Hearst publicity men. Some of it was not. By now the public's acclaim was coming in such massive doses, it was difficult for Marion to know what was real and what was created. It is possible she did not know until some years later that the film was not the great money-maker that Hearst said it was.

For Hearst, there was no retreat—not as yet—into more modest territory. He decided that *Yolanda* had been too much like its predecessor, and what the American public really wanted was an epic treatment of its own history. With no more than two weeks between productions, most of which was spent by Hearst in New York State searching out locations and setting up advance units for another film and by Marion getting fitted for more than a dozen costume changes, they moved into production of a movie even more sweeping in scope and pictorial excitement than either of the two earlier spectaculars, the difference being that this time it was all about America and the Revolution. Marion had become, for Hearst, like the Gish sisters in *Orphans of the Storm:* vulnerable humanity swept along by history. What was more important to her career was that she had become human before the camera. She was able to project innocence, lovability, and poignancy. If she seemed less vulnerable than Lillian Gish, that was simply the old Douras pluck shining through, and then, of course, she always managed to come out on top and her audiences came to know this. If there was anything lacking in Marion's movies of this time, it was suspense, the not-knowing whether she was going to make it or not. Later, there would be suspense to spare in her comedies, but in 1924 she was still known as a dramatic star, the way Hearst wanted it.

Janice Meredith, Hearst's major excursion into American history, had a great deal going for it. Perhaps there was a bit too much solemn historical fact, such as a fifteen-minute long sequence involving George Washington at Valley Forge; and it had a tendency to include everything, from the Boston Tea Party to the final triumph of freedom from English rule. But the big Griffith-like recreations of history's great moments dominated the film, and it was to Marion's credit that she was compelling enough on the screen not to be overshadowed by troops of Hessians, the whole rebel army, and enough snow to send an audience out temporarily blinded. Typically, Hearst had moved Marion, his cast, and an army of technicians from Plattsburg,

New York, to Lake Placid, when Plattsburg suffered a thaw. The film negative cost came to between half a million and a million dollars, making it another Hearst super-spectacle that would have to become a smash hit to recoup. Unfortunately, despite glowing reviews from everywhere, it did not succeed in this except in New York, where it was a road-show attraction for several months, following reviews such as that of *The New York Times*, which said, "No more brilliant achievement in ambitious motion pictures dealing with historical romances has ever been exhibited."

The year 1924 was shaping up as Hearst's most difficult in following his impulses, fulfilling his desires, and not caring very much what was said of him. An accretion of public hostility going back to his pro-German attitudes during the war finally had overflowed and he was no longer given even grudging respect. Increasingly, he was depicted by editorial cartoonists as an overgrown, oafish, power-crazed brute. His defeats in the political arena were inspirations to these artists. Hearst tolerated this without losing his temper, but he believed that he was immune to vilification over his private life. He became a very angry bear indeed (cartoonists were fond of rendering him as a bear or as an octopus) when Marion and Millicent were maligned because of their association with him.

The first indication of incipient scandal came when, at Hearst's instigation, *American* reporter Nat Ferber was assigned by managing editor Victor Watson to find out who was protecting the "bucketshops." Behind Hearst's courageous action in behalf of the public was a private and overwhelming desire to "get" Big Tom Foley, who had backed up Al Smith in Smith's political crucifixion of Hearst the previous year. "Bucketshops" were brokers' offices run by stockbrokers who pretended to buy stocks for clients on margin, asking that they pay ten percent down and charging them six percent interest on the balance. They did not buy the stock in most cases, but collected their clients' interest illegally and for services unperformed. Foley's involvement in the racket was principally with a firm called Fuller & McGee, two crooked gentlemen who were brought into court by outraged, fleeced clients again and again and never prosecuted. Foley, who had tremendous influence over the courts of New York City, had been paid generously for this favor, in one documented instance $10,000. A photostat of the check was made by reporter Ferber and shown to Hearst.

Ferber exposed eighty-one bucketshops in the pages of Hearst's *American*. This was one of numerous public services performed by Hearst during his publishing career that very nearly made up for his irresponsibility and recklessness. If reading one of his newspapers was "like watching a screaming woman run down the street with her throat cut," as one of his staff colorfully remarked, this time he had something to scream about.

In nearly all of the bucketshops' dealings with the law, the name "Fallon" appeared again and again. The *American* next learned through a former assistant of Fallon's, Ernest Eidlitz, that Fallon once had bribed a juror by the name of Charles Rendigs in order to win an acquittal for his client, the Fuller & McGee partnership.

When Hearst found the jailed Fuller and McGee in a talkative mood, he persuaded the authorities to transfer them to a floor of the McAlpin Hotel he had taken over as their "cell block." Mrs. McGee (musical comedy star Louise Groody of *No, No, Nanette* fame) came for visits, as well as Fuller's girlfriend. Hearst also took over a floor of Brooklyn's Hotel Bossert in the Heights as a safe place to store his pigeon Ernest Eidlitz.

Gene Fowler wrote a brilliant account of lawyer Fallon's life, *The Great Mouthpiece*, filled with devastating observations on Fallon's flamboyance. One such comment occurs during Fowler's chapter on the Hearst exposé: "Referring to himself in the third person, as was his court-custom, Fallon shouted: 'It's a plot to get Fallon out of the way. The Hearst papers are looking for a goat. So they choose Fallon. It is a gigantic conspiracy.' . . . He intimated that Mr. Hearst had personal reasons for wishing him out of the way."

During the trial, juror Rendigs had turned State's evidence, pleading guilty to the charge of accepting the bribe. Still incarcerated after Fallon's acquittal, he felt that his own conviction was a miscarriage of justice. He began talking in detail to Federal authorities, revealing how he had been in financial trouble and Fallon had offered him $5000 for his vote to acquit Fallon's clients. "Half the money," said Rendigs, "never was paid."

When Rendigs was brought into Criminal Court for sentencing, Fallon was in the building and was given the facts about Rendigs' telling all. He fled from the building and holed up in the apartment of his mistress, the actress Gertrude Vanderbilt.

One of many girlfriends Fallon had along with a wife, Miss Vanderbilt was the most useful and faithful of all of them. Being typically Hearst, the publisher ran an *American* front page showing Fallon in a mock-up "Wanted" poster: "Fugitive from Justice—Wanted by U.S. Government—William J. Fallon."

Fallon was indicted while in hiding, caught after several days of the police following his mistress; his bail was fixed at $100,000, and, in default, he went to the Tombs. It was the beginning of the end for Fallon, whose health was already failing as a result of alcoholism. In desperation, he played one last card. He said he was building his own case slowly during his trial, but when the judge cautioned him about his attacks on the court and said that his "back was to the wall," Fallon shouted to the jury: "Fallon's back is not to the wall. He is in the front line."

Then Fallon took the stand in his own defense and began talking about publisher Hearst and his moral behavior. Fowler wrote:

> With characteristic bravado, Fallon in advance let it be known to the offices of the *American* that he was going on the stand to allege certain scandalous matters. He hinted at the nature of the charges broadly enough to cause excited huddles in the offices of the newspaper. There was a telephone call to the San Simeon ranch of Mr. Hearst. . . .
>
> A worried editor informed Mr. Hearst by long-distance telephone of the probable Fallon outburst. Mr. Hearst replied:
>
> "Well, then, you won't be in doubt as to *what your headline will be for tomorrow's paper*."
>
> Mr. Hearst is entitled to a monument for *never having bored* anyone that worked for him.

In later testimony, again quoting Fowler, Fallon asserted, concerning his ex-colleague Eidlitz's confession:

> Eidlitz said to me that he told Watson [editor of the *American*] he was fearful he would be arrested, and that he [Eidlitz] knew I had the birth certificates of the children of a moving-picture actress, and that I knew Mr. Hearst had sent a woman, who pretended to be a countess, to Florida to get evidence against his wife. He said he had told Watson that I intended to use that information to blackmail Mr.

Hearst. . . . Eidlitz said he told Mr. Watson that I had the
number of the car and the name of the man who went to
Mexico with the same party, the same moving-picture actress. He said a few days later Hearst communicated with
Watson, and said to Watson: "Fallon must be destroyed."

There was no doubt in anyone's mind about who the motion-
picture actress was. If there had been, it was dispelled when
prospective jurors at Fallon's trial were asked, "Are you ac-
quainted with Marion Davies?" Marion's photo appeared in non-
Hearst papers from coast-to-coast, and her career seemed threatened. Reporters converged on the Bedford Drive house which
Marion had rented upon her return to Hollywood, but there were
too many Dourases screening her for any of them to get through.

Hearst was sick with apprehension about her. Perhaps he
thought that he could modify the deal with the Goldwyn Company, which was about to merge with Metro, and turn over her
career to Mayer and his able directors. On an impulse, Hearst
sent off a letter to Marion, written on the cheap, yellow-lined
pad he so often used for memos, telling her that he had decided
to go out of moving pictures. His reasons were, he said, that
the work was too hard and the compensation too little.

There is considerable rue in the tone of this letter, regret
that all of his publicizing in her behalf may have led only to
notoriety and scandal. He seemed to be saying, "When a man
has tried very earnestly to accomplish a certain thing for over
five years and finds everything exactly as it was when he started,
it's time for him to stop." He told her that, apparently, he was
not suited temperamentally to pictures, but that she was. She
liked that kind of thing. She had advanced every day in her
profession, in his opinion, and now she was at the top. It would
be easy for her to go still further and be the greatest of all moving picture stars past or future. He declared that this was no
idle hope. He *knew* that it would be so.

Marion put aside her fear of an accidental encounter with
Millicent and phoned Hearst at San Simeon. She told him that
she had no intention of remaining in films if he got out; that
it was all his idea in the first place. She was not treating her
film career lightly by doing so; she was declaring herself and
her feelings. "I've done this to please you," she told him, "and
it doesn't matter that it began to please me, too." Without Hearst,
she would have no more fun making movies. Of course, the fun

had always been behind his back and sometimes at his expense, but she could not imagine her life as a star without him.

Hearst's mood, as it so often did, swung wildly into elation. Of course he would stay in films if it meant that much to her. And now *he* had made a declaration. He was staying in films because she wanted him to. It was the sort of subtle seesaw they enjoyed riding.

At San Simeon, Hearst escaped from the reality of the Fallon trial as he would from every other exterior event until the advent of the Second World War when he was to fear an attack upon the castle by artillery from Japanese submarines and reluctantly take flight. In a letter to Marion, he described his sensations on a moonlit night, describing the sea below as calm and smooth with the moonlight making a broad path upon it like a silver road to the land of their dreams. He remarked on the beauty of the distant lighthouse flashing its beam and the long sloping hills that seemed to have lain down to sleep and to have wrapped themselves in the mantle of the night. He said that he thought and dreamed of her and wished that he could hold her hand and wander together along that silver road.

Marion thought it was beautiful and put it away along with the rest of Hearst's poetry and correspondence (she never threw away anything from Hearst). Along with the poesy, he cautioned her about their behavior during the trial. Against Fallon's wild-eyed talk about her "children's birth certificates," he suggested that she stay in seclusion for the time being. Instead, she went partying every night, joking about her alleged offspring, and prompting Hearst to send her a special delivery letter, discreetly using secretary Joseph Willicombe's name, in care of the Palace Hotel, San Francisco, as the return address. "Big Joe" Willicombe had been a Hearst reporter for nearly twenty years until the death of Hearst's previous secretary, L. J. O'Reilly. Hearst called Marion a "little bum" and said that she was having a grand time and not missing him a bit. He insisted that she was out nights until five in the morning and then slept until one o'clock next day and nobody could get her on the telephone, that she was running around with all her old beaux and a lot of new ones. (Hearst was getting detailed reports on Marion's activities through Louella Parsons.) But he complained that moving-picture stars and queens and goddesses were too swift for him, that what he really wanted was a quiet little girl out of the Follies or the Winter Garden or the Columbia. He said that he wished he might find some affectionate "little flapper" innocent enough to appreciate someone as devoted as himself, and he concluded hoping that her conscience would bother her "knowing" that she didn't have any, and that if she read of a swain disappointed in love committing suicide, it would be "W.R." Despite the threat of public opprobrium if Fallon turned out to have the alleged documents, Hearst persisted in his nineteenth-century style, the eternal gallant in spite of everything including old age.

There was some panic among Hearst's executives in New York over Fallon's charges, and a Hearst attorney asked the court to disregard the personal attacks upon Hearst. Since Fallon had implied that the unnamed actress had gone to Mexico to have her children delivered in secret, there was no way of verifying his charges or denying them. Judge McClintic then shut up Fallon by saying: "There has been a great deal said about an alleged conspiracy of the New York *American* to get Fallon. Newspapers have aided public authorities before, and their motives are of no consequence if the man should be found guilty. There is no evidence in this case to show improper motives of the *American*." Indeed not. It is immediately clear from the foregoing account that Hearst had set out to get Big Tom Foley. In his pursuit of vengeance, Hearst had lifted the lid on one of the most notorious rackets in "legitimate" business since the Teapot Dome scandal earlier that year, and thus rendered the public a lasting service. The "bucketshop" exposé largely put such operators out of business for good. Fallon, in spite of his attractive Irish charisma, was a chronic liar and an outrageous tamperer with juries. He was acquitted only after long, agonizing hours by a jury whose emotions had been caught and played upon by Fallon, an acknowledged virtuoso. Rendigs, the confessed acceptor of the bribe, drew a two-year *suspended* sentence.

Within three years, forty-one-year old Fallon suffered a gastric hemorrhage and a heart attack and died, played out after the nervous strain of his two trials and more than a decade of intense dissipation.

The *American*'s editor Watson had gone through hell during the trial, knowing that every non-Hearst paper in town was watching his columns to see how he would evade the testimony by Fallon. While newspapers across the land headlined the accusations against Hearst and publicly ventilated what was known of his private life, including his association with Marion and his marriage with Millicent, Watson published headlines such as "HOTTEST DAY KILLS FIVE," with the Fallon trial relegated to an inside page and the Hearst remarks deleted. It is said that Millicent blamed Watson for starting the noisome affair in the first place and asked her husband to fire him. Instead, he was demoted to the editorship of the Baltimore paper.

Reporter Ferber, in a memoir published some years later, said that he went through birth records to determine whether there were, in fact, any illegitimate children—a seemingly impossible task, since he would have to assume that the actress was Marion and that any possible births could have occurred at any of a thousand places from Mexico to California, or from New York to Europe. He also asked Gertrude Vanderbilt, who told him that her late lover had had no birth certificates. The rumor was not to die there, however, and, as the author of this book, I am constantly approached by people wanting to know if I found out about "those children."

In Adela Rogers St. Johns's autobiography, *The Honeycomb*, she dismisses the possibility by saying that if Marion ever had had any children, they would be right there with her. I'm not convinced that the question is resolved that easily. Marion said in her memoirs that she did not especially care for children. We should take her word for this, despite her polite interest in the children of her friends and her being the doting aunt to Charlie and Pepi Lederer and Patricia Van Cleve. During the thirties, a male member of Marion's family told her that a young man he knew had "got a girl into trouble," and he was desperate to find a solution. Marion lightly told her relative to give him the name of Dr. So-and-So. "He took care of all of mine," she said, and she wasn't laughing. But as we know by now, Marion was a cool lady with a joke, and after a few martinis she often would say just about anything good for a laugh or a shock.

VII

Marion never was a full-blown flapper, but there were times when she looked and acted the part. As a wild, impulsive child and then an irrepressible teenager, it should have been expected that she would have lived through the twenties with the abandon and recklessness of a Zelda Fitzgerald, but there were carefully-drawn boundaries to her freedom with Hearst.

Walter Lippmann, in writing of the young in the twenties, was to point out plaintively: "It is common for young men and women to rebel, but that they should rebel sadly and without faith in their rebellion, that they should distrust the new freedom no less than the old certainties—that is something of a novelty." But when Marion rebelled, it was frequently not against the times but against her lover. Hearst's habit of working at his publishing or movie interests at any hour of the day or night infuriated her. In his autobiography, Charlie Chaplin mentions an occasion when Marion's annoyance became unalloyed rudeness. It shows both the depth of Hearst's feelings and the random, impulsive peeves Marion sometimes let others see. The incident was to occur approximately two years after the opening of *Knighthood* when Hearst had moved his film operations to the West Coast.

Two or three times a week [writes Chaplin] Marion gave stupendous dinner parties with as many as a hundred guests, a melange of actors, actresses, senators, polo-players, chorus boys, foreign potentates and Hearst's executives and editorial staff to boot. It was a curious atmosphere of tension and frivolity, for no one could predict the mercurial temper of the powerful Hearst, which was the barometer of whether the evening would go or not.

I remember an incident at a dinner Marion gave in her rented house. About fifty of us were standing about while Hearst, looking saturnine, was seated in a high-backed chair surrounded by his editorial staff. Marion, gowned a la Madame Récamier, reclined on a settee, looking radiantly beautiful, but growing more taciturn as Hearst continued his business. Suddenly she shouted indignantly, "Hey! You!"

Hearst looked up. "Are you referring to me?" he said.

"Yes, you! Come here!" she answered, keeping her large blue orbs on him. His staff backed away and the room hardened into silence.

Hearst's eyes narrowed as he sat sphinxlike, his scowl growing darker, his lips disappearing into a thin line as his fingers tapped nervously on the arm of his thronelike chair, undecided whether to burst into fury or not. I felt like reaching for my hat. But suddenly he stood up. "Well, I suppose

I shall have to go," he said, oafishly hobbling over to her. "And what does my lady want?"

"Do your business downtown," said Marion disdainfully. "Not in my house. My guests are waiting for a drink, so hurry up and get them one."

Hearst obediently tended bar. The executives present doubtless despised Marion for humiliating their "Chief," and understandably. But everyone in the room knew that Hearst *had allowed* her to do so. It was one of his many compensatory tributes to his sweetheart. It was, in a sense, a game in which both knew the rules. And when one of his staff seized an occasion such as this to urge that Hearst return to Millicent whom the executive believed to be always gentle, Hearst simply looked at him with incredulity. When the staff member persisted and began talking about morality, Hearst cut him off quickly, replying, "I'm not saying it's right. I'm saying that it *is*."

Bad manners were tolerated in the twenties just as drunken guests were. People were "letting off steam" from the restrictions of the recent war and, before that, the stifling pretensions to morality of the Victorian era. Marion doubtless humiliated Hearst publicly more than once, but she is not remembered in Hollywood for ordering Hearst about. Perhaps those who liked her have blocked out memories of little acts of hostility and rebellion and recall instead her gaiety and the way she had of seeing that everyone had a good time. She was Hearst's social buffer—his pained smile at large parties masked an innate shyness. Marion dissipated the tension that surrounded Hearst with laughter and stammered concern about their guests. Their mutual devotion was never more evident than when Hearst was running off one of her films for a gathering of friends. Ilka Chase in her memoir *Past Imperfect* recalls such an occasion at San Simeon with everyone bundled up against the chill—Miss Chase says it was because of the wet plaster in the new castle theater, but Anita Loos insists that there was always a kind of Stygian gloom in the place—and, as Miss Chase writes, "They [Hearst and Marion] would sit close together in the gloom, silhouetted against the screen, and bundled in their fur coats, they looked for all the world like the big and baby bears."

Hollywood suited Marion. It was a mutual love affair. Beverly Hills was very much like a new upper-middle-class English suburb with lots of timbered Tudor-style buildings and small shops, a pretentious air of being an established community belied only by the spanking newness of everything. Marion never had been impressed by antiquities, but she enjoyed her studio life where she was surrounded by fake relics and props. In a sense, Beverly Hills was one huge set, a piece of English countryside recreated in a much more salubrious climate. She loved every stuccoed bit of it.

A white stucco mansion situated on the top of a rise just off Sunset Boulevard came on the market. Marion and Mama Rose went to look at it and they were impressed at once by the size and proportions of the rooms. It was as grand as any of the other stars' homes. Perhaps it was a challenge to Hearst to make good on his promise to set her up as chatelaine of the castle, but when she phoned him in San Francisco to tell him that she wanted to buy 1700 Lexington Road, Hearst merely told her, "Let Mama Rose buy it in her name." If he feared legal repercussions from Millicent's corner when it was discovered that he had helped Marion to acquire a piece of California property, he would get over it within a year. Then Marion would begin acquiring property in Beverly Hills and Los Angeles that eventually would make her the richest leading lady this side of Mary Pickford and, by the time of Hearst's death, even richer than that.

The legal owner of the house rarely came downstairs. The film community was not her world and never would be. Mama Rose felt ill-at-ease throughout her five years in Beverly Hills and, removed from her small circle of friends back East and having to contend with continuous party noise coming up the stairwell, it may have shortened her life.

Marion recalled that "We used to have, let's call them 'friends,' at night, you know, playing cards, laughing. Then we'd turn on the victrola or the radio and drive her [Mama Rose] crazy. She couldn't sleep. So one night, she lost her temper. She leaned over the balcony and she said, 'Everybody go home please.' "

Louella Parsons, recovered from a year-long bout with tuberculosis after a stay in the dry air of Colton, California, at the expense of Hearst, came into Hollywood for the first time with her young child Harriet and no place to go. At Hearst's suggestion, mother and daughter put up at the Lexington Road house with Marion and Mama Rose. Louella wrote that she ar-

rived in the film capital "in the days of Prohibition, the old Montmartre Cafe, the Cocoanut Grove, the Charleston and the Black
Bottom. . . . Bands were playing 'Yes, Sir, That's My Baby.' The
girls were wearing knee-length evening gowns and big bows on
high-heeled slippers. Clara Bow was the biggest box-office star."
What she didn't write was that she was upstairs in the Douras
mansion, in Marion's words, "Tick, tick, ticking on the typewriter, six o'clock in the morning . . . enough to drive anybody
nuts."

Mama Rose complained to her daughters, "I do wish that
she would start her work a little bit later." Marion was busy on
her first Hollywood film and desperately needed her rest after all
that dancing the night before. Many of the parties were celebrating Louella's recovery, but after two months the celebration
was wearing a bit thin.

According to Louella, the parties were a never-ending round
of festivities involving Charlie Chaplin, Rudolph Valentino, and
assorted actors, actresses, polo players and chorus boys. They
had been going on when she and her daughter arrived at the
Lexington house and she was invited simply because she was on
the premises. Marion's story that they were in Louella's honor
was a fiction, according to Louella, to cover herself whenever
Hearst happened to return from New York.

Marion recalled that Louella was distressed the evening
Hearst was expected. "What are you afraid of?" Marion asked.
"There's nothing wrong."

"There've been so many parties," Louella said. "I don't think
he's going to like it."

"Well, dear," Marion told her, "the parties were given for
you. What should he be annoyed about? He won't mind that."

When Hearst finally arrived, he was wearing a tuxedo. Marion wanted to know if it was an occasion of some kind or a joke
in very poor taste—and she noticed Louella looking rather uncomfortable. He told her that Louella had wired him, telling him
there was going to be another party.

In the car on the way to the party, Hearst reached into his
pocket and handed Marion a gift of pearls and diamonds worked
into either a brooch or a bracelet—Marion wasn't sure in recalling this; her interest in her growing collection of jewelry was
always vague and a little careless. Marion said, "Very nice!" Louella, sitting on the opposite side of Hearst, then remarked (in a

nervous way she had of filling pauses) with the comment, "She doesn't deserve it. She's been a bad girl. She's been dragging me to parties all the time."

Hearst told Louella, "Anything that Marion ever does is all right with me. She's a good girl," and he patted Marion's hand, as he would that of a mischievous daughter.

Louella then said with all due contrition, "I'm sorry, Chief."

Marion was in a state by this time. She despised being treated like a child. "Take it back!" and she was in tears now. "Take the junk back!"

"Don't pay any attention to Louella," Hearst said gently. "She hasn't got any brains." Or so Marion recalled that he said. In any event, Louella subsided and never raised the subject again. And Hearst, for his part, was ever on the defensive about gifts to Marion. There was always a look on his face, the one he wore when he felt left out of things, a look that suggested a small shy boy leaving Mayflowers on a girl's stoop and running away.

PART THREE

LIFE AND
SUDDEN DEATH
IN
HOLLYWOOD

I

As in any industry, there are strata of the very successful, the moderately successful, and a substratum of failures in the film community. With the exception of a handful of tough-skinned executives, the very successful behave with the least maturity. The stars, writers, and directors, and even a few producers, indulge in a gamut of excessive emotions, sulking, planning pranks, loving nearly everybody, hating a few. Hollywood is an aberrant kindergarten and the studio head often takes the place of the hated teacher or principal. "Kiddy" is a favorite word, as well as "Baby," both used in addressing other adults as forms of endearment. But real children usually relate to one another with some sensitivity and regard for the other's needs. Egocentric children who want everything for themselves often wind up without any playmates.

In Hollywood, it is expected that if you are moving in the very successful crowd, you will think of yourself first. You are a star or a famous director, something special, with the prerogatives of an elite. When you begin to slip and move into the society of the moderately successful, reality enters your life once again and, while you may still use them, all those "Baby's" and "Kiddy's" begin to sound a little forced, as though you are speaking a foreign tongue.

Marion and Hearst were, of course, in the top stratum from the beginning of their Hollywood years until some years after her retirement. Until quite recently, it had become fashionable to denigrate Marion's and Hearst's role as society leaders in the film community—a dismissal of all the facts of their era as ignorant as the misconceptions about Marion's film career, and both alterations of Hollywood history growing out of the mythic legend of *Citizen Kane*. In some ways, Marion seemed a typical Hollywood star; her fourteen-room "bungalow" and her privileges at Metro even elevated her above that level. For long periods she thought only of herself, of her own affairs, and the attention she paid to those who counted most—Mama Rose, and even Hearst

—was scant. But while Mama Rose remained quiet in her neglect, Hearst did not. He wrote her notes of complaint, phoned to
scold her, gave her expensive gifts with notes appended saying,
"I love you anyway."

Hearst himself was a special case. He was not a tough-
skinned producer. His feelings were easily hurt. But he had
great faith in himself, sufficient to allow him to feel at ease
with Marion's friends, and his devotion to her was deep enough
for him to overlook the occasional verbal abuse he took from
her in and out of her presence. Sometimes, Marion would be
quoted as having called him "an old bastard" by someone whose
primary loyalty was to Hearst, but this person soon learned that
their tale-bearing was not appreciated by Hearst, so in time
most of Marion's coarser epithets went unreported.

Marion's occasional "cussing-him-out" may have been the
cause of her falling out with Arthur Brisbane, Hearst's closest
colleague in his publishing empire. She knew that Hearst loved
Brisbane in a fashion that is best described as brotherly affection of the deepest sort. She resented him, and she was more
reckless in railing at Hearst in Brisbane's presence than with
others. Doubtless Brisbane warned her, but she probably told
him to mind his own affairs. For a number of years, until Brisbane's death in 1936, there was a nervous truce between them.

But those who were less emotional in their feelings for
Hearst could see that Marion was the perfect foil for him in
that frantic heyday of the twenties in Hollywood. If he was the
lord seigneur of his publishing empire and sprawling California
domain, she was the gayest girl in town; everybody—or nearly
everybody—loved her, especially the members of her "chowder
crowd," so named by Hearst because these actors and actresses
were newly risen to great affluence, but had the manners of
boarders in an Irish rooming house.

Marion craved sensation in a sensation-drugged age, and
she found it. Hearst, who had been spoon-feeding sensation to
a public that had been serenely complacent in the nineties at
the beginning of his "scare-them-silly" newspaper approach, now
was seeing daily events match in horror or shock his old fantasies and exaggerations. There was the "rubbing out" of Chicago ganglord Dion O'Bannion as well as nearly four hundred
other lesser gangsters in the same town, all in 1924; and that
same year there had been the thrill murder of young Bobby

Franks in Chicago by two university students, Loeb and Leopold. And Hearst was uncomfortably aware that there had been considerable shock value in the stories coming out of the Fallon trial.

Despite the tight control over film content exercised early in the twenties by the Production Code Authority under Will Hays, Hollywood's notables continued to live keyed-up lives. Only drugs were considered a forbidden distraction. There were a few stars like Alma Rubens—still a Hearst star and in Marion's circle—who remained heavy users, but (in Miss Rubens's case) very privately. Bootleg whiskey continued to be the preferred social lubricant and general antidepressent (although predictably it gave them the "blues" afterward for too many hours) for the Dourases, and for many others in the film colony. Despite his personal aversion to it, Hearst was forced to have liquor delivered in wholesale quantities to supply Marion and her various family households as well as his own social needs.

Just as Hearst found it impossible to police either the behavior (excluding obvious drunkenness) or the intake of his guests, the internal force of the moral revolution going on in the twenties could not be contained by the Hays office. Before the decade had ended, collegiate films were showing college boys in their underwear making mad love with coeds wearing nothing more than "step-ins," an abbreviated undergarment. Joan Crawford and other "jazz babies" of the time were not above dancing around the screen clad in such attire. So uninhibited had the movies become for many moviegoers there was something refreshing and reassuring about Marion's and Mary Pickford's on-screen personalities, projecting as they did such glowing purity.

Marion, like the others, drank, but it did not begin to show until very late in the twenties, and her principal high was obtained through being in a crowd of people she liked. One of her friends, more objective than most, saw her incessant party activity, her always being the life of any party, as a cover for her profound disenchantment. But she knew that she would have to put a stopper on her ebullient spirits soon. She had to learn to be serious even though she was by nature wildly impulsive, for she was the companion of a sixty-one-year-old man whose health was becoming precarious. More and more, Hearst was "rationing" his time with Marion, possibly on the advice of his physician. It was his tendency to keep pace with her whenever they were together and, if no limits were set, it could prove fatal.

When she wasn't doing an exhibition dance with one of her friends—the Charleston or the Black Bottom—she was performing in pantomime or planning elaborate gags. A typical one had Harry Crocker, her new crony from San Francisco, appearing in her drawing room dressed as a waiter with a bulbous red nose and a napkin over his arm. Crocker asked a British Earl, one of Hearst's friends, if he would like some champagne. When the Earl said, "Yes, a drop," Crocker emptied the glass over the Earl's head and elegant Bond Street tuxedo. Stunts such as this broke up Marion, and, after she stopped shaking with laughter, she apologized and made sure that something else happened to another guest so the Earl would not feel he had been singled out as a victim. She patted these dupes on the arm and said with warmth, "It was only a ga-ga-gag." Then she laughed so infectiously, the victim usually joined her. Occasionally she would wonder aloud about her need to have things happen around her. She envied women who were quiet and composed, but emulated them only in parody—Shearer or Gish, for example. The taboo against thinking or speaking about death must have reached deep and made her jig a little whenever it crossed her mind.

Most of Marion's entertaining at the Lexington Road place was done in a huge ballroom which had been attached to the house in less than a week by a crew of carpenters and masons working around the clock. While the castle at San Simeon was nearing a state where it could be occupied, the ballroom was ordered by Hearst the moment Marion said that she needed one. No one ever observed any second thoughts in him about needless expense.

And before the Lexington Road mansion was ready for entertaining, there had been an enormous party at the Ambassador Hotel given by Hearst to welcome Marion back to Hollywood. Everyone of any prominence at all attended—over five hundred guests—and the evening was marred only by a drunken hobo in tattered clothes believed to be the real thing by Marion, Hearst, Chaplin, and others, asking for a handout. A gracious refusal or even a few coins would not shake the man off and he was finally tossed out. When, the next day, a film company on location at a nearby pier began getting anxious about its star, John Barrymore, who hadn't shown up by noon, someone was sent to his home to fetch him, and he was found still in his hobo costume, sleeping it off.

When production began on Marion's first Hollywood production, *Zander the Great,* Marion tried to discipline herself and retire early since she had to leave for the United Artists studio by six o'clock in the morning. (Metro's own studio facilities were not yet available to Hearst and Cosmopolitan, although they were financing the production.) But it was difficult for Marion to break away from the congenial atmosphere of her living room, where the fireplace would be going and the radio playing the latest tunes by the Cliquot Club Eskimos, while sisters Rose, Ethel, and Reine flirted in the approved, open manner of the twenties flapper with a handsome succession of beaux.

"It was gay," Marion recalled. "I didn't mind it so much, but I thought, 'Oh, Lord! I gotta join the party, and if I do, I won't be on the set in the morning.'" Then a favorite fox trot would blare from the radio and everyone would dance, and Marion would clap her hands and exclaim, "This is just so peaceful!" Peace for Marion was a roomful of noisy friends.

She usually made it to the studio on time, although there were a few occasions when she would appear at eleven. Director Hill circumvented a shutdown of production at such times by getting rid of the dress dummy that was only good for testing the lighting in stationary set-ups and hiring a young lady, Vera Burnett, who closely resembled Marion. Miss Burnett would walk through the action prior to Marion's arrival so that shooting could begin as soon as Marion reached the set. Soon, nearly all of the female stars had stand-ins.

Zander the Great once again cast Marion as a girl, an orphan with pigtails and freckles named Mamie Smith. Written by Frances Marion and Lily Hayward and directed by George Hill, the film might have become a brilliant comedy despite Marion's visible maturity (she was approaching twenty-eight), but Hearst was tampering with the script by way of ten and twelve page telegrams sent from San Simeon. In effect, these would be scenarios of what would be shot that week, with the ladies' screenplay put to one side. As an example, Hearst wanted to use a sandstorm to enable Mamie to escape a band of outlaws (a climax which a critic later called "claptrap hokum" that buried Marion's fine acting). Hearst wanted a big effect "like Griffith's storm," with sand flying, trees bending and breaking, the outlaws' blankets and things blowing away, cattle being blinded by sand and stampeding. His vision of a film he was making often spilled from him like a revelation, and he would not forget one word of it; there was hell to pay if it was ignored. The rushes or daily reels of completed action would be sent by special messenger to San Simeon, where they were run off in Hearst's study at Casa del Mar. Sometimes too much footage would be used for a relatively simple scene and he would send an explosive telegram to production manager, Dr. Goodman. Sometimes Hearst's instincts were sound. He was one of the first to see that Marion could supply her own comic relief in her films, and in *Zander* he asked that she have some absurdly terrified reactions and perform some agitated, trembly things. Instead of going to the window and staring out in a melodramatic fashion, he wanted her head to come up above the curtain with her eyes saucer-wide on the lookout for some desperate deed. Hearst knew all the idioms of the silent screen.

But there were times when his orders baffled his directors. On another film, he asked that an ancient warship be painted with gilt rather than with monotones, even though the film was in black and white, at a cost of several thousand dollars, so the actors would be more enthusiastic in their roles. No one would venture to ignore such an order or to make any changes without his specific authority. Nor did Louis B. Mayer ever interfere with Hearst's productions. It is likely that this first Cosmopolitan film to be financed by Metro and produced in Hollywood was done at the United Artists studio so that there would be no interference from anyone at Metro. When visiting studio executives carried back to Culver City stories of Hearst's "reasonableness," he finally was invited to shoot all of his future films there. Irving Thalberg, who had come to Metro as production chief in 1924, admired Marion both as an actress and as a person. He wanted her to rise as one of the screen's great comediennes and most of the properties he sent along to Hearst and Marion for their consideration were comedies. He believed that Mabel Normand's premature retirement had left the field clear for Marion.

Zander the Great was a modest success, attributable, according to one non-Hearst critic, to Marion's "gorgeous comedy." She was compared in this film to Colleen Moore and, to her intense sorrow, to Mary Pickford. As nearly always, her supporting cast was a strong one (Hearst always saw to it that Marion was surrounded by the finest actors available), including young

Jackie Huff as Zander and Hedda Hopper as Marion's mother. Miss Hopper would become close to Marion during the production and their friendship would survive until Marion's death. When talkies were well established, Miss Hopper would be launched with Marion's help as a Hollywood gossip columnist and the toughest competition Louella Parsons was ever to encounter.

There was a scene in *Zander the Great* in which orphan Mamie, played by Marion, comes upon a circus. The sequence had little motivation; it was there for the sake of suspense. Mamie was supposed to enter the lion's cage and say, "Hello, boy," the tenuous connection with her own situation being, I suppose, that the lion was an orphan, too, far from home.

Marion was terrified and wouldn't go near the cage. Director Hill reassured her, saying the lion had no teeth. This was just another gag (gags were plentiful on a Davies picture): the lion had a full set, but Hill had placed a thick plate of glass between the lion and where Marion was supposed to stand and lean over and kiss him. She entered the cage, the lion let out a roar, displaying a magnificent set of incisors, and Marion ran screaming toward her dressing room.

Chaplin liked Marion's company so much that it soon became obvious to their mutual friends that any party thrown by one of them would include the other. Hearst was as aware of this as anyone else and at first he thought it was a tribute to Marion's gay personality. But Marion could not avoid being as flirtatious with Chaplin as she was with other attractive men and shortly he was reacting to it. Chaplin frequently picked Marion up after her day at the studio, on his way from his own studios where he had begun production on *The Gold Rush*. Hearst was still at San Simeon, but Marion had worked out a signal to be used by the guard at the front gate if he should pay a surprise visit to the set when Chaplin was there, so the comedian could leave by the rear gate. All of the cast and crew of *Zander* were aware that something was going on, but Marion was far too much like Chaplin for it to have been a meaningful affair. In the presence of others, they clowned together like an affectionate brother and sister, and it is difficult to imagine them being very different when they were alone together.

Marion told Chaplin about the lion with teeth. "Th-they're t-t-trying t-t-to get rid of m-me," she told him. "With W.R. out of town, th-they're t-taking advantage." After Chaplin had stopped laughing, he told Marion that he had a nice gentle old man of a lion down at his studio. Anyone but Marion would have doubted that the great Chaplin would take time out from a strenuous schedule to deliver her an animal, but, through her long association with Hearst, she had got used to being catered to. If she later were to ask George Bernard Shaw to write a comic screenplay for her, she would be watching the mails.

When Chaplin failed to appear the next morning and director Hill began looking anxious, Marion was afraid that Hill would go ahead with his own lion. She fled to an adjoining studio stage, where her pal Connie Talmadge was starring in a Graustarkian romance with Ronald Colman. Miss Talmadge was incredulous when Marion told her that she was being ordered into a cage with an angry lion, but when she saw the evidence (Hill's caged beast), she told Marion that she was a sap to even consider it. Then Marion said that Charlie Chaplin was supposed to bring his own lion.

Miss Talmadge thought this prospect was equally dubious, and she proposed that Marion get into a disguise of some sort. Within minutes, the two of them were in black-face, Marion's string quartet had been cued, and they shuffled onto the *Zander* stage singing *Mammy*, the old Al Jolson tune.

"Very funny. Very funny," said Hill.

Meanwhile, next door they were calling out "Where's Miss Talmadge? Miss Talmadge wanted on the set." Hill chased the star off his stage and turned to Marion: "Listen, punk," he told her. "Get that goo off and come back here as fast as you can."

While Marion was cleaning up and putting on fresh makeup, Chaplin appeared with a circus wagon containing his lion. Suddenly director Hill saw what Marion's delaying tactics had been leading up to. Chaplin entered the lion's cage and played with the beast for several minutes. The crew crowded around, and then Marion appeared. "See?" Chaplin told her. "He's like a kitten."

Marion was appreciative and impressed, but still unconvinced. In recalling the incident some years later, Marion said that Chaplin wasted no more time, but asked to borrow her costume and wig, telling director Hill to shoot from the rear, and he proceeded to do the scene for her. Miss Burnett, Marion's stand-in, remembers it quite differently and insists that she herself doubled for Marion in one shot, and then a professional lady animal trainer put on Marion's costume and did the rest of the scene inside the cage.

II

Away from the studio, Marion was surrounded by girlfriends who were free in spirit: Constance Talmadge, Dorothy Mackaill, Eileen Percy, and Anita Loos; but she needed no encouragement from them to declare herself her own person, and not owned body and soul by Hearst. It was a fantasy that she might do so, but, for a long time, she persisted in it.

Charlie Chaplin, too, was fighting to save his freedom. Between wives, he had been seeing a great deal of young Lita Grey, who was acting with him as the dance-hall hostess in *The Gold Rush* (she was replaced later by Georgia Hale). The affair may have gone sour when Miss Grey became pregnant. Miss Grey says that she was offered "a dowry" of $20,000 by Chaplin and his help in finding her a young man closer to her own age to marry her. She turned down this offer, her family holding out for a wedding.

During this desperate time, Chaplin increasingly sought out Marion. She could be gay in the face of the most dire events. Although many of their meetings took place at the studio—in Hearst's absence—and at Chaplin's house, they began going out publicly. Grace Kingsley, a Hollywood columnist for the New York *Daily News*, mentioned them as a couple on November 16, 1924, the item suggesting that the friendship might be serious and that it had been going on for some time: "Charlie Chaplin continues to pay ardent attention to Marion Davies. He spent the evening at Montmartre dining and dancing with the fair Marion the other night. There was a lovely young dancer entertaining that evening. And Charlie applauded but with his back turned. He never took his eyes off Marion's blonde beauty. Miss Davies wore a poudre blue dinner dress and small blue hat and looked very fetching indeed." Chaplin had been taken at once with Marion's wit and her impudent way of needling the pompous asses among them. Many leading ladies in Hollywood took themselves as seriously as did Pola Negri, with whom Chaplin had

had an affair prior to Miss Grey's advent. Once when he had addressed Miss Negri as "sweetheart," she took him aside and scolded him. "How dare you insult me in front of my friends!" she told him.

Marion knew that Hearst had a great fondness for Chaplin. She could not have known whether this affection would allow him to overlook what was rapidly being gossiped about as a romance. It is certain that Hearst had a great admiration for Chaplin's talent, but he knew that there were two sides to the comedian's personality in his presence: he was sober and interested in film production and world affairs with Hearst, and a much more youthful man who found nearly everything a laughing matter around Marion.

There is no evidence available as to how seriously Chaplin took the relationship. In any case, the romance in this intense phase was aborted by circumstance. But Marion was beautiful and girlish with her frequent laughter and her stammer, qualities that fascinated Chaplin, and she was more intelligent than the average Hollywood beauty. This must have been the first instance in Chaplin's life when he began seeking a woman who had wit as well as attractiveness. There were times when he found Marion's sense of humor uncivilized, however, such as when she asked Albert Einstein, "Why don't you get a haircut?" but even this appealed to his love of the outrageous.

Earlier that fall of 1924, Hearst had written Marion a note which gave her a clue as to his state of mind. The brief letter must have been the product of a suspicious day. Apparently he had been trying to get her on the phone and by telegraph, with no luck. His feelings were pushing toward a crisis between them; he wanted to know where she had been for over a week and what was going on. Aware from almost the beginning of their alliance that he must remain gay and bantering, he recommended that she get a copy of Al Jolson's record *I Gave Her That* about an ungrateful sweetheart.

Hearst must have been nearly ill with frustration. He had been spending much less time in Los Angeles and with Marion since the Fallon trial. Circumspection had been called for, but not this. He followed the affair from his mountaintop and from New York; there were spies on the staff at Cosmopolitan Films (later Marion was to say that secretary Ella "Bill" Williams was his most important secret tattler), and he even hired an outside detective agency to keep tabs on her. Chaplin himself reveals some of this background in his *Autobiography*, writing that during one dinner party at Marion's house, Hearst had phoned from New York, confessing to Marion that he had had her watched. She was furious as Hearst read her a detective's report of her comings and goings. When she got off the phone, Marion told Chaplin that Hearst was returning to Los Angeles to settle up his affairs with her and end their relationship. But Hearst did not come back to California then.

Chaplin has attempted to purge his memoirs of any suggestion that his friendship with Marion was anything other than platonic, but, as Dorothy Mackaill remarked, "He must think we all have very short memories," and then there were all of those gossip items—a particular sore point with Hearst since journalistic ethics usually call for restraint in printing items about rival publishers, and anything concerning Marion, he believed, concerned him.

Hearst, wounded in spirit and fretting over what he should do, remained in New York only briefly. Marion alternated between moods of relief and acute depression. She was like a canary let out of its cage that flies right back and perches on top of it. She sent off a wire to Hearst, telling him, "It's a balmy day in Los Angeles. Hurry back."

Hearst's next move is difficult to explain or comprehend. He came back to the Hollywood area ostensibly to patch things up with Marion and to have final conferences with Thomas Ince about having Ince become an active producer for Cosmopolitan Pictures at Metro. Their differences seemed to be basically over a matter of salary for Ince and over just what Ince's function would be in the new post. Hearst was reluctant to relinquish control over his film product, but Ince was not used to sharing production authority. Hearst invited Ince early that third week of November to join him and Marion aboard the Hearst yacht, the *Oneida*, and Hearst also invited Chaplin. Perhaps he thought that it was safe to do so, if he believed that he had broken up the romance; or he may have wanted to clarify Marion's status a bit with Chaplin, since Chaplin seemed to have some doubts about it.

Thomas Harper Ince had entered movies as an actor for the I.M.P. Company in 1910. Later that year, he made his first attempt at direction with a one reel *Little Nell's Tobacco* (his wife was known to her friends as "Nell"). By 1911, after an abortive effort at making films away from the Patents Trust

(Edison *et al.*) in Cuba, he was one of the first film men on the West Coast, arriving two years before Cecil B. De Mille. In California, Ince hired Miller Brothers' 101 Ranch Wild West Show at $2500 a week and began shooting westerns on 18,000 acres of leased land. By 1913, when De Mille did his *The Squaw Man,* Mutual released Ince's first feature, *The Battle of Gettysburg,* personally directed by him, while his studio was grinding out three short westerns a week. Ince hired a number of directors to keep up with the demand—Frank Ford (John's brother), Henry King, Frank Borzage, John Griffith Wray, and Fred Niblo. His studio complex was known as "Inceville," and he became highly regarded within the industry for his emphasis on a strong scenario and thrilling action in contrast to the improvised, static scenes of many other early producers.

After more than three years as a partner with D. W. Griffith and Mack Sennett (the Triangle Corporation), he produced films for Paramount, then Metro, and finally Associated Producers, Inc., which merged with First National in 1922. Throughout those years of various affiliations, he continued making westerns with William S. Hart. Hart and Ince had trouped together before their Hollywood years and eaten beans from the same can. When Hart was down on his luck, Ince put him on salary at $5 a day. Hart's salary as the world's favorite cowboy was increased to many times that figure through the next half-dozen years, but Hart made $6,000,000 for Ince while, according to Hart, winding up with only $5000 for himself when he quit Ince's employ. Because he had quit to make his own films for Paramount, Ince filed suit against Hart, but the producer lost. It would make Hart and Ince lasting enemies, and there were others in Hollywood who were almost equally bitter about Ince. But Hearst did not require his executives to be popular—he had numerous enemies of his own. At only forty years of age, Ince had discovered more stars than any other film executive except Griffith, some of them being Charles Ray, Florence Vidor, Mary Astor, Clive Brook, Ian Keith, Buster Collier, Warner Baxter, and Jacqueline Logan. There was every possibility that with Hearst, Ince would come back to renewed prominence. At the time he was conferring with Hearst about taking over production of Hearst films, Ince's reputation had dimmed slightly as more sophisticated films, those of Constance Bennett, Gloria Swanson and Pola Negri, were in vogue. There would be a swing back to the spectacular action film in the late twenties

(*The Trail of '98, Wings*), but Ince would not survive to see it. Hearst was also drawn to Ince because the producer looked at the screen medium much as he did himself. This is confirmed by John B. Richie writing about Ince in *Films in Review:* "He was one of the first to perceive that screen drama must consist of vivid, flashy incidents, hurrying restlessly on to a final and cumulative crisis."

The alliance with Ince sought by Hearst probably would not have advanced Marion's career. Marion was headed in a different direction, and by the late twenties would become unique in the vital comic force she projected. She was by then a subtle blend of the bounce of Clara Bow with the cool wit of Carole Lombard. Her films where the action dominated were, as a rule, her weakest ones, while those where her personality carried the film (*Little Old New York, The Patsy, The Fair Coed, Beverly of Graustark, Quality Street, Show People, Peg O' My Heart, Blondie of the Follies*) hold up exceedingly well even today. Ince was important historically, more so than any other American except Griffith, but Marion needed a light hand to guide her. Ince might have seen, as Hearst did not always, that she needed to be in the hands of truly sensitive directors such as King Vidor and Sidney Franklin, two men responsible for five of her best films, and not studio ringmasters who turned out slick films. But no one will ever know how Marion might have fared with Ince since the veteran producer died suddenly and mysteriously that November.

The yacht party was a typical Hearst impromptu affair. It came in the middle of the week (Tuesday, November 18) and everyone, including Marion, had to drop his routine for a couple of days. At least fourteen guests were invited, including Louella Parsons and Chaplin, both of whom dropped by the United Artists studio that Tuesday afternoon to pick up Marion on the set of *Zander the Great*. Miss Parsons and Chaplin later denied that they were aboard, although Marion's stand-in, Vera Burnett, distinctly recalls that they appeared at the studio, ready for departure. Other guests were the actress Seena Owen; Theodore Kosloff (the ballet maestro who had taught Marion in her early years); the writer and aspiring social dictator Elinor Glyn; Hearst's chief secretary Joseph Willicombe; publisher Frank Barham and Mrs. Barham; sisters Ethel and Reine; niece Pepi; and Dr. Daniel Carson Goodman, Hearst's studio manager.

Marion recalled that they had an uneventful dinner. "*We drank water* [italics mine] and I remember one thing Tom Ince said: 'I would like to drink a toast to my son's birthday.' And Elinor Glyn said, 'Don't drink it in water. It's bad luck.' " After dinner, according to Marion, everyone went to bed expecting to sail the next morning to some moorings south of San Diego. But it was not a quiet night for several of the guests, and the passage of nearly fifty years has compounded the mystery surrounding that night.

Marion, reciting what became the "authorized" version of what happened, said that Tom Ince had been vomiting all night; Willicombe thought that he had ptomaine poisoning and recommended a hospital. This diagnosis was later altered to read "acute indigestion." Dr. Goodman, in this version, agreed to take him first to a hospital and then to his home in Beverly Hills. In Marion's account, Ince is said to have died two days after returning to his home because "there was a member of his family who was [in] Christian Science and didn't want a doctor." Newspaper accounts in New York and Los Angeles, published November 20, 1924, are all consistent in stating that Ince died the same day he was removed from the yacht, the longest survival time being ten hours.

But there is something disturbingly wrong with some of the early newspaper accounts of Ince's death. The first story sent out over the wires and clearly coming from Hearst sources had a sub-headline reading, "SPECIAL CAR RUSHES STRICKEN MAN HOME FROM RANCH," and falsely says, "Ince, with his wife, Nell, and his 2 young sons, had been visiting William Randolph Hearst at his upstate ranch for several days previous to the attack. When the illness came upon him suddenly the film magnate, stricken unconscious, was removed to a special car attended by 2 specialists and 3 nurses, and hurried back to his canyon home. His wife and sons, and his brothers, Ralph and John, were at his bedside when the end came." When it became evident that this story would not wash since eyewitnesses had seen several of the yachting party depart for its pier in Santa Monica, the ranch story was abandoned, but a typical Hearst touch remained, "He was unconscious until a few minutes before he died. He smiled and tried to speak to his wife."

In Hollywood today, all of Marion's family and friends recall the death of Thomas Ince, but few agree as to the cause of it. Nephew Charlie Lederer says that the rumor that Ince was shot by Hearst aboard the yacht is absurd. But three or four of Marion's friends who will speak on the matter (some will not) believe that Ince died aboard the yacht and that he was shot. Marion denied that there were any weapons aboard and posed a question, "So if he'd been shot, how long can one keep a bullet in his system?" As any forensic medical practitioner knows, bullets have remained in a person's body for long periods of time, sometimes years. As for a weapon being available, biographer John Tebbel writes that Hearst was expert with a gun, either revolver or rifle. "It amused him to surprise guests on the *Oneida* by knocking down a sea gull with a quick hip shot." If true, this would account for a revolver having been in Hearst's possession aboard, but it contradicts all the evidence, including some in Tebbel's own book, concerning Hearst's reverence for wildlife and animals. Yet Hearst was full of contradictions.

Eleanor Boardman recalls that Kono, Chaplin's secretary, told the Japanese staff at the Chaplin home, and the story was carried by them out to other Japanese domestics in the Hollywood area and thus to their employers, that he personally saw a bullet hole in Ince's head as he was removed from the ship. Since Kono was one of the most discreet of employees, only the shock of a traumatic experience could have made him this incautious. Elinor Glyn told Miss Boardman that everyone aboard was sworn to secrecy, including the crew. Such an oath must have appealed to Mrs. Glyn's feeling for high drama, but why such an extraordinary step should have been taken if Ince had died either of ptomaine poisoning or of acute indigestion (the final "official" cause of death) is difficult to fathom and only serves to reinforce the rumors that rocked the film colony for weeks, caused Hearst to stay away from Ince's funeral (although it should be mentioned that he had an aversion for them), and left a cloud around the reputations of Hearst, Ince, and Louella Parsons, who, another rumor asserted, got a lucrative position with the Hearst syndicate for remaining silent about the affair (successfully refuted by Louella in her autobiography in which she documents her initial hiring by Hearst as being in 1922). Louella's power in Hollywood did become greater in the mid-twenties, which would be almost immediately following the death of Thomas Ince, and her syndication expanded, but one can only assume that this was coincidental.

The murder rumor is substantially the same in all of the accounts given to the author by those surviving members of the Davies-Hearst circle who will discuss it, excepting one detail: whether it was a case of mistaken identity or not. Thomas Ince bore a strong resemblance to Chaplin (see photographs); they both had large, handsome heads with wavy hair of the same color and trimmed in much the same fashion. The story places Marion and Ince in the lower galley sitting at a table, talking. The galley light was relatively dim and Ince's back was to the galley steps or "ladder." Hearst, it was said, suddenly missed Marion and his suspicions got the better of him. He began searching the vessel for her, saw her engrossed with someone whom he immediately took to be Chaplin, pulled out a pistol, and shot him. In other versions, Hearst's jealousy was allegedly inflamed by Ince himself. In denying this rumor, which Marion heard many times in the years to come, she said, "There were no weapons aboard, ever. So who could have shot him? Margaret Livingston was not on the boat. I didn't even know her." But here, Marion is muddying already turbid waters. The name Margaret Livingston crops up several times in her recital of the events of that night. The only woman by that name living in Hollywood at the time was an actress who faded out of films soon after talkies came in. At the time of the boat tragedy, it seems clear from Marion's account, Miss Livingston was Thomas Ince's girlfriend. According to Marion, Nell Ince (the widow) asked her, "Was Margaret Livingston on the yacht?" and Marion told her "No . . . I don't even know the girl." Remembering Marion's habit of "prettying up" the truth to spare herself or others —in this case, the widow—perhaps Miss Livingston was a fifteenth guest.

The overriding question today, with all possible evidence successfully suppressed (if, in fact, there is anything to suppress), is simply "Why did such a rumor begin? Where did the story about a shooting have its origins?" Men had died on Hearst's junkets before (witness publisher Guy Barham in London only a year earlier) and nothing had been made of it. But even today the death of Thomas Ince remains a delicate subject. Adela Rogers St. Johns in her autobiography quotes from a letter she received from Ince's widow:

> . . . so you see, Adela, all those who wanted the truth could have found plenty of testimony. Why did no one ask me?

Do they think, could anyone think, that I would have remained silent if there had been any truth in his having met
with foul play on the Hearst yacht? Anything else you ever
want to ask I can take it—the only thing I haven't learned
to take—it still happens so often even after *forty years*—is
to meet someone who says sweetly Are you any relation to
the movie producer who was shot by Mr. Hearst? That one
I could shoot. Forgive me if I have spouted off too much.
When I think of skunks like deMille and Bill Hart admired
still and all these lies cooked up about Tom I do get enraged. I am so glad you will be writing of WR in your book.
None I have seen do him justice at all, they give no conception of the dynamic and fascinating man he was to
meet and know. A delightful dry sense of humor I found,
and such kindliness—and such a splendid *dancer*. . . . Adela,
I am writing this carefully because I do hope for the sake of
my children and my beloved grandchildren no such belief
in such a weird and silly story will continue down into the
generations.

    An inquest into the death of Thomas Ince would have set-
tled the matter quickly and it is extraordinary that none was requested, not even by the coroner of Los Angeles County, where
his body—living or dead—was taken, or by the coroner of San
Diego County, where Ince was taken off the boat. The rumors
began almost at once, apparently fanned by an item in the Los
Angeles *Times* in which the headline allegedly read: "MOVIE
PRODUCER SHOT ON HEARST YACHT." The item, it is said, appeared in only one edition, having been killed by the next run of
the presses. Such an inquest either would have laid to rest all
rumors or opened up a scandal of legendary proportions. It was
not allowed to happen, and Ince's body was cremated on Friday,
November 21, two days after the incident, because, in the
widow's words to Mrs. St. Johns, "It was our considered opinion
and belief that it was the best way. . . . We had promised each
other."
    The death certificate was signed by Dr. Ida Cowan Glasgow,
Ince's private physician. Possibly under pressure brought about
by the fleeting item in the *Times,* Chester C. Kempley, the district attorney of San Diego, investigated the incident and said, "I
am satisfied that the death of Thomas H. Ince was caused by
heart failure as a result of an attack of acute indigestion." Ince's
body was then examined by the Chief of Homicide of Los Angeles

County and by Dr. Day, of Day and Strother, the mortuary where Ince's body was taken. It is difficult to believe that all of these people became part of the conspiracy of silence. It is equally difficult to understand why there were so many contrary statements made later by those who had been on the yacht.

Chaplin wrote that he went with Hearst and Marion to see Ince at his home two weeks before he died and that he was glad to see them and thought that he would recover. A curious lapse of memory on Chaplin's part when every newspaper in the country carried a photo of Chaplin himself grieving at the funeral of Thomas Ince, the photo appearing just three days after the tragedy.

Chaplin made a final decision that weekend of Ince's funeral. He sent off Lita Grey and her mother to Guymas, Mexico, and on Sunday (November 23), he was on his way south by train to marry her.

Hearst left Hollywood, too, sending Marion word that he thought it best to go East, since the situation in California was "so unsatisfactory." He frequently told Marion that time was always on your side if you didn't make an issue of something. He was to survive Ince by over twenty-six years, and time would prove him right. But in those days immediately following Ince's death, Hearst must have felt acutely uncomfortable in a community where doubt and suspicion were visible in nearly everyone's eyes. A woman who had a real and lasting affection for Hearst said recently, "Yes, I had doubts. When a man of such enormous power as Hearst gets into grave trouble, nothing comes of it. That's the trouble with too much power."

Noel Coward's Melanie in *Conversation Piece* says, "This adventure must be gay and funny. We will cheat and lie and pretend to everyone because that is agreed, but there must be truth between us, ourselves." With Hearst and Marion, quite often an unattractive fact was elaborately disguised or, whenever possible, ignored. If Ince, who had ulcers, drank whiskey aboard the *Oneida*, he surely knew the possible consequences. And if Ince received a bullet wound that proved fatal, it was simply a ghastly accident. Marion's life with Hearst was quite often a masque, with all the lines and actions carefully measured. Her spontaneity would break through at unexpected moments, giving Hearst an occasional fright, but it was useful, as it served to break up the ritual of their life in Hollywood and San Simeon. Whatever

happened on the *Oneida*, that ritual closed in around the survivors, and life moved on.

III

The aftermath of the Ince scandal-that-almost-broke was a chill
between Marion and Hearst, lasting until the Christmas holidays. If there was a crime, there was no repentance. When
Hearst returned from New York, he contacted Marion to tell her
tersely that he was stopping at the ranch, that he was ill with a
heavy cold. He ordered her to come up to San Simeon aboard the
Oneida on the weekend. Did he consider such a method of trans-
portation easier for Marion or was it further punishment for *her*
crime? Whatever his motive, all endearments were missing from
his wires and letters; the tone was cold.

But there was a thaw during the holidays even though they
celebrated a little in advance because Millicent and the boys were
on their way west. Hearst and Marion were always terribly sentimental about Christmas. Mountains of gifts would be piled about
a two-story tree in Marion's living room and later in the castle,
where garlands of holly were strung from every beam. From
Christmas Day to New Year's, Hearst spent the week with his
wife and sons, but shortly after New Year's Day in 1925, he sent
Marion word that she might go ahead with her good times. He
told her, in effect, to forget about her "grandfather," who would
rather have her going out than staying at home praying to go
out. There were hints, however, that his tolerance had its limits;
he no longer shuffled over like a country bumpkin to do her bidding and nearly all of his communications to her in early 1925
were signed simply "W.R." or even "Hearst."

Hearst's changing attitude toward her had one visible effect
upon Marion: she no longer looked so innocent, and photographs
taken from 1925 on clearly show the change. Perhaps, at twenty-
eight, this was only natural, but it may have been brought about
by the boat tragedy and the sense that her devotion to Hearst
had entrapped her. To those in Hollywood who believed the
rumor that Ince had been shot because of her, she was now
looked upon as a *femme fatale* when what she really wanted was
to remain an effervescent girl-about-town. Shed of her inno-

cence, there was a certain "don't give a damn" quality to many of her actions. Her flirtations became a little more open and Hearst looked the other way whenever she got moderately involved with one of her leading men, something that would become *de rigueur* on a Davies film. This would surprise many of these actors, especially if they were new to Hollywood, and they would ask, sometimes in trepidation, "But what will Mr. Hearst have to say about *that?*" But Hearst had little to say anymore about her alliances. The spy system was still in force and he followed her every move —and she knew it. Sometimes she would say defiantly, "This will give him something to think about." Doubtless it would, but there were no more confrontations over her male encounters. The truth will be hard for the sentimental to accept but Marion loved Hearst too much to leave him and she loved life and its sensual pleasures too much to abandon them.

Hearst had had his first financial crisis in 1924, and by the summer of 1925 he had floated his first series of bonds, raising $15,000,000 for working capital. He had hired a former reporter from the San Francisco *Bulletin,* John Francis Neylan, to see him through this financial stress (and through several more such near-collapses besides). Neylan had left journalism for public office in Sacramento and then a law practice in San Francisco. He became Hearst's most-trusted executive, granted the privilege shared only by Marion among those in Hearst's inner circle of saying "no" to the Chief. A mutual resentment developed almost immediately between Neylan and Marion, deeper even than that she felt for Brisbane. She could joke with Brisbane almost until the end of his life, but never with Neylan. Despite his Irish ancestry, Marion thought that Neylan could not be trusted, an error in judgment which Hearst listened to but managed to ignore. It was a trait of Hearst's always to hear a person out as though he were in total agreement and then go ahead and do something quite opposite in his own unobtrusive way.

Hearst had been nursing his wounded spirit through a buying spree, following his brushes with scandal, insolvency, and Marion's self-assertiveness, and in the spring of 1925, he had all of the rooms redecorated at the Clarendon in New York—still considered his New York residence since his family was there, but only when Marion was not with him. French and Company handled the whole job and it was costly, but it was an outlet for his pent-up feelings just as redoing one of the rooms at the castle always was. When he complained to a friend that it was becoming increasingly hard to find fine things, the friend resisted an impulse to say that most of them were already in his hands. He looked, too, for some eighteenth-century silver serving plates for Marion, finding a handsome old English period room for himself during his search.

Mama Rose had been ill with a heart condition, possibly aggravated by Marion's strained relations with Hearst. While she had begun to look upon Hearst's largesse as excessive, the arrival of the silver plates from New York was a signal to her of renewed harmony, and she was able to get on her feet for the first time in several weeks. Marion took the train eastward as far as Arizona and met Hearst at the Lodge on the rim of Grand Canyon, where they spent several days. They both loved "making up."

Marion's friendship with Chaplin was changed into something more durable. With his marriage to Lita Grey, he was no longer a threat to Hearst, and, besides, his screen image as a vulnerable innocent could not withstand the obloquy that surely would follow any attempt to resume publicly his interest in Marion following the boat episode. So Chaplin stopped seeing her at the studio and in his own home, but came by Marion's house frequently whether Hearst was there or not. Their friendship would survive until he drifted so far to the left politically it was impossible for Hearst to keep his papers from editorializing about it. By then, Chaplin's cronies were no longer the fun crowd that surrounded Marion anyway; they were intellectuals of the first rank. But throughout the late twenties and early thirties, Marion and Chaplin were "pals." She watched his startlingly accurate mimic portraits of their friends and enemies, and soon she was able to do her own. One of his most biting portraits was of Lord Duveen, the British art dealer who had sold so much to Hearst at inflated prices. Chaplin walked along Marion's private gallery and paused before each painting, making some absurd comment to an absent Hearst. Marion was enchanted, and by 1927 she would feel expert enough to display her own talent for parody in films with an especially deadly burlesque of a leading lady she considered a little too sober, Lillian Gish.

On the evening of July 6, 1925, Marion and Hearst joined nearly everyone else of prominence at Hollywood's Egyptian Theatre to attend the premiere performance of the picture Chaplin said he wanted to be remembered by, *The Gold Rush*. It was one of those rare moments when everyone present realized that they were in the presence of a comic genius. From the opening trek up the snow-encrusted mountainside to the triumphant fadeout with "multimillionaire" Charlie kissing his old Gold Fields' Dance Hall hostess in a final surprising reunion, the audience was lifted from one level of anxiety or hilarity to yet another, and it knew that what was happening to Charlie, from his shoe-lace "spaghetti" dinner to his big gold strike, was a wistful comment on every man's ups and downs. (How total is an audience's identification with Chaplin when he is "dancing" the Oceana Roll, using bread rolls attached to forks as his legs!) Hearst would laugh until he wept at Chaplin's films, and doubtless seeing *The Gold Rush* redeemed Chaplin once again in his eyes.

Marion's last meeting with Chaplin occurred in the early 1950s soon after Hearst's death. Chaplin was dining with his friends, the Frank Taylors, when the phone rang. One of Chaplin's servants told him that it was Marion and Chaplin got on the phone and told her how much he had missed seeing her during the past decade or so. Marion wondered if she might come over with a friend and, in a half-hour or so, there she was. A Southern novelist, Speed Lamkin, whom she had recently befriended, escorted her and half-supported her in a little dance she did as she came into the room singing "Let's do it like we used to do it . . ." and ending with a kootch roll of her hips. Chaplin said later that he was nearly heartbroken to see how his old pal had declined in health, while he was still vigorous and recently had married the young daughter of Eugene O'Neill, Oona. It was difficult for Marion to bridge those many years of silence between them, and she saw almost as soon as Chaplin did that it was hopeless. She was helped to her feet and across to Charlie to kiss him good-bye.

Before the end of 1925, the castle was ready for occupancy after Miss Morgan had worked a crew of a hundred men on double shifts to complete the job. It was not finished; it never would be, for Hearst felt that if he ever completed construction at his castle site, he would die.

Before Millicent departed, Charlie Chaplin was the guest of the Hearsts. The zoo had been installed and wild animals in herds pounded over the dusty hills surrounding the castle and the villas. In December 1925, Hearst had purchased forty buffalo; there were also zebras, ostriches, elk, and deer running the

slopes behind miles of fencing. After dinner, Chaplin and Millicent walked through the unfinished gardens surrounding the
castle.

> From the zoo [Chaplin writes] the occasional roar of a
> lion could be heard and the continual scream of an enor-
> mous orangoutang, that echoed and bounced about the
> mountaintops. It was eerie and terrifying, for each evening
> at sundown the orangoutang would start, quietly at first,
> then working up to horrific screaming, which lasted on into
> the night.
> "That wretched animal must be insane," I said.
> "The whole place is crazy. Look at it!" she said, view-
> ing the chateau. "The creation of mad Otto . . . and he'll go
> on building and adding to it till the day he dies. Then what
> use will it be? No one can afford to keep it up. As an hotel
> it's useless, and if he leaves it to the state I doubt whether
> they could make any use of it—even as a university."

The year 1925 had become a year for clearing the air, for
resolving old conflicts. A more specific arrangement was made
with Millicent whereby she would remain in New York and he
would live at San Simeon. The servants were told that they were
shutting up the ranch for a while when Millicent was sent East,
and Hearst moved to his suite at the Palace Hotel in San Francisco. But nothing could keep him away from San Simeon for
long and soon he was back, just in time to celebrate his sixty-
second birthday, furiously sentimental and feeling alone and
abandoned, despite steady waves of young guests—his sons
and their friends. He was too restless even to sit through the
nightly movies in their entirety. He was seen going off into his
hills with a gun or a fishing rod, again surprising in the light of
his years of propaganda against vivisection—a campaign begun
at about this time in the Hearst press—but one of many para-
doxical actions he was to perform in his lifetime. His life, ever
threatened by scandal or financial improvidence or Marion's real
or imagined infidelities, was cushioned by the dark-paneled walls
of San Simeon. The ranch had become something mystical to
Hearst: all of his roots, all of his hopes for a calmer life were
there. It had been his mother's favorite retreat—her old ranch
home still stood on the hillside—and Hearst's deep attachment
to San Simeon doubtless represented his own retreat to the protection and security he had known as Phoebe's "Billy Buster."

The upsets in Marion's life were absorbed by friends and family, by taking a bottle of gin into her bedroom. They were certainly made less painful when she was within the walls of her exquisite new "dressing room" bungalow on the Metro lot. Of course, it was not a bungalow at all, but a Mediterranean-style villa, consisting of fourteen spacious rooms, one of them to be used frequently by the studio when entertaining important guests. There was a master bedroom where Marion could sleep over when she was working late on a film and a study which was to become Hearst's Los Angeles headquarters. But his rigging-out of the studio bungalow with a switchboard connecting him with the far corners of his empire did not happen right away. He was not yet back to being Marion's constant companion after that chilliest winter of their life together. When Alice Head, his managing director of publications in England, visited New York, he trained East to entertain her at Millicent's temporary apartment in the Ritz. At her Whitechapel flat in London many years later, Miss Head was to say, "Marion was busy making pictures, although we later became good friends. I don't think she was in very close touch with Mr. Hearst at that time." When Miss Head did meet Marion a year later, she was to be struck by Marion's genuine unselfishness, a side of her known only to her friends. "She will give the clothes off her back to anyone she thinks needs them, and has to be forcibly restrained from distributing most of her possessions." Hearst was as gallant as ever during this meeting with Miss Head. In her memoir *It Never Could Have Happened*, she describes Hearst as a man who "listened with close attention to everything I had to say, made friendly comments, told a few funny stories and left me feeling very happy that I was working for so natural and unalarming a person. . . . He likes his own way and on occasions can be so beguiling that it is hard to refuse him anything, but sometimes, as I have told him, he is not stern enough, and then I have to supply the granite. The contrast between the real man and the public conception of him is quite shattering."

When Miss Head returned to London, Hearst cabled her to buy St. Donat's Castle in Wales, a nine-hundred-year-old fortress-like structure on the coast west of Cardiff built in Norman times and closely resembling one of the colleges at Oxford University. Miss Head quickly put in a bid on the property in the name of the National Magazine Company, Hearst's British subsidiary, and by early fall St. Donat's belonged to Hearst, although he had no notion as to when he would be free to stay there. Marion was not consulted and she must have been apprehensive since she had not yet spent much time in the guest houses at San Simeon. It is impossible to determine just what triggered this desire in Hearst to have a home abroad. Certainly he was not very happy roaming his San Simeon parapets alone and his future with Marion was a dubious concern. But another fortune began pouring into the restoration of St. Donat's. A swimming pool was to be installed next to the sea with a *cabaña* fashioned out of an old seaside cottage. The North Court would have eight large bedrooms and marble baths, and the old armory was to be made the pride of the castle just as it had been for its early owners.

St. Donat's was to be reserved for Marion and himself, and Hearst had taken another step in ensuring their future together. At sixty-two, he still thought of his own life in terms of decades rather than "remaining years." Marion sustained the youthful juices in him by her lively presence and—in a strange way—by living out in reality the fantasies in which Hearst indulged himself. When he told her to go ahead and enjoy herself, she understood that he was with her in spirit. The years did not diminish his enormous zest for living—what he could not do, Marion could. It was his way of "mellowing."

When *Zander the Great* was released in May 1925, one of the movie reviewers working for Hearst gave it such faint praise Marion phoned Hearst with a bad case of the blues. He immediately "fixed" the review and wired her that she must have got an early edition. "The folks at the *Examiner*," he said in his down-home way of speaking of his newspaper employees, had told him that there had been an error in the first run of the presses and that their critic really had said that *Zander* was "a big story and a big picture." He asked her to look at a later edition. In this instance, Hearst was right in calling for a fairer opinion of the movie since most non-Hearst reviewers around the country praised the film's comic moments, which were numerous, and Marion's performance in particular. But it was Marion's custom through the years to tell Hearst when a review or a story seemed wrong to her, just as it was Hearst's to call up the newspaper and get it "fixed." That the "fixing" was a kind of censorship or control over what Hearst's writers were putting into their columns never seemed to occur to Marion.

That spring Hearst spent much of his time at the ranch,

doing his very best to keep from rushing to Marion's side. He told her he had decided to cut down on the nightly movie screenings as a way of relaxing—away from Hollywood and Marion's friends, much of his interest in films declined.

There was something woebegone about his efforts to entertain himself. He sensed that Marion was equally as important as his castle in keeping old age at bay. He clipped out a poem by an anonymous author and sent it to her, its rhymes mirroring his regret at not being with her:

> Twelve o'clock and all is well
> Is the cheerful tale the watch should tell
> But sorrowful thoughts crowd through my mind
> Of the land and the life I have left behind
> Of the shimmering pool and the shining sand
> Of the turbulent sea and the sun lit land
> Of the beauties of earth and sea and air
> Spread in reckless profusion everywhere
> From morn till the sun sinks wrapped in red
> When I seek my room and my four post bed
> With its spotless linen smooth and white
> And the girl who lies by my side at night.
>
> Oh the night is blue and the stars are bright
> Like the eyes of the girl of whom I write
> And the day is a-glimmer of golden light
> Like the locks of the girl of whom I write
> And the skies are soft and the clouds are white
> Like the limbs of the girl of whom I write
> But no beauty on earth is so fair a sight
> As the girl who lies by my side at night.
>
> Then carry me speedily over the plain
> And carry me speedily back again
> To the sun lit land of love and light
> And the girl who lies by my side at night.

These verses convey Hearst's feeling for California ("sun lit land of love and light") and Marion as well as anything he could ever write himself. Since he had it printed up for possible distribution to close friends of his and Marion's, he was obviously pleased with the effect. But for Marion's eyes alone, he added some handwritten couplets in which he mentioned her blue-eyed baby stare, now mostly a memory as she was beginning to look her age.

The tension began to ease, Marion was never a good correspondent and she relied heavily upon personal contact where she would nearly always shine. Besides, Hearst had told her that he was forced to destroy all of her letters to him soon after their arrival out of fear that they might fall into the wrong hands.

Nephew Charlie Lederer already had graduated from college, one of the youngest graduates in the history of the University of California, and he was befriended by writer Ben Hecht, who wired his wife Rose, "I have met a new friend. He has pointed teeth, pointed ears, is nineteen years old, completely bald and stands on his head a great deal. His name is Charlie Lederer. I hope to bring him back to civilization with me." Probably Charlie was two or three years younger than Hecht believed him to be.

Charlie was something more than just a prodigy that summer of 1924. He did not seem to be conscious of how bright he was, but he was bored with his peers whom he found to be lacking in wit. He still adored his Aunt Marion, whom he must now have seen as someone less intelligent than himself but very nearly as clever. Although it was never articulated, he was her knight-errant and no one, not even Hearst, ever reckoned with Marion alone from then on; they knew that they were dealing, too, with nephew Charlie.

Marion welcomed Charlie's arrival back from school as a besieged army would the relief troops. He dazzled her with his precocious, acidulous wit and his zany, unpredictable impulses. It was a combination that appealed not only to Marion, but to Hearst, who loved having him around. Marion needed all the laughs that Charlie could supply.

Following the Goldwyn Company's merger with Metro and the death of Thomas Ince, Hearst decided in 1925 to take the final step in his alliance with the new and powerful company, and he brought his stars, Marion, Alma Rubens, and Lionel Barrymore, who was doing a picture for him that year, into the Culver City studio. He told Louis B. Mayer, who had become head of the studio under terms of the merger, that he was giving up his status as an independent producer with great reluctance. Mayer quickly assured him that he would have total freedom in

selecting properties and full control over his productions. In exchange for Hearst's promoting all of Metro-Goldwyn-Mayer's
films and stars in the Hearst media, Mayer agreed to finance
Hearst's films and pay Marion's and Alma Rubens's salaries.

Mayer, a Polish Jew from Minsk, who was once a junk
dealer and beachcomber, admired Hearst inordinately. He saw
Hearst first of all as a patrician, the scion of a wealthy family.
Hearst did not enjoy having his wealth admired above himself,
and he told Mayer that his father George had known the same
early poverty and reverses as Mayer, but Mayer was not interested in such a comparison. Mayer was a short man who wore
carefully tailored clothes that gave him the look of a bantam
rooster, and he was often to be seen strutting about his studio
domain like the ruling cock in a barnyard. He reminded Hearst
of Papa Ben Douras, and, like Papa Ben, Mayer had an eye and
a weakness for a pretty face. He was impressed sufficiently by
Hearst's very public double life to launch a series of affairs of
his own, nearly all of them in the open. He would not divorce his
wife Margaret until he was sixty-five and nearly out of touch
with Hearst. Obviously, he saw that he had his own Millicent-
relationship, but his Marions kept changing. And like Hearst, he
told Frances Marion that he was only going to make pictures that
he wouldn't be ashamed to let his children see. Frances must
have learned to keep her sighs to herself as she was given those
lectures in film content by powerful men who, in her presence,
were more often with their mistresses than with their wives.

When Hearst's ban on amorous closeups threatened to damage one of her films, Marion told him, "Look. There's always a
happy ending."

"But children don't like it," Hearst said. "I'll prove it to you."
And when his grandson Bunky, John's son, was visiting next
time, a romantic film was shown and as the lovers went into a
clinch, Bunky said, "I don't want to look at that. That's awful!"
Hearst felt Bunky's distaste soundly backed up his case, but
then, observing Marion's look of incredulity, he declared, "Mary
Pickford's always made very fine, clean pictures. And I want you
to do the same."

Mary Pickford, who had become Marion's close friend, was
still a professional sore point. Marion was constantly pressuring
Hearst to release her from the "Pollyanna" mold. "What's wrong
with kissing?" she asked him with some heat. "Germs?"

Hearst had a firmer grip on his emotions, or, more accurately, was able to project a calmer surface than Mayer, but he was far more profligate with money. With *Little Old New York*, Hearst had produced a film on a high, but not unreasonable, budget. Mayer had a keen eye for production values and he knew what they cost. It was not until he first visited San Simeon that he would be stunned by the extent of Hearst's store of treasures. On a slightly smaller scale, he would seek to emulate Hearst's life-style. There were to be a series of Mayer mansions, including one which he rented from Marion. And Mayer was to die with few friends to mourn him, but with a number of dignitaries present as befitted his station in life.

The deal with Mayer's company was to bring a measure of financial relief to Hearst personally and corporately. Even his successful newsreel (known now as *Hearst-Metrotone News* and the longest surviving newsreel in America) was to be financed by Metro. Cosmopolitan Pictures had been a deficit operation almost since its inception through no fault of Marion's, with profits from successful films being plowed back into expensive failures. Now the burden—especially the $10,000 weekly being paid Marion and her $100,000 annual salary as company president—was going to be assumed by a going firm that could withstand the strain. There was nothing nebulous about the setup; it was quite specific, and in 1927 production chief Thalberg would send a wire to Hearst complaining about the poor publicity given a film which Hearst felt was bound to fail, no matter how it was promoted.

Mayer was convinced that all Marion needed to make her one of Metro's top-grossing stars was another tender comedy like *Little Old New York*. A sequel of sorts was fashioned out of a play, *Merry Wives of Gotham*, and the title changed, not surprisingly, to *Lights of Old Broadway*. Conrad Nagel, newly arrived from the stage, was signed as her costar and the direction was assigned to Monta Bell, who was to direct Greta Garbo later that same year in her first American film, *The Torrent*.

Lights of Old Broadway told the story of twin sisters (both played by Marion), Irish immigrants born into poverty, whose luckless father gives up one of them to wealthy New Yorkers. "Fely" remains with her father (Charles McHugh), while "Anne" goes with the de Rhondes. Young Dirk de Rhonde is fond of his foster sister Anne, but he falls in love with Fely during an Irish uprising in the city in which Dirk finds himself fighting on the

side of the outraged poor. In order to escape the wrath of the
mob, who see his fine clothes as the badge of their oppressors, he
is helped by Fely into the tattered work clothes of a fallen comrade. The film is swift paced, and there are some remarkably
contemporary touches such as the use of a fire hose on the mob
and a five-minute technicolor sequence, featuring Nagel and
Marion, color as natural and ungarish as the finest to be developed many years later. *Lights of Old Broadway* was one of
Metro's most successful films that year. It solidly established
Conrad Nagel as a popular leading man, and soon he, too, would
be working with Garbo.

Some of Hearst's old enthusiasm for the movies returned.
Sidney Franklin, rapidly becoming the most sensitive director on
the Metro lot, was signed to direct Marion in her most sophisticated film up to that time, *Beverly of Graustark*, a satire of European court intrigue in which Marion would be impersonating a
crown prince through half of the film.

That fall, George Van Cleve came West on business for
Hearst. Distressed over his wife Rose's affairs with other men
and feeling helpless after attempting in vain legal steps to regain
custody of seven-year-old Pat, Van Cleve "kidnaped" his own
daughter and took her back to New York.

Rose phoned Marion at her dressing bungalow in a state
and said that she was too upset to call the police. Marion phoned
Hearst, who was in San Francisco at the time, and it was
Hearst's suggestion not to bring the matter to the police or into
the courts. He had long had grave reservations about Rose, her
drinking, and her men. He must have seen her as a distorted
image of himself—self-indulgent, reckless, and impervious to
the opinions of others. He could recall with wry amusement the
numerous occasions when Rose would come around to Marion's
in a wheel chair (because of that childhood injury caused by the
demented nurse), either to make up with Marion or to seek a
favor. A favor could mean anything from paying off some astro-
nomical bills to renting her a beach house for the summer.
Hearst believed that Rose was faking the leg injury, and thought
he was proved right when Marie Glendinning told Marion a
story, which Marion repeated to Hearst, about a visit by Rose to
Marie's tiny Hollywood house. "She was wheeled into the living
room by her handsome chauffeur," as Marie recalled it. "Soon
there was a pounding on the front door. It was Rose's husband,
Louis Adlon [related to the Berlin hotel family], who had quar-

reled with her about the attentions she was paying the chauffeur. Rose panicked and leaped through the bedroom window with no apparent injury to herself, running off down the block."

Marion and Hearst were to spend large sums of money and considerable personal energy in the attempt to find Pat and her father. Van Cleve had quit his job with Hearst and gone into hiding with a Japanese servant named Taka. According to Pat Van Cleve Lake (she was to marry Hollywood actor Arthur Lake in a ceremony at San Simeon in 1937), the little family group would move on whenever Hearst's detectives seemed to be closing in. They lived during the next five years in New York, in Minneapolis, and in a suburban house in Maryland. Several times detectives would stop Pat on her way home from school and ask who she was. She was instructed by her father to say, "I'm Nancy Applegate."

There was a rising murmur of resentment among New York City's voters over the way Hearst was attempting to run their political life from his mountain retreat in California. His man, Mayor Hylan, was defeated by a man of much less integrity than Hylan but with the color and adaptability to the times which sometimes can combine to make a legend. Jimmy Walker's election virtually spelled the end of Hearst's political connections in New York.

It was also the beginning for Marion and Hearst of a warm, new understanding that would survive until his death. They seemed to have come to an agreement about their problems: he would overlook her occasional straying and her drinking, and she would not complain about fitting herself into the corners of his busy life.

One evening in May 1926 Hearst picked up Marion at her house on Lexington Road and drove her to the beach at Santa Monica. In those days before air conditioning, it used to get torrid in the flatlands of Beverly Hills where Marion lived, and they often would go to one particular spot along Ocean Front Road and sit on the sand, holding hands. Earlier that week, evangelist Aimee Semple McPherson had gone swimming nearby and had vanished. The most colorful religious leader of the day, "Sister Aimee" regularly "saved souls" in her huge Angelus Temple, the great white wings of her flowing robe illuminated by spotlights. She made converts drunk on visions of salvation. Marion studied the waves washing the beach a few yards from them. "Nasty bad

waves," she said, "to kill a nice person like Aimee Semple Mc-
Pherson." And then suddenly a huge wave swept toward them
and nearly knocked them over.

"Why are you blaming the ocean?" Hearst asked her as they
moved up to a safer spot.

"The wave hit me," Marion said, "there's something wrong.
I don't believe the ocean did it." She was referring to Sister
Aimee's possible drowning.

(A little later Marion was proved right when the evangelist
turned up in the desert, the "victim" of a kidnaping that never
happened. She had really run off with the handsome radio operator at Angelus Temple.)

Hearst was more interested in the site than in Sister Aimee's
disappearance. "Do you like it?" he asked her.

"It's fine," she told him. And as simply as that it was agreed
that she would move out of Beverly Hills to the beach at Santa
Monica. In the back of Hearst's mind, according to Charlie Lederer, was the hope of ridding himself of some of the Dourases.
Marion's home was overrun by them, and it was an uninhibited,
gregarious family whose friends were so numerous Hearst told
her it was "open house, every day."

The beach house was begun later that year—a white Georgian style structure. It would have a dining room for 25 guests;
37 fireplaces, some 250 years old; a gallery for Marion's growing
collection of art treasures; a gold room finished in gold leaf; crystal chandeliers from Tiffany's; and a library with a motion-picture
screen that would rise out of the floor by pushing a button. In another version of the beach house's origin, there were two identical
Georgian structures on the coast road, which she had joined together with a hallway under the overall supervision of architect
William Flannery.

If Marion feared that Hearst was abandoning his plan for
them to share the castle at San Simeon, he never indicated by
word or action that it was so. Marion was moving beyond her
"chowder friends" and becoming a leading hostess of the community. Hearst could not be satisfied just in establishing her in
a home more elegant than Pickfair, Beverly Hills' standard of
excellence. He wanted her set up in the largest beach residence
on the West Coast. Before it was considered "finished," it had
cost nearly $7,000,000 ($3,000,000 for construction and $4,000,-
000 for the furnishings and art works).

The beach house barely had been opened and Marion settled when it became clear that Hearst was spending more and more of his time at the ranch. It was simply another wry turn such as the one when he found Casa del Mar ready for occupancy at the same time her Lexington Road ballroom was rushed to completion, the one in which he asked her to come to California a few months after her Riverside Drive home was totally renovated back in New York. But this was far more devastating to Marion than these smaller coincidences. San Simeon was becoming his mistress. Before her thirtieth birthday, Marion was to realize that her rival was no longer Millicent; it was La Casa Grande, and it was being built for the ages as well as for reasons of personal vanity. It would be difficult to flail at a monument.

PART FOUR

SAN SIMEON-
THE
GREAT
DAYS

I

The rise on which the castle stood was called La Cuesta Encantada (the Enchanted Hill), and there *is* a look of wonder in Marion's face in an old photograph taken the day she first toured the castle. It is a faintly baffled look, as though she were looking into a slightly clouded mirror.

But it is not an especially happy person we see in this photo. She had achieved a sane balance in life by living each moment as it came. Possibly it was the only way she could survive as mistress to such a man. But there was a timelessness to this monument he had created for them to live in, and that bothered her, as did, perhaps, its immensity. She could walk from the great hall a hundred feet before reaching the other side. Some of her friends helped to give her a temporary sense of ease with all those assorted treasures of the old world by calling the over-scaled sofas and chairs "early Barker Brothers," after a famous Los Angeles department store dealing in good solid furniture for the home. Then, too, those many marble maidens, columns, and other gimcrackery from the Renaissance and Roman periods that crowded the lush landscaping for attention outside were often out of focus due to wisps of fog (or was it clouds?) that could be seen beyond the leaded window panes.

She never could come to like the carved saturnine faces adorning the great, walk-in Stanford White fireplace, and she wasn't fond of the dark walls, made so by skilled artisans with their paneling of rich walnut and mahogany. But she was awed by the floor of the vestibule when she learned that it came from a recent excavation at Pompeii where it had been buried under volcanic ash since A.D. 79. "People died on this floor," she would tell visitors. In time, she got used to living with relics and soon she would be screaming with laughter as two of her pals did a little dance atop a priceless chest dating back to the Middle Ages. Hearst turned pale but did nothing to stop them.

If Hearst was a Renaissance specialist, Marion was a nearly pure product of the twentieth century. She smoked more than

was good for her, abused the freedom to drink as much as a
man, and enjoyed wearing trousers nearly as much as Hearst
liked seeing her in them. It was a delight for many seeing her
drinking and smoking and wearing her slacks in a room filled
with antique choir stalls and hung with a series of seventeenth-
century Flemish tapestries once owned by the Spanish royal family, depicting the great moments in the life of Scipio Africanus,
the Roman general.

In time, she no longer noticed the candelabra, gold-framed
diptychs, antique tables, and Oriental rugs, although she enjoyed
cracking jokes about the metal figure of a suited knight standing
in the corner of the billiard room like an eternal kibitzer. What
she did feel more than anything was the chill. It gave her ample
excuse for a couple of toddies before turning in and she told a
friend, "It must be all that stone." The feel of dampness was
never to leave the place; a mixture of old dank stone, fresh
mortar, and probably the breath of hundreds of mice who inhabited the place, the question being, were they plain old American field mice come in out of the cold or imported European
mice brought in all of those crates?

Getting Marion into his furnished castle was a happy
achievement for Hearst. But hovering near her and observing her
reactions to the castle on that first exhaustive tour was a strain
on him. It is said that on their first night together at San Simeon,
he fell asleep in his four-poster bed ahead of everyone else.

In Hearst's bedroom, there were fading photographs of his
mother Phoebe and his father George on the wall above a night-
stand. Hearst's inexpensive camera lay on the dresser. His life
with Marion from this time on would be the most fully recorded
affair in history, with literally thousands of informal photographs in every conceivable setting surviving. The story, circulated for many years, that Hearst refused to be photographed
with Marion out of deference to Millicent is wholly false.

A small parlor divided Marion's bedroom from Hearst's. It
had a low gilded ceiling with angel heads on the beams, brought
in from a Spanish nunnery. A small and cozy stone hearth held
a low fire, kept burning as long as the master was in residence.
An open balcony with a ribbed, fanlike canopy shielding it from
the elements ran along that sitting room, and Marion was to
discover that she could look down from there to the esplanade
below and watch guests arrive. This private suite was where
Marion would spend much of her time while at San Simeon. It

had the feeling of an elegant country house and was quite in contrast to the museum gallery look of the ground floor rooms. But this country place had phones concealed behind rocks, on mountain paths, at the two swimming pools, for Hearst's constant use.

To a sensitive, detached observer, there seemed to be a purpose behind this inhabited monument. With all its eclectic treasure—the armor, rare books, marble statuary, priceless Gobelin tapestries, monastery beams, parchment shades and illuminated manuscripts, banners of knighthood hanging in the refectory over the English silver, and church choir stalls rendered black from antiquity—the whole seemed a highly personal statement. If it was madness, then it was all a piece, like the Watts Tower. Some master plan in Hearst's mind had tied it all together and made incongruity meaningless. Even the insipid maidens of white marble staring vapidly in the gardens seemed to belong there. Nearby were other ancient dwellings brought intact from their original sites in Europe—Norman farmhouses with overhanging eaves, Irish farmhouses with thatched roofs, an Andalusian house, an English manor, one typically Dutch—and all blended perfectly with the Spanish castle itself and seemed to belong against that fold of mountain ridge and sky that was their background. Hearst sought a quick response of staggering beauty and perfection from his guests, and while opinions differ sharply as to the extent of his achievement, he would get unfailingly a quick intake of breath and a stunned look from everyone who came up his hill. Marion's own taste was bourgeois and inclined toward overdecoration. She rarely saw simplicity as a virtue in her rooms or when she was "dressing up." But Hearst had a sharp sense of what was intrinsically beautiful. One visitor was to describe the expression on the faces of guests he watched stepping gingerly over the ancient Pompeiian floor of the vestibule as "the look of sinners entering paradise." Beside him was a philistine asking, "Loew's?"

It was relatively simple for guests to be patronizing toward the castle. It was not "pure" anything, and it was sure to outrage the sensibilities of those whose taste had been carefully schooled in what one *ought* to like. But for those whose minds and sensibilities were open to a new experience, a weekend at San Simeon meant a few days of immersion in a world of Hearst's own fashioning.

Those who became regular guests—Anita Loos, Eleanor

Boardman, Dorothy Mackaill, Eileen Percy, Elinor Glyn, Charlie
Chaplin, Rudolph Valentino, Ben Lyon, Bebe Daniels, Constance
Talmadge, John Gilbert, and a strange little boozing gagster who
walked in off the street by the name of Eddie Kane—would go
to the castle "for a rest." But no one ever came without an invitation or, if they made such a mistake, they were denied entrance. Invitations usually came over the phone from secretary
"Bill" Williams. The most exciting event would be when a guest
made the mistake of smuggling in his own whisky and suddenly
became obviously drunk. Then his bags would be packed and he
would find himself in a limousine being chauffeured to the train
depot at San Luis Obispo.

Gloria Vanderbilt, Sr., writing in her memoir, *Without Prejudice,* gives a vivid portrait of the man and his "principality":

> The things that impressed Nada and myself most were
> his Madonnas—one finds them everywhere: on wardrobes,
> on tables,—in every imaginable corner where they can be
> placed. He is a lover of the Italian Primitives—that is plain
> to be seen.
>
> The guest houses are generally composed of two bed-
> rooms, two bathrooms, and a large sitting room filled with
> his objects of art. Here one finds a catalogue bound in old
> Levant or missal-decorated, containing information of where
> in Casa Grande his chefs-d'oeuvres may be found. . . . Life
> in this Hearstian empire is lived according to the discipli-
> nary measures laid down by its dictator. No one is permitted
> to bring one's own personal maid—a maid or valet is as-
> signed you immediately on your arrival. You are permitted
> to do as you like in the mornings; there are only two things
> asked of guests at San Simeon—that you appear promptly
> in what is called the Great Hall each evening about twenty
> minutes before dinner, there to wait for your host . . . it is
> an understood thing that no drinks are ever served until
> just before the dinner hours, and then only in the Great
> Hall . . . an interesting and unusual room, for on one of
> the walls is an enormous jig-saw puzzle the height of a
> man, and all the guests stand about the faience bowls that
> hold the pieces and try to put them together.

Mrs. Vanderbilt described Marion as having no equal in her capacity of making the guests of the castle feel it is the one place
they want to be at that particular moment. "It is Marion Davies'
personality that has made the Rancho Casa Grande's house par-

ties rare. She has that deep intuition which is a gift, of asking groups that partition well with other groups. Besides that she has the tenderest heart to be found on this globe."

Marion's sisters and their children were often at the "ranch," as Hearst democratically called it, and they mingled on intimate terms with Hearst's five sons. The sons enjoyed Marion's sunny temperament and began calling her "Daisy" once they had heard Connie Talmadge address her by this nickname. Charlie Lederer was disappointed to discover that Hearst's boys were not on his own intellectual level at all, and he would eagerly await the arrival of anyone whose reputation for original thought had preceded him (or her), such as Chaplin, Herman Mankiewicz, Ben Hecht, or Dorothy Parker. To young Charlie, raised among show people, these were the real stars and soon he and his close friends would hang around them for hours waiting for some witty intimation of their keener minds. He was equally attendant upon inflated egos such as Elinor Glyn and Arthur Brisbane, hoping to witness their deserved comeuppance, a form of buzzard-circling of which Hearst probably was unaware and Marion aware and indulgent. Hearst worked long hours at San Simeon with secretary Willicombe and a staff that transmitted his orders and decisions, gathered news clippings, and came and went night and day. He was probably unaware of much that went on under the castle roof.

Hearst seemed far more concerned with his newspapers, the physical environment he was creating at San Simeon, and his film productions, in about that order. The towers of La Casa Grande had been torn down just prior to Marion's arrival and replaced with ones of a Moorish derivation. Within a year, Samuel Goldwyn would back his car into an oak tree and Hearst would have it moved at considerable cost to a safer place several yards away. Building and changing and remodeling would continue for more than two decades until Hearst's health began to fail seriously, and he was forced to leave his hill for good. His intuitions about San Simeon as a hold upon life would turn out to be correct. He was to die a year or so after his final purchase for San Simeon, some Arabian stallions.

Ben Lyon, an actor much in demand in the twenties and early thirties, remembers vividly his first weekend at the "ranch." He was engaged at the time to another star on the Warner Brothers–First National lot, Bebe Daniels, who was one of Marion's pals and who had come up to the castle soon after Marion's first visit. Lyon and Miss Daniels were sent an invitation along with two railway Pullman tickets with instructions to be at the Glendale station at a certain hour on the night of their departure. There Hearst had his own train, consisting of a couple of sleeping cars and a diner, waiting for some seventy guests, including such other film favorites and Hollywood notables as Hoot Gibson, Jack Mulhall, Howard Hughes, and Garbo. There was also a club car for cocktails, where the guests imbibed freely— all of them knew that no liquor was allowed to be taken into the castle and consumption while there would be limited to two cocktails and some sherry before dinner. Smuggling was rife, however, and scotch and gin would be wrapped in pajamas and shirts in suitcases. Whenever a guest told one of the staff, "I'll unpack that," the maid or valet would know at once that there was liquor inside. Rarely was anyone reported to Hearst, however. Hearst's ban probably led to heavier consumption than would have been the case had liquor been allowed—precisely the same effect as legal prohibition, which was then being violated by at least eighty percent of the population.

A fleet of cars from the castle would meet the train at three in the morning at San Luis Obispo and drive the guests along a winding seacoast road to La Cuesta Encantada. If fog, which was frequent and deadly in the area, forbade this, then the guests would sleep until seven-thirty in the morning when breakfast would be served in the diner, and they would get into the cars around eight-thirty. The drive in clear weather took an hour and a half.

Lyon was impressed by the announcement from the chauffeur that they were entering Hearst's property, for the castle was not yet in view. They drove for seventeen miles before they caught a glimpse of it—the acreage then was 350,000. Various gates separated different species of wild animals; American buffalo, giraffes, zebras, emu, camels, moose, yak, Barbary wild sheep, elk, deer, eland, goats, and ostriches were allowed to roam freely, and signs were posted along the drive saying "Animals have the right of way." Louella Parsons would one day fret inside her car for nearly an hour while waiting for a moose to leave the roadway just in front of her limousine and a lawsuit would be filed against Hearst by a workman claiming to have been trampled by an ostrich.

During Lyon's first night in one of the guest villas or "bungalows," as Hearst called them, he awoke at three in the morning "scared out of my wits by a lion roaring, and I thought it was just below my window." The following morning, Lyon made a personal survey of the area about the guest house and discovered Hearst's private zoo about sixty yards from where he had been sleeping. Here were lions, tigers, panthers, leopards, and chimpanzees behind a moat and bars. One chimpanzee named Jerry was offended by the sight of all human beings, especially Hearst, and would race up and shake the bars whenever the master appeared. Anyone especially colorful or distinctive in appearance attracted his profound attention, too. Elinor Glyn wore trailing scarves and veils of various hues as well as a turban. One day when Mrs. Glyn was visiting, Jerry defecated and threw it at her, a "comment" much appreciated by onlooker Billy Haines, a popular film star, who had been told by Mrs. Glyn that he didn't have *it*. "It" was Mrs. Glyn's odd word for sexiness, possessed by the Prince of Wales, Gary Cooper, and Lord Beaverbrook, and the title of a film starring Clara Bow (later known as the "It" girl). "Now you have *it*," said Mr. Haines to Mrs. Glyn. The same treatment was accorded Marie Dressler, that lovable elderly comedienne, and Countess Dorothy di Frasso, but Miss Dressler shared one quality with Mrs. Glyn and the Countess—she preferred the company of the rich and famous. Perhaps Jerry was making some comment of his own.

Hearst had a Germanic sense of humor, which is to say he found life more melancholy than funny; his laughter was often forced. He disliked off-color stories. When Marion told him amid fits of laughter about Mrs. Glyn's misfortune with Jerry, he looked back at her in shock and said, "That's the third time. Jerry must go." He apologized profusely to Mrs. Glyn, and soon a home was found for Jerry in a Midwestern zoo.

Marion sadly watched the crated animal as they loaded him into a truck for the trip down the hill to the depot. She felt responsible for Jerry's bad luck and the loss of one of the few sources of merriment at San Simeon. "After all," she told William Haines, "I goaded him into behaving like that; we all did, making faces at him and giving him the raspberry." And, while she seemed to go out of her way to be hospitable to her, Marion really had no great love for Mrs. Glyn, who was often a threat to her friends' careers. Contracts lapsed after some whispered few words into a producer's ear; Louis B. Mayer followed her advice slavishly, convinced that she had occult powers. She *did* have an interest in the spirit world and spoke of vases that talked back to her, and there were any number of the disaffected who hoped some-day to feed the vase its lines. The author of *It* and *Three Weeks* and the vaunted authority on romantic sex in the twenties saw her own personality problem with considerable perception when she wrote in her memoirs, "The early symptoms of the disease [the "California Curse"], which break out almost on arrival in Hollywood, are a sense of exaggerated self-importance and self-centeredness which naturally alienates all old friends."

II

Beverly of Graustark, Marion's only film to be released in 1926, was a sad letdown financially after *Lights of Old Broadway.* Its sometimes delicious spoofing was lost on most audiences. The reviews were fine, but the public stayed away.

But she was too caught up with her new toy—the beach house—to care very much; or at least she *thought* she didn't care. Later evidence would show that her film career was the animus of her life. She moved to her beach villa—as large as many fine hotels—in the summer of the year, carrying her bull-dog Buddy in her lap. Mama Rose, who was ailing, was left in a Bel Air mansion with sister Ethel and Reine's daughter Pepi (the Dourases were a nicely confused family). Reine and Rose were settled in other houses, all paid for by Marion and/or Hearst. Hearst was rid of the Dourases, but he had a new and built-in irritant in the beach house—there were often as many as four different parties going on in the house on an average day: after-tennis parties, cocktail parties, dinner parties, and movie parties.

Hearst had intended Ocean House to be a gathering place for Marion's friends, who now numbered several hundred. When the din became too much, he could always take off for San Simeon. Weekends at the castle the merry turmoil would begin again. While he was a man whose enthusiasm for the pleasures of this life was boundless, Hearst was not a social animal. And there is some evidence that this enthusiasm was his way of coping with mortality, that premium God had placed upon life which would fall due eventually. He was not stoical about this situation; he was in rebellion against it until nearly the end. But there was a visible strain in nearly all of his relations with others except for a handful of cronies and Marion. While he loved his sons, he was often awkward in their presence as though fatherhood was not a role that suited him. He seemed to believe his chronic sense of desolation and loneliness was somehow unhealthy, and he treated this "illness" with massive doses of parties and people, made bearable by Marion's sunny and ameliorating presence.

At those San Simeon dinners, he would sit quietly, rarely having much to say, reminding Gloria Vanderbilt, Sr., of "those big structures I have seen in Europe that have weathered the attacks of centuries and remain imposing and strong." Alone with Marion or an intimate circle of two or three cronies, he lost his diffidence, impressing them all with his boyish delight in each moment, especially when they were spent in Marion's company. He occasionally kidded his guests, once telling actress Fifi D'Orsay, who had thin, weak wrists and was a consistent loser at tennis, "Maybe 100 years from now you will be a champion." Marion would tease him back and she would carry on long conversations with Fifi in nonsense French, saying, *"C'est aujourd'hui, n'est-ce pas? Mais certainement sur la table. C'est aujourd'hui parce que c'est l'hiver."* And Hearst was forever convinced that she was fluent in French.

The "understanding" with Millicent was beginning to work, or perhaps Hearst was becoming less concerned with appearances as his sons were growing up and his political fortunes were at their lowest ebb. He was quietly proud of Marion's beach house. Architect Flannery had made it a showplace, and numerous large parties were planned to show it off. Three hundred or more guests were not uncommon (there were 2800 lockers for visiting bathers), especially if the guest of honor happened to be Charles Lindbergh, back from his solo flight to Paris.

Joseph Kennedy was a frequent guest. Marion got on well with him, and there was no doubt about his admiration for Hearst's life-style. There was in both men the same restless drive for power with only a thin veneer of the democratic spirit required in America when power is finally won. Kennedy's charm for Marion was in his Irish self-assurance as a man despite his air of preoccupation—doubtless derived from his near manic obsession with reaching the top. He was often in the company of actress Gloria Swanson, whose hauteur and pretensions Marion knew to be fraudulent—Miss Swanson's emotional crutch in dealing with her studio and her fans. The actress was a small lady who arched her head back regally and was not unused to having her hand kissed off-screen, and Marion was to revel in a slightly malicious portrait of her within a year or so in *Show People,* which was to be widely accepted as Marion's finest screen performance.

There was talk about Kennedy and Miss Swanson, more perhaps than there normally was about Marion and Hearst. Kennedy rapidly had won a reputation for success in films, something that Hearst had yet to do, and he had made a profitable business out of modest-budgeted "second features," produced one-a-week in assembly-line fashion at the FBO studios, a predecessor of RKO. Miss Swanson had taken Kennedy on as her advisor since she had formed her own production company. It was a brief partnership, and four years later they would part company. "I questioned his judgment," she told Kennedy's biographer, Richard J. Whalen. "He did not like to be questioned."

It could be argued that Marion was out of her depth. Removed from the context of her life at the castle and beach house, her opinions and her day-by-day response to life seem almost banal. But in the flesh, with all of her vitality and exuberance, she successfully refuted such an impression. Most often, she disarmed the skeptical upon first meeting.

While Marion liked to parody the pretentious, there was something in her that responded with childish delight at mingling with the world figures who were walking into her drawing room. She had a tremendous curiosity about other people, and if they happened to be Calvin Coolidge, Albert Einstein, George Bernard Shaw, Lord Mountbatten, Andrew Mellon, Herbert Hoover, Charles Lindbergh, the King of Siam, or Winston Churchill, she felt a sense of fulfillment which no film success ever could give her.

Hearst's elevation of her to the position of being one of the world's most favored and interesting hostesses, the social peer of prime ministers' wives and duchesses, did nothing to alter her fundamental naiveté. She considered that position as a kind of accident rather than her due and sometimes she would kid about it with her friends. If these world figures came away with an impression that Marion was vain about her achievement, it was simply because they had spent very little time with her and hadn't got to know her. The accouterments of vanity were mostly Hearst's idea—those larger-than-life paintings of her by Henry Clive as she appeared in various roles (*When Knighthood Was in Flower, Little Old New York,* and *The Red Mill*), hanging on the ballroom walls at Ocean House with additions to the collection as her career advanced; the jewelry, which Marion wore as proudly as any badge of honor; and the grand scale of her rooms and houses.

The hired help knew her to be most democratic. It was a strange experience for a newly hired maid to find their mistress asking if her feet hurt after a grueling party night or telling the sort of joke usually heard in the back kitchen.

Perhaps it was the knowledge that she had an excess of riches. Certainly she had to be aware of the extravagance of the life she was leading. But whatever triggered it, something awakened her social consciousness at about this time. She began looking beyond the Dourases for worthy causes. She undertook to educate the daughter of her cook, a girl named Mary Grace. In mid-1926, soon after she moved into her beach palace, she purchased several acres in Los Angeles as the future site of what was to be known as the Marion Davies Children's Clinic. She began giving large sums to other institutions helping the children of the poor. On the set, when she learned that an electrician had a crippled son, the boy was sent to specialists at her expense. By 1927, she was spending far more on her philanthropies than on her homes or entertainment.

Marion's sudden involvement in philanthropy and good works rather neatly paralleled wife Millicent's. Millicent had married Hearst in 1903 and a dozen years later became active in New York charities. During World War I, she headed a committee that distributed soup to hospitals and homes of the poor; then the committee moved along to securing milk for every child. Millicent's work with the Milk Fund was to continue for several decades. She organized annual benefit nights at the Metropolitan Opera House for the Fund.

Marion had met Hearst in 1915 and by 1926 she felt compelled to give others some of the riches that had come her way. It is interesting, too, that she should choose children for her chief charity. As we have already observed, she was never especially fond of children as individuals, excluding her sisters'. No one ever observed any latent motherly instincts in her. Did she resent Millicent's motherhood and her own deprivation in that area? Probably not, although there are conflicting opinions about this among her friends and family. All that seems clear is that Marion liked children in the abstract and wanted to help those who by chance were born into poverty.

As Marion's philanthropies multiplied over the years, she was to acquire a reputation for being Hollywood's most generous star. The minority who condemned her as a latter-day Madame du Pompadour declared that she was attempting to buy back the name of a decent woman. But most saw this pursuit as a further extension of Marion's rather unique lack of selfishness, rare among actresses. It was something that had been apparent for a long time among her friends and now she was widening her horizons. Most importantly, it was all done on a personal level with the checks signed by Marion herself. The big tax bite had not yet come, and she was not motivated by possible large tax deductions won so often today through charitable gifts (usually through attorneys) by film stars, some of whom have no idea of the names of the recipient organizations.

It is likely, too, that Marion had wearied of having the Dourases as her single biggest beneficiary. She had set up all of them in regal establishments. They were all on handsome allowances. Some at least, Charlie Lederer among them—were aware of her impatience with their taking her wealth for granted. With Charlie's gesture toward finding suitable work, his genius for designing new pranks to keep the action going around her, and his visible admiration for her, it is easy to see why Marion turned to Charlie more and more for advice and consolation in the years ahead.

III

Hearst's relationship with Marion might have seemed to many—by 1926—to be a prolonged exercise in gallantry, the mood of a lasting marriage, but his feelings went far beyond that. He was instantly ready to protect her, sometimes from herself. He was no longer terribly concerned over her constant partying but he was upset to see the skin under her eyes become puffy and the eyes themselves bloodshot. When she "dried out," it was never out of self-preservation but because "W.R." told her to. The small trinkets from Tiffany's continued, jewelry and silverplate, and sometimes a painting, usually a portrait of a lady, would be tagged by his art dealers to be sent along to Marion.

Marion's curious off-handedness continued in her relations with Hearst even though he had moved into all of her dependencies; he was lover-father-mother, as well as her conscience. "W.R. wouldn't like that," became a frequent comment, said mostly to herself. But she pretended that she was not on a rather long leash and she had her brief flings with her leading men and with a few others and nothing ever came of any of them. Perhaps she deliberately sought out men who were, for one reason or another, unavailable on a long-term basis. To compensate for Marion's partial inability to fulfill herself romantically, a situation for which he largely blamed himself and his years, Hearst continued to supply all the romantic touches he and his checkbook could manage—a gondola ride through Venice's canals would be coming up soon and was typical. Marion had acquired a large reputation for being romantic. She spent much of her time away from the camera hatching elaborate plots, often resembling a story by Robert W. Chambers, to prod those she liked into an intense affair or a marriage.

One of her closest male friends was Rudolph Valentino, who treated her like a beloved sister and who understood the source of her unhappiness better than most. Around Marion, Valentino laughed more than was his custom and he frequently played the clown in her presence because he sensed that she had been locked into a situation in life that gave her everything but the freedom to make of her life what she would. Valentino *knew*, because a succession of women had done the same thing with his private life and an intense public adulation was doing the same with Valentino, the star.

When Valentino asked Marion to introduce him to the great continental beauty, Pola Negri, who had become an important leading lady at Paramount Studios, Marion set up a number of rendezvous, but Miss Negri, playing the unattainable, would always phone her regrets. Finally, at a costume ball at Marion's beach house where everyone was to come as his or her favorite character, Valentino arrived as a matador, a role he had played successfully on the screen, escorting the blonde silent film queen Vilma Banky, and Marion whispered to him that the elusive

Pola was going to show up. "I told her that if she didn't, Bill would be very hurt," she told him, using the name for Hearst that had become more popular than "W.R." or "Willie" since he had become such a pal to her friends during that marathon period of socializing in the late twenties.

As Miss Negri writes in her memoirs, "Rod La Rocque [who had become a second-string Valentino in films] was invited to be my escort but when he arrived at my house on the evening of the ball he was not in costume. He said forcefully, 'I'm not going to that damned party and neither are you.'

" 'Oh yes I am. I'm not going to disappoint Marion.' "

La Rocque knew that her real reason for going was to have her much-postponed first meeting with Valentino. Pola finally went alone and Marion greeted her at the door, telling her, "I was just about to send out the Texas Rangers." Valentino was just behind Marion and bent to kiss Miss Negri's hand and took her off to dance the tango while everyone watched them smoldering together on the ballroom floor. From that moment on, Marion did all she could to promote the romance, but apparently little help was needed, and soon a torrid love affair was going on, with Miss Negri hurt and angry over his every glance at another woman and Valentino prostrating himself at her feet and insisting that she had no rival.

When Valentino died suddenly in the summer of 1926 following an operation in New York for ulcers and appendicitis, Marion was between films and staying at the castle. Her first thought was of Miss Negri and she feared that she would be inconsolable. If she felt some guilt because she had pushed for their meeting, she must have realized that Valentino would have used another avenue if she had failed him. He had been a man of a certain willfulness until a strong attachment with a woman was established. It seemed evident that he wanted to marry Miss Negri upon his return from the east coast.

Marion drove down as quickly as she could to Miss Negri's large house near her own place at Santa Monica and found her surrounded by overemotional friends and her mother, all from middle Europe. Marion sat embracing Miss Negri and comforting her until a doctor's sedatives put the grief-stricken actress to sleep.

But there were moments of comic relief at San Simeon. One frequent visitor was Winifred Bonfils, who suffered from diabetes and very carefully avoided any foods containing sugar.

However, it was a Sunday ritual at the castle to have heaping bowls of ice cream in the evening, and Mrs. Bonfils could not resist. The dessert first made her ill, then delirious. She told Marion, who had come into her room to see how she was feeling, that a little man named Eddie, a carpenter she thought, had come up to her bedside with a tape measure and had told her that he was measuring her for her coffin. "Wasn't that a rude thing to do?" she asked Marion. "I hope he doesn't come around again."

Marion told her pals Eileen Percy and Eddie Kane, and from then on, whenever anyone began to get out of line, Marion would say in mock-ominous tones, "Send for Eddie."

IV

Charles Lindbergh had landed in Paris on May 21, 1927, at Le Bourget Airfield near Paris, after over thirty-three hours of flying alone across the Atlantic. He was something more than just the hero of the hour. He somehow fulfilled all of the frustrated hopes of humankind; he gave the frantic twenties a keen look at the direction in which they were headed and millions of people throughout the world a focal point for much of their often misguided enthusiasm. It had been a long time since everyone on this planet had agreed upon a hero—there had been none in the twentieth century unless one counted the late President Woodrow Wilson, whose investiture, it seemed, was done with only a few catcalls coming down from Boston but was meant for a season only.

President Coolidge had sent the cruiser *Memphis* to bring home Lindbergh from France. The reception in New York Harbor was the most turbulent and rousing affair ever. Marion had become so enthusiastic over "Lindy," as she and all of the newspapers were calling him now, she rushed through the retakes on her current film and told Hearst that she simply had to be in New York to greet the hero.

Marion gave a detailed account of that rare reception in a letter which she wrote to Louella Parsons following the arrival itself and a subsequent reception Marion had prepared for Lindbergh at the Warwick Hotel, an elegant establishment Hearst

had acquired and which he would deed over to Marion before
his death.

Dear Louella:

I know now what it is to be a fan, and to get an autograph of your favorite star, and to do all the rest of the
things that fans do. I am a Lindy fan.

When Lindy came to town, a party of us went down
the bay on a yacht to be among the boats that met him.
The bay was full of boats—ocean steamers, excursion
steamers, tugs, yachts, launches and rowboats.

Everything was gaily decorated, and the whole bay
seemed dotted and checkered and striped with multi-col-
ored flags. Lindy was late. We watched the skies for him
for about an hour. Then out of the blue came a little speck
of an aeroplane [the *Memphis* had docked in the Potomac
and Lindbergh already had received the most exuberant embrace and welcome Calvin Coolidge was able to muster
during his entire lifetime; Lindbergh then flew to New York
in an army pursuit plane as the *Spirit of St. Louis* had developed a sticky valve, transferring in the city to a seaplane
to justify all the fuss New Yorkers were making in the
waters of their harbor] that grew bigger and bigger until
we could see the American flag flying from it and knew
that it was Lindy. . . .

The big steamships roared, the tugs bellowed, the
smaller craft shrieked, and the little boats lost their voices
entirely trying to make themselves heard.

. . . He is a very tall, very slender young man, with
clear blue eyes and blond hair, generally tousled. He stands
very erect and looks straight ahead in an almost military
manner.

He would seem quite a severe young man if it were
not for his smile. He has a wonderful smile—a glorious
smile. His smile wins everybody at once. There is no re-
sisting it. . . .

People were massed on elevated road platforms. It
seemed as if the multitudes of New York had been used by
a master hand as decorations to Welcome Lindy. . . .

Into this picture came Lindy, ever calm and smiling,
while everybody else went mad with excitement and enthusiasm and waved and cheered and threw hats and hand-
kerchiefs in the air, and many cried—actually cried—in
the intensity of their emotions.

And some women fainted and some men fell off railings, and the long lines of police could hardly control the surging, shouting stampeding crowd.

Altogether, Louella, you never saw anything like it in your born days, and none of us will ever see anything like it again—I am sure of that.

Why did they [the estimated 5,000,000 people] stand there for hours without food or drink or rest, merely to get a glimpse of him?

Why did some of them stand so far down side streets that they could not even get a glimpse of him, or hope to get a glimpse of him, and satisfy themselves with shouting themselves hoarse and throwing their hats somewhere in the direction where they imagined he might be when the procession was passing?

. . . It is the personality of the boy, and the fact that he is a boy, and the further fact that he is a typical American boy, and that there are millions of other American boys just about like him, capable of doing some such glorious deed if occasion demanded it.

We know now, and Lindy has made us know it, that the country is safe in the hands of this splendid young generation, this young generation which we have all been criticizing too much and appreciating too little.

Hurrah for Lindy!

. . . Lindy's success is our success. He is our boy. America's boy. That is why we love him.

I have seen Lindy several times since this first day, and I have had no occasion to change my first impression of him. I met him at my party in the Warwick, and again at a luncheon on the yacht. He is a simple, natural, admirable American young man.

"He knows his groceries" as far as his business is concerned. Flying is his business, and he attends to business. In fact, he does not attend much to anything else. He does not drink, and he does not smoke. He thinks girls are all right in their way, but they should not get in his way.

In June, Lindbergh reached Hollywood during his summer-long triumphal trip through America's cities. He was invited to the usual celebrity luncheon by Mayer, a tour of the studio and a look at Marion's dressing room bungalow. The opulence surrounding Marion appeared to puzzle the young aviator, since she seemed so much more human than the other film stars. He had, he confessed, preferred her to all of the others. But he had acquired along the way two business advisors named Bruno and Blythe, who doubtless gave him the background of Marion's relations with the studio and with Hearst. It may have made him all the quicker to turn down the half-million dollars Hearst offered him for the right to film his life story.

Marion gave a tea dance in Lindbergh's honor, with Mary Pickford and Norma Talmadge assisting at the young man's request. Despite her selection as assistant hostess, Mary could not make much headway in charming Lindbergh. "I hear you don't smoke or drink," she told him. "I smoke," Lindbergh admitted, then returned his gaze to Marion. Mary was not used to such neglect and she tugged him on the sleeve. "What do you think of our Hollywood air?" she asked. "Purified," was all she could get out of him. Mary gave up and began dancing.

It was one of the quieter afternoons in Lindbergh's summer. Marion was able both to thaw out the stiff reserve in the flier and keep him from being bothered too much by the small group of celebrities. She even kept reporters away by telling them, "Now, b-b-boys. Colonel Lindbergh is here as guest of the movies and I want him to enjoy his t-t-tea. You know he hates to be photographed. Won't you please take your cameras and go away just this time?"

On the following day, Lindbergh watched a scene being filmed on the set of Marion's movie, *The Fair Coed*. Mayer's first lieutenant Harry Rapf noticed his eyes blinking. "Do the klieg lights hurt your eyes?" Rapf asked him. "No-o-o. It isn't the lights," Lindbergh explained with a glance at the actresses performing in a basketball game wearing "peek-a-boo" gym bloomers.

Marion had no time to feel especially unhappy when "Lindy" left California. His final weekend had included a quick trip by air to San Simeon, where he was photographed next to his delighted host. Hearst had made excuses for Marion, who did not accompany them and who was furious about it. *The Fair Coed* had been too much delayed because of Lindbergh and a much more ambitious film (*Quality Street*) loomed just ahead with an even longer shooting schedule planned.

In late September, Marion was a bridesmaid attending Norma Shearer at her wedding to Irving Thalberg. Louella Parsons described the affair, using a phrase that was later much ascribed to her alleged Epiphany-in-print of Marion: "Never has Norma Shearer looked lovelier. Many, many times she has been called upon to play the role of a bride, but yesterday (the 29th) she gave her most realistic performance." Marion and Miss Shearer would become neighbors as the Thalberg home was not far from the beach house in Santa Monica. But they never did get to be bosom pals. Marion believed that the new Mrs. Thalberg *thought* too much and swore that she sometimes could hear the wheels turning in her brain. And this was long before the intense rivalry was to begin between the ladies.

Marion's principal upset that fall came when she learned that a young Denver "gold digger" was going around New York and Long Island impersonating her and reaping a harvest of bracelets, earrings, and necklaces from gullible "sugar daddies." The girl was finally arrested and exposed.

Repelled and a little sickened by this echo of a part of her past she would like to forget, Marion sat down and wrote out a check large enough to get her Children's Clinic started on the land she had bought in the Sawtelle section of Los Angeles. The medical facility was to be part of a Children's Home on Louisiana Avenue which initially would cost Marion a quarter of a million dollars.

In the wake of this gesture, which was not very well publicized (Marion's charities rarely were), Irving Thalberg told the ubiquitous Louella Parsons that Marion was the most finished comedienne in pictures. But, he added, the studio could not always be sure of getting a story with the whimsical qualities of Barrie. He summed up Marion's success as being a combination of beauty, personality and an ability to characterize.

V

The ex-Follies girl had come a long distance by 1928. In *Variety*'s January list of Metro's top stars at the box office Marion appeared in fifth place, right after Norma Shearer and Lillian Gish, but ahead of Garbo, Crawford, and Dressler. She was making over half a million dollars a year as a leading lady of the screen and she was at least an acquaintance if not more of a majority of world figures in the western hemisphere. The Prince of Wales called her "Marion" and thought she was very gay when they met for the first time later that year—an earlier meeting had been prevented by Hearst in 1916 when the handsome young heir to the British throne had visited New York to help rally Americans to the Allied cause. Marion was doing a matinee and Hearst had picked her up on a wintry afternoon to take her home. On the way, he stopped at Cartier's and when he came out he was carrying a small package. He asked her if she was going to General Vanderbilt's party for the Prince, and she said that she was. "Well," he asked, "would you rather have jewelry than go to the party? Bird in the hand, you know," and he showed her a black pearl bracelet and a black pearl and diamond ring to match. "If you don't go to the party, these are yours." Marion took the jewelry, thinking she would double-cross him, keeping the bracelet and ring and going to the party anyway. But Mama Rose and Hearst jointly kept her honest, Mama Rose warning her that she must not break her promise to Hearst unless she gave back the gift and Hearst hiring detectives to patrol the walk in front of the Douras home. It may have been the beginning of his mistrust of Marion, although he was suspicious by nature of nearly everyone—the sole exception perhaps having been his mother Phoebe.

At the castle, there was a steady stream of notables, nearly all of them carrying away an impression of Marion as an amusing hostess who gave their visit some point, since more often than not, after a quick visit of the castle and grounds, these guests were put completely on their own, and it was Marion who saw that their time was pleasurably filled. The tall young millionaire Howard Hughes allowed her to set up dates for him with such beauties as Billie Dove.

If she sometimes made a social mistake, it was never a petty one. When Mary Pickford invited her to Pickfair to meet the King of Siam and she rushed breathlessly into that mansion and dropped her ermine coat in the arms of a uniformed man near the foyer, of course the swarthy little man in the bright red jacket had to be the King and not the butler.

While Marion called herself "just another dumb blonde," and few of her close friends ever thought of her as being brilliant, it took a person of an unbending intellectual snobbery to find her dull. Such a man apparently was future college president Robert Hutchins who found Marion's experiment with vegetarianism a stupid pose and displayed his testiness around her by hitting her in the forehead with a ping-pong ball using an overhand delivery that was against all the rules. When he was labeled a social ingrate by Eleanor "Cissy" Patterson, the publisher, who was also a guest, he promptly packed his bags and left in the middle of the weekend.

Despite Hutchins' opinion, Marion had an intelligent grasp of things. She liked to poke around, to find out what made this person behave as he did or that thing work as it did. She knew the newspaper world better than most publishers' wives. Her real estate purchases had a way of appreciating in value when they came into her hands. She had a refreshing openness of mind except where Hearst was concerned, when she would become defensive.

And she was just as open in spirit. She had some of the basic earthiness of a Lulu White or a Texas Guinan, but with less taste than Lulu and more graciousness than Texas. There were never to be any tucked-away apartments for her, no elaborate dodges to conceal her arrangement with Hearst. Once Hearst got used to the idea that most of his time would be spent with Marion and very little with Millicent, he was as delighted as a small boy turned loose from school. At an age when most other men were preparing for retirement, Hearst entered into the maddest social whirl of his life. Even at sixty-four, a boyish smile would peel away a dozen years whenever he introduced Marion to visiting world figures.

At thirty, Marion was still delicately beautiful, reminding her friend Pola Negri of a Greuze painting. When Marion began collecting Greuzes, filling up the walls of her beach house with handsome French ladies, it was not so much vanity that moved her as it was reassurance. Much of her charm resided in her lack of pretension. She seemed never to know how truly attractive she was.

Her laughter had a trace of the hoyden in it and her hair was usually not her own—she would rather send a wig to the hairdressers than waste the time to go herself (her own hair was baby fine and worn in a short bob). In the late twenties, her preferred costume, slacks, became her trademark in Hollywood long before Dietrich ever reached America. Hearst's penchant for seeing her in trousers now sparked a rumor that he would buy any film property in which Marion was called upon to wear trousers. His scenarists usually obliged him. In *The Red Mill*, they were Dutch, ballooning near the ankle; in *When Knighthood Was in Flower*, she wore tights with knee-length

boots; in *Beverly of Graustark,* a snappy lieutenant's tunic, jodh-
purs, and cap; in *Operator 13,* a similar Confederate officer's
uniform; and in *Little Old New York,* she impersonated a young
man through three-quarters of the film. If the obligatory pants
seemed to threaten the plot line, the desperate screen writer
would come through with *something,* like the yacht party in
Blondie of the Follies, where Marion engages in a cat-fight with
her girl-friend Billie Dove and they both fall overboard, calling
for Marion to wear a borrowed sailor suit while her dress dries
out.

Her reputation as a serious actress, which Hearst tried so
hard to foster, suffered occasional setbacks brought about by
Marion's continuing love of practical jokes. But as she grew older
her practical jokes were directed oftener than not at deserving
victims. Venice Amusement Park had opened in the twenties
several miles below Ocean House. When Mrs. Glyn's hauteur
became more than any of Marion's friends could bear, she plot-
ted to escort that lady to Venice for an evening of "fun." Miss
Negri, who recalls that evening in her memoirs, writes that "We
were about to illustrate how right the distinguished novelist was
in her indictment of our barbaric American lack of sophistication. John Gilbert was in command." When a jet of air in the
fun house blew Mrs. Glyn's skirts over her head, Gilbert told
her, "Elinor, what lovely legs you have." On other occasions,
Marion would "test" her daring by riding the roller coaster again
and again, once until dawn. One of Clark Gable's most vivid
memories of Marion was of an evening when he and Carole
Lombard joined her on the Venice coaster, with Marion sitting
alone behind the couple "screaming her head off."

In many of her pleasures, she was observed to be without
a male companion. It was not for lack of available men, and
her small amours were all conducted with such discretion that
it would have meant a serious breach of faith for Hearst to
mention any he came to know about. Doubtless he knew about
nearly all of them. Likewise with her drinking—she drank as
much openly as she could manage before Hearst's understanding
wore thin and then she would retire to the lady's powder room
at Ocean House or at San Simeon, where she always kept a
bottle of scotch or gin cooling in the water tank of the toilet.

Some of James M. Barrie's *Quality Street* was supposed to
have been shot in London on location, at Hearst's suggestion,

but, if so, it is not especially visible in the charming production made of the play. It was a turning point for Marion, since *Quality Street* called upon talents unsuspected in her and closely approaching if not surpassing the work later done and redone by her rival Norma Shearer. But despite a major campaign by Metro and the Hearst publicity machinery to promote this modest but affecting comedy of manners as a "distinguished stage classic," only the more sophisticated moviegoers in the large cities of the East and West Coasts appreciated Marion's touching performance as a young woman whose lover is gone so very long in the Napoleonic wars that she appears to have lost her beauty by the time of his return. Conrad Nagel is equally appealing as her lover, and Marion handles the careful switch from plain schoolmarmish looks to radiant beauty again—pretending to be her own niece in a test of Nagel's faithfulness—with a tinge of pathos that elevates this film to among her finest. Sidney Franklin drew a shattering performance from her, and the film has far more life and brilliance than a later talking version with Katharine Hepburn.

Unhappily, the film—her finest dramatic performance—failed at the box office. It was her second failure in a year (*The Red Mill* had not recouped its huge cost), and she was not the only one bewildered by this succession of financial clinkers. The films themselves varied from competent to excellent and she still had thousands of fans who had got to know her as a saucy young woman with her heart in the right place. But they were now seeing a maturing Marion doing roles that required something more than mere perkiness and unpredictability. This was not the Marion Davies who had charmed them with *When Knighthood Was in Flower* and *Little Old New York.*

At a Metro sales meeting that year, a Philadelphia salesman asked Louis B. Mayer directly why Metro handled Marion's films. Mayer, unprepared for this broadside, first praised *Lights of Old Broadway* (six pictures back), which had made some money (*The Fair Coed* and *Tillie the Toiler*, both substantial successes, were overlooked in his panic) and then extolled Hearst in such hyperbole it resembled a eulogy.

Mayer knew that at the time of this attack Marion was involved in the first of three comedies she was to do with director King Vidor, namely *The Patsy*. It was the sort of thing she did best and, if he had not been thrown off balance, he probably would have reminded his salesmen of this. What he did not

—could not—know was that *The Patsy* would become a major success, putting Vidor "in solid" with Hearst, and by the late 1960s a favorite silent film of film scholars and film buffs in general.

Perhaps the Philadelphian had been lying in wait for this moment. Philadelphia is not a place known to be charitable to mistresses, nor actresses either for that matter. The distribution system in the twenties and thirties called for theaters to accept a block of films, and the salesman's complaint was that the theaters had to take a Davies film in order to get a Garbo. What is most interesting about this complaint is that during her reign as Metro's most prestigious and sensational star, Garbo was not a great financial success in the United States where block booking prevailed. Some of Garbo's films would have been losers had there not been a European audience where lines would form in front of any moviehouse playing them. Marion's successful and break-even films (roughly half of her total film production) outnumber all of the American films Garbo ever made. This comment is not meant to elevate Marion Davies above Garbo in audience appeal. Garbo's films have become increasingly popular in revival, and Marion's best comedies only recently have been taken out of the vaults and revived.

Hearst was in even greater difficulty at about the same time. He had become concerned about his Mexican properties. His ranches had been raided and looted as the peons began getting crumbs at last under President Calles and his agrarian reform acts, and they began acting like revolutionaries. Documents turned up that were alleged to prove anti-United States plots by the Mexican government. Edward Hardy Clark, who now was active in managing Hearst's Mexican properties, told Hearst about the documents. Using a private espionage team, including one dubious Mexican-American named Miguel Ávila, Hearst set out to get his hands on the documents. Conveniently, Ávila began "obtaining" them one after the other in Mexico and in New York City and was rewarded handsomely for his services. The documents ostensibly proved that Mexico planned to stir up a Central American war against the United States; they named four American senators—William Borah, George Norris, Thomas Heflin, and young Bob La Follette—as takers of bribes from Mexico totaling over a million dollars, and other equally outrageous acts against its northern neighbor.

...ion poses in high-fashion clothes for Metro's photographer, James Manatt, 1931.

Some of Marion's many hat
(At left) A Garbo slouch
1932; in a straw at San Simeon
1933; and challenging a
comers in a picture hat, 193

(Top) Former Broadway showgirls Eileen Percy, Marion, and Dorothy Mackaill on the tennis court at Marion's Santa Monica beach house, 1930. (Bottom) Marion rarely had her eyes closed, but she obliged photographer Melbourne Spurr, 1927.

(Top) Marion wrote on the back of this lively pose: "This is the me I like and which the boss said was alright," 1930. (Bottom) Marion at the height of her fame wears a "poor boy" cap, 1933. (At right) Clark Gable used to ride the Venice roller coaster with Marion and his wife Carole Lombard. Here they are in their second appearance together, *Cain and Mabel*, 1936.

(At left, top) Half a dozen Metro stars in the commissary for a scene from *Show People*. From left: Karl Dane, Estelle Taylor, Mae Murray, George K. Arthur, Rod LaRocque and Marion, (1928). (Middle) Charlie Chaplin visits his pal Marion on the set of her film, *Blondie of the Follies*. From left: director Edmund Goulding, Marion, Chaplin, and Billie Dove, 1932. (Bottom) Producer Thomas Ince watches his three sons "make a movie," 1923. (Below) General Douglas MacArthur visits Marion on the set of *Bachelor Father*. The living room closely resembles the great hall at San Simeon, 1931.

(Above) Marion and the silent camera, 1928. (Bottom left) Rescued! Marion and George K. Arthur after being pulled from the river in *Zander the Great*, 1925. (Top right) A drudge in *The Red Mill*, but Marion attempts to lighten her work load by "skating" over the floor with scrub brushes. The St. Bernard is there to precipitate disaster, 1927. (Bottom right) Antonio Moreno counsels the Prince in *Beverly of Graustark*, her first film to be directed by Sidney Franklin (1926). Hearst loved to see Marion in uniform or trousers.

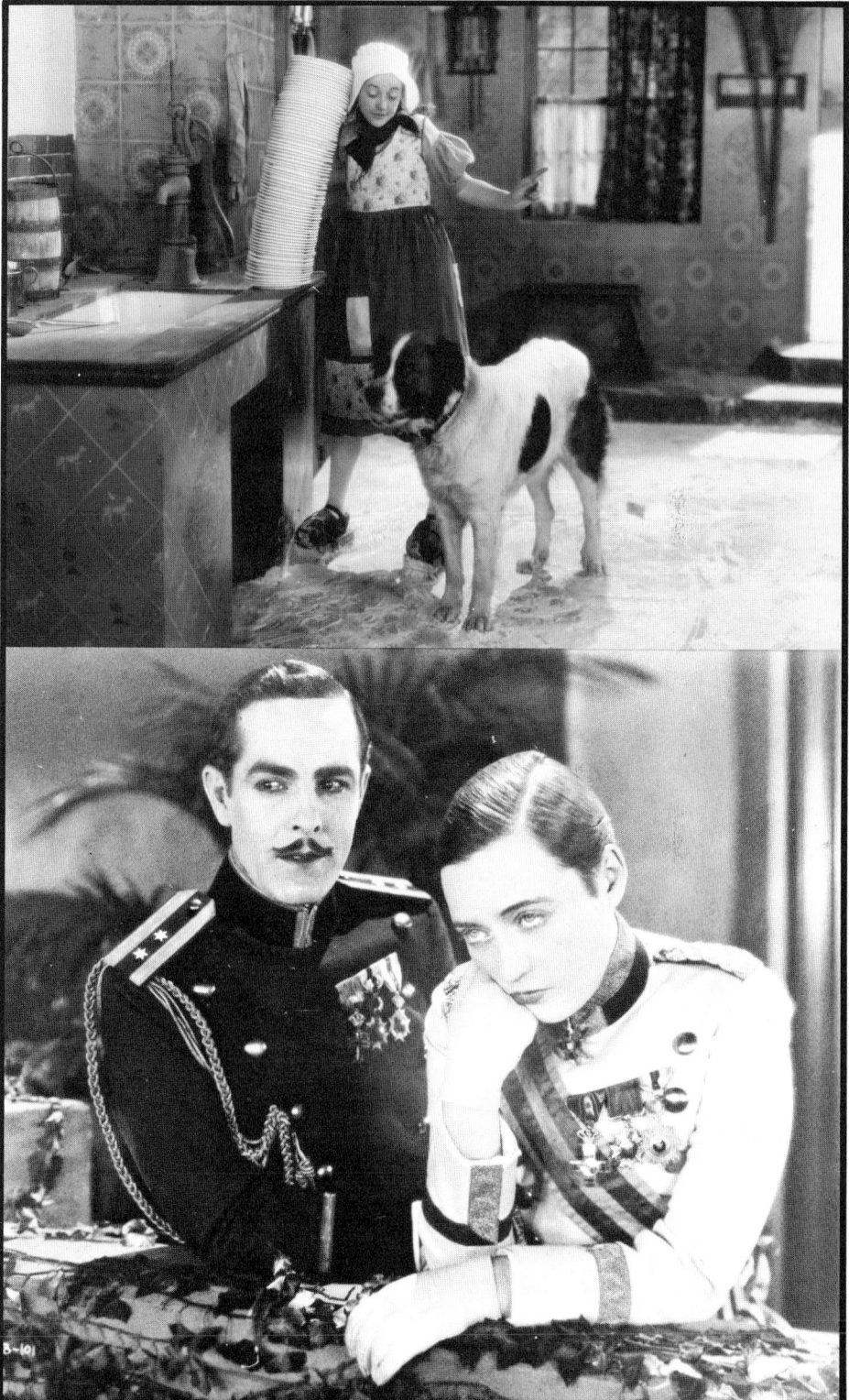

Marion's finest dramatic performance—sensitive schoolteacher Phoebe Throssel in *Quality Street*, directed by Sidney Franklin, 1927.

(Top) William Haines as Billy Boone is delighted to see Marion finally react to his ardor in *Show People*, 1928. (Middle) Tillie the Toiler tries to read back her steno notes with the help of the office boy, 1927. (Bottom) Johnny Mack Brown carries Marion to her dorm room after a slight injury on the basketball court. *The Fair Coed*, 1927.

(Clockwise) Another uniform for *Marianne,* Marion's first talking picture. Robert Edeson plays the general, 1929; Charles King joins Marion in a publicity duet for *Five O'clock Girl,* a musical never released, 1930; and Leslie Howard sits in a rooftop restaurant with Marion until a very late hour in *Five and Ten,* 1931

(At right) Marion leaves her slum home after the death of her father in *Blondie of the Follies*. Billie Dove waits at the car, 1932. (Below) Bing Crosby and Marion sing "We'll Make Hay While the Sun Shines" in *Going Hollywood*, 1933.

Two scenes and two rol
for Marion in *Operator*
with Gary Cooper. As a
blonde actress-spy (top
and (bottom) disguised
as a mulatto servant,
1934. (At right) With
Dick Powell in *Hearts
Divided,* her second film
for Warner Brothers,
1936.

(Top) Hearst had the canals of Venice re-created for Warner's *Cain and Mabel*, 1936. (Middle) The first of the Vidor comedies, *The Patsy*, with Lawrence Gray, who appeared as her leading man three times, 1928. (Bottom) On a Warner sound stage, Marion in her "ugly duckling" outfit for *Ever Since Eve* with leading man Robert Montgomery, 1937. It was her final movie.

The documents were published day after day in the screaming headlines for which Hearst was famous, but were suddenly
questioned by angry senators in Washington who sought an
investigation. During that Senate probe into one of the most
irresponsible of all of Hearst's acts as a publisher, Hearst was
questioned and it was discovered that he privately did not believe that the four senators accused of accepting bribes ever
had taken the money despite his headline smears against their
reputations.

Marion must have been aware that her companion had been
caught in a lie, but it was not allowed to register in her mind.
She had a self-censoring faculty—inherent in all of the Dourases
of screening out the bad in anyone she loved.

VI

About making movies,
I don't think financially Marion had to;
Emotionally she didn't have to.
She probably did it a lot
to please Mr. Hearst.
                    —King Vidor to the author

Director Vidor's opinion about Marion's motives for remaining in films when she was worth at least a couple of million
dollars was shared by a few in Hollywood who worked with her,
but it is not the view of Vidor's one-time wife Eleanor Boardman.
Miss Boardman believed that Marion enjoyed making films so
much that she was lost when she went into retirement. Marion
often said that she was happiest when she was on the set with
the crew and cast. "We were one big happy family," she insisted,
on each and every film apparently and quite apart from the
quality of the film being made. And she did not seem to mind
the hours, rising at dawn and working until after seven in the
evening many times. Studios worked a six-day week when she
was active.

What Vidor is suggesting is that her social activities had
become more significant to her than her standing in films. It is
true that she could count on "a good review" following her parties. Even in the fan magazines, there was far more social chat-

ter about Marion than comment about her films. Hearst is rarely
referred to in these items and then only as "Miss Davies's
friend," but he and Marion had moved into the void created by
Mary Pickford's troubles with Douglas Fairbanks and they
reigned as the imperial pace-setters of Hollywood society, the
difficulty being that their pace could not be met by any other
host in the community excepting one or two millionaires such as
Atwater Kent.

They were a public couple, and if that seems brash, those
who knew them all agree that the most embarrassing element in
their relationship was the sentiment. Most men who have mistresses confide in them, love them, and help them pay the rent,
but they send the Valentine flowers and candy to their wives. But
not Hearst, and for his mistress it was Valentine's Day 365 days
a year. If Marion found this a mite excessive, she was mostly
quiet about it. Sometimes she would confide to Anita Loos or
Frances Marion her impatience with the imperiousness which
was so interwoven with his devotion, but she made her comments without much heat, as though she was seeking to establish that her protector was not a god but mortal and fallible like
the rest of us. To some of her friends, it seemd a suffocating cage
and they couldn't see how she could bear it. But as with most
other creatures, conditioning made the cage not only bearable
but the world outside terrifying.

And there may have been another element that kept her
tied to Hearst's side for more than three decades. In her memoir
Past Imperfect, Ilka Chase touches upon it:

> From the feminine point of view there is much to be said
> for William Randolph Hearst. Power and ruthlessness have
> ever appealed to women and whatever his shortcomings, he
> has certainly loved in the grand manner and he has forced
> the great of the earth to accept his mode of living and the
> lady of his heart. He has enveloped her in luxury unique in
> our era, and her jewels are the talk of a community where
> the Koh-i-noor would rate no more than a passing glance;
> everyone has twenty-carat diamonds, but Mr. Hearst's lady,
> in line with his flamboyant patriotism, sports among other
> bijoux an American flag tastefully done in diamonds, sap-
> phires, and rubies. He has heaped her with more fame than
> infamy and has disbursed fabulous sums that her artistry
> might be well spoken on, although the pathetic thing about
> that is that had her pictures been produced with less money

and more intelligence and taste, Marion might well have developed into an enchanting light comedienne.

Miss Chase's tone is only slightly patronizing, and it had become the fashion in the forties when her book was published to put down Marion as an actress. *Citizen Kane* had been released in all major American cities and Marion's fictional counterpart, "Susan Alexander," had virtually destroyed her film reputation. No one sensed after the steady decline in quality of her last films that the earlier ones might merit revival. What is more, Marion was forever too insecure as a performer to do anything but agree with Miss Chase's put-down of her acting and she was close enough to her showgirl origins to be gratified that her American flag brooch was recalled.

"I was no Sarah Bernhardt. I was no great actress," Marion was later to insist. During those weeks in 1952 spent with Stanley Flink's tape-recorder, she felt compelled to lubricate her memory with large drafts of vodka. Sometimes, she would become unintelligible as the words began to slur, to run together. Sentences would break apart, her thoughts fragmented. "As a matter of fact, I doubt very much whether I was an actress or not. I might have been a character . . . and I thought, 'Well, this is handicapping me because I can't possibly live up to it.' Nobody could. . . . If you over-advertise a thing, like, for instance, television. Pardon me, but those commercials! They go a bit too far sometimes. . . . But if you're underadvertised, from a personal standpoint, let the public find out if they like you or not." Fragmented, but out of an old despair.

King Vidor was Marion's most important director. There were others who did one or two films with her whose place in the American film is equally secure: Sidney Franklin, whose work with Marion won them both critical accolades but failed to make money; Raoul Walsh, Allan Dwan, and Sam Wood; and certainly Mervyn LeRoy and Richard Boleslavski—but Vidor did three films with Marion in 1928–30 and they were all successes. They have become known in Marion's film dossier as "the Vidor comedies." They were unique even in Vidor's career, for he was never to surpass their airy lightness of touch and elegant clowning. Vidor is considered a giant in American film history by the Russians and the French, and in recent years, through several retrospectives, he has been rediscovered in his native land.

Vidor was born in Galveston, Texas, the same year as Marion. As a teenager, he was handling a motion picture camera shooting Texan disasters and other happenings for the old Mutual Weekly Company, a newsreel producer, at 60¢ per usable foot of film. By the time he was seventeen he was on his own in Houston, where he had his own newsreel company. He was learning his craft from every angle. By 1915, he had outgrown Texas and relocated in Los Angeles, together with his ambitious wife, Florence Vidor, who went on to become a leading lady.

Vidor was an extra and production assistant for several years, during which he observed D. W. Griffith directing *Intolerance*. Then in 1919, he did his first feature, *The Turn in the Road*, a film on Christian Science backed by nine doctors. The picture made money and he went on to direct his own wife, Florence, who had become a star, in *Jack-Knife Man* (1920), a sentimental but moving story of an orphan boy and an old man. In the mid-twenties, there was his major war film, *The Big Parade*, followed later by *The Crowd* with his second wife, Eleanor Boardman, and *Hallelujah*, his first sound movie, utilizing an all-Negro cast, a film that holds up as well today as when it was made. Vidor's career in films was one of Hollywood's most durable, continuing through the thirties and the forties with *The Champ* (1931), *Street Scene* (1931), *Bird of Paradise* (1932), *The Citadel* (1938), *Comrade X* (1940), and *H. M. Pulham, Esq.* (1941). He was still making major films in the 1950s with *Duel in the Sun*.

The Marion Davies comedies were a high point in his career as well as hers. Nothing Vidor had done before prepared the critics for their light touch and nothing Marion had ever done suggested her total expertise at frothy comedy. The suggestion that Vidor be hired by Cosmopolitan Productions had been Hearst's. He had much admired *The Big Parade*—Marion later remarked that it was her favorite film of all time—and doubtless he may have seen Marion as a glorious successor to Renee Adoree of that spectacle, but the Metro executives and Vidor pushed for comedy and convinced him.

Marion had been moving in the direction of the buoyant comedy of *The Patsy* with comic moments in *Little Old New York*, *Lights of Old Broadway* (her famed teetering scene atop a three-story scaffold was one), *Beverly of Graustark*, and *The Red Mill*. None was farce, and although there is some slapstick in the Vidor comedies, they are not so much farce as they are comedies of manners—the manners of socially ambitious middle-class

America in *The Patsy* and the bizarre manners of Hollywood folk in *Show People*.

The Patsy made Marion safe for a while. It restored her fans' confidence in her ability to delight. In this adaptation of the Barry Connors play, Marion was teamed with Marie Dressler as her mother, and Miss Dressler's great talent did not eclipse Marion's. At one wildly comic moment, Marion skips and trips into the town's yacht club, trailing her sister's hand-me-down Spanish shawl while her sister queens it in Marion's new evening wrap, an ill-afforded luxury which Marion has bought for herself after saving for months. When her sister's boyfriend, for whom she has a secret yen, ignores her suggestions to dance, her delicate fingers begin an hilarious tango on the tablecloth, reminiscent of and probably inspired by Chaplin's "Oceana Roll" in *The Gold Rush*. Finally, desperate to arouse some ardor in another of her sister's beaux, a drunken playboy, she sees portraits of his favorite film stars in silver frames about his living room and she begins at once a parody of Mae Murray, projected with deadly accuracy right down to the pouting cupid's-bow mouth, followed by a wistful, shawl-draped Lillian Gish that has a delicate shade of woebegone sadness in it, and then a scowling vamp, unmistakably Marion's friend Pola Negri, with a knife between her teeth instead of a rose.

The reviewers were unanimous in their praise of Marion's droll, put-upon younger sister. The intense and mannered performances of Marion's screen beginnings were forgotten as she continued in a series of sharply delineated comic roles through 1928, 1929, and 1930—or until Hearst's insistent voice could no longer be drowned out by the applause—so that by the time of the talkie, *Five and Ten,* she was again a poor little rich girl of the Fannie Hurst variety, the point of which seemed to be that it was foolish to be rich. Of course, it was even more foolish to be sad and unfunny.

Before *The Patsy* went into release, a bit of Marion's world —never very secure—crumbled away. Mama Rose died suddenly of heart failure in the early hours of January 25, 1928. It was thought by Marion and the other girls that her condition had improved, but then the call had come through to the beach house that she was "very low." She was, at that moment, already dead, but Ethel thought that Marion might become hysterical if she were told by phone.

Marion hurried to the house on Lexington Road in Beverly Hills which she and Hearst had bought for Mama Rose and the family. She knew when she saw the face of one of the household staff who opened the door that her mother was dead, and she did become hysterical, screaming and cursing, railing at what seemed to be her fate—the loss of every worthwhile human being around her while her wealth continued to climb.

During her Hollywood years, Mama Rose had become a dim and silent figure at those parties of Marion's she had managed to attend. It was usually Ethel's idea that she be brought to sit in on them, a kindness that Marion was often too busy to observe herself. Mama Rose was relatively young—56, according to her burial records—but she had achieved all the goals she had set for her daughters. She had begun to feel relatively useless once Marion began running the family's affairs. When the struggle began on that night in January, there was small motive for her to fight an adversary who was bound to come sooner or later and her cushioned days had become so much alike, survival had lost its point.

Marion's hysteria was to be repeated each time death called, and she couldn't tell you why she lost control. She did not seem to fear death so much as to despise it. She was robbed several times during her life, but death was really the greatest thief of them all, for Marion's life was structured not around herself and her career, despite the joy she took from making movies, but around her loved ones, including Hearst. When one of them was taken, the void seemed impossible to fill, and when Hearst was finally lost to her, a major part of her crumbled away, and—for many—she was a ghost of what she had been.

With Mama Rose's death, the last connection with Marion's girlhood was gone. Mama Rose symbolized Brooklyn and Manhattan, Chicago and all those blissful nights backstage at the *Follies,* where she had looked after her "girls." Marion no longer had needed the comfort of Mama Rose's shoulder when she was blue. Any of half-a-dozen friends were available to come at her bidding during those moments, or, when not, a bottle could be opened. But the barrenness of her mother's last years struck her with such starkness that night, it was nearly unbearable. Mama Rose had become a revered furnishing of her Beverly Hills mansion, neatly gowned by I. Magnin, but depersonalized.

In death, Marion's wealth and fame thrust Mama Rose into the limelight. She was laid out at Pierce Brothers Mortuary in

Beverly Hills in a handsomely carved mahogany coffin partially covered with a blanket of white gardenias accented by orchids sent by Hearst.

Hearst phoned Charlie Chaplin and asked that he be a pall-bearer along with Hearst himself, his son Bill, Jr., Harry Crocker, and former Ambassador to Spain Alexander Moore, who had become a family friend. With the Hearsts and Crocker, two of the wealthiest families in California were represented among those who bore Mama Rose to her grave. She was buried in the new white marble Douras mausoleum by a still pond in Hollywood Memorial Park. It was announced that the nondenominational cemetery burial was temporary and that Marion was having a mausoleum constructed at Calvary Cemetery, a Catholic burial-ground in Los Angeles, but the transfer never was made. Actor William Haines was there and both Louella Parsons and Hedda Hopper, and Frances Marion came to mourn a friend who had been delighted to have been approached in her living-room corner to exchange kitchen recipes.

The four Douras daughters—Marion, Rose, Ethel, and Reine—came in two limousines to the funeral chapel, and all were in black with veiled faces, and all wore large diamond pendant earrings swinging from their lobes and diamond neck-laces of the choker variety at their throats, badges of their comforting immersion in Mama Rose's beliefs. Once inside the ante-room of the chapel, Rose and Ethel in a kind of ritualistic gesture opened up their purse compacts and glanced at their makeup, Rose giving her nose a swipe with a powder puff. They were not being thoughtless—in their minds, quite the contrary—and they had not even consulted one another as to what to wear. It was a Davies coincidence inspired by the woman who lay dead.

VII

On July 20, 1928, Hearst and Marion sailed for Europe. They went on separate ships, Marion taking the *Ile de France*. *The Patsy* had opened in April and was playing to crowded houses around the country, but the Philadelphia salesman's challenge to Mayer still rankled. Even Marion was not aware that, with her last three films and continuing on through *Show People* and half a dozen others, she was far along the way to total critical acceptance. There was drama in them as well as comedy, so it was not acceptance with reservations. Reviewers from *The New York Times* to the *Los Angeles Times* had come to expect engaging and often exciting performances from her in just about everything she did. In reading these reviews of ten of her films done over a period of six years, the later distortions and absolute falsehoods seem appalling, revealing as they do how easily history of any sort can be distorted. Taken as a group, these ten films compare favorably and often excel in quality and performance those of nearly all of her peers, including Lillian Gish, Pola Negri, Norma Shearer, Joan Crawford, Colleen Moore, and Constance Bennett. If this surprises some film scholars or some who were around the castle or the beach house when Marion was so terribly social, but not taken very seriously as an actress, let them look at the record—the releases of these stars at the time Marion had reached her peak—not because as her biographer I seek belated tribute to Marion but simply to set the record straight. There were successes and mediocre films scattered through all of these ladies' careers at the time (and Marion's last films in the 1930s as well), but somehow for six straight years Marion was endowing all of her movies—with the exception of the 1928 *The Cardboard Lover*—with some of her off-screen desire to give everyone a good time. Swanson and Garbo were too extraordinary to be considered along with the others, although Swanson was about to enter into a twenty-year period of decline and semiretirement with the advent of sound.

The wonder is that Marion was able to carry her film career so far in the face of the intense resentment that was building both in Hollywood and among movie audiences over that unremitting publicity she was receiving, and the many hours she was spending frolicking on the set and off, with parties for four or five hundred guests at a time. What would have happened if she had broken with Hearst in 1924 when relations were so strained between them and he brought up the matter of parting? It was just at that time that her success in *Little Old New York* had prompted Mayer to give Hearst a nearly blank check in underwriting her future films. What if Hearst had bowed out and all of her films from then on had been made for Thalberg and Mayer? The chances are better than 50–50 that she would have abandoned all of the Robert W. Chambers stories and done nothing but brisk comedy. Comediennes as attractive as Marion are a rarity, and even Hearst seemed to have sensed that during those "golden" six years. But old age was to catch up with him several years before she retired, and she would be forced to turn back the clock of her screen career and do one of those films again with "overstuffed emotions and costumes" Frances Marion had warned him about.

She had become Hollywood's busiest hostess because, as she told a friend, "When I'm entertaining at home, no one can ever tell me to get out." Her equivocal place in Hearst's life reinforced old insecurities even though no one can recall a specific instance when she was humiliated while with Hearst. But in the studio, she had felt on firmer ground. While she thought that Hearst overrated her abilities, she believed that she was someone of value in films—until that spring when the salesman had directed his diatribe against her movies (and how ironic it was that, from *The Patsy* on until *It's a Wise Child* in 1931, all of her films except *The Cardboard Lover* were to make money for Metro and Hearst!).

The Hearst tour party that summer of 1928 was a large one. When the group sailed for Europe, Hearst saw that Marion was surrounded with good friends. Each one was made to feel that she "needed" them along to cheer her. They were put up at Hearst's expense at the Hotel Crillon in Paris with a retinue of valets and maids. Hearst guests were always transported, housed, and fed at his expense. His sole compensation, as he frequently told them, was that they should take something home with them in the way of a new cultural experience.

Alice Head, Hearst's publishing director for the British magazines, was coming over from London to join the group. Miss Head believed that she was going for the weekend and took just a small overnight bag, but she was not to see her home again for six weeks. Miss Head writes:

> Four large touring cars were drawn up outside the hotel the following morning and we set forth, first to Versailles, and then to Rambouillet and Chartres, where the lovely cathedral with its fabulous stained glass, seen at the sunset hour, left an undying impression. As we came out of the cathedral, Mr. Hearst remarked: "Well, children, shall we dine here or shall we go on to Tours?" One of the girls in the party replied: "We don't care *where* we dine, but we *must* find the ladies' room." . . . After leaving the chateaux country we struck diagonally across France and stopped the first night at Vichy. I may add that, as the party included some extremely beautiful and attractive girls from Holly-

wood dressed in the smartest of summer frocks from Magnin's, the arrival of our cars in French villages always
caused something of a sensation.

On the trip that summer, there was more family along than
film stars. There were even two relatives of Millicent's in the
party: Mrs. Sadie Murray and her daughter Anita, whom Marion
liked very much—not an unusual situation in Marion's life with
Hearst. There were also sisters Rose and Ethel, Pepi and Charlie
Lederer, and Hearst's son John and his bride Gretchen, for whom
the trip was a honeymoon. Among the nonrelatives were Lloyd
Pantages, of the Los Angeles theater family, Harry Crocker, who
was now employed by Hearst as a social secretary, and Maury H.
Biddle Paul, of the Philadelphia Biddles, who since 1917 had
been "Cholly Knickerbocker" for the Hearst papers and a part-
time social mentor to Millicent. There were others joining the
party along the way, including Papa Ben, who turned up in Italy,
so that the complexion of the group was constantly changing.
According to Anita Loos, who recalled one such trip, the
Hearst cars making up his motorcade were purchased casually
by Hearst. He would see what he wanted in a showroom window
and walk in off the street and buy them. It was a remarkable
sight to see the Hearst caravan lined up in the morning ready
for departure. Box lunches were prepared by the hotel chef and
their arrival meant that Hearst was on his way down from his
rooms. He seemed rejuvenated by the prospect of seeing his familiar old cathedrals and ruins again.
Vichy was then a lively little spa wholly innocent of any
vestige of the grimness of its not-too-distant role in the history of
France. The entire party drove around the city that night in open
horse-drawn carriages. After Grenoble, they moved south to the
Riviera. It was no wonder that the French villagers (and Spanish
and Italian) came on the run when the Hearst convoy entered
their villages. Many of them were sufficiently impressed by a
glimpse of the smiling, gaily-clad film people to bring cameras,
but few realized who Hearst was. He took Miss Head by the arm
and said: "We're *much* the most important people, but nobody
wants to photograph us!"
In Italy, they stopped at Viareggio where Marion and the
other sensitive-skinned ladies were plagued by mosquitoes. No
netting could be found at any price. Then they went on to Pisa,
where Marion entered the tower, her arms straight down at her

sides, her body at an appropriate variance from the vertical. Finally they reached Florence, which Hearst considered to be the crowning experience of their continental tour. He had been taken by his mother Phoebe on educational tours of Europe as he was growing up, and now it was one of his chief pleasures to give those he liked the opportunity to see those historic places, the jewels of that world he had sought to recapture at San Simeon.

By the time they reached the Lido outside Venice, they had been traveling four weeks without a break, and Hearst felt that Marion and her pals deserved a little fun. He recessed his vagabond college and rented Cole Porter's dance barge for an evening of music and dancing through the canals. The notoriously much-married Peggy Hopkins Joyce, who had been a high-ranking showgirl when Marion was in *The Follies,* joined them for the night, and the two ex-Ziegfeld girls sat out most of the dances and reminisced.

Then at the Taverna, they all paid their respects to Princess Jane di San Faustino, an aging American lady who had become a Venetian monument. The next day, the white-haired Princess made a spectral appearance on the beach in a flowing white gown. Used to American tourists looking much like the ones before them, she was attracted by the color and splash made by the Hearst party. "I'll just sit here and listen to the silly, idiotic conversation that I'm certain is going to go on." Marion found her fascinating and her candor refreshing.

Sister Rose was not interested in taking the "cure" at Bad Nauheim, so she and Lloyd Pantages returned to Paris. It was an indulgent Hearst who allowed them to go. There had been occasions when truant guests, who declined to take on any more cathedrals or museums and chose instead to sit them out in a tavern, were summarily dismissed from the tour and sent home.

It was in Bad Nauheim that nephew Charlie shaved off all his hair (it was already thinning prematurely) and appeared before his Aunt Marion and the others at breakfast wearing a bedsheet around him Gandhi-style. Marion screamed and laughed in turns, and Hearst was concerned for a moment for Charlie's sanity. When the young man appeared later in the day wearing a Harpo Marx wig of golden curls, Marion told him, "You looked better bald."

When they were in Florence, the view from the Piazzale Michelangelo of San Miniato had moved Hearst to say to Miss Head, "One simply can't help feeling sentimental!" Charlie knew

Hearst well enough to be quietly reverent there. But Bad Nauheim was a functional place where pranks were tolerated by
Hearst. His principal worry was that his guests would be bored,
and his chief concern when Charlie appeared half-naked in his
improvised loin cloth was that he might catch a cold. He was not
surprised later that week to learn that Charlie had come down
with tonsillitis.

At the German spa, the Hearst party set up headquarters at
Deske's Grand Hotel. Everyone knew that they were there chiefly
for Hearst's sake. Bad Nauheim's dullness was accepted as a
courtesy to their host. The only entertainment was a German
band in the village square each Sunday. Their daily routine called
for them all to have massages at eleven in the morning followed
by carriage rides, and the carriages would drop them at the bath-
houses. As Marion recalled the "cure": "You walk into these
wooden tubs and you lie down and it's all bubbly like White
Rock. And you have to watch this clock. Eight minutes is the
longest that you can stay there. Then you ring the bell and the
Fräulein rushes in and she gets you out and she wipes you down,
and then you go back into the carriage to your hotel, and you're
supposed to sleep for one hour. And whatever you want to do for
the rest of the day is all right, but no coffee, no tea, but a little
Rhine wine."

In their free time one day, Marion, Hearst, Bill, Jr., Harry
Crocker, and Jack Hearst and his bride Gretchen visited a local
winery and its "tasting room." Earlier, they had been given lunch
by a millionaire wine merchant who had served cocktails, dulling
their taste buds for the wine. As a consequence, Marion and
some of the others drank quantities of the wine instead of just
tasting it. Shortly, they had a game going, begun by Bill, Jr., who
decided that he could climb through one of the huge empty wine
casks. When Marion attempted it, she was gassed by the smell
and came out groggy. On the way back to the Grand Hotel, she
sang the old Helen Morgan song *Why Was I Born?* and Hearst
asked if she was tight. "Not any tighter than you are," she told
him. Hearst, mildly annoyed, said, "I didn't drink a bit of wine."
And, of course, he hadn't.

Hearst's German doctor, a man by the name of Heinz Groedel, was distressed to find everyone but his patient drunk. He
chose to call Marion "Nurse Davies" because she was usually at
Hearst's side, and now he said, "Nurse Davies, I said a *little*
Rhine wine."

Meanwhile, Charlie Lederer, rendered vulnerable perhaps by his appearance as "Gandhi," came down with his tonsillitis. Dr. Groedel fussed over him and Hearst, but that only took up part of his day, so he suddenly suggested for no apparent reason that all of the Hearst party have their urine tested. "Nurse Davies" was asked to go through their wing of the Grand Hotel and pick up the samples and label them. The filled bottles were in her suite just long enough for ailing Charlie to have a go at them.

The next day, Dr. Groedel phoned Marion and gravely informed her that Hearst had one of the worst infections of the kidney that he had ever encountered. He wanted another specimen, just to be sure, but Marion said she was embarrassed to ask Hearst to fill the bottle a second time. With some reluctance, she rapped on Hearst's door and said that Dr. Groedel had "found something" and wanted another specimen. Hearst knew his physical condition as well as any of his doctors and said, "Whatever he's found, he's mistaken," but he grudgingly supplied her with another filled bottle.

Dr. Groedel was amazed to find that Hearst's condition had cured itself overnight, and proved it by showing Marion the two bottles, one brownish and the other pale yellow. Finally it dawned on Marion what had happened. "My nephew," she told Dr. Groedel, "has had kidney trouble for a long time."

Marion's gift for exaggeration was never more richly employed than in the telling of an incident that occurred at Bad Nauheim late in her stay there. She wearied of the daily soaks in the old wooden tubs, but she had heard that there was an "Emperor's Bath," and she asked one of the *Fräuleins* if she might use that. The Emperor did his soaking in an elaborate mosaic design, and Marion felt especially favored as she lay back, feeling the warm bubbles seep upward around her. But the Emperor's clock, it turned out, was not working. After what was no more than an hour but much more than the prescribed eight minutes, the *Fräuleins* remembered her and pulled her out. One of Hearst's doctors examined her back at the hotel and, in her own words, "he told me that I have no heart. . . . 'Oh, I see. It's the size of a dime.'" Then she explained that the idea of the baths is "to shrink the heart down. Mine was the size of a dime. . . . I'm still alive, but it's a wonderful cure."

A miniature dachshund had been left behind at the Deske Grand Hotel by his owner in default of a bill of nearly five hundred dollars. Harry Crocker learned of the dog and told Marion. The orphaned puppy was frightened and sat quivering in a corner of the manager's office. Something about the dog reminded Marion of the gentle and undernourished Mahatma Gandhi, then so much in the headlines with his hunger strikes and only that week the inspiration for one of Charlie's pranks. "Come here, Gandhi," she said, and she turned to Harry Crocker and Martin Bonfils and told them, "I want the doggy."

Hearst bought the dog for Marion, paying a little extra "because Marion likes it so much." He was underestimating Marion's feelings for Gandhi. An eleven-year attachment was begun that day in Bad Nauheim between Marion and her dachshund. They were to become inseparable, even more so than Hearst was with his Helenas, a royal succession of dachshunds he had until his death. Hearst had begun breeding them in the 1920s, and at one time had fifty or more, kept in a large kennel near the castle at San Simeon, where they would yelp for some affection and attention, which they crave more desperately than do most dogs. It was not uncommon for a guest to be distressed by the sight of dozens of small dachshunds scrambling over one another at the fence trying to lick a human hand. When at dinner one night Anita Loos asked Hearst why he kept so many of them, he said, "Because I love them."

Returning to Paris to pick up Rose and Lloyd Pantages and catch the boat train that week to England, Hearst and his party were invited to lunch at the Foreign Ministry as the guests of Aristide Briand. The Mexican film star Dolores del Rio was among the other guests. She had recently completed a big western spectacle, *The Trail of '98,* and she and Marion chatted about their prospects in the new medium of sound, Marion hiding her fears that she would be out of it all.

Marion sat next to a Parisian journalist by the name of Roger Delaplanque and they conversed amiably through the luncheon. Champagne was poured as quickly as a glass was emptied, and Marion enjoyed the privilege of sitting across from Hearst, downing the champagne freely with the knowledge that he was helpless to restrain her.

After coffee, everyone got up to go into an adjoining sitting room. Marion recalls in her unfinished memoirs that she mumbled an excuse to Delaplanque that she needed to find the ladies' room. If we are to believe Marion's account of what happened next, then a significant detail in the biography of Hearst is corrected. Since her accounts are often colored by fantasy, it would be easy to dismiss her story as just another wild fable. Charlie Lederer seems inclined to dismiss her version as just another of her inventions. Perhaps it is; no one can ever document the details that she gives us.

Alone in the dining room, Marion says that she saw a half-opened door along the inside wall. Her curiosity impelled her to swing it all the way open, revealing a small chamber containing a safe. The safe door, too, was not securely closed, so she opened it. Inside, she found a document tied with a colored ribbon.

That same intense curiosity that had plagued her ever since she peeked at W. C. Fields from the wings recurred and she slipped the ribbon off, unrolled it, and saw a great deal of small print in French, which she could not read. Just before lunch, she had been talking with a young French diplomat, and he had asked her what she thought of the Japanese. She had told him, "They're all right. I don't know many except the ones who work for Charlie Chaplin," but she thought the question odd. Now as she glanced at the document in her hands, she somehow believed that it had to do with Japan.

The document had nothing to do with Japan. It was a secret pact concerning Anglo-French naval deployments. Marion then said that she raised her dress and stuck the papers inside the elastic of her "sissy-britches" or panties. She didn't consider what she was doing an act of thievery. She thought she was being "clever," and she had no idea what it was.

That afternoon Hearst took the party to another museum and Marion forgot about what she had done. When she went to take her bath that evening, she recalls that the document fell to the floor, and she suddenly regretted her act and thought to herself, "Oh, what a nuisance!" Then she sought out Hearst, coming right to the point and telling him that she had taken something from the Foreign Ministry.

Hearst was shocked and asked her why she had done such a thing.

"You should know by now," Marion said, "that I'm no kleptomaniac," but she told him that her curiosity got the better of her. She was distressed that she had given in to a childish impulse when so much might be lost if she were exposed. She was so ashamed of her act, even Eileen Percy and Dorothy Mackaill never knew that Marion was involved—if her story is, as she insists, an accurate one.

Then Hearst explained that they were in great trouble; that the French government had missed the document already and they suspected him, since he was the only one present who would have anything to gain by taking it. A representative of the government had phoned Hearst and asked him if he had taken the document. Hearst said he had told the man, "I haven't got it," but apparently he took the papers from her and allowed one of his own men to take the rap for the crime—at least temporarily —until he had made full use of the document's headline value.

Hearst had been given one hour to leave Paris and France, and special gendarmes were searching his suite at the Crillon. "So we're already packing," he blithely told Marion. "I promised I'd be gone in half an hour."

In Marion's account, Hearst's attitude seems surprisingly indulgent. Very few Americans considered him a responsible publisher; he had published false documents, created sensations out of fiction, manipulated emotions in his readers to such a degree he was even held accountable for the assassination of President McKinley. But around Marion, he seemed far more reliable. Most of his instincts within her orbit were decent ones. And yet when she confessed that she had stolen secret state papers of France that had resulted in his own expulsion from that country, all he could say was, in effect, "I'm on my way." Then he instructed Marion to stay behind and finish getting the clothes she had ordered. Maintaining the composure that marked his behavior during most crises, he left her, the document apparently concealed on his person.

Meanwhile, back in London, Alice Head had received a telephone call from Paris and a voice had informed her in broken English that somebody or other was coming to London immediately. Since Hearst was the only person she knew of who would call her from Paris, Miss Head assumed that it was someone he was sending over, so she went to Victoria Station that night and met the boat train. "Out of the train," Miss Head writes in her memoirs, "stepped Mr. Hearst and Colonel Willicombe and Harry Crocker. My chief followed me straight into my car, after just a word of greeting, and we drove off to the Savoy. As soon as we were clear of Victoria Station I remarked: 'Something has happened.' 'You're right,' he said calmly, 'something *has* happened. I've been turned out of France.'"

The document was immediately published in the Hearst press, provoking the French government to take more extreme measures. They arrested Harold Horan, the Hearst correspondent in Paris, and he was questioned for hours about the theft. He had attended the luncheon, of course, and he was an obvious second choice after Hearst for a thorough investigation. The government was embarrassed because Foreign Minister Briand had been opposed to the treaty and there was some suspicion that he had deliberately leaked it in a successful effort to defeat it. Horan was expelled from France and the government then arrested journalist Roger Delaplanque and the diplomat with whom Marion had chatted at the luncheon. These gentlemen were charged with having passed the document to Hearst or Horan.

Marion and sister Rose attempted to remain in Paris until their wardrobes could be finished by their *couturier*. All of the friends who had treated them with unstinting hospitality earlier drifted away with the exception of Mrs. Otis H. P. Belmont. "She stayed in the apartment with me," Marion recalled, and she told her that she would get the gendarmes away from her door. And soon Mrs. Belmont had succeeded in this effort and even managed to get Marion out for some fresh air. Still, gendarmes remained posted outside the door at Rose's hotel, and she was quite vocal in her sense of outrage.

Within a few days, Marion, her sister and Maury Paul rejoined Hearst in London. Hearst shared a suite with Marion at the Savoy overlooking the Thames. He seemed to have forgotten all about the treaty episode and was eager to get on to Wales to have a first glimpse of the Welsh castle he had asked Miss Head to purchase for him in 1925. Like her late predecessor, James Y. McPeake, Miss Head was not only director of Hearst's British publications but his principal buyer of British relics.

In 1928, St. Donat's was in the final process of restoration under the direction of Sir Charles Allom, Royal Architect. An additional forty-seven bathrooms were being installed, elevators added, and walls torn out to make some rooms more spacious.

It was getting dark when they arrived, but Hearst did not seem to mind the eeriness of the place at dusk. It was Marion who noticed the cobwebs in the corners of the unfinished rooms and spoke of bats. Hearst walked ahead of Marion and Miss

Head, delighted as a small boy with a Christmas sled.

St. Donat's had been owned by an aristocratic couple named Pennoyer, who had vacated prior to its sale. The castle dated back to the eleventh century, although the main portion, which was built around a quadrangle, was not constructed until some centuries later. For six hundred years it was in the possession of a family named Stradling, one of the few castles in England continuously inhabited. In her memoirs, Miss Head writes: "It is a place of breath-taking beauty, especially in the moonlight, and the terraced gardens that slope down to the Bristol Channel could only have been planned by someone with a real genius. . . . Each enclosed garden is a lovely picture, and the whole landscape provides a setting worthy of the uncanny beauty of the Castle."

Marion was more impressed with its *oubliette*, a medieval dungeon which usually has an opening only at the top but at St. Donat's had one exit to the sea, for those prisoners who wished to commit suicide. The place inspired endless spooky gags. The ghost of an ancient Lady Stradling was supposed to begin haunting the castle if it should ever change hands, but Marion never caught even a glimpse of the wraith. Instead, she sometimes got herself up in a sheet and ran hooting through the upper hallways at a late hour, a thirty-one-year-old prankster playing at Halloween.

There at St. Donat's Marion was more truly the mistress of the castle than she ever had been at San Simeon or Wyntoon. Millicent was not especially welcome there and it always would be Marion who would be at Hearst's side to entertain the visitors who came up—George Bernard Shaw, Lloyd George, Lord and Lady Plunket (she was the daughter of Fannie Ward), the Mountbattens, Alice Head, Elinor Glyn, and scores of others. Mrs. Glyn by now was considered a regular in Marion's and Hearst's circle. Later that year (1928) on a visit to California, Marion would insist that she stay at Ocean House for six weeks because she thought the busy novelist looked overtired. Apparently she had reconciled herself to Mrs. Glyn's imperious manner or perhaps Mrs. Glyn herself had mellowed.

Traveling on those exhausting "educational" tours of the continent always made Marion edgy and eager to get back to St. Donat's to recover. It was a restful place, despite the many guests, with much fewer demands upon her as hostess than at Ocean House or at San Simeon. On that first visit, the quiet days gave her time to sort out her thoughts about the recent past and her future. She was clearly at the end of an epoch in her life; the matriarch of the Douras clan was buried and the silent picture era was winding up. She told Eileen Percy that she felt very uncertain about everything except "W.R."

When Hearst spoke of going home, Marion seemed reluctant for the first time on their several trips abroad. But he soon learned the basis for her anxiety. It was not the loss of Mama Rose that disturbed her now. It was *sound*. The talkies. Al Jolson's *The Jazz Singer* had created a stir a year earlier, but Marion had tried to ignore it. With another Jolson film, *The Singing Fool*, attracting crowds everywhere, a whole flood of films with "sound effects" and with "added dialogue in sound" were coming out. Given her stammer, Marion couldn't see herself in talking pictures. And without her role as film star, her life seemed insufficient. Hearst had cast her in that part and had given her no options.

VIII

It was Hearst's idea that Marion and his guests would return to Germany and fly back across the Atlantic in the dirigible in which he had a financial interest, the *Graf Zeppelin*. Much to Marion's relief, technical difficulties prevented this, and the party sailed for home on the *Berengaria*, reaching New York on October 5.

On their way to the Ritz Tower, a Hearst hotel property (one of four New York hotels he owned at the time), all Marion could see were the marquees of the movie palaces heralding the advent of sound. She believed that it had taken over New York. "I'm ruined," she kept saying over and over again.

The real transition had come that summer. *The Jazz Singer* (1927) had not convinced everybody in the industry that talking pictures were more than a fad. Even Charlie Chaplin considered sound a novelty that had nothing to do with the true art of film. He had had a mild dispute with Hearst about it, Hearst insisting that there was something to be said for sound, and that it might have to be accepted by all. Chaplin's attitude was not a careless, emotional one. Early talking pictures would prove to be vastly inferior on the whole to the better silents. The first sound cameras were encased in huge booths that were practically im-

mobile. Many films were little more than photographed plays as
the actors moved about small areas. The fluid poetry of the silent
camera disappeared for a time. Evocative images were displaced
by actors in closeup speaking words, words, and more words.
Imaginative use of the new medium was very limited when it
existed at all. The moviehouse was no longer a dark retreat of
silence and graphic poetry in motion, or, in the expressive words
of silent star Louise Brooks, "the movements of thought and soul
transmitted in a kind of intense isolation."

Jolson's second immersion in bathos, *The Singing Fool,* was
a primitive version of *Love Story,* with little Davey Lee playing
the four-year-old doomed son, as opposed to the doomed wife.
Like *The Jazz Singer,* it was showing twice a day and there were
long lines at the Winter Garden, where it was playing. It is not
a film that has aged very well. Its emotions seem spurious when
they are not banal, but in its day sound added an additional tug
to its story of alienation in marriage. The public was enthusiastic
and accepted its banality because of the novelty and excitement
of hearing a voice break through grief or the sudden relief of
someone's laughter. Marion tried to persuade Hearst to accompany her, but Hearst said, "I've got things to do. You and Maury
[Paul] go."

Marion stared at the screen and listened, convinced that her
career was wrecked by this technical advance. With Jolson's
major song—

> *When there are gray skies,*
> *I don't mind those gray skies—*
> *You'll make them blue, Sonny Boy.*

—Marion began sobbing, her mascara running, and whispered
to Maury Paul, "I'm ruined. Ruined!"

When Paul returned her to the Ritz Tower Suite, she was
still crying. "What's the matter with her?" Hearst wanted to
know.

"*Sonny Boy* got her down," Paul told him.

Marion was defensive and said that if Hearst had been
along, he would have been crying, too. And, of course, he would
have been.

Marion and Hearst returned to the West Coast to find Metro
no longer ignoring the shuttle of limousines between the Warner

Brothers–First National studio and the train depot at Pasadena, where press agents and chauffeurs were picking up Walter Huston, Ruth Chatterton, and other actors whose voices were familiar to theater audiences. Mayer and Thalberg were renting an outside studio with sound equipment to attempt their first part-talkie, *Alias Jimmy Valentine,* with William Haines. The studio atmosphere was tense as Metro's stars were being tested in relays for their adaptability to sound.

Still apprehensive about her speech problem, Marion spoke of retirement, but Hearst said that he would find a voice coach. And she was not alone in her anxiety. Silent actors frantically sought to rid themselves of Bronx, Brooklyn, and European accents, and to lower and strengthen voices that sounded effeminate and weak. Marion's voice, despite her impediment, was of excellent timbre for talking pictures. It was slightly lower than contralto, what is sometimes described as a "whiskey voice," with a tinge of humor in it much of the time. Hearst and her friends convinced her that it was an asset rather than a liability. Upon her first contact with sound equipment, however, she lost whatever confidence she had.

When Marion's sound test scene arrived, she read it with growing incredulity. The dialogue was absurd beyond belief, something like, "Do you think it's nice to be in a river with a caterpillar?" She turned to her leading man in the test, comedian George K. Arthur, who had been one of her fellow players in *Lights of Old Broadway* and again in a cameo role in her recently completed *Show People,* and told him, "We're going to ad lib."

"What for?" Arthur wanted to know.

"When you get stupid dialogue like this," she said, "why not? It's like a Wassermann. It's just a test. I don't care whether I live or die."

"But what about me?" Arthur asked a little indignantly.

"Just follow me," she said, "I'll lead you along." And picking up a thermos of champagne she carried for courage, she walked with Arthur to the sound stage.

The sound camera rolled and, improvising on the basis of their costumes and the set (a dining room, and Arthur was in evening dress), Marion began: "This is a dinner party where there're *er*sters . . . Brooklyn *er*sters. Sit down."

Arthur complained, "There's no chair."

"Well then, fall down. What's the difference?"

Marion was sure that the test was a disaster. Shivering back in her dressing room bungalow waiting for the ax to fall, Marion told Norma Shearer's brother Douglas, who was a sound engineer in charge of her test scene, that she had decided to go back to Europe. "I don't care for this climate out here. It's so . . . so sordid . . . this idea, sound. I don't care for it."

"It's all right," Shearer told her, reassuringly. "You'd better go home now."

"Yes," she said, "but first I must get reservations for me to get aboard a plane or a boat, yes, a *slow* boat to China."

When she got back to her Santa Monica beach house, Marion's whole family had gathered and they stood there near the door, looking at her wonderingly, since this was such a critical day—her half a million dollar annual salary might well stop. Marion told them to go away. "Don't ask anything. Don't talk to me, please. I don't care for this idea at all. I'm going to sleep now, and I hope I never wake up."

The next day at noon Thalberg was telephoning her, asking that she come to the studio immediately.

"Irving, I can't. I'd rather have my contract broken right now."

But Thalberg wouldn't relieve her anxieties by phone and insisted she come over to his office. "Whatever you did," Thalberg told her when she arrived, "you're one of the few who's getting a new contract. You stunned the other people with that test. Yours was the best. You want to see it?"

Marion, stunned a bit herself, told him, "No!"

"Who wrote your dialogue?" Thalberg then asked. "I'll have him promoted. How'd you memorize so quickly?"

"Because it was a great writer," Marion said, hoping to kid herself into accepting what Thalberg was telling her.

"I'll raise his salary," Thalberg declared.

IX

To go backward in time for a moment, Metro had purchased a mildly successful stage comedy entitled *Polly Preferred*, which had as its heroine a successful stage actress. Laurence Stallings was asked by director King Vidor to do something with the comedy. Stallings was the scenarist on *The Patsy* whose specialty was writing about the "doughboys" of World War I (his screenplay of *The Big Parade* had been widely acclaimed—the first major American film to debunk war and phony patriotism). Word had just come down from Mayer and Thalberg to "throw something together for Marion." She was restless, they said, and didn't wish to be idle. It would be her third film that year (1928). Although no one knew it at the time, this was to be her final silent film.

It would be Marion's second film for Vidor. She was accepted by him as someone who was more than simply competent. While it was the habit of some of Marion's earlier directors to act out scenes in advance for their performers, Vidor depended upon a personal rapport with them. John Gilbert, star of *The Big Parade,* described it as a form of "mental telepathy."

As Vidor remembers it, "the stage comedy, *Polly Preferred,* was too weak to hold up on the screen. So we transferred the whole thing to Hollywood and paralleled the fanciful life of Gloria Swanson, who had recently returned from Europe with her fifth husband, the Marquis de la Falaise." Miss Swanson's marriage to the French nobleman had taken place in 1925 and her first appearance with him at the New York opening of her film, *Madame Sans Gêne,* had caused a near riot with thousands of the curious pushing toward the Rivoli Theatre to catch a glimpse of the high-toned couple. The theater had been decorated with French tricolor streamers and Napoleonic soldiers stood guard outside two sentry boxes in front. When Miss Swanson reached the West Coast, her studio, Paramount, had all of its executives lined up in a kind of parade review for her to greet and allow to kiss her hand.

Gloria Swanson was earning the highest salary ever paid by Paramount, but her start in films had been as a Mack Sennett bathing beauty when she was married to one of her early husbands, a not yet famous and inelegant Wallace Beery. Vidor found this background and the story of her rise to the equivalent of royalty precisely what he wanted for his comedy, the name of which had been changed to *Show People.* He borrowed the vacant Mack Sennett Studio for the filming of the early years of his heroine, now called "Peggy Pepper," and returned to his home lot, Metro, for the film-queen scenes.

For several years now, Hearst had ridiculed the fashion of famed film queens marrying European noblemen. Pola Negri recently had married a French aristocrat and had given out an interview in which she told a reporter that such men made better husbands. "Pola is nutty as a bed-bug," Hearst told Marion. "How do these foreigners hypnotize these gals?" he wanted to know. He jokingly asked her if she had in mind finding herself some "Count Bunco" and then "in addition to having a Princess De Damloony and a Marquise De la Foolish de la Krazy Kat, we will have a Countess De Bonehead de la Bughouse" as well. Constance Talmadge had recently divorced her titled husband and Hearst said that "she knew her delicatessen when she dropped her liability into the ash can." He had not been as excited about a screen property in years as he was about *Show People*. He thought the satire of Hollywood and its socially ambitious leading ladies was not only on target but was close to the attitude toward society which he had had for nearly a lifetime.

Vidor's work with Marion in *The Patsy* had convinced him that she was a natural comedienne and gifted mimic. She would often regale her studio companions with spur-of-the-moment takeoffs on some of Metro's super-luminaries. When Garbo visited the set of one of Marion's films to watch Jetta Goudal perform, Marion thought the Swedish actress had come out of friendliness to her since Garbo had spent a few weekends at San Simeon. This proved not to be the case, and when Marion naively returned the courtesy by walking onto Garbo's closed set next door to hers, Garbo stopped performing her love scene to growl in deep guttural accents, "Dere's a stranger-r-r on dis set. Ged-out, whoever you are!"

When Marion was hurt or depressed, she often would attempt to lift her mood through telling a story or doing a little dance or a parody of someone. Now her mimicry of Garbo was perfection, down to the last roll of the "r," although her performance was still mixed with a little pain and surprise. In *Blondie of the Follies*, she would play Garbo to Jimmy Durante's "John Barrymore," and when she tells him, "Ay vant to be alone," Durante pleads with her for just a little time together. "Garbo" concedes, "Vell, maybe for a veek."

Barring Garbo's closed set, Marion roamed rather freely through the Metro studios as a sort of semi-official hostess. Anyone who came under contract at Metro was invited to San Simeon. For this reason and others, including the number of high-caliber performers gathered under that studio roof, Metro was considered the elite place to work and its stars were a little snobbish about it.

Vidor had wanted as Marion's leading man a handsome, melancholy Irishman by the name of James Murray, who had costarred with Eleanor Boardman in *The Crowd,* a pitiless study of the grinding abrasion of love by poverty. But Murray's alcoholism (unlike Marion's, which never got out of hand during her film career) had undermined all of his discipline as an actor. When the call from Vidor came, Murray was off on a bender. He failed to show up for the part, drifted away from Hollywood, and shortly thereafter died a suicide.

With early shooting on *Show People* already begun, Vidor sought Thalberg's help in finding another suitable leading man. William Haines, who had come up with hits in *Tell It to the Marines* and *Brown of Harvard* and whose breezy optimism (before the stinger in the script caught up with him) was his trademark, was recommended and signed. Haines, with the same self-assurance off-screen he displayed in his films, later insisted that he was signed in order to give Marion's career a boost through his own recent popularity. With her success in *The Patsy* looming just ahead upon its release, this probably would not have been necessary.

Show People is the penultimate screen comedy about the movies. It is so perfect in all of its parts, it rivals *The Crowd* or *The Big Parade* in being King Vidor's finest achievement during his long career. Its humor is leavened by a genuine humanity, by a sense that this comes very close to being what Hollywood is all about. It is as evocative of a place as Chaplin's later *City Lights.* In recent years, new audiences are discovering the film. It is always included in any Vidor retrospective, and Vidor himself has come around to the view that the film has far more merit than he believed it had at the time it was made.

In it, Peggy Pepper (Marion) reaches Hollywood in a battered Model T Ford driven by her Georgia Colonel father (Dell Henderson). The Colonel drives his overdressed daughter, who is done up in ribbons and bows, to the gate at Metro-Goldwyn-Mayer only to be turned away. The early scenes of 1928 Hollywood have a tingling excitement and wry humor, almost a satirical documentary quality. The satire of the community is not broad; it is tender and sad. Marion as Peggy Pepper is warm and touching in her attempts to break into the movies. Chaplin and

Marion frequently performed together at parties, so it is probable that much of Chaplin's utilization of the small gesture, his mixture of pathos and humor, had colored Marion's acting technique.

The Colonel and his daughter meet an outgoing Mack Sennett–type comedy actor (William Haines) in a studio commissary. Billy Boone, as the actor calls himself, agrees to take her to his boss, a comedy director whose zany slapstick comes from a mind that is perilously close to the borderline of insanity. Peggy wears her finest party dress for the test scene, naively unaware that she is to be soaked by a squirting seltzer bottle. Her shock, registered on camera, gives way to tears, and she is nearly inconsolable in the dressing room, where Billy tells her she has to learn "to take it on the chin." Originally, Peggy was to have been struck by a custard pie, but Hearst refused to allow it. Vidor thought the pie was necessary and there was a conference in Louis B. Mayer's office about the matter. "You're right," Hearst told Vidor, "but I'm right, too, and I'm not going to let her be hit by a pie." The seltzer bottle was a compromise and, in one way, it was an improvement, since Peggy Pepper's pretentious, frilly costume is wrecked along with her composure.

Peggy and Billy have a romance, but her rise to prominence as a comedienne is rapid, and when she is cast in her first dramatic role, her leading man, a phony count who used to wait tables in a spaghetti joint, tells her that she is now too important to bother with the old Mack Sennett crowd; she must mingle with only "the best" of Hollywood society, since she has an image of glamour to live up to. Peggy changes her name to Patricia Pepoire, exposes her upper teeth like a rabbit gently nibbling a piece of lettuce *à la Gloria Swanson,* buys an expensive foreign limousine, a house with a foyer resembling Grand Central Station, and acquires a droll snobbish maid (Polly Moran). She stops returning Billy Boone's telephone calls and gets engaged to the phony count. At a dinner prepared by Billy in his modest kitchen, the perplexed old Colonel wonders what Hollywood is doing to his innocent daughter.

What it is doing is ruining her career. Letters come in from exhibitors complaining and asking the studio to please not send any more Patricia Pepoire features, "the public is tired of her." The sequence is a unique example of Marion's ability to laugh at herself, since it followed by only a few weeks the Philadelphia salesman's complaint about her own films. When the studio head tells her to "come down to earth and be old Peggy Pepper and give up the Patricia Pepoire business," she flounces out of his office and soon is in a wedding gown about to be married to her phony count (the publicity, he assures her, will put her on the top again). But Billy Boone comes to her home, where the wedding is to be performed; denied entry by a guard, he goes in through the back door with a laundry basket. He demands to see Peggy, and her shocked maid tells her mistress that "that low comedian is downstairs and won't go away." Peggy, in her wedding gown, goes down to the dining room where he is waiting—more at home with the pastry and custard pies. Billy tells her that she must wake up before it is too late, that she is ruining her life and career through her pretensions. She is furious at having the truth told her so harshly and picks up a custard pie to heave it at Billy, but the door opens as the phony count searches for his bride and gets the pie full in the face. Peggy suddenly sees the absurdity of it all, doubling up in laughter as her phony count gravely insists on going ahead with the ceremony, ignoring his custard-whitened face. Peggy flees the scene with Billy.

Show People was released in November, a month after Marion's return from Europe and during her preparations to enter talking pictures. (Warner Brother's *On Trial,* a talkie with Pauline Frederick, opened that same week.) Marion's movie satire was even more successful than *The Patsy,* and once again reviewers compared her with Mabel Normand, who was now nearly off the screen completely as a result of ill health and continuing repercussions following the William Desmond Taylor death. Forty years later, the Vidor satire on Hollywood would be revived at the New York Film Festival, a film-wise audience excited by their discovery of how very talented Marion was, and a few years after that it would be the opening night attraction of the most comprehensive Vidor retrospective ever shown in the United States at the Los Angeles County Art Museum.

The irony in having her last silent film reveal her to be one of the most deft comediennes in silent pictures was not lost on Marion. In the decade since *Runaway, Romany,* she had grown from a stiff mannequin into an actress who gave off as much vitality and spontaneity as anyone performing on the screen.

But her security in knowing that was gone almost as soon

as the rave reviews were pasted into her scrapbook. She was going to have to learn an entirely new medium or retire. Hearst insisted that all she would have to do in front of the sound camera was to be herself. That was not very reassuring as Marion always had needed props to keep "herself" going. Despite her reputation for gaiety, she was far from being an untroubled human being. Her love for Hearst had become more a mood than an emotional involvement; it was like a familiar room to which she could return whenever she was depressed or frightened.

She was not ready for retirement. Work at the studio kept her life in balance and, though it would be foolish and untrue to say that she did not drink at the studio bungalow, she drank less there than when she was between pictures and idle. She knew that her drinking bothered Hearst, and there were times when she drank *because* it bothered him. The bottle had become a subtle weapon when her hothouse existence became a little too much, a bit too stuffy. If she didn't have those respites from heavy drinking of her weeks at the studio, her life with Hearst might go completely out of kilter. And, too, the studio had been a retreat away from the Dourases and their problems. Rose still had her beaux, and there was always something wrong with them—they were exploiting her wealth (and that, of course, meant Marion's wealth) or they were smalltime gamblers or bootleggers. There were Rose's "martini storms" when she would break things. And by 1929, Patricia Van Cleve had been "missing" with her father for nearly five years. Marion and Hearst had spent a fortune hiring detectives who, in Marion's opinion at least, seemed to do little more than make contact somewhere —usually in the Middle West—with Pat and her father, George Van Cleve. By the time Hearst had secured a local attorney to press for the child's return, they had moved on again. Here again, one wonders if this was not all a big performance for Marion's sake or "for the record." When Hearst finally made an intelligent move toward Pat's recovery, it was accomplished quickly. There was a rumor much circulated during Marion's lifetime that Pat was really her child by Hearst. It was one of half-a-dozen such rumors and it only gains some small credence through the fact that Pat was never very close to her mother, Rose, and she (superficially at least) resembled Hearst.

Hearst decided to call in his trouble-shooting editor Walter Howey to help recover Marion's niece. Howey was a gruff veteran of the Hearst press and an archetypal city-room man who had inspired the central character in the play *The Front Page:* Adela Rogers St. Johns described Howey as having one glass eye. "We assumed," she wrote, "that someone had shot it out during the back alley circulation war when he was on the Chicago *Tribune* before Mr. Hearst lured him away. It was hard to tell which was the glass one. Ben Hecht said it was the *warmer* one, and finally Jack Clements, Howey's favorite reporter, asked the undertaker, but that was too late to do anybody any good." Howey's approach to the problem was simple and direct. He traced Van Cleve and his daughter to a current address and offered him an editorial job at $500 per week, which was still cheaper than the retainer fee at the detective agency.

With Mama Rose gone, Papa Ben soon would retire from the bench and come West to join Marion's other "problem-children" among the Dourases. As long as Marion lived, there would be something happening to her family that had to be remedied either financially, medically, or emotionally. She was always drawn to help them, and if she retired she would be totally available. Her motives to succeed in talking pictures were much stronger than any she ever had had to advance on the stage or in her early movies, but, curiously, they were to be blunted by the new physical working environment of the "sound stage." Marion never would be able to adjust to its requirements, its inhibiting demands for "silence on the set."

X

The Broadway Melody opened at New York's Astor Theatre on a two-a-day schedule on February 8, 1929, a week after its gala premiere at Grauman's Chinese in Hollywood. According to Benjamin B. Hampton in his *History of the American Film Industry* (first published in 1931, less than two years after the event), Hearst had produced it, although it was released without the Cosmopolitan trademark. Possibly it was only partially a Hearst film since Irving Thalberg had taken a personal interest in it and reworked it.

While its backstage story is threadbare, *Broadway Melody* had a number of assets besides being the first musical film to come out of Hollywood. There were three durable song hits: *You Were Meant for Me;* the title tune; and *The Wedding of the*

Painted Doll, a number filmed in Technicolor not quite as satisfactory as that Hearst had used in two sequences of Marion's *Lights of Old Broadway* four years earlier when the color process was first introduced. Not every critic endorsed the musical. Mordaunt Hall in *The Times* said it was "raucous, talking, singing and quarreling." But it made a great deal of money.

Several months later, in *The Hollywood Revue of 1929,* Hearst attempted to duplicate in films what Ziegfeld had achieved in the theater. A collection of skits, blackouts, and songs and dances with no overall theme, it still emerged with considerable style. There were twenty songs used, the best of which, *Singing in the Rain,* survives. Most critics considered the film an advance over *Broadway Melody,* and Marion was surrounded by her fellow Metro stars: Norma Shearer, Joan Crawford, John Gilbert, Lionel Barrymore, Laurel and Hardy, Buster Keaton, Cliff "Ukelele Ike" Edwards, and Marie Dressler.

Marion's particular contribution to the film was a dance number with a chorus of men dressed as Grenadier guards. At the opening, she is a lilliputian figure among brobdingnagian soldiers, but she grows up to natural size—one of several technical effects employed in the film. She was also in the chorus in a yellow slicker for *Singing in the Rain.*

The week *The Hollywood Revue* opened, Hearst was deeply involved in the details surrounding the Hearst-Zeppelin "flight around the world." He had hired Lady Drummond Hay, Karl von Wiegand, and the arctic explorer Sir Hubert Wilkins as flight correspondents who would be "flashing daily news dispatches," informing the world of what was happening during the flight from the *Graf Zeppelin's* berth at Friedrichshafen to Tokyo. As a small boy in Des Moines, Iowa, I was taken to see the musical film on a Saturday and later that month watched the *Graf Zeppelin* ponderously move across the skies over my town—thus the pervasiveness of Hearst's enterprises in American life at the time. In New York City or a dozen other places visited by the dirigible, I might have added a third: I could have read about what I had seen in a Hearst newspaper.

Marion's life in 1929 resembles a speeded-up silent film from this distance in time. Her days were more than crowded; they were frenetic. The fight over niece Pat's custody had not turned out to be a simple one. Van Cleve was not happy over his daughter's absence, even with a high-salaried job as compen-

sation. Because of Rose's continuing misbehavior and alcoholism, Van Cleve left his position with the Hearst press and won
a court order at San Simeon returning custody of Pat to him.
However, before he could reach the entrance to the castle, word
was received there that he was on his way with legal papers. Pat
and her Aunt Ethel got on horseback, with Marion frantically
urging them to ride into the hills. "He'll never find you out
there," Marion told them—words that soon began troubling the
runaways as they rode deeper into the wilderness. They came
back to the castle under the cover of darkness to find Van Cleve
waiting for them, and father and daughter again disappeared.

That was in August, and then on Friday the thirteenth of
September, Winston Churchill and his eighteen-year-old son
Randolph visited San Simeon. Churchill had been out of office
(as Chancellor of the Exchequer) since May, when a Labour
government had come into office. Hearst informed Marion that
he would have to let Millicent preside at the castle for that weekend and that he would bring the Churchills down to the beach
house later the following week.

Predictably, this did not especially please Marion. She had a
fairly wild party that Saturday, knowing that they would not be
visited by Hearst. Late in the evening, Marion was heard to say
that the Churchills "should have come down here. They'd have
had a lot more fun." She was not far wrong. Randolph, in his
memoir on his growing up years, recalls that Millicent Hearst
was "quite too charming." He also writes: "Old Mrs. Hearst tonight made a most wonderful remark which shows that even the
nicest people out here suffer from megalomania and overween-
ing pride. Speaking of Arthur Brisbane—Hearst's right-hand
man and who writes syndicated leaders for all the yellow press—
she said, 'The relationship between Voltaire and Frederick the
Great is not unlike that between Brisbane and Mr. Hearst.' "

On Wednesday, Hearst kept his word and brought the
Churchills to Los Angeles. They were taken directly to the Metro
studios for a lunch hosted jointly by Hearst and Mayer. "There
were about 200 people at the lunch," Randolph recalls, "mostly
film stars and producers. We met Marion Davies—Colleen Moore
—Anita Page—Joan Crawford—Douglas Fairbanks, Jr.—Ramon
Novarro, and many others of whom I had not heard. I thought
Marion Davies was the most attractive. After lunch during which
an orchestra of about 20 played continuously, various stars appeared on a stage at the far end of the room and performed. It

really was astounding. They had a beauty chorus of 25 all of
them infinitely more attractive than the best in London. A man
sang who is paid a thousand pounds a night in New York and
there were various other turns of exceptionally high order."
When Churchill made a little gracious speech, a man proposed a
vote of thanks and said, "I can only say that I would like to hear
it again, and I dare say Mr. Churchill could bear a little of it!"
and through a hole in the roof, it was all played back again.

Whatever vestige remained of Hearst's much-touted "anti-
British" feeling was nonexistent during the Churchills' stay. He
was completely won over by the elder Churchill, and when he
was told that Churchill would enjoy the proceedings more if the
speeches were kept to a minimum, Hearst said it was "like the
man who did not take his wife abroad as he was going for pleasure." Randolph especially found this a rich remark, "Considering
that he had just left Mrs. Hearst and was in Los Angeles with
his mistress—Marion Davies. . . ."

The following afternoon, the Churchills went to Marion's
beach house to swim, Randolph describing it as

> a magnificent place looking on the sea, with a wonderful
> marble swimming bath of great length and very well heated
> —all provided by William Randolph. Marion had collected
> a dinner party of 60 for us. . . . The stars included Pola
> Negri, Charlie Chaplin, Harold Lloyd, Billie Dove and Diana
> Ellis. I failed to recognize either Charlie or Harold, since
> moustache and horn-rimmed spectacles were missing.
>
> After dinner we danced and then Marion stimulated
> Charlie into doing some impersonations. She did Sarah
> Bernhardt and Lillian Gish, and then he did Napoleon,
> Uriah Heep, Henry Irving, John Barrymore as Hamlet and
> many others. He is absolutely superb and enchanted every-
> one. He also did terribly complicated patter dancing as also
> did Marion. She is delightfully stimulating and must have
> danced and frolicked around for about 1½ hours after a
> hard day's work.

The Churchills wound up their stay in California with a
fishing excursion on Hearst's yacht, followed by a premiere party
thrown by Marion for the movie starring Victor McLaglen and
Edmund Lowe, *The Cockeyed World*, which Randolph called "the
worst film I have ever seen," although it was a huge success commercially. The French boxing champion Georges Carpentier was

a guest along with Chaplin and everyone of any importance in the film world.

Marion had been impressed by Churchill's down-to-earthness, and they had shared a wink over their seventh or eighth drink in the beach house, a wink that said that they were drinking mates. Several years later, she and Hearst would be invited to go down from London to Chartwell, Churchill's estate, where she was particularly taken with Churchill's plebeian hobby of laying bricks. She would refer to him always as having had "the common touch," and she was thinking of his decided taste for gin, that brick wall he had put up around his estate, and the many perfectly understandable and representational paintings he had done of landscapes, apples, and an occasional gin bottle.

Two of Churchill's swans got into a fight while Marion watched, horrified. "Oh, you bally bloaters!" Churchill shouted, and he began picking up stones and throwing them at the combatants. When blood began to flow, Marion ran to the house, and in a few minutes, Churchill came in with the news that one was dead. "Why do you have swans that fight?" Marion wanted to know, and Churchill said, "Just show me one that doesn't fight."

One of Marion's difficulties as a film queen was the gossip about her wealth. Much of the public had been surfeited with references in the fan magazines and movie columns to her jewelry, the number of her servants, or how many bathrooms she had. The extent of her charities was not sufficiently publicized to counteract this. Just ahead was an economic convulsion in the country that would intensify this situation and there is small doubt but that public resentment of her lifestyle contributed to her film decline in the 1930s. But by now she was too immersed in her gilded environment to notice how unique it all was—she had been living in luxury for well over a decade. And Hearst, with such a sensitive finger on the public pulse in other directions, was even more out of touch with the average man's lot than Marion was. During the reckless twenties, he never questioned the indices of "prosperity" for a moment, no doubt needing to believe in them. Almost alone among America's wealthiest men, he seemed to have no guilty conscience over being rich.

They were insulated not only by money but by Marion's deep involvement in costly Metro productions. In October 1929, on the day of the Wall Street Crash, Marion's first full-length talking picture, *Marianne,* opened in New York. It had been inspired by

King Vidor's popular film of World War I, *The Big Parade,* and Hearst had asked that film's author, Laurence Stallings, who had also written *The Patsy,* to write the dialogue for it. What emerged was an extraordinary musical comedy brightened by Marion's cool wit and, incongruously at times, put aside in favor of the new realism then beginning to exert an influence on films. But in *Marianne,* the "doughboys" of Stallings seemed to have girls on their minds rather than the Germans, which was doubtless quite true in many cases, although it gave a comic opera aspect to what was essentially a world tragedy—Hearst's pleasure once again in things military overriding his judgment.

The film had been begun even before Marion had done her routine in *The Hollywood Revue,* and she had insisted that she was not yet ready to do a talkie. She did an entirely silent version with Oscar Shaw as her leading man. Before its release, sound was almost universally accepted—at least in all the major first-run houses—so, following *The Hollywood Revue,* Marion was forced to repeat her role, this time with Lawrence Gray in the lead (for reasons unknown, since Oscar Shaw was a veteran of Broadway musicals and had a perfectly acceptable speaking and singing voice). Both versions were released, the silent one distributed to the small towns and villages not yet equipped for sound. Only the talking version survives today.

In an effort to keep the war in some kind of solemn perspective, Marianne is given a French lover, André, whom she believes dead in battle, but who returns blinded by the war. The American doughboy gives up Marianne in a heroic gesture which Stallings and his collaborator, Gladys Unger, ensure is only temporary. For laughs, there is Marion's fractured English (she was to speak her first words on the screen with a pronounced French accent); a baby pig; and comics Benny Rubin and Cliff "Ukelele Ike" Edwards. Gray was given a love song to sing *Just You, Just Me,* and it became a standard. Hearst was so insistent in seeing that only the best talents he could find went into Marion's films that her composers were the most successful in the field. There was at least one popular standard coming out of nearly every one of her talking pictures.

Irene Thirer writing in the *Daily News* said that Marion was a joy. "The dialogue prepared for her is screamingly funny . . . dandy entertainment." The *Times* man, Mordaunt Hall, was more reserved than usual, complaining about her pronunciation of French, but he conceded that it "drew waves of merriment from the audience." Marguerite Tazelaar wrote in the *New York Herald Tribune*, "Miss Davies gives an emotional performance of such genuineness and yet restraint that it turns the prankish comedy for a moment into tragedy—heart-breaking, lyrical tragedy." Hearst needed none of his staff tub-thumpers to beat the drum for Marion now that she had a voice. The non-Hearst press was doing it for him, and the reviews in other cities were much the same. It was a week of triumph for Marion while the nation was plunging into the deepest depression it had ever known.

PART FIVE

MR. SHAW'S FAVORITE BLONDE

I

The Great Depression did not alter Marion's and Hearst's life-style to any detectable degree. The spending went on. While a number of poorly managed newspapers and a few excellent ones folded in the United States between 1929 and 1933, none of the Hearst papers was lost. Studs Terkel, writing in his brilliant documentary of the Depression, *Hard Times,* recalls one instance of a long and critical strike against Hearst's *Chicago Herald-Examiner.*

> Outside the building [he writes] journalists picketed. The Hearst delivery trucks were manned by a hard lot; some I remembered as alumni of my high school; some with syndicate friendships. They were employed in a dual capacity: as delivery men and as terrorists. Whenever the situation presented itself, they'd slug a journalist-picket . . . a pale, bloodied reporter lying on the pavement as colleagues and passersby stare in horror. In the middle of the street stands a squat heavyweight, an auto jack in his grasp. His arms and legs are spread-eagled. He appears to be challenging all comers. Yet I see, quite unblurred, the terror in his eyes.

This sort of violence went on far from San Simeon and seldom, if ever, was noted on secretary Joe Willicombe's clipboard of important messages for Hearst. But it is impossible to believe that Hearst was ignorant of it. He was the extremely sensitive and vulnerable child of his late mother when he felt he could expose what he considered to be his true self, but from his distant mountaintop he could manage never to be touched by the bloodshed and injuries wrought by a Hearst policy many miles away. Expanding his philanthropies, he was spending a fortune on breadlines during the Depression. The most spectacular one was in New York City, but there were smaller ones in Chicago and Los Angeles. Song writer Yip Harburg remembers—also in *Hard Times*—a skit in a musical in which Mrs. Ogden Reid, of the *Herald-Tribune,* is jealous of Hearst's "beautiful bread line."

It was bigger than her own, and Harburg and Jay Gorney wrote a song for the skit which echoed a phrase heard on every street corner in America at the time, *"Brother, Can You Spare a Dime."*

Hearst's fortune remained at around $200 million although some of it was mortgaged then and would be increasingly as the 1930s advanced. Marion's personal fortune was in the several millions—a conservative estimate places it at five million, but others insist that it was at least twice that—some of it in jewelry and bonds, but a good deal in real estate in Beverly Hills and New York. Her Children's Clinic had become a busy reality, and she was continuing her casual charities at the studio, underwriting an eye operation for a cross-eyed young prop man at Metro, sending her cook's child Mary Grace to a finishing school, paying the family's expenses for a movie technician injured and laid off, and there were always several down-on-their-luck ex-vaudevillians who considered Marion a "soft touch." Some of the prouder ones like Joe Frisco, the stuttering comic, never had to come around for a handout. Marion would get in touch with them to see how they were doing. Frisco was an inveterate gambler and, when Marion asked if he was all right, he told her that he was about to be thrown out of his apartment because his rent was in arrears. He said that with five hundred dollars he could satisfy the landlord and not suffer such a humiliation. Marion wrote out a check for $1,000 and handed it to the comic, who immediately rushed to the nearest poker table and proceeded to lose it all. When a friend told her what had happened, Marion made out another check for the rent and told her informant, "Wh-whatever J-J-Joe does with it, it's all right with m-m-me. It's his m-m-money."

Hearst was diversified long before the term became economically fashionable. He had 28 newspapers, 13 magazines, 8 radio stations, 2 movie companies (Cosmopolitan Pictures and Hearst–Metrotone News), New York, California and Mexican real estate, 14,000 shares of Homestake mining preferred stock (which had been the nucleus of his father's fortune), as well as his huge herds of cattle and his personal treasures. However, he was still in the habit of spending to the very limit and borrowing beyond that. In a sense, he was a country unto himself with his own built-in economic stresses and strains, and by the late 1930s he would suffer his own personal depression at a time when

Roosevelt's Herculean efforts to turn the economic tide in the country were paying off.

In 1930, a fire destroyed the old "castle" at Wyntoon. It had been his mother Phoebe's original home there, and Hearst was distraught. He immediately dispatched little Miss Morgan to go over the ruins, and she began the lavish Bavarian village that rose in the pine forest there. Hearst wanted a fairy-tale atmosphere, and Miss Morgan achieved this with Bear House ("Papa Bear" and "Mama Bear"), where Hearst and Marion would stay, away from the other guests. And there was Cinderella House with Willy Pogany murals on the *outside* walls; a large building called The Bend farther down the McCloud River; River House; and The Gables, where guests were entertained and fed.

According to some of Marion's friends, she liked the unbroken peacefulness of Wyntoon very much, but grew restless if her stay was prolonged. Others insist that she was nearly always bored there and denigrated it, calling it "Spittoon." Hearst seemed as much at home there as he did in his cherished castle. Some of the most relaxed snapshots of the couple were taken at Wyntoon cookouts. Hearst himself would hand out the hotdogs, and there is a serenity visible in Marion not seen on any of the European trips and rarely at San Simeon.

In looking back on those years when his Aunt Marion was in her prime, Charlie Lederer recalls the mood of the time more distinctly than specific events. Early in 1930, the mood was jazzy and fulfilling. Marion ran from one movie (*Not So Dumb* with three leading men) to another (*The Floradora Girl*). What kept it from becoming exhausting was her sense of freedom on a movie set; there, she was truly out of her cage, and then, too, the reviews from every corner were glowing. Her basic insecurity would return, however, as she left the studio gates and whenever she read some "outside" favorable comment on her acting in *The New York Times* or elsewhere, she couldn't wait until Hearst had read it, too.

In *The Floradora Girl*, she was teamed again with Lawrence Gray, and he was becoming such a fixture in her films, there was talk of an affair. Gray was undeniably handsome, having a sober gravity that nicely complemented Marion's perkiness—there was still a bubbly effervescence about her, a holdover from the twenties. Still under a doctor's care, Hearst may have looked the other way during this dalliance, and Gray later married one of the Figueroa sisters.

The New York writer and sometime actress Ilka Chase was in the cast of *The Floradora Girl,* and in her autobiography she writes:

> ...when Hearst kept his finger out of the pie, things went very well. Harry Beaumont, who directed ... devised a simple and ingenious trick for keeping the boss from underfoot. When the red light is on outside the door of a sound stage it means a scene is shooting, and God himself can't come in. Harry posted scouts at all the approaches to the stage, and as Mr. Hearst advanced upon it, he would promptly order the doors closed and would then rehearse his scene in peace while the mighty one cooled his heels. There was one sequence, however, where this ruse failed. The "Tell Me, Pretty Maiden" scene was shot in *glorious* technicolor, and because of the blazing lights the stage got so hell-hot the doors couldn't be kept closed longer than five minutes at a time, and in would nip old Nosey Parker.

Marion's decline in popularity was steady but not alarming. Both she and Hearst believed that she was solidly established in the talkies. She had made a long series of excellent comedies, nearly long enough, but not quite, to give her a substantial niche among Hollywood's legendary stars. There were no audible murmurs of protest from Metro salesmen as her comedy-dramas with incidental music went into release. They played the major Loew houses such as New York's Capitol, and often there would be lines during their runs there. They were nearly all brightly written and crisply edited so that few audiences were bored during a Davies film. There were other stars faring much worse. Among them was the legendary Broadway dancing star Marilyn Miller. The most dedicated of artists, she had become New York's darling and the brightest dancing star in America. She had been one of Marion's classmates at both Kosloff's and Ned Wayburn's. Marion recalled trying to "out-dance her" and failing. Now they met as fellow stars when the dancer came for tea at Marion's bungalow on the Metro lot. Unexpectedly, Miss Miller had been badly handled during her brief try at the movies. She was poorly photographed, possibly because someone believed that her gossamer quality might best be captured by underlighting, and she became one of Hollywood's most surprising failures. After a year or so, the famous star of *Sunny* and *Sally* returned to Broadway, where she was again a smash in *As Thousands Cheer*. During her Hollywood stay, she had become attracted to Marion's nephew Charlie, then a very urbane young member of the "Algonquin Round Table West," hanging out with Dorothy Parker, Ben Hecht, Charlie MacArthur, and Herman Mankiewicz. He was a singular youth, prematurely balding and with an equally premature disenchantment with the more serious philosophies of life. He felt that his mind was given a far more perceptive view of life by standing on his head than by reading Santayana. Like Marion, he felt that sober-sided citizens should be sent to Siberia or at least to Keokuk. Miss Miller, who resembled a twinkle-toed fairy on the stage, was drawn to Charlie's inverted and refreshing sense of values, but she was also the target of some of his wry comment. Before leaving Hollywood, she attempted to convince him that he had no rival for her affections, but he was sure that he had and told her that her denial was so much "horseshit," underscoring his hurt feelings by having a truck-load of steaming horse manure piled below her hotel windows. Then back in New York, according to Ben Hecht, he dined with her at the exclusive Colony Club and sat "listening owlishly to a lecture from her on how to live properly. It was necessary, she said, to get up before noon and find some work to do. As the lovely girl came to a finish in her discourse on right living, Charles, who had sat seemingly spellbound, arose and handed her his trousers. He had removed them surreptitiously during her lecture. 'Here,' he said, 'you wear these,' and walked coldly out of the restaurant in his shorts."

At Marion's bungalow, the ceremonial visits never ceased. Former President Calvin Coolidge and his wife Grace were touring the United States in the Summer of 1930 and came to Hollywood at Hearst's personal invitation. Lunching in Marion's bungalow, Marion slipped Coolidge, a teetotaler, a glass of Tokay wine, thinking it a great joke. She told him that it was a fruit drink, which it was, and he liked the tumbler-full so very much, he asked for another and even a third. "I don't know when I've had anything as satisfying as that," he told her.

Marion and Grace Coolidge made an interesting contrast. Marion so spirited and winning in her extralegal role by Hearst's side and Mrs. Coolidge attempting to be jolly and nearly succeeding, *and* tactfully accepting Marion as Hearst's companion without a hint that it was not completely respectable. Invited to San Simeon, the Coolidges arrived just as a storm was breaking. Mrs. Coolidge, doubtless exhausted by the "grand tour" of the premises, its treasures and exotic creatures, wanted to retire right after dinner. They had been given the "Celestial Suite"—magnificent rooms in one of the towers with broad expanses of glass on three sides, affording a breathtaking view of the Pacific and the mountains north and south of the castle. The storm broke as the ex-First Lady was ascending to the Celestial region in the intimate two-person elevator. All of the lights went out at the same time, but candles were brought quickly to the scene so that Coolidge could reassure his wife. He stood on a winding stone staircase nearby and told her, "They're fixing it. The lights will be on soon, dear." And Mrs. Coolidge, much cooler than her husband, said, "It's all right. I'm perfectly happy." The storm continued all night and it is unlikely the former President or his wife got much sleep since the tower rooms were designed to include the skies outside —now split by bolts of lightning—as part of the atmosphere. Possibly longing for the quieter meadows of Vermont, the Coolidges departed the next morning.

Marion appeared to enjoy such visits, but she much preferred the intimate, congenial parties where there were no dignitaries. On April 16, 1930, on the occasion of Charlie Chaplin's and Fifi D'Orsay's birthday, a very old friend turned up—Flo Ziegfeld, without his wife Billie Burke. Ziegfeld repeatedly told Hearst how proud he was of "discovering" Marion, and graciously included Fifi in his compliments, telling her that she reminded him of Anna Held.

As Marion's position in films became increasingly unstable, it would seem that she didn't care very much whether "school kept or not," since she and Hearst would shut down production for a yachting cruise or a two-week trip to Mexico. But there is strong evidence that she cared very much about her role as film star. She was known by her directors as a perfectionist. Always early on the set, she left late, after viewing the daily rushes and agonizing over them. Those who thought she took her career lightly overlooked her professionalism. All of the "high-jinks" were now engaged in only between takes, and when "Miss Davies" was called to the set, the respect felt by all the crew and cast as she stepped into the shooting area was genuine and spontaneous. Some of her directors were a little afraid of her, possibly because she had more power than the average leading lady. She had matured in films right alongside Hearst and after more than thirty films she knew a great deal about every phase of production. She ran "Marion Davies Productions" with a firm hand and even Hearst always deferred to her judgment.

She felt fiercely competitive about certain other Metro leading ladies, especially Norma Shearer. With the release of *A Free Soul,* in which Miss Shearer played a sensual young society girl taken with a roughneck (Clark Gable), an intense rivalry surfaced between the two studio "queens." The rivalry was first felt by Miss Shearer (who had become Mrs. Irving Thalberg) as early as 1928 when it was announced in the annual "press book" of forthcoming Metro productions that Norma Shearer would star in *Polly of the Circus.* Marion and Hearst complained to Thalberg that Marion was much more suited to the role of the circus girl with the tough exterior than Miss Shearer ever could be. Four years later, Marion did the role as a talkie. But *Polly* proved to be a token concession by Thalberg and, in the early 1930s, Marion discovered that the best properties at Metro were no longer available to her, that they were all presented first to Miss Shearer for her consideration. Marion did not immediately realize what was happening. The production chief had been more enthusiastic than anyone else about Marion's dramatic performance in *Quality Street* and he had been instrumental in getting the services of director Sidney Franklin for that film and for *Beverly of Graustark,* which had preceded it. It was a role far closer to Miss Shearer's later tear-drenched performance as Marie Antoinette and more convincing than any critics have had the wisdom to point out.

But Thalberg's first loyalty was to his wife after she showed herself to be an exciting leading lady. Finding the best parts for her available anywhere became a major preoccupation with him. The effect of this policy on Thalberg's part was that there was a subtle but visible decline in the quality of Marion's scripts beginning in 1931 and continuing throughout the last of her Metro years. It was one of Thalberg's few mistakes (there were others, such as his mishandling of Scott Fitzgerald and other gifted writers) and has never been mentioned in print before because most film critics have never compared a comprehensive body of Marion's films with Miss Shearer's and because there have been few dispassionate studies of Thalberg's life and career.

There were a number of stage hits emerging at this time—the Hecht and MacArthur comedy, *Twentieth Century,* for example, admirably suited Marion's talents, but none of them reached her hands as screen properties. Her films were all discovered either by Hearst or herself in magazine stories, the melodramatic novels of Robert Chambers, all of which seemed to have been optioned by Hearst, or twenty-five-year-old plays (*Peg O' My Heart*) which Hearst still considered worth remaking. And a case can be made for Thalberg's situation at the time. Nominally, the Marion Davies film unit (Cosmopolitan) functioned as a separate entity and had total freedom to pick its own properties. The trouble was that over the years at Metro, Hearst had come to rely increasingly upon Thalberg's own story editors. It was a wise decision until Norma Shearer emerged from the ranks of ordinary leading ladies into being a front-rank movie queen with *A Free Soul,* and Thalberg invested a great deal of his time and energy in seeing that she remained up there.

There was little malice in this rivalry, even though Marion took great satisfaction from seeing reviews that praised her performances—sometimes in second-rate material. She always hoped that Miss Shearer would see the notices. The ladies continued to meet socially, and at one of Marion's and Hearst's great parties on his birthday, Miss Shearer arrived wearing the costume and white wig of Marie Antoinette, although the party was supposed to be American in theme. Her skirt was of such width, one of the doors at the beach house had to be removed before she could enter.

Thalberg, unlike Hearst, rarely carried his private life over into his movie work. But Miss Shearer was the exception, and nearly every major stage and book property with a substantial feminine role was earmarked for her. The silent rivalry went unnoticed outside of Metro, but the other leading ladies and men there as well as Mayer and the top production staff knew about it. Sometimes, open hostility would erupt between Hearst and Thalberg as it did over cuts in *Five O'Clock Girl,* a musical film by Guy Bolton and Fred Thompson with music by Bert Kalmar and Harry Ruby, and with Charles King of *Broadway Melody* fame as Marion's leading man. Marion's performance in this should have been vintage Davies, since it was the sort of thing she did so well and she was in complete command of her talent, but there was a quarrel over the rough cut of the film and Louis B. Mayer ordered it permanently shelved. There is no print of this picture in Marion's own collection and possibly the negative was destroyed.

II

Sometime in the middle of 1931, Marion, Hearst, and Harry Crocker were spending a quiet weekend at the castle when a transatlantic phone call came through for Hearst. "You take it, Harry," Hearst said, since that was a time when Crocker was often on the staff as Hearst's personal aide.

Crocker returned and, through fits of laughter, told Hearst that there was a syndicate of men in London whose spokesman wanted to know if Hearst would like to buy London Bridge. Crocker and Marion both stopped laughing when it appeared that Hearst was seriously considering the offer. Today, of course, London Bridge spans an artificial river at Lake Havasu, Arizona, having been purchased by a syndicate of promoters in the United States. What finally changed Hearst's mind about it seemed to be that his only river-front property was Wyntoon, and its Bavarian architecture would scarcely go with London Bridge.

His largest purchase that year was a turreted Norman-style estate at Sands Point, Long Island, for Millicent. It was huge and graceless, but it somehow satisfied both his wife's sense of fair play, since she no longer was especially welcome at San Simeon except for very special occasions, and Hearst's guilt pangs, which were minimal by this time. It was the least of his castles and he would spend even less time there than at St. Donat's abroad.

San Simeon was the hub of his business empire and his social life with Marion. There was even a rather rigid propriety at work there and certain ceremonies were carried out—state dinners for visiting nabobs, riding excursions into the mountain fastness, movies right after dinner—with any upset to this ritual deeply disconcerting to Hearst. One such episode occurred later that summer with the arrival of a yacht owned by a French Baron, who knew one of Marion's friends in France. According to Henri d'Arrast, a director who had become a member of the castle's inner circle along with Crocker, Eddie Kane, and Lloyd Pantages and who was to marry Eleanor Boardman following her divorce from King Vidor, the Baron had murdered his father in order to get his inheritance. After hearing this, Hearst declined to join the others at luncheon on the yacht. Marion went chiefly out of curiosity, but was disturbed by the sudden appearance on deck of a young French girl no more than fourteen years old, wearing a sailor suit. The Baron ordered her below, but her presence made the yacht and its owner even more sinister than before. That night, Marion told the Baron that she was sorry that there was no room for the Baron's party at the castle. In fact, she asked the Baron if he could accommodate a couple of her own guests. Lloyd Pantages volunteered to sleep aboard the yacht, but he soon regretted it for in the middle of the night there was a piercing scream, and he rushed topside where he learned that the fourteen-year-old girl was being raped in turn by all hands. The explanation for this bizarre occurrence was as peculiar as the act itself. The child had begun to take a bath but she had failed to turn off the water, and the tub was overflowing. When the water threatened the safety of the ship, the sailors broke into the bathroom, and it was at that moment that they all set upon her and she began screaming.

The experience unhinged the girl, and she was pronounced insane by a psychiatrist, who said that she would have to go to a sanitarium. By this time, the Baron and his party had sailed out of San Simeon Harbor on their way back to France. Within a day or two, word reached Marion that the psychiatrist himself had attacked the girl. Hearst, who had kept his distance from the entire group, was appalled by this turn of events and contacted the district attorney. County officials located some of her family in France, and she was sent home. When the matter was nearly forgotten, Hearst received a bill from the mind doctor for $6000, and Marion told him not to pay it, that the doctor had raped the patient and surely that was sufficient reason not to pay. But by this time Hearst was used to paying off all sorts of weird creatures just to keep scandal away, and doubtless he paid the rapist-psychiatrist as well.

The French baron later allegedly became an acquaintance of heiress Barbara Hutton, who seemed to have a penchant for attracting unusual characters to her side at that point in her life. In any case, Miss Hutton had made a great splash in the tabloids at the time, following her debut in 1930 at a $60,000 supper dance and several years of expensive wilfullness during adolescence when she bought her own private railroad car and a New York penthouse. In 1931, she was presented at the

Court of St. James's; and she was the probable inspiration of a story by Fannie Hurst about a dime-store heiress and her family, unhappy all, entitled appropriately *Five and Ten*. The story was bought for Marion and one of Metro's most popular slick directors, Robert Z. Leonard, was signed to stage it.

The theme was not a new one—that of the rich having no positive goals and drifting into profound unhappiness as a result —and Marion, in the part of the heiress, Jennifer Rarick, was forced by her part to be *down* much of the time, so her usual *champagne sec* style was curbed. The story itself was a faint echo of the later highly stylized and vigorous *Citizen Kane*, except that it focused on the empty-headed, vapid heroine rather than the tycoon. Jennifer is winsome, stupid in an appealing way, and restless, as she tries to break out of her boredom. Despite the limitations of the part itself, Marion is convincing. The happy ending is almost impossible. Leslie Howard, in the role of the architect with whom Jennifer has fallen in love, rushes to the dockside (as Jennifer's boat is about to leave for Europe) to finally declare his love for her, with absolutely no motivation except that she has persuaded him to seduce her earlier but he has married another. But then his bride has ludicrously offered to sell him to the Raricks for their daughter for $100,000 and he has lost faith in her. *The New York Times* said that "A somber contemplation of the above [story] suggests that without Miss Davies and Mr. Howard 'Five and Ten' would be only a something reminiscent of the old flickering days of the movies. But the two are supported by a good cast—Irene Rich, Richard Bennett, Lee Beranger and Mary Duncan among them— and manage to move the picture along its bright way until almost the end." Audiences came and approved. The film made some money for Hearst and Metro.

It was now routine on a Davies picture to rehearse at the castle. There had been a magnificent little theater there for several years with walls paneled in red brocade and a private telephone for Hearst next to his front row seat. When Leslie Howard arrived at the castle theater for their first rehearsal, Marion was dismayed to discover how short he was. Unhappily, she rarely kept such disappointments to herself and when Howard heard about it he stood on a platform for their love scenes, without a trace of vanity.

Some of her friends recall that there was a small romance with Howard during the filming, although it must have been dif-

ficult for him since Mrs. Howard, a very gay and sociable lady,
had come along. Doubtless Mrs. Howard must have been indulgent, for Marion did show all the signs of being deeply infatuated, the British lady aware that her husband's contract would
be up in a matter of a few months. Howard enjoyed teasing
Marion, and he would jump into the splendid Roman outdoor
pool and say he couldn't come out because he had lost his trunks.
Mrs. Howard, who humored him, told him he was a "bad boy"
and ordered him to come out. As an actor, Howard was easy, effortless, and, as Marion said, his dialogue came out of him just
like ordinary conversation. *Five and Ten* helped to establish
Howard in American films less than three years before his great
hit in *Of Human Bondage*. His sure professionalism was to give
Marion lasting confidence. By the time of his death in a lost air-
craft during World War II, she was out of touch with him, but
she felt his death keenly.

Sister Rose, possibly following in Marion's footsteps once
again, had been seeing a great deal of the publisher Edward
Beale McLean. In the summer of 1931 McLean was in Riga, Lat-
via, attempting to get a divorce from Evalyn Walsh McLean.
Marion stood by Rose's side as Rose held a press conference an-
nouncing her impending marriage to McLean. But a hitch developed and the divorce was never finalized. For the next decade,
until McLean's death in 1941, Rose spent most of her time with
the publisher, staying with him whenever he was in California
and visiting him in the East. When McLean died of a heart attack ten years after his alliance with Rose, he left her $300,000
and described her in his will as "my common-law wife, who has
given me her association and affection." Mrs. McLean, who was
wealthy in her own right and the owner of the Hope Diamond,
was left only her dower rights. It was her second financial blow
in the past decade—in 1933 she had given the embezzler Gaston
B. Means $250,000, believing that it would result in the safe
recovery of the kidnapped Lindbergh baby, who was soon thereafter found dead. But for Rose, the legacy represented the largest
fortune she was ever to receive at one time even though Marion
gave her several times that during their lifetimes. Rose had won
a publisher of her own and become his heir.

Marion pretended not to notice Rose's fierce competitive-
ness. Hearst, however, was very upset about the whole affair. He
saw it as a flagrant parody of his relationship with Marion.

In September 1931, Rose's affair receded into the background
as the Federal Bureau of Revenue climaxed months of investigation into Marion's tax situation by demanding that she pay over
a million dollars owed for previous years, including penalties. It
has been said by many of Marion's friends that she was generous
to such a degree she had to be restrained from giving away her
fortune. What the government failed to recognize was that she
had given away all of her available cash—or perhaps they
wanted to be the chief recipient. She went by train to Washington, one of three trips there, and spent a day wrangling with tax
officials over deductions for makeup and trips by car in connection with her screen work. The government refused to allow her
any of the normal deductions granted an actress and Marion
probably rightly believed that she was being made the victim of
a political vendetta by a tax commissioner who was out to establish that she was not legitimately an actress at all, but something
like a paid companion. It made her ill to think about it, and she
hurriedly left the interrogation room to run to the ladies' wash-
room, where she vomited for several minutes. One of the secretaries came down to see if she was all right and commiserated
with her for a short time before running back to inform the commissioner that Miss Davies was ill. When she returned to the room,
the commissioner told Marion that he was prepared to let her off
if she would hand over a certified check for $950,000 and an-
other one for the penalties totaling nearly $100,000.

Since she had given away nearly all that she had in her
checking account, it would take several weeks to sell the necessary bonds, some of her jewelry and a parcel or two of her real
estate, so she phoned Louis B. Mayer and told him what she
needed. She said that she would work for a year or two for nothing, if he would send on the check. Mayer complied, and Marion
actually worked for a year and a half at no salary at a time when
she was going from one production right on to another.

This personal harassment did not alter her custom of continuing to give away much of her income. She sent off a $1000
check to Actors' Equity telling them, "If there are similar evils
[to what then existed on the stage] in the moving picture business, I hope that Equity will be able to correct them."

But with the year nearly over, there was still another shock
ahead for Marion. During the Christmas holidays, she came
close to being the victim in a homicide attempt. On December

21, she asked her butler to open a small parcel wrapped in brown paper that had been among a pile of gifts meant for needy children. The address had been typed by someone who could not spell properly and this vaguely bothered her. It was labeled "Personal Only for Marion Davies." Inside the wrapping was a casket such as jewelry might be kept in with a key fastened to its side. When the butler touched the key, smoke began to pour from the casket and Marion screamed at him to throw it out of the house. He tossed it onto the beach and the sheriff was called. After soaking the device all day, the casket was opened and was found to contain a powerful explosive. The sheriff's office announced on Christmas Eve that there had been an attempt on Marion's life. It was a sordid end to a bad year, and Marion fretted for a long time over the fact that there was someone unknown who resented her enough to take her life.

Following that year of calamities, Marion still was able to project an outer calm, braced only slightly by scotch. Some of her friends and staff remarked on her "bravery," and certainly some of the old Douras spirit was visible. But mostly she was emotionally detached, a trait she shared with nephew Charlie, perhaps derived from Mama Rose's stoicism. They both appeared to have the ability to look upon the most distressing events other than the death of a loved one with a certain cool objectivity.

Throughout 1932, Hearst was deeply involved in national politics as the Depression deepened and his own breadlines lengthened. He no longer had ambitions for himself. He said, in fact, that if anyone tried to give him a political office, he would murder him and "consider the deed justifiable homicide." Louis B. Mayer had appealed to Hearst to support Hoover, who had become a close personal friend of Mayer's, for a second term, but Hearst wired the studio chief that Hoover's name had become anathema to the American people and told him that the Republican president was a lost cause. When it became clear to Hearst that Republican leaders were in agreement with Mayer, he lost all interest in the Republican convention and began putting his power and influence behind John Nance Garner of Texas, who eventually became the Vice President. Hearst let it be known, too, that he was not opposed to the nomination of Franklin D. Roosevelt, if Garner failed to hold up during the early balloting. When the showdown came on the third ballot, with Roosevelt desperately needing the California delegates' votes, which were controlled by Hearst and nominally held by Garner, Hearst telephoned Chicago and instructed California to go over to Roosevelt, an action inducing Garner to release the Texas delegation to the New York governor. Thus, Roosevelt owed his nomination to Hearst's last-minute decision.

Marion was at his side throughout these maneuverings, recovering from an arduous production schedule on *Polly of the Circus,* for which she had captured Clark Gable, late of Norma Shearer's successful *A Free Soul,* as her leading man. As in so many of her films, this tight and modest melodrama had renunciation as its principal theme. It was a quality that Hearst wished to see stressed in her films. He finally was permitting her to play "ordinary" women, such as circus performers, but he wanted them to be touched with nobility. The ban against kissing her leading men on screen seemed to have been dropped with *Marianne* in 1929, and this element added persuasion to Marion's early talkies.

Marion truly felt—and said so repeatedly—that she finally had been allowed to be human in her film roles and, for a time at least, this rounded out her rather extraordinary off-camera life. But this was a dangerous illusion. There were walls between herself and ordinary humanity and even her gift-giving was often taken over by hard-boiled Ella "Bill" Williams, who decided how much would be spent and who the recipients would be. It was not that Marion ever felt superior to others less well-off than she. She simply had no way of reaching them except on isolated occasions. This was Hearst's way and it perforce had to be hers as well. Doubtless, her sense of guilt contributed much to her drinking problem.

The illusion on screen, however, was successful and in *Polly,* when Marion tells her unemployed minister husband (Clark Gable) that she doesn't need a mansion as their first home together, since her past has been spent sleeping in "just a bunk in a circus car or a room in a theatrical hotel," the lady of the castle at San Simeon is totally convincing.

III

The year 1932 was turning out to be very nearly as exhausting
for Marion as 1927 had been (when the nonstop partying was
going on at Ocean House and at San Simeon during intervals
between the four pictures she did that year), but there were
compensations. Her Children's Clinic had expanded to such a
degree that it could no longer be managed through random dis-
bursements by Marion. The Marion Davies Foundation had been
set up earlier to take over the financial and administrative end
of her principal charity, and from then on Marion sent them
large amounts of money in advance of their needs on a regular
basis. She had been very excited about "becoming a Foundation,"
as she put it. More than the several homes and properties she
owned, more than Hearst's efforts to stand beside her publicly,
even more than her celebrity, this Foundation had given her a
sense of being respectable at last. It went farther than anything
else in making her feel that she was a legitimate part of society
and not just a wealthier-than-usual backstreet girl. The Foundation now was getting far more of her income than the Dourases
or any hangers-on.

She was really earning her huge salary at Metro of over
half-a-million dollars a year. Her production schedule had been
rugged—nearly seven months of shooting with no vacation, if
one did not count the frequent days off for picnics or extended
weekends.

But by summer, *Polly of the Circus* was released, the public
was responding, and they were in the homestretch on an equally
important film, *Blondie of the Follies*. *Blondie* had excited Hearst
more than anything since *Marianne*. He called it the "chorus-girl
story" and he asked his favorite screenwriter Frances Marion to
make the story topical and Anita Loos to give the Follies girls
the proper gold-digging lingo. Real issues and backgrounds had
become popular despite, or perhaps because of, the Depression,
which still held the country in its thrall. Early that summer, over
20,000 unemployed veterans had moved on the nation's capitol,
calling themselves the Bonus Expeditionary Force, setting up a
makeshift camp and demanding immediate payment of a proposed bonus for service in the First World War. President Hoover
had called in the troops under General Douglas MacArthur to

rout them with tanks, tear gas, and bayonets (MacArthur had become friendly with Hearst and Marion the previous year when he had visited Hollywood and spent half a day watching Marion perform in *Bachelor Father*). Slum conditions and other social realities, as well as frank depictions of male-and-female relationships had become the vogue in films—there was almost a revolutionary alteration in the subject matter. (This had been brought about in part by the success of King Vidor's 1931 movie *Street Scene*, based on the Elmer Rice play and adapted without compromise. It was a healthy change, and the many film people brought over from Europe in that period returned to the mature themes they had built their reputations on back home. In one season, a whole flood of adult pictures moved into release: *I Am a Fugitive from a Chain Gang*, Katharine Hepburn's *A Bill of Divorcement*, Paul Muni's *Scarface*, Leslie Howard's *The Animal Kingdom*, Joan Crawford's *Rain* (with Walter Huston's memorable Reverend Davidson). Thalberg hastened to bring Metro into step with Vicki Baum's bestseller, *Grand Hotel*, starring Garbo, Joan Crawford, the Barrymore brothers, and Wallace Beery. The book's Continental urbanity was preserved by director Edmund Goulding, and it was a rich brew of human frustration and recognizable sinners. It had wit and great style, and it won the Academy Award as best picture of the year. Almost simultaneously, Jean Harlow's steamy jungle affair with Clark Gable, *Red Dust*, went into release, and Metro had an answer to Paramount's Mae West.

Hearst knew that Marion would have to keep pace with this new maturity in films if she were to remain a star, and he had sought King Vidor's services as director. Hearst told Vidor, "This is Marion's own story combined with all the drama of *Street Scene*." There was even a role based loosely on Hearst himself (played in the film by Douglas Dumbrille). Unfortunately, the director had a commitment with David Selznick to do *Bird of Paradise*. Edmund Goulding, whose prestige was very high following *Grand Hotel*, was next on their list. Goulding accepted.

Blondie was no *Street Scene*, but it was a successful film, and it carried Marion even farther away from the Pollyanna (and the later madcap flapper) roles of her silent career than had *Polly of the Circus*. All of the scenes set in Blondie McClune's slum home have a sense of sharp reality about them. (The beautiful Billie Dove appears in one shot on the front steps of a tenement building in which she strikingly resembles Estelle Taylor as Mrs. Maurrant in *Street Scene*.) The reviews were all on the plus side, *The New York Times* saying,

> ... the assumption in *Blondie of the Follies*, which was jamming the auditorium of the Capitol yesterday, is that there is something to record about the life of a Follies girl. Whether one accepts this premise or not, the film does offer a number of good features. Jimmy Durante pops in irrelevantly for three minutes or so, which is long enough to him to break up the show. He sings one of his "disa and data" songs, heaps vigorous and naughty scorn on his imaginary enemies and does a mad impersonation of John Barrymore in which Marion Davies figures as Greta Garbo. ... Marion Davies and Robert Montgomery are completely satisfactory in the leads. Both are light comedians and as seriously disturbed and frustrated lovers the two players are admirable.

Marion's life long ago had fallen into a pattern. The week she finished a film, she would leave Ocean House, where she stayed throughout her film activities, and go up to the castle, ostensibly to get some rest. Possibly it was quiet there when Hearst was alone but rarely when Marion was in residence. She complained later that the routine at the castle began to pall after a few years of setting place cards and handling large dinners, but in the early 1930s she was content, surrounded by her friends: Eileen Percy, Charlie Chaplin, Dorothy Mackaill, Fifi D'Orsay, Eddie Kane (whose origins and occupation remained a mystery even to Marion), her sisters, niece Pepi and nephew Charlie, and intimates Constance Talmadge and Marie Glendinning. Hearst worked long hours there, but he would join the crowd for dinner and the evening movie—often one of Marion's, but not always, contrary to legend, since he made three or four other features without her each year, and all of these were shown as well as major Hollywood features. After the movie, Hearst often would go into the kitchen and whip up a welsh rarebit, which he did masterfully. Marion could not cook anything, including, she said, boiling an egg, and she was usually the first to suggest to Hearst that he treat them to one of his special dishes.

One of the more exotic elements of a visit to San Simeon was the tinkling sound of a dinner bell being rung by a servant running through the halls of the castle and guest houses at meal times. Once Hearst arose at dawn to see a sprinkling of snow on some crimson camellias that were in bloom, and he began ringing a large dinner bell to arouse everyone before the sun could thaw this sensation of nature, a gesture he cut off suddenly when he saw that someone had put bras and panties on his marble maidens against the chill. Although Eleanor Boardman, Gene Markey, and several others were present at the castle, Hearst accused Marion and Eileen Percy of the crime, while Charlie Lederer insisted to the author that he had done it.

Sometimes, an illustrious guest interested Marion so profoundly, a correspondence would follow with occasional personal contacts over the years. The unlikeliest of these friendships grew out of the visit of the George Bernard Shaws. Shaw and his wife Charlotte had come to the United States on his one and only visit in April 1933. When Hearst learned of his plans for an American trip, he quickly dispatched an invitation to San Simeon to the playwright and, to the surprise and chagrin of "New York leftist intellectuals," Shaw accepted.

It was not Shaw's first contact with Hearst. In his "autobiography" put together by Stanley Weintraub, Shaw said that when Lenin came into power, he was offered a very handsome commission by Hearst to go out to Russia and describe what there was to see there, but, he said, "I refused because I knew only too well that what I should see was Capitalism in ruins and not Communism *in excelsis.*"

Shaw's visit to San Simeon was a typical "state" affair. A crowd of some seventy guests, all carefully chosen by Hearst and Marion, went up to San Luis Obispo on Hearst's leased train. There was no snobbery motivating their choices—one or two vegetarians were thrown in, known alcoholics whose behavior was unpredictable were excluded. Metro executives Thalberg (with his wife Norma Shearer) and Harry Rapf mingled with Jack and Harry Warner. Old regulars Frances Marion, Kathy Menjou (divorced from Adolphe), Lloyd and sister Carmen Pantages Considine, Eileen Percy, the King Vidors, William Haines, and Marie Glendinning sat together in one of the private cars and shared a laugh over the "command performance," the cream of Hollywood society going up to Hearst's mountain to pay their respects to the grizzled and caustic literary lion.

There was so much tension at the long trestle table in the

high-beamed dining room that Mrs. Shaw ate the white orchid
on the gold-rimmed saucer next to her table setting, thinking it
was salad. Marion sat at Shaw's right and looked at him ador-
ingly. "I have two great heroes in literature," she told him.

"Who are they?" Shaw asked, turning to glance at her sideways like a petulant rooster.

"You and Shakespeare," Marion said.

Shaw looked disappointed. "Oh. Why mention me in the
same breath with Shakespeare?"

"Well, *Androcles and the Lion.*"

Now Shaw was skeptical. He was also looking murderous as
a huge platter of bloody roast beef was brought in and placed
practically under his nose. Frances Marion, who shared with
Hearst a love of rare beef, caught Shaw's reaction across the
table from her and guiltily lifted a couple of slices to her plate,
feeling like a werewolf.

"Did you read that?" Shaw asked Marion. "I didn't think you
had the intelligence."

"I have the intelligence to read it, but I haven't got the
intelligence to understand it. Now you explain it to me."

Shaw smiled, and a waiter, cued and as guilty-looking as
Frances Marion, skillfully moved the roast beef platter to the far
end of the table and replaced it with a mushroom dish surrounded by attractive vegetables. "Pretty shrewd you are, young
lady."

Marion was pleased. "Thanks for calling me a young lady."

By now nearly everyone was looking toward Shaw and Marion with the quizzical blankness of perfect ninnies. Frances Marion was relieved to have Shaw's attention diverted from the rare
roast beef she was eating. Eileen Percy watched the scene in
obvious delight at seeing the whole Hollywood zoo—especially its
lions, wolves, and jackals—put in its place by her girlfriend.

Early the next morning, Shaw met Frances Marion as he
was returning from his stroll. He glanced at her sternly, and she
was convinced he could see blood dripping from her carnivorous
lips. "You look as keen-witted as anyone around here," he told
her. "Tell me. Who is Lou-alla?" and he pronounced the name as
though it were some sort of oversized African game.

"That must be Louella Parsons, the columnist," said Frances
in some relief.

"Well, Miss Davies has asked if I won't grant her an interview. I've told everyone since I've come to America 'No interviews' but now my hostess is seeking a favor. She said I'd be doing a wonderful thing. I'm trapped."

At that moment, Louella entered the hotel-sized front parlor, carrying a lined note-pad and beaming.

"You interrupted my morning walk," Shaw told her.

"You're very kind," Louella said, still beaming.

"Kind!" Shaw said, and whatever patience Louella had hoped for seemed exhausted in advance of a single question.

Frances Marion discreetly moved toward the "morning room" beyond the parlor. "Don't leave me!" Shaw said loudly, and his words were more of a command than a plea. Frances came back to a chair a few yards away from Shaw and his eager interviewer, and he nodded in relief, as though he wanted an intelligent witness to whatever was said.

"Now," he asked Louella, "what do you want to know?"

Louella asked him if he might give her a few remarks about his friendship with Ellen Terry. "That is none of your damned business," Shaw told her.

"Is it true that you wrote *Cashel Byron's Profession* for Jim Corbett?" she then wanted to know. James J. Corbett, world heavyweight champion, had been cast in the leading role of the gentleman boxer in Shaw's play when it was first done in New York.

"My dear Miss Lou-alla, I wrote *Cashel Byron* before Jim Corbett was ever born." Something of an exaggeration, this, but Shaw was never comfortable away from the British Isles, and the more alien his environment, the sharper his tone.

Shaw's only interview during his visit to the United States continued in this fashion. When asked for his opinion of Sarah Bernhardt, he said that she reminded him of his Aunt Georgia, whom he detested.

Louella added a description of Shaw as she saw him—"A jolly Santa Claus in a white beard on the outside," and she made several futile attempts to describe her reactions to his "inside." Finally, she turned the whole notepad over to him and Shaw began to rewrite it in longhand, leaving only the remark about the jolly Santa and then signing his name.

When Marion looked in on them to see how everything was going, she saw Louella seated dutifully with her hands folded in her lap as Shaw was slashing through every line. But Louella nodded eagerly, aware of the prize she was receiving in exchange for a big slice of humble pie.

Katherine Menjou wanted desperately to get a snapshot of Shaw, but had to content herself with a rear view as he walked down a lane with Marion and Constance Talmadge. "I won't turn around," he told Mrs. Menjou, "because I will not have myself photographed, and I don't like people who do things like that." But, of course, he was photographed several times when he visited the Metro studio, once over the lunch table, a particular intrusion, but Mayer wanted it all recorded for posterity.

The Shaws were an hour and a half late for that Metro luncheon because fog had forced down Hearst's pilot at Malibu Beach. They were both covered with mud and sand when a car finally got there to pick them up, and they were soaked by an unusually heavy April thunderstorm. Marion cleaned up Mrs. Shaw in her bungalow, while Mayer, Clark Gable, John Barrymore and other Metro luminaries fretted. Marion was delighted when the demoralized woman asked for a nip of scotch, and she thought that it was Mrs. Shaw's "little secret," since Shaw was a teetotaler.

Shaw sat next to Marion at the lunch table and told her, "you've got a rotten pilot. The stupid so-and-so could have landed us someplace else. . . . I've got sand in my pants. . . . And it's raining."

"Look at all those newspapermen outside, standing in the rain," Marion told him in her most mournful tones "And you're here in this nice warm room . . . Would you let them come in for one minute?"

"Well," Shaw said, thawed by her charm. "Who said they couldn't? I'm not eating anything. I don't like your food."

When John Barrymore came up to Shaw and asked if he would sign a little album for his son, Shaw wanted to know how old the boy was. "Six months," said Barrymore. "Sorry," Shaw told him dismissively, "he's too young to appreciate it." Barrymore left the room in a rage. As they were leaving the commissary, Cecil Holland, a studio makeup man, came up to Shaw and asked if he would sign his cowboy hat. "Who is he?" Shaw asked Marion. "He's an artist," she said quickly. And Shaw signed the hat.

The first movie set they visited was that of *When Strangers Meet* with Ann Harding, Robert Montgomery, and Alice Brady under the direction of Sam Wood. Everyone was awed by Shaw and the cameras stopped. Ann Harding rushed up to him and said, "Mr. Shaw, don't you remember me?" He said he didn't. "I did *Androcles and the Lion*." And Shaw looked at her icily and said, "It must have been a pirated version." Miss Harding seemed about to swoon and ran off to her dressing room. Hysterical weeping could be heard from inside, which Shaw managed to ignore, but in the next day's *Los Angeles Times* there appeared a story headlined "George Bernard Shaw Insults Ann Harding."

Marion steered the Shaws through all of this dizzy-headedness with composure. She corresponded with him until his death, and once he came for a visit to St. Donat's, making it clear that he wanted to see Marion again. When he lay dying at Ayot-St. Lawrence, Marion wrote to Alice Head and told her to take a particular gold watch to Shaw and give him "our love." Miss Head did so. Shaw expressed his gratitude to Marion and to Hearst; he died that same month. Marion felt genuine sorrow at his passing and wondered if perhaps he should not have been a vegetarian, forgetting that Shaw had died in his ninety-fourth year.

IV

In 1933, Marion was reelected President of the Motion Picture Relief Fund, an industry-wide charitable organization. It was her fourth successive term in that office. No one challenged her ability to manage it; it was well-known by now that she had given away millions, both to worthy causes and to show business figures down on their luck.

Ironically, there was a pressing need for cash much closer to home. A month before Shaw's visit, Hearst had been forced to find another huge sum of money to meet his current personal expenses. There was no more money available from his inheritance, and so he had gone to a Los Angeles bank and sought $600,000, putting up the castle as collateral. Unluckily, it was just at that moment Roosevelt chose to declare a bank holiday, but one of the officers of the bank, who knew Hearst as a professional colleague, advanced him the money personally. That man was Harry Chandler, publisher of the *Los Angeles Times* and Hearst's rival for the newspaper market there for many years. It is said that Hearst did not know that Chandler held the mortgage and not the bank itself, but such innocence of pertinent facts would not be typical at all of Hearst. It is likely that he knew Chandler was loaning him the money, but he would rather not dwell on it.

Immediately after the Shaws' departure, Hearst and Marion threw their traditional huge party to honor his seventieth birthday. The motif was Pioneer America, and a covered wagon was among the props the guests—including Richard Berlin, Townsend and Constance (Talmadge) Netcher, Irving and Norma (Shearer) Thalberg, Anita Loos, Joe Mankiewicz and his brother Herman, Walter Wanger, Harpo Marx, and about two hundred others—found especially amusing. Marion wore a gingham dress and a sunbonnet and Hearst was decked out as a riverboat gambler with a fancy vest.

Marion had finished *Peg O' My Heart* earlier that spring and the dance orchestra played the film's theme song, *There's a Light in Your Eyes, Sweetheart Darling,* a lilting ballad in the manner of an old Irish air, often enough to send everyone to bed with a tune in their heads. The song was destined to become even more popular than the picture and soon became the number one song in the country. The wisdom of having thirty-six-year old Marion play a girl in her late teens was questionable, although she made the audience forget her years through much of it, pouring considerable Irish charm and vitality into her role. Frances Marion had attempted to bring the old J. Hartley Manners play up to date with an adulterous couple and their exposure as one of the subplots. At least a generation had passed since Laurette Taylor's memorable stage performance of her husband's hit play and Hearst may have been right in reviving it as Marion enjoyed a modest success. In the film, when Peg comes into her fortune and moves into the old family estate, she is perhaps more Marion and less Peg (Marion dancing a jig at San Simeon would be the perfect parallel in life), but the seamless sentimental comedy still worked and technically it was a great advance over her earlier talkies.

Peg O' My Heart represented Hearst's rebellion after seeing Marion play brash blondes (with gold-plated hearts) in half-a-dozen talkies including *Five and Ten, It's a Wise Child, Polly of the Circus,* and *Blondie of the Follies.* In *Peg,* she was back in the equivalent of a sunbonnet walking down a country lane or helping villagers bring in the day's catch of fish. It was his last chance to see her perform as a young girl, and he saw that it was polished to a brightness that nearly made the film one of her best. In this musicalized adaptation, there are moments—especially when the villagers are singing *We'll Remember*—when melodically and in appearance it is remarkably like *Brigadoon,* a Broadway musical that appeared twenty years later.

Some of the party guests stayed on at San Simeon after the birthday celebration, among them Kathy Menjou, who had obtained her formal divorce decree from actor Adolphe. She was very pleased with the settlement she had received, since it included about four hundred shares of General Electric stock, which along with other "blue chip" stocks had begun a climb back upward following the crash of '29. Marion observed Kathy running into the office wing at the castle several times a day to have a look at the tickertape machine installed there, and Kathy's obsession with her stocks inspired Marion to play one of her pranks. She rigged the tickertape machine in such a way that General Electric began a dramatic slide downward almost at once, falling to a shocking 24 by the following day. When it reached 17, Kathy began shouting that she was ruined and took to her bed, where she remained, so near unconsciousness it was almost impossible to make her understand that it was all a joke.

With no more than a one- or two-week interval, Marion was back at Metro playing opposite a new leading man, the crooner Bing Crosby, in Frances Marion's Hollywood satire, *Going Hollywood.* It was not as bright in its humor as *Show People* had been, and its comedy did not have that film's poignancy, but it was a smoothly tooled entertainment, Crosby's fourth feature after three successive hits (*The Big Broadcast, College Humor, Too Much Harmony*), and a Hearst movie again had supplied the nation with its number one popular song in *Temptation.* The musical score by Arthur Freed and Nacio Herb Brown was one of their finest and included other lesser hits: *We'll Make Hay While the Sun Shines, We'll Make Love When It Rains, After Sundown,* and *Our Big Love Scene.*

Marion looked better on screen in the Crosby film than she had in several years with soft makeup and a natural hair style that happened to give her more youthfulness in her role of a young woman than she had been given as a girl in *Peg.* Some of her bounce, so apparent on the screen, came from her obvious delight at playing with the leading popular singer of the day. It

was her idea that they be teamed, and it was clear from the first
day of production that she and Crosby had much in common.
Crosby wrote the author:

> Marion Davies, as I remember her, was a very warm-
> hearted lady of abundant good humour, who loved func-
> tions and festive occasions more than most.
> She loved festivities, and was a marvelous hostess.
> Always had some local jokes and pranks to play on the
> guests.
> The experience of making a picture with her, was
> probably the last of the halcyon days. She always had a five
> or six piece orchestra on the set, to play the current hits of
> the day, between takes.
> Sometimes the intervals between takes became quite
> lengthy.
> Our schedule, on the picture I made with her, stretched
> to unbelievable lengths—but it was a real joy working with
> her.
> She was extremely kind to members of the crew, and
> thoughtful, too. She always remembered birthdays and an-
> niversaries, and was most charitable.
> She was always surrounded by a coterie of old vaude-
> ville performers and indigent actors who were fun.
> All in all, an association long to be remembered.

Marion recalled the experience with as much warmth in
later years and added that Crosby was "so crazy about Dixie [his
wife]." It was not pure joy for Hearst, however, since Marion
often would return from the studio terribly hung-over and unable
to do anything beyond retiring to her rooms, where if all went
well she would recover by the next morning. Although those were
Crosby's heavy drinking days, it was not his fault that Marion
seized upon her association with him in a movie as an excuse
to celebrate nearly every day. And if Hearst was partially the
source of the underlying problem that led to the marathon
drinking sessions, he was helpless in finding a remedy. Fifi
D'Orsay, who played the Hollywood actress in the film, recalls
that they would all gather for drinks in Marion's portable dressing room on the set—Marion, Crosby, and Fifi—but when the
signal came to Marion that Hearst was entering the sound stage,
the signal transmitted by secretary Ella "Bill" Williams or by a
member of the crew whom Marion had enlisted in this small

conspiracy, then everyone would dump the glasses, hide the whiskey, and pretend to an innocence that Hearst would gallantly accept as genuine. Whether Hearst was present or not, work was always suspended at four for a "tea break," which might last for an hour or more. There was the usual gossip about Marion's little affair with her leading man, this time blunted by the spirit or spirits prevailing on the set and by Crosby's determination to go home to Dixie, whatever the hour might be.

Going Hollywood was the Christmas week attraction at the Capitol and Loew's Metropolitan theaters in New York. It marked the feature film debut of Broadway comedienne Patsy Kelly, who was soon to win a wide movie following in a series of comedy shorts with Thelma Todd. In contrast to most movie musicals of the time, it was welcomed by audiences and critics for its modest smaller and more human scale. Fifi D'Orsay who was known as the "French bombshell," but who was born in Montreal of French-Canadian parents and who never had seen "Paree," was a protégée of Will Rogers, one of Fox's biggest stars. She had asked for her release from a lucrative Fox contract to do some personal appearances on the RKO theater circuit and at the end of the tour found herself an unemployed star. Marion had interceded in Fifi's behalf and the part of the eccentric film queen went to the American-born "Parisienne" rather than to Hearst's first choice, Lili Damita, while Crosby was cast as a famous crooner and Miss D'Orsay's boyfriend. In the movie, the two of them are on their way to Hollywood to make a picture together, when Marion, a schoolteacher and a super-fan of Bing's, spots them and follows them all the way across the country. The predictable twist in the plot has Marion achieve all of her heart's goals, taking the place of flighty Fifi D'Orsay in Bing's picture and in his affections as well.

The movie had some formidable competition the week of its release in New York. There was Eddie Cantor's *Roman Scandals*, written by no less than three of the country's finest playwrights: George S. Kaufman, Robert E. Sherwood, and George Oppenheimer. But Marion's movie proved to be more popular than the Cantor film and a star-studded production of *Alice in Wonderland*, starring Charlotte Henry as Alice. *Going Hollywood* even competed nicely with the brand-new Radio City Music Hall's Christmas show, *Flying Down to Rio*, starring Fred Astaire and two leading ladies, Ginger Rogers and Dolores Del Rio.

Joan Crawford was being given a massive build-up as a musical comedy queen at the time, and her film *Dancing Lady* had preceded Marion's into the Capitol Theatre. Perhaps overburdened by all the talent and money going into it (its songs were written by Rodgers and Hart, Jimmy McHugh and Dorothy Fields, *and* Burton Lane and Harold Adamson), it further escalated Miss Crawford's career and it is remembered today chiefly for one of its songs, *Everything I Have Is Yours*. Miss Crawford was not one of Marion's studio pals, although they had appeared together briefly in *The Hollywood Revue*. She was a fan of Crosby's, however, and she would rush from the set of *Dancing Lady* to sit near the camera setup on *Going Hollywood* to watch him perform. Marion said that it was nearly impossible for Crosby to do his scene with those great "owl eyes" upon him. Miss Crawford had some reservations about Marion's professionalism (although none about her philanthropies and was quick to give her full credit for those) and once, when Marion came visiting on one of her sets, she shut down production and chatted with her until Marion left twenty minutes later. She rarely visited San Simeon, although she was seen there several times with her husband Douglas Fairbanks, Jr., and she shared William Haines's brotherly affections with Marion. She had her mind on her job—as a film queen—almost to the exclusion of all else, and Marion could not resist on at least one occasion doing an impression of her—in makeup—with a great slash of red lipstick and enormous eyes.

The madcap social life of Hollywood seemed a little excessive by the mid-thirties, and Hearst began to spend more and more time with Marion at Wyntoon, where there were no news photographers and the only pictorial record of their good times was being taken by Hearst himself and by close friends with box cameras.

The year 1934 had been one of stress for both of them. Niece Pepi was having emotional problems. She had broken with her closest friend and had fallen into a profound melancholy. Marion wanted to get her off to Europe, and she even looked forward to taking her to the Black Forest and Bad Nauheim, which she now looked upon as a cure-all. That section of Germany had the pine-scented charm of Wyntoon with those medicinal waters that shrank down the heart and, as Marion hoped, some of the heart's problems.

But she was having trouble getting away. Her film with Gary Cooper, *Operator 13*, was running over schedule as Hearst kept tampering with it. Hearst was also nearing a showdown with Irving Thalberg over *The Barretts of Wimpole Street,* the successful Broadway and London play, which he wanted for Marion and Thalberg said was purchased for his wife, Norma Shearer. Bosley Crowther writes in his biography of Louis B. Mayer: "In one crisis, however, Mayer backed up Thalberg. That was a difficult contention with Hearst as to who, Norma Shearer or Marion Davies, would be given the enviable assignment of playing the heroine in *The Barretts of Wimpole Street.* The popular play had been acquired for Miss Shearer. Then Hearst got the notion that it would be an appropriate vehicle for Miss Davies. *Why he or his blond protégé should have remotely assumed that she could play the delicate role of the invalid-poetess, Elizabeth Barrett, is hard to understand. . . .* [Italics mine.]" Crowther perhaps had never seen *Show People, The Patsy,* or either of her Sidney Franklin films prior to having written his book, but not to have properly researched Marion's acting skills seems nearly as careless as the manner in which Orson Welles later denied that the sources for *Kane* were anything but fictional—almost as though the damage which Welles knew had been done to Marion's career was a trivial matter to a genius.

As *Operator 13* reached the finishing stages, Norma Shearer and Charles Laughton were cast as daughter and father in *The Barretts* film and Hearst went into a rage, offended to the point of an open break with the studio. He had been having secret conferences with Jack Warner, and Marion's future was up in the air.

And Marion was tired. She badly needed a vacation from film-making. Finally, after several months of production (one of the longest shooting schedules of her career), *Operator 13* was finished. The result was satisfactory, but not brilliant. Despite their opposing views on horses (she still hated riding), she had got on well with Cooper. He and his wife "Rocky" had become regular guests at San Simeon. Cooper and Marion were drinking companions, but there is no evidence that their friendship ever went beyond this. He could hold his liquor better than she could (although drinking often put him to sleep), and Hearst had a special fondness for him, perhaps because he treated Marion and her drinking rather like an indulgent older brother might. Cooper and Hearst sometimes would go out riding over the hills together.

There had been tension on the set, however, much of the time, and disputes usually wore out Marion. Director Boleslawski and Hearst had not seen eye-to-eye on certain scenes and, in one instance, Hearst had stepped in and directed a scene himself. He knew a great deal about military history, the Civil War in particular, and he saw the film as a panoramic drama covering the whole war. It was an approach he had used earlier in *Janice Meredith*.

Operator 13 has an exciting opening montage of Civil War scenes, thanks to Hearst's military preoccupation, and moves along swiftly to its climax. Many moments in the film are handled with a documentary realism in the Griffith manner of dealing with historical events. It was to become Hearst's favorite of all of Marion's films, but Marion plays the key role with a brittle weariness and the movie dramatically reveals what was happening to her career.

Marion plays two roles in *Operator 13*, although they are one and the same person—an actress who becomes a spy and assumes the disguise of a mulatto girl. As the actress, Marion was given the first of a series of appallingly artificial blond wigs to wear (three others would follow in her Warner Brothers films), her makeup is harsh, her true age (thirty-seven) made all too apparent by an ineptitude in the makeup department that flaws this last film for Metro, and the effect is so much a caricature of what Marion used to be it seems almost a plot against her. It had nothing to do with Marion's own appearance or the inroads of her age or her dissipations since, as the brunette mulatto girl, she is very much her old self—flirtatious, with a slightly wicked humor, the same attractive, sensual kitten she was in more than a dozen films during the 1920s. This must have resulted from the iron hand of an aging Hearst coming into open conflict with a skillful director, Boleslawski, who was only then discovering his touch for lighter things (he would direct Irene Dunne in the classic comedy, *Theodora Goes Wild,* the following year). The dominance of the blond actress was insisted upon by Hearst over the sparkling and marvelous mulatto girl. Gary Cooper's response to the two women is barely credible: he falls hopelessly in love with the blond actress, who seems to have ice in her veins, and he all but ignores the sensual mulatto. The film could have been brought into balance, the romantic moments made as persuasive as the battle scenes, if Cooper had been allowed to react as any virile male would have to the coffee-skinned girl, and if Marion, as her blond self, had been given the same natural treatment from the makeup department which she had been receiving for nearly a decade at those same Metro studios.

The moment Marion was free, Hearst began pulling together a congenial group of guests to accompany them to Europe. Eileen Percy, Harry Crocker, Mary Carlisle, Buster Collier, secretary Ella "Bill" Williams, and three of the sons—Bill, Jr., George, and John and their wives—along with Pepi Lederer, comprised most of the group. Retired star Dorothy Mackaill, who was in New York at the time, said that she would join them in the East, but Hearst would have none of it. "We're going to stop off to see the Chicago Fair," he told her, "and we'll do it together." The Chicago Exposition of 1933 was then in its second year. So Miss Mackaill flew back to the Coast to join the party, as instructed.

They drove through Spain in a caravan of seven open sedans. In Barcelona, all of the party except Hearst and Marion went to the bull ring. The couple shared an aversion to such bloodletting. The entourage stayed no more than three or four days there, and then the group was off for a new point of interest. On several occasions, Hearst would ask Crocker, who was acting as his social secretary on the trip, Marion, and Buster Collier to sit in the rumble seat of one of the open cars while he sat in front next to the driver and acted as tour guide, giving them a knowledgeable account of the mountains, villages, history, and politics of the countryside through which they were driving.

Hearst, Marion, Pepi, Crocker, and Collier left from the Madrid airport for London in a chartered Fokker plane. His sons and the others went by car across France. The French government, possibly under some pressure from dealers in antiquities, had told Hearst that he was welcome, but he icily declined their invitation. He had contacted Hugo Eckener to see if the *Graf Zeppelin* could come down and pick them up—his financial stake in the huge dirigible and its maintenance was still substantial—but it was then involved on a mail route out of Bremen and could not oblige him. The Fokker ran into rough weather over the ocean a hundred or so miles from the British coast, and the pilot told Collier, "We are losing our ceiling." Hearst and Marion were not informed of the trouble until the pilot decided to make a forced landing when he determined that they were over British soil. They came down in a hilly pasture, making a belly landing and killing eight sheep. All of them except Hearst kissed the ground. He took near-calamity in stride, and he calmly asked Collier to go into the nearest village and find some cars to take them on to London. Marion said nothing, and the others thought she was being very brave, but she later said that she was simply paralyzed by fear. They missed a reception for them at Claridge's by nearly ten hours, and they were a wretched lot as they dragged themselves into the Savoy Hotel at three in the morning.

Reporters converged on the Savoy early the following morning wanting to get some comment on a great art controversy that had broken out in Venice over the hanging of an oil portrait of Marion there in the 19th International Biennial Art Exhibition. The large portrait by the Polish artist Tade Styka appeared mysteriously one day hanging with the American collection sent by the Whitney Museum of American Art. The study shows Marion with short, wavy blond hair in a classic cut looking off to the right of the picture, her hands crossed over her breasts in a slightly protective manner. She wears a single strand of matched pearls and a silk sleeveless dress. It *did* capture Marion's beauty but little of her high spirits. At the time it was painted, in 1928, Styka said that Marion was "supremely beautiful" because in her features "there is the contrast of the whirlwind and the soft sunshine," but Mrs. Juliana Force, director of the Whitney Museum, was not interested in either the beauty of the subject or the quality of Styka's work (he was highly regarded as a portraitist in the twenties and thirties). The painting had been hung without her museum's knowledge and it was not part of their collection dispatched to Venice. She ordered it removed, but the Italian authorities refused to do so. Then Mrs. Force ordered all of the American collection crated and sent home, but the Italian art show officials declined to let the pictures be taken down. Tempers rose and the secretary of the show, Antonio Maraini, was sent to Rome to confer with high Fascist officials as to what course he should follow. It is possible that both Countess Dorothy di Frasso and Count Ciano were consulted. Maraini came back and the following day, the portrait was scheduled to be moved to the Venetian Pavilion of Decorative Art. On the day after that, with Mrs. Force fuming back in London where she was visiting, the president of the exposition, Count Volpi di Misurata, announced that the portrait would *not* be moved after all but would remain in the American collection and that "Italian authorities will resist taking down other pictures." Following this, Mrs. Force filed a suit against the Venice art show officials to restrain them from continuing to exhibit what she plainly felt was a "contaminated" collection from America, but the show went on. The suit moved ponderously through the Italian courts and finally, after the exhibition closed, was dropped in November.

The Hearst party stayed in London for several days and then Lord Louis Mountbatten entertained them at his country estate. After that, they spent nearly two weeks relaxing at St. Donat's in Wales, returning to the Continent in late July. They spent several days in Holland and Belgium and moved on to Switzerland by car. Marion had her dog Gandhi with her, and she kept the dachshund close to her everywhere they went. Many photographs survive from the trip showing Marion walking Gandhi at filling stations and along mountain paths en route. Both mistress and dog appear to be near exhaustion from their travels through the Alps. The beautiful Dorothy Mackaill, too, appears equally travel-worn in many of the snapshots taken by Hearst, Collier, and others in the party.

In Rome, all but Marion and Pepi managed to be among the crowd watching Mussolini as he harangued the populace. Marion was staying close to her niece, attempting to cheer her, but she was not having much luck. Whenever they were with the group, however, Pepi attempted a mood of gaiety and seemed not especially depressed to the others. Marion cursed her luck for having missed seeing *Il Duce*, but Buster Collier had his camera with him and took an excellent photograph of the Italian dictator. The invasion of Ethiopia was a year away.

On the way north again to Germany by way of Venice (where Marion made a quick visit to the art show) and Salzburg, the party stopped at a mountainside restaurant, and Marion liked the Rhine wine that was served so much that, out of Hearst's earshot, she asked for a bottle to drink along the way. Buster Collier asked how she could manage that when Hearst was sitting directly in front of their rumble seat, and she said, "Leave that to me." For the rest of the journey, she and Collier sipped at the wine from two straws in a coke bottle, giving an occasional swig to Harry Crocker. By the time they reached Salzburg, the three of them were laughing uproariously at some private joke and slapping one another. Hearst smiled in that tentative but hopeful way he had when he thought he was being left out of something and asked, "What's got into you?" The question sent Marion into additional fits of laughter, and Hearst got the joke finally and took a sniff of the coke bottle.

Louis B. Mayer forgot their studio differences long enough to wire Hearst to please see Hitler while he was in Germany and urge the German dictator to stop his persecution of the Jews. Hearst wired back that he would do what he could. But once in Germany, even Hearst was shocked to see how far into military preparedness the Nazis had gone. A small platoon of soldiers stood at the border and an officer among them stepped forward to join them as their guide throughout their stay. Marion and Miss Mackaill thought it was very unkind of the German government to have this sober-faced captain spying on them every moment, for no one in the party was taken in by this "courtesy." Wherever they went, even in Hearst's beloved Munich which once had been so gay, there were soldier guards with shovels at their shoulders, paying token obeisance to the treaty. Marion kept thinking, "This is all due to one man," and her curiosity about Hitler began to override her fears.

Ernst (Putzi) Hanfstaengl, a high-ranking Nazi who was half-American and whose family was in the publishing business, came to Bad Nauheim to speak with Hearst. According to Marion, Hearst refused to see him, but, in all likelihood, this is Marion again being protective. Hanfstaengl arrived with several Nazi bodyguards. He knew that it was Hearst's intention to have a personal interview with Hitler, and he told Hearst, in an off-hand way, that he would set it up. Hanfstaengl patronized Marion and spoke of her films, which he said he admired very much, and she responded to him more warmly than did any of the others. She was not remotely in touch with the political realities of Germany or Europe; it was all a rather exciting spectacle. She spent several days at Bad Nauheim "working on W.R.," attempting to persuade him to take her along on his visit to Hitler. She even asked Harry Crocker to intercede for her, but neither of them got anywhere. "Have a heart," she told Hearst. "I want to see this mysterious person."

Finally, Hearst consented to having Marion accompany

them to Berlin. She believed that his resistance had crumbled and that this meant that she would accompany him into Hitler's headquarters as well.

Hearst, with Harry Crocker, Hanfstaengl (who was to act as interpreter) and Marion took off for Berlin. At the Berlin airport, a friend of Marion's, Ruth Selwyn, suddenly appeared and, catching Marion by the arm, said in a desperate manner, "Marion! I can't get out of the hotel. Could you come over to the Statler?"

"Look," Marion told her, equally desperate, "I have a date."

But Harry Crocker told Marion to go ahead. "We'll go on," he said. "And then you meet us at the Brown House." And he gave her the address of the "Brown House" and got into a taxi with Hearst.

At the hotel, Marion's friend, who was Nicholas Schenck's sister-in-law, said that she had called up "Nicky," but that he wouldn't give her anything toward her hotel bill, which was $700. "I haven't got a cent," she said, "the house maids won't help me pack my things, and I can't get out."

In Marion's mind throughout this episode was the elusive image of Hitler, looking, she imagined, "like Chaplin—possibly worse." Then Miss Selwyn asked Marion to help her pack and when she offered her a drink of brandy, Marion began to smell a rat.

In half an hour or so, the room buzzer rang and a voice downstairs said that "Miss Davies' party was waiting."

When Marion got down to the lobby, she found Hearst and Crocker waiting for her. They already had been to see Hitler and they said their plane was waiting. When Marion became furious, Hearst said, "I just went in for five minutes and then left."

Marion didn't speak to Hearst or Crocker for two days.

During the brief interview, Hearst had told Hitler that National Socialism would win more friends in America if the anti-Semitism would stop. Hitler then asked Hearst, "But what about the American Indians?" Hearst attempted to explain the difference, although this was difficult, but he told Hitler that the persecution of the Jews was indefensible to nearly all Americans and that this was the twentieth century. Hitler then reportedly assured him that the measures against the Jews were temporary, and Hearst went away with the feeling that the exchange had helped in some small way to ease the tension in

Europe. A photographer was waiting outside Hitler's headquarters, and a picture was taken of Hearst with Dr. Alfred Rosenberg and other Nazi leaders. The photograph, together with some of Hearst's dialogue with Hitler lifted out of context, became a sensational item in the American press.

V

Within three years of the universal acceptance of sound, the silent queens began to be aware that their films were failing at the box office. The first to go was Mary Pickford, who had won an Academy Award for her first talkie, *Coquette,* but who was quick to sense rejection just ahead. Much against her better judgment, she would come out of retirement two or three times after 1929, only to have her conviction reinforced when the public stayed away. Pola Negri, with enormous faith in herself and her fans, played *Madame Bovary* as late as 1935, but it was a dismal failure. Eleanor Boardman never returned to films after 1932. Gloria Swanson decided that *Music in the Air* was her swan song, unaware that she would make a startling comeback as a washed-up silent queen in *Sunset Boulevard* sixteen years later. Vilma Banky's last successful film had been *The Winning of Barbara Worth* (1928). Betty Compson, Claire Windsor, Clara Bow, Aileen Pringle, and Renee Adoree joined the exodus in the early thirties.

Marion was a special case. She probably had the best voice of any of the female stars mentioned above. She was only thirty-two when she made her first sound film (1929). Unlike Garbo, Joan Crawford, and Dolores Del Rio, each of whom had a unique screen image going for her, Marion could only survive on her talent and personality. But she realized that she had to have stronger parts. When in late June 1934, she and Hearst returned aboard the North German Lloyd liner *Europa* (a typical bad publicity break for Marion brought about by Hearst's contempt for public opinion, since America by now was inflamed against the Nazis), they decided that she would give Metro one last chance. She would stay if Thalberg would consent to giving her the role of *Marie Antoinette* in the studio's announced production of the Stefan Zweig biography. They would ask Sidney

Franklin, who had done so well in directing her in *Beverly of Graustark* and *Quality Street*, to direct.

Thalberg's first reaction was negative. He had no intention of conceding this "plum" to Marion; he had intended it for his wife. The surprising truth was that given Franklin to direct and soft and natural makeup on Marion to compensate for the artificial powdered wig she would have to wear, Marion could have made Marie Antoinette an intelligent extension of her gentle Phoebe of *Quality Street*. Franklin was enormously capable and managed to get onto the screen all of the warmth and pathos that had marked her best serious films. As it turned out, the film would be made by Miss Shearer within four years, planned by Thalberg but only completed after his tragic, premature death in 1936. It was not a substantial success and was marred by a one-key, dolorous performance by Miss Shearer, who saw only tragedy in the Queen of France.

It is only fair to point out that the career of Norma Shearer was a splendid one. Her most impressive quality was delicate grace, and from her first talkie (*The Trial of Mary Dugan*) until her retirement in 1942, whenever the role called for "a lady" she was usually properly cast. She was inadequate to any real comedy demands upon her, however, making *Idiot's Delight* (1938) something less on the screen than it had been as a Lunt-Fontanne stage vehicle.

Finally Thalberg wired Hearst, according to Marion, that Marion could have the role if she wanted it. But Hearst had not reckoned with Louis B. Mayer, whom he considered a close friend. Mayer told Hearst that Marion could do *Marie Antoinette* if Hearst paid the cost of production. This was contrary to their original agreement, and Metro had financed Marion's last twenty-three films completely. With his own difficulties in finding ready cash for his castle treasures, running his several establishments, and staking a dozen or more guests to tours such as they had just concluded, Hearst was quick to refuse.

Negotiations with Jack Warner were resumed again and finalized. Warner Brothers would finance Cosmopolitan Pictures, and the studio would receive all the publicity Metro had enjoyed from the Hearst publications. Marion's fourteen-room bungalow was sliced into three parts and trundled up the road to Burbank, a distance of fourteen miles. For Marion, it ended an era. She was never to feel completely at home at the Warner studio, and she would give up in three years.

Mayer wept as he saw the strange caravan moving out through the studio gates, and he turned to Marion, who had come to say goodbye, and said, "The Queen has left the studio today."

"Not the Queen," Marion told him. "The *King*."

Tragedy had delayed for several weeks settling these difficult matters with Marion's career. Pepi was so emotionally disturbed by the time of their arrival back in Los Angeles that she was taken to the psychiatric section of Good Samaritan Hospital. Before any therapy could be undertaken, Pepi leaped through a window on the third floor of the hospital building and died.

Marion and Hearst had gone to San Simeon immediately upon their return. It would be easier to settle her career difficulties from there. Even phone calls—to Jack Warner, for example—carried far more weight and authority when they came from the castle. It was always Hearst's base of operations when he was handling delicate business. They were sitting at their usual place in the middle of the long refectory table when word of Pepi's suicide was brought to Hearst by secretary Willicombe. Earlier, the family had been told that Pepi could not have any visitors for the present, and Marion had convinced Reine that she should come with them. Hearst informed Reine, who took the news more calmly than Marion; Marion lost control, as she always did when confronted by death. In this instance, because of Pepi's extreme youth and their closeness, she could not accept it at all. She never had been concerned about Pepi's earlier tomboy ways, the boys she had "beaten up" when she was small, the impression she often gave of being an "outsider." Marion, too, had been an outsider for years because of her stammer, and she had been far wilder as a young girl than Pepi ever had been. It was the cruelest blow she had suffered in life or ever would —until those strange and nearly sinister hours following Hearst's death. Her drinking soon got out of control, and there were days when she could not get to the Warner studio until noon, other days not at all.

Even though Jack Warner had paid part of the cost of transporting the bungalow and had ordered two new rooms to be added onto it (Marion said he had thrown in a Rolls-Royce as well), she was reluctant to go to Warners because she had spent over a decade at Metro and, as she said, "I wouldn't know anybody." This was not exactly true. Mervyn LeRoy, who was to direct her first picture there, *Page Miss Glory,* had been at the Metro studios for a number of years prior to joining Warners, and he had been a frequent visitor to the castle and the beach house.

Director LeRoy considered Marion a "woman with a heart bigger than herself, with a great sense of humor." He had reservations about her acting ability, based upon her recent Metro films which he had seen. But it should not be forgotten that the crisis with Metro had been over her ability to do drama, and much controversy had raged in Hollywood pro and con about her dramatic gifts. For this, Thalberg was chiefly responsible. It was not just *The Barretts* and *Marie Antoinette* of which he had deprived her, but half a dozen other properties as well, in which her dramatic talents would have been put to the test. If he had conceded her even half of these, and if her performances had measured up to her work for Vidor, Goulding, or Franklin, there would have been no controversy. As it was she was being measured against a long string of dramatic performances by Norma Shearer going right up to the present, and few in Hollywood recalled the poignancy of her work in the late 1920s when her career was moving along flawlessly. Memories are extremely short in the film colony.

Hearst was on his best behavior with *Page Miss Glory.* He stayed away from the set most of the time, and he cheerfully agreed with all of LeRoy's concepts. There was only one small disagreement when Hearst wanted a song introduced into the story which Marion could sing. This had become standard practice in nearly all of her Metro films. But LeRoy told Hearst that the film story had been adapted from a successful Broadway play and there was no place for music anywhere. Surprisingly, Hearst backed down, although a title song was injected along the way. There was no other friction.

Knowing Marion's taste for gags, one evening about eleven o'clock when they were shooting late LeRoy was able to get in only one "take" a scene in which Marion was to come by taxi some distance into the set, moving around a darkened corner into the light. But LeRoy told her that she would have to do it again, and Marion gamely returned to her remote corner out of sight while LeRoy got everyone, crew, cameramen, absolutely everyone, off the set, and Marion rode around her corner into a lighted empty sound stage and thought she had lost her wits.

Her leading man, Dick Powell, attempted at first to keep a certain distance from Marion except during their scenes together. He said that he was afraid of "Mr. Hearst." But Marion became fonder of him than she had been of any of her leading men since Lawrence Gray, and there were numerous visits to San Simeon and to Ocean House. He was then separated from the actress Joan Blondell, who later became Marion's good friend.

Powell would call Marion's private number at Ocean House or at the castle and have long conversations with her, and once, it is said, she asked him if he loved her and he quickly assured her that he did. But he was not above joking about their "affairs" or giving his locker-room pals at the country club all the latest details.

Marion insisted upon doing another film with Powell immediately following *Page Miss Glory*, a romantic drama set in the time of the Napoleonic wars entitled *Hearts Divided*. It had the fine acting talents of Claude Rains as a stern-eyed Napoleon, Marion as a lovely young blonde from Baltimore being courted by no less than three of Hollywood's finest comic character actors: Edward Everett Horton, Charlie Ruggles, and Arthur Treacher, as well as by Captain Jerome Bonaparte, Napoleon's brother, played by Dick Powell. Warner's makeup department did better by Powell than they did by Marion, and he was quite beautiful with curled hair and epaulettes, but the film was not very successful.

Marion's friendship with Powell did not terminate when she learned of his careless betrayal of their relationship. "I'm 'The Patsy' in such things," she later told her husband during her last decade. Characteristically, she didn't blame Powell but her situation in life. She was vulnerable to almost anyone who wanted to take advantage of her delicate mistress-celebrity role. But her friendship with the singing actor did change, and once in a great while Marion would allude to their old intimacy in his presence with a few well-chosen bawdy words and sardonic laughter. Part of her motivation in keeping Powell on as a platonic and congenial friend was Hearst's admiration for him. During Marion's protracted and fatal illness many years later, Powell was a solicitous and welcome friend. Within a period of eighteen months, he did three films for Hearst—the two with Marion and a highly successful musical, *Shipmates Forever*.

As she grew older and death began to claim members of her family, one after the other, Marion became far more tolerant of occasional pettiness in others than she had been as a young chorine. It was as though she felt that she needed all the friends she could get as insurance against that future time when Hearst, too, would be gone. By 1935, she was beginning to feel an ominous dread that death was going to take away everyone she loved and leave her alone in that enormous beach palace, for on April 26 Papa Ben died. He had come out to California in 1930 following his retirement from the magistrate's bench. It was three days before Hearst's seventy-second birthday, and the usual large party was canceled.

Papa Ben was eighty-two, and the death certificate said that he had died of complications resulting from cirrhosis of the liver. Fortunately, it was not a long illness, and he had been on his feet until two weeks before the end. He spent his last days sitting around San Simeon and the beach house telling stories to anyone who would listen; he still enjoyed a conversation with a pretty young girl, and there were always a number of them at both places. And when he was stricken and carried to bed, he told Marion once again that she was the one thing in life of which he was proud. She understood at once what he was implying—that she was decent and had a great heart, and convention be damned.

Hearst and Marion made up for that lost party the following year on the occasion of his seventy-third birthday. Painted scenic flats were installed in the lower rooms of the beach house, converting it into a hacienda. The theme was that of a Spanish fiesta.

It was also, by chance, a wedding celebration for composer Harry Ruby and his bride, Marion's old and dear friend Eileen Percy. Hearst had flown them to Yuma, Arizona, in his private plane for the ceremony, and the pilot had brought them back to Santa Monica. Marion had worked hard to encourage the match. It was a weakness she could not help. She looked upon marriage as far more desirable than fame or wealth, and since marriage is often such an uncertain proposition and not the state of bliss Marion liked to believe that it was, her matchmaking must be considered as a serious fault. At least three weddings, if not more, grew out of her careful plotting at San Simeon.

She rarely mentioned her own unmarried state. During one evening at Adela Rogers St. Johns's home when she and Hearst were guests, along with Tom Mix and his wife, Buster Collier and Connie Talmadge, Marion was advising Hearst to take a firmer hand with his sixteen-year-old son, Jack, who was in constant trouble. Marion told him that people who are divorced are always too soft with their kids—they all have guilty consciences.

"But," said Hearst, "I am not divorced and I do not have a guilty conscience."

Marion burst into tears. "Sometimes I don't know what to do," she said, forgetting they were not alone. "You know you can't live without me."

Then he set her straight. "I would _prefer_ not to," he said.

"I won't let you get a divorce," Marion said. "I've told you before and I tell you again. You're a great man. . . . You must have dignity. They can attack your politics and throw dirt and all, but you mustn't ever give them anything that could—could make you lose your dignity. It is all right—it's sound historically, or traditionally, and dramatically, if it _is_ wicked—for you to have a Follies girl and blond movie star as your mistress. Look at Louis XIV and Charles II and Herod! If you divorce your wife, the mother of your five sons, to marry her, a girl younger by twenty years, they can make you look like an old fool. You can live down being thought old-fashioned and even immoral but no man, you say it yourself, has ever lived down being ridiculous. I'd rather take our chances this way."

Hearst must have been disturbed by this conversation. It was clearly a lamentation rather than a declaration that all was well. He probably knew that it was said as much for Adela's sake as his own and that she really resented deeply his failure to legitimatize their long relationship. Soon after this, Marion embarked upon her second film with Clark Gable, a comedy entitled _Cain and Mabel,_ and Hearst seemed obsessed with the idea that Marion had to be put on a pedestal so that the world could see her purity of spirit. He ordered a spectacular musical number, which became—as his visions expanded and multiplied— an absurd apotheosis of Marion. Alabaster palaces arose beside Venetian canals, with banks that floated together to allow a modern ballroom ensemble to sway while a male chorus offered a few bars of the song _Who?._ The lords and ladies of Le Petit Trianon then appeared in the conventional Versailles setting, that scene dissolving to reveal Marion as an imperious Madame Du Barry. Wildly anachronistic, a wimpled company then was seen in front of such a mighty pipe organ that Hearst had to have the roof of the Warner studio raised to accommodate it. The pipe organ divided at that moment so that a *corps de ballet* could leap forth. The ballet company seemed much agitated by some sight off camera—Marion materializing from a heap of Arthurian finery as the Lady Guinevere.

That one scene added half a million dollars to the movie's cost, and it was all to be lost. When it became evident that *Cain and Mabel* was winding up in the red, Marion seemed upset by it. It was the first time that she had shown any concern over the box office. Some of her friends frankly hoped that she would retire before matters got even worse with her career. She was now forty years old; she had forty-six features behind her. And she was the richest woman in Hollywood.

Hearst had not been really involved with Marion's films since *Operator 13*. Feeling the weight of his years, he was reserving his energies for his newspapers and, once again, politics.

By 1936, Hearst believed that Roosevelt had carried the country too far into socialism. His tone in his papers against Roosevelt was no longer mildly critical. Hearst's enemies were quick to call him a Fascist, forgetting that only three years earlier he had suggested that the government take over the railroads —part of his crusade against the "railroad trust" that went back several decades. In any case, he proposed that his old enemy, Al Smith, toss his derby into the ring, and, realizing at once that this was a lost cause and knowing the Democrats were dedicated to Roosevelt, he turned to the Republicans. Hearst was among those supporting the bland Governor of Kansas, Alf Landon, for the Presidency. When Landon was overwhelmed in a Democratic landslide, Marion was worried about what the weeks of attacks against Roosevelt in the Hearst press might have done to their friendship with Anna Roosevelt Boettiger and she phoned Hyde Park on the night of Election Day. She finally got through to publisher John Boettiger and told him that "We love you and Anna very much. All that newspaper business was just politics." Then Hearst got on the line and said, "Well, I just wanted to repeat what Marion said, that we have been run over by a steam-roller, but that there are no hard feelings at this end." He backed up this declaration within a short time by hiring Boettiger to run the Seattle *Post-Intelligencer* at a salary of $37,500 a year.

When *Ever Since Eve*, Marion's fourth film for Warner Brothers, was completed and she held her traditional end-of-the-picture party, none of the guests suspected that it was any different from the forty-odd other such parties she had given during her film career. Marion was, in fact, gayer than she had been during the film's production.

Jack Warner grinned at her whenever she glanced his way —the Levantine smile of a tough bargainer at the rug auction, only the product was celluloid and not Karastan. Warner had no complaints, despite the declining box office on Marion's Warner films. *Ever Since Eve* had been booked into the prestigious Radio City Music Hall and for four years now Warner Brothers films, all thirty or forty of them a year or whatever huge number the Warner stock company was turning out, were getting magnificent exposure in the Hearst media.

But Marion had plenty to complain about. The scripts she had been doing since she left Metro had deteriorated steadily in quality. There seemed to be a conspiracy to undermine her career through miscasting. So similar was the theme of *Ever Since Eve* to *Page Miss Glory* they might have been written by the same inept scenarist. In both, Marion was supposed to be a plain jane who suddenly becomes the sexiest dame in town. But she looked her years now; erasing the tell-tale shadows beneath her eyes no longer concealed her early surrender to middle age. Leading man Robert Montgomery had walked through his role of novelist with an annoyingly patronizing manner, as though he were simply fulfilling a contractual obligation. Admittedly, his lines were dreadful and no one could possibly believe that such a witless human being could be a published writer. More implausibly, Marion's "ugly duckling" disguise with horn-rimmed glasses and school-marm hair turned out to be more striking and chic than her "transformation" into a beauty. She had been getting thick-waisted throughout the thirties, and she didn't care enough for her fading career to go on any crash diets for Jack Warner.

The comedy at times promised to be funny whenever Louise Fazenda, as an early feminist publishing head, was rampaging through Montgomery's penthouse, vainly attempting to extract some manuscript from an obvious loser in her stable of authors. But even Miss Fazenda had to rely upon inflection and exaggerated outrage to win smiles; there was no humor to be found on those pedestrian bypaths.

Doubtless the Eastern premiere at the Radio City Music Hall had been the result of Marion's friendship with the Rockefellers. She had been seeing a great deal of Winthrop and his sister Abby, and "Bobo" Rockefeller, Winthrop's wife, would sit out the weeks of waiting for her divorce at Marion's home several years later.

Marion had told no one that *Ever Since Eve* was to be her valedictory to a long and largely successful career as a leading lady. But she was a shrewd professional in films, and she knew better than anyone that in every one of her four Warner films, she had played a woman half her age. Part of her willingness to participate in such a bankrupt effort was Hearst's visible anxiety. He seemed desperate to surround himself with youth as old age overcame him. Even at forty, Marion was his little girl, his blond playmate. If she were to perform on the screen as a middle-aged woman, it would shatter his dream of her as the maiden with golden hair who made him forget his years. And, as a star, she had to remain virginal. The Warner studio announced that Marion was signed to play the girl in *Boy Meets Girl*, a Broadway comedy hit of a recent season. Marion forgot retirement for a few days and seemed excited by the prospect. But then Hearst read the script and thought it was too outspoken. Marion quietly announced that she had changed her mind, that she now believed it was not the sort of property she did best. Immediately following this disappointment, George Bernard Shaw wrote her asking if she would be interested in playing Liza Doolittle in a film version of *Pygmalion* which his new friend Gabriel Pascal was planning to make. Marion was flattered and awestruck, desperately wanting to go to England to do it because it would be a challenge and because she had come to love England and had many friends there. It was a role that closely paralleled her own early years. But something happened to kill the prospect—perhaps Pascal's lack of enthusiasm since her last three or four films had been so far below her own standard of excellence —and Wendy Hiller got the role.

This blow did not devastate Marion as the loss of the part of Elizabeth Barrett had. The truth was that after twenty years of one film after another she was tired, and if she was to be rescued professionally, she needed the hand of a strong director who could shake her out of her lethargy and tap some of that energy still visible to her friends on certain party occasions.

Anyone who recalled Marion's subtle and tearless heartbreak in *Quality Street* when she believed that her lover, returned from years as a soldier, saw her as plain, her beauty lost, or her status-driven film queen in *Show People,* knew that her versatility had begun to be overlooked around 1930 soon after talking pictures came in.

And sometime in 1930–31, Marion began to lose some of the ingratiating, kittenish appeal she had throughout the last half of the 1920s. Much of the fun had gone out of making movies when sound arrived and silence prevailed on the set a great deal of the time. It was as though an unseen hand had wrapped itself around Marion's mouth to keep her quiet. She said then that making movies was becoming "a factory business." She did not enjoy speaking in whispers or tiptoeing through *anywhere.*

She attempted to cover her exit from movies with an acceptable alibi. She explained, "I'd been working so long, and I felt that I would rather be a companion to him [Hearst]. . . . I thought I might as well take it easy and rest for a while and have some sort of companionship with the one that I loved. So I got out—made up my mind just like that."

VI

It is not unusual for a wealthy actress to retire at forty. What is unusual is for her to make a success of her retirement. After years—usually twenty or more—of being in the limelight, of being everybody's darling, of carrying the burden of whole productions on her shoulders, suddenly she is in the middle of that wasteland of her private self. The result can be tragic, when it is ill-planned. The fans and the hand-kissers must be supplanted by a circle of friends who are willing to give love, encouragement, and support in place of adulation.

Security and self-confidence are rarely experienced by film stars, and in their retirement they often seek out equally insecure souls. Aging actresses will often accept the company of a circle of either their own kind—other actresses living in the past, homosexuals, or alcoholics. Sometimes they will seek the approval of God. Marion was to do all these things in turn, having in addition Hearst's devotion and that of her own family.

Marion said at first that she looked forward to her retirement, that she couldn't wait, that she needed a rest. She was going to travel and read and play with her dog. For "serious" consumption in gossip columns, she said that she was going to help others find careers, as she had done so often. She was going to look after the sick children of the poor, as she had in the past.

As one of the two richest actresses in American history (Mary Pickford was the other), she should have had no worries. The nation was in the darkest heart of a cruel depression, but it had not seemed to have affected the film industry appreciably and millions of Americans had sought out the local moviehouse as an oasis away from reality. So Marion began living out her days of leisure in her old film community that was as out of touch with reality as its product.

But as Marion had feared, retirement plunged her precipitously into a half-way house of fading fame and family problems. Although she could have retired following her last Metro film, *Operator 13*, with her fame intact, since it was acceptable entertainment, her career at Warner Brothers had taken her four pictures away from that distinction. She did not know it then, but it had set her up for nearly total destruction of her film reputation within three years.

Shortly after she had finished her last film, Hearst's closest editorial collaborator and friend, Arthur Brisbane, was stricken with a series of heart attacks. Hearst dispatched his Bad Nauheim specialist, Dr. Heinz Groedel, to Brisbane's bedside, but on Christmas Day 1936 Brisbane died. He had been ill in Europe, where he had spent part of December with Hearst and Marion in Venice and at Countess Dorothy di Frasso's Villa Madrone.

Marion felt considerable remorse since she and Brisbane had been at each other's throats throughout much of the trip. At the Villa Madrone, where Count Ciano, Mussolini's son-in-law, was a guest, Brisbane wanted desperately to get a newspaper story out of Ciano, but Marion was seated at Ciano's right at dinner and Brisbane was far away, at the other end of the table next to Hearst. Marion asked Ciano, who spoke no English, why the Italians "teased" the Abyssinians, using her schoolgirl French. Brisbane was watching this, overhearing the accent if not the words, and noticed that Ciano looked offended. Ignoring Marion's question, Ciano began talking to the woman on his left. Brisbane whispered to Hearst that he was sure that Marion was telling Ciano "American secrets" in French. Hearst sent Marion a note warning her not to talk about such matters to Ciano, and this inflamed Marion, who knew no special secrets about her country. After dinner, Marion walked up to Brisbane and tucked the note in his handkerchief pocket, telling him that he might save it for posterity. Marion managed to keep Ciano dancing until the party broke up, eliminating any chance for Brisbane to get to him for a story.

Brisbane's illness had begun at the Lido, and Marion believed that it had started with a high temperature. Marion and Alice Head, who had come down from London, took turns at his bedside, since Brisbane insisted that his illness was not serious and had refused to get a nurse. Then, with the help of Prince Alexis M'divani, who had been divorced from Barbara Hutton only the year before and was $3,000,000 richer thereby, Brisbane was ferried across to Venice, then carried aboard an express train to Paris, where his condition worsened. It was then decided to rush him by fast liner to New York.

Eleanor Medill ("Cissy") Patterson, publisher of the Washington *Herald* (formerly a Hearst paper, but she had been allowed to lease it from Hearst and publish it as her own) and much admired by Hearst, phoned Hearst's suite at the Ritz Tower Hotel that Christmas morning. Marion answered as Hearst had been with Brisbane the night before and was himself exhausted by the death watch. "Good Lord, Cissy," Marion said, after hearing of Brisbane's death, "aren't we in enough trouble?" Hearst was standing just behind her and asked her to give him the phone. Tears were pouring from him. Christmas often made him terribly sentimental and sad, and this was the saddest Christmas of his life.

Marion and Cissy Patterson went on that snowy morning to Brisbane's home at 102nd Street and Fifth Avenue, where Phoebe Brisbane invited them in to see her dead husband. Marion recalled that he was lying with an encyclopedia open in front of him. Outside in the living room, the Brisbane family was drinking sherry and, before she left, they tried to pump some good cheer into Marion, who was terribly depressed. "It was practically an Irish wake," she said of the gathering in the Brisbane home.

Marion said that later that day Hearst received a call from John Neylan, who had resigned as Hearst's chief legal aide and business manager exactly a year earlier. In a broken voice, Hearst asked Neylan to help him, but, according to Marion, Neylan said, "I've got you where I want you. I've waited for this day." Marion grabbed the phone from Hearst's hand and said,

"Look, you louse, don't you dare come near here and don't you dare go to Arthur Brisbane's funeral!" There was a pause at the other end of the line, and then Neylan said, "I didn't know he was dead." Marion then told Neylan that he didn't know he (Neylan) was dead, but "you're dead from the neck up."

Hearst protested what he took to be a verbal assault on Neylan and wanted to know why she had done such a thing to one of his former most-trusted aides. Marion told him, "My God! Don't you realize when you've got an enemy in your camp?"

Marion was plainly seeing most of Hearst's business aides and high executives as out to bring him crashing down. At seventy-four, he was in desperate trouble financially. Two years earlier, an exhaustive study of his empire and finances had been published in *Fortune* Magazine, but it failed to show that much of his personal property was heavily mortgaged. The deception was not the magazine's but the work of Hearst's staff. Beyond this, many of his newspapers began to lose money and he was reluctant to give up a single one of them. His attempt to hang onto all of his possessions was as feckless as was his attempt to have Marion cling to youth. It was foredoomed, and in early 1937 everything collapsed.

Hearst had spent his way into insolvency. He had been borrowing heavily for years for his personal "needs" such as a collection of rare pewter or a block of ten paintings released by an estate, and the notes, most of them held by Canadian banks where the Hearst enterprises got their newsprint, were being called in. The Hearst organization formed a Committee from among the executives to help stave off disaster for their Chief. This Committee would remain active for nearly ten years attempting to hold back financial ruin and within three years would call upon the services of Wall Street banker John W. Hanes, that former college stagedoor johnny who had hung around Marion during the run of one of her shows in New Haven.

Within less than a year all of the measures taken by the Committee had failed to satisfy Hearst's many creditors and part of his huge collection of European treasures was taken from the warehouses in the Bronx and at San Simeon wharf for sale in department stores in major cities. It was a terrible wrench for Hearst seeing them go; he could no longer sit down with his card file and order one period room exchanged for another.

But he was allowed to keep all of the things he had been living with at San Simeon and in Marion's beach house, so some of the sting was taken out of the ordeal.

Marion's enemies were few, and they were all in the East, and they were all Hearst executives. She said she had no love for Dick Berlin and apparently the feeling was returned. And years after the debacle, she was blaming John Francis Neylan, the lawyer who had been juggling the pieces of the Hearst empire for years to keep the wolf from the castle door, for Hearst's near ruin. Neylan was Hearst's Brutus in Marion's mind, and she even quoted Hearst as saying to Neylan, "And you, too, John?"

It was rare for Marion to condemn others for weaknesses that were her own, but she claimed that Neylan drank heavily. Frances Marion, who shared Marion's low opinion of Neylan, spoke of one instance when Neylan was at San Simeon "loaded, and he staggered into the living room and said, 'Where is Hearst?' " This informality distressed Frances and she told Neylan, "I don't know where *Mr.* Hearst is—I call him 'Mr. Hearst' because I worked for him for a long time and have great respect for him."

"I still call him Hearst," Neylan said, a trifle belligerently. Frances ignored this and told him, "Mr. Hearst's gone to bed a long time ago and you're drunk."

According to Frances, Neylan then said, "I'll get that son-of-a-bitch if it kills me. I've always hated his guts." Frances protested, saying, "He's done everything for you."

"That's it!" Neylan allegedly declared, and here anyone close to Hearst might agree that Neylan deep in his cups would allow some of his resentment to surface after years of stifling much of his own ego in the presence of his employer. But Frances saw this resentment as a betrayal, and she then says that she asked Neylan if he wanted some of the power that had been denied him through that working lifetime of holding Hearst financially intact.

"Yes," Frances quotes Neylan as having said, "and I'm going to get it."

Perhaps this happened. Frances's memory is accurate in most areas. But this shocking betrayal of one of Hearst's closest friendships could not have occurred at the time of Hearst's imminent bankruptcy, and Neylan could not have been, as Marion believed, the cause of his downfall, since Neylan already had resigned from the Hearst organization because, as he wrote biographer Swanberg, "the strain was so unbearable that had I not resigned I would have been dead before 1940."

What is significant to our story is that three top Hearst executives, Berlin, Neylan, and Brisbane, were nearly as close to Hearst as Marion was, and she resented this intimacy and came to hate them. It was in later years that she "fixed" her memory of that financial debacle and came around to blaming Neylan, who was a year out of the picture. And there is no question about Berlin's feeling and Brisbane's, too, when he was alive, that Marion was the greatest threat to the magazine and newspaper empire. Neylan's retirement and Brisbane's death would leave the field clear for Richard Berlin to remain Marion's chief nemesis and the man she later would accuse (to her friends only) of the "murder" of her beloved companion on that August night in 1951. It was not hysteria that prompted such an accusation but the troubled mind of an emotional woman who was trying to make sense of that chaotic last night. *Why did Berlin and two other Hearst executives come to the house just before he died? Why was she given an injection? Why did they steal his body out of the house while she was under sedation?* Marion never saw herself as a threat to the empire or to anything else. She was, in her mind and in fact, an extension of Hearst—as much his creation as the castle itself.

So when Marion accused Neylan of this betrayal long after his retirement from the field, she was attempting to even up old scores. Neylan was the one who first had urged Hearst to cut down on his spending, and Marion knew, as Hearst himself had known, that keeping the money *flowing out* to galleries and dealers and to the huge staffs at San Simeon, Wyntoon, and St. Donat's was a vital part of the old man's "circulation." To deny him this was worse than rendering him a blow as physical as a stroke. Marion knew better than anyone that if all the spending stopped, Hearst might lose all interest in life and quickly sicken and die. To Marion, Neylan was an angel of death in the guise of the man Hearst asserted was "my best friend."

The true villain in fact was Hearst's fiscal dipsomania. His personal expense was running to $15 million a year. His expenditures for art and relics came to more than $1 million each and every year until the Canadian banks blew the whistle in 1937 and threatened to foreclose on the notes they held in payment for newsprint. Liquid capital was needed fast. There appeared to be none available since Hearst was mortgaged to the very limit. "I guess I'm through," he told Marion.

Marion asked how much he needed, and she was told "at least a million." Actually, he needed more than that, and Marion eventually was compelled to seek help from friends. She was in far healthier financial condition than he was at the time. She had stocks; she owned real estate in New York and California, plus some huge land holdings in the state of Vera Cruz, Mexico, grazing land next to Hearst's own—some of it gifts from Hearst, tokens of reassurance that she was loved, but much of her wealth was derived from her own earnings.

Marion did not hesitate, and she condemned Millicent for not coming to her husband's rescue with "some of her millions." Marion had to liquidate her stock and some of her real estate in a short time. She asked Hearst's film chief, Edgar Hatrick, who had become her financial advisor, to liquidate as many of her assets as he could. "I've got to have a million dollars in a hurry," she told Hatrick. "I don't care what you do, but get it for me."

The Committee was to meet with Hearst in New York later that week. Several high-ranking executives in the empire were with him aboard the train going East. Marion, who had no official title except that of Editorial Consultant, was among them. Her worst moment was when she was ready with her surprise. "You don't have to worry," she told Hearst and then handed him the certified check for a million.

"I won't take it," Hearst said. He had heard from his general manager, Thomas Justin White, that Marion was carrying the check with her.

"Now look. . . ."

"I'm sorry, Marion," he insisted. "I won't accept it. Here, I'll take it but I'll tear it up."

"No, you won't!" And she gripped the check so tightly, it was permanently wrinkled.

Hearst told her emphatically that he wouldn't think of accepting it. Then Marion got up, and she sought out White and handed the check to him. Bill Hearst, Jr., and Richard Berlin were witnesses. White's first reaction was to tell her that it was a kind thought, implying that it was not enough to save Hearst. But then when he saw her keen disappointment, he added that the idea wasn't such a bad one.

Marion asserted that following this episode no one among the Hearst hierarchy spoke to her again during the journey. "They were hoping," she said, "to take the lamb to the slaughter."

Marion and Hearst went to their apartment at the Ritz Tower on Park Avenue. Hearst had acquired the building from Arthur Brisbane in 1928. Brisbane had built the luxury apartment hotel in 1926 with $4 million of borrowed money, and it was running at a huge loss. The favor to "Artie" was now another debit venture for Hearst, but at least he and Marion could be comfortable whenever they were in New York. He had given up the charade of appearing at social gatherings in New York with Millicent. Their meetings now were only to transact family business.

The Hearst executives met with their Chief in Marion's drawing room, that being the most spacious room available. The proposal made by Berlin and others was to give Marion the two Boston papers—both money losers—as collateral. Hearst strenuously objected and said, "Give her the magazines."

Meanwhile, Joseph P. Kennedy, who had not yet been appointed as Ambassador to Great Britain, came by to offer $14 million for the magazines. He had been tipped off about Hearst's financial difficulties. This offer was quickly rejected since the magazines earned that much each year.

Marion was eavesdropping outside the closed door and praying that no one would open it suddenly. She could hear great sighs from Hearst and then a noisy argument going on over what collateral to give her for her million-dollar loan. Hearst was hotly defending Marion as someone especially dear to him and not to be treated as an impersonal outsider. Finally, Marion was too embarrassed to listen to more and quietly walked back to her bedroom.

Hearst came to her there and said, "Well, they want to give you the two Boston papers for collateral."

"I don't want any collateral."

"You've got to take them. I don't think it's any good. I wanted to get you some decent collateral, but they seem to think that this is all right. I know it isn't."

"Listen," Marion told him, "if that's what's worrying you, I'll take them. Just as long as I don't have to pay the expenses of what is in the red."

The following day, Walter Howey, Hearst's specialist for

ailing papers, dropped by to see Marion. "Hey, Boss," Howey
began. "You know I'm in charge of the Boston papers. You own
them, right?"

Marion set him straight on her involvement and then
Howey said, "I'm going to Boston and take those papers out of
the red." And in five months time, he had done just that, the
Hearst organization pressuring Marion to give back the newly
prospering members of the Hearst chain. She obliged them, and
part of her million dollars was returned to her with the balance
following later.

The night after Marion's money was accepted, she lay sleep-
less in her room, wondering why Hearst hadn't come by to kiss
her goodnight. This night of all nights she expected him to be
warm, considerate, and even grateful. She had spent the day lux-
uriating in her good deed. After twenty years of having millions
showered on her, she finally was allowed to give something back
beyond her presence and loyalty. When Hearst failed to appear,
she got up and walked to his room. She could hear him pacing
up and down. She rapped on his door and wanted to know what
was the matter.

Hearst opened the door, and his expression was grim and
despairing. "It hasn't worked, dear Marion," he told her. "The
banks want more money."

"How much more?" she asked.

"At least two million. I've put in a call to Cissy. She's going
to call me back." He last had seen Cissy Patterson at Brisbane's
funeral, but she was a very special person to him. Whenever she
would come to San Simeon in her private railway car, Hearst
would have all the castle guests lined up on the esplanade holding out flowers to her and, at least once, singing a song of welcome. Despite the fact that she was also part owner of the rival
New York *Daily News* and the Chicago *Tribune*, she was eternally grateful to him for letting her have the Washington *Herald*,
which she had made indispensable to anyone in Washington
society. "I'm going to leave it up to her to decide on how much
she can manage," Hearst explained.

The call came through and Cissy Patterson said she could
loan him a million. She told him she didn't want any interest
paid on the sum, but Hearst insisted on 5 percent.

Marion ran to her room and rifled her drawers and jewelry
case, dumping the pearls, diamonds, brooches, earrings, beads,

and bangles into a scarf and then hurried back to Hearst. She dumped the dazzling heap onto a table and asked, "How much will this stuff bring?"

Hearst said nothing, but he began weeping at the sight. "You always come out the loser at the pawnshop," he said. "We need a million dollars more."

Marion left him suddenly, grabbed a sable coat from her closet, and in a few minutes she was on Park Avenue hailing a cab. She went to the apartment of Abby Rockefeller, a close friend, who unhesitatingly agreed to advance Hearst over half a million dollars. Miss Rockefeller was the lone sister to the five Rockefeller brothers. Marion described Abby as "a very beautiful little girl—I must call her a little girl because she's very short and all the boys are tall. She is very kindly and reticent and sweet and just as nice as anybody could be."

Marion spent all of the next day mortgaging her New York real estate, selling her jewelry, and coming up with the balance needed in cash. Then she collapsed in her room at the Ritz Tower, her nerves, body, and mind exhausted. Hearst was never to forget her successful efforts to save him.

In the first flush of gratitude over Marion's gesture, Hearst in typical fashion made an effort to bring other elements in his life into harmony. During one evening that week, he told Marion that nearly everything in their life together was perfect "if we could lick the booze" and then suggested the Keeley cure, a now outmoded method of withdrawal that sometimes cured alcoholism but was a period of hell for the patient. Marion bridled and ran out of the room. She tossed everything in her own room she could pick up against the door separating their rooms, then, half out of breath, she phoned Millicent Hearst.

"You can come and get your boy," she said. "I don't want him." What Millicent replied is unknown, but certainly she was more composed than Marion. She must have politely declined Marion's "offer."

Marion's drinking had been a source of friction between them for a very long time, but since her retirement from the screen it had become so serious, nearly all of Hearst's friends had heard his lamentations about it. "What can I do?" he would ask. "I try to cut off her source of supply but it never works." Hearst was perceptive about human failings and undoubtedly knew that the only thing that would work would be to cut off the source of her unhappiness. She insisted even to him that it was no longer marriage that she wanted. Then, he must have wondered, *what was it?* She had immense wealth despite her generous gift of all her liquid capital and much of her collection of diamonds and emeralds. She had more friends than anyone in Hollywood. She was surrounded by family, even though they were dying off at an alarming rate. If she was involved in an affair with somebody else, he knew nothing about it, and even if she were, they were almost invariably futile—with married men or with actors so involved with their own egos not even Marion could take them seriously.

VII

Refusing to be cowed by reality, Hearst and Marion returned to the Coast early that spring to begin planning their most magnificent party ever. It was to have a circus theme, and they persuaded Jack Warner to lend them a carousel from Warner's back lot. There were sideshows, and Hearst's huge birthday cake for the assembled five hundred guests was in the form of a circus tent. Marion wore a lady bareback rider's costume with plumed hat, while Hearst wore a clown suit without the white-face makeup. Recklessly spendthrift, he was yet a conservative about his person.

There is an interesting photo of Maureen O'Sullivan and her director husband, John Farrow, as they rummage through a trunk of costumes at the beach house, searching for something appropriate. They both look bemused by their situation—quite obviously, neither one had much use for this sort of fantasy. The costumes for such affairs came from Western Costume and were always sent in lots of a hundred to the castle or to Ocean House for those big annual celebrations of Hearst's natal day. Bette Davis thought it was all too childish and came in an evening gown, but late in the evening she donned some whiskers and made an appearance as the Bearded Lady. Marion rode the carrousel half the night and kept trying to catch the brass ring. Once she caught it, and everyone applauded her good fortune.

With such rituals, Marion and Hearst returned to the old tolerances, the old forebearances. He was now rabidly against the President he had helped to power and even joined forces with his old enemy Al Smith to denounce Roosevelt, but Marion liked Eleanor Roosevelt and spoke of her admiringly. Anna Roosevelt Boettiger and her publisher husband from Oregon were frequent guests at the castle and at Wyntoon. Marion had begun to dislike the columns of the arch-conservative and rancorous foe of communism Westbrook Pegler and came very close to pressuring Hearst to get rid of him. She detested anyone whose opinions were full of bile and hatred, so Hitler, who was also something of a bogeyman to her now, joined Pegler on her undesirable list. She was only rarely heard to echo Hearst's growing blasts at the Reds in America and abroad. Politics were still rather tiresome to her, but now she blamed most of what was wrong in Europe on Hitler, and both she and Hearst were concerned about the fate of St. Donat's if England were engulfed by war. It was not the treasures accumulated there that they were anxious about but the place itself—that place of such restorative serenity to which they looked forward every summer.

By June 1937, Hearst was forced to relinquish financial control over his publishing empire, surrendering it to Clarence Shearn in New York. Shearn shut down Hearst's own favorite, the New York *American*, merged its features and facilities with the *Journal,* and the *Journal-American* would survive another thirty years, or until a massive newspaper strike forced it out of business. The Rochester papers were shut down, and Hearst took a pay cut from half a million a year to $100,000. But the nightmare went on. In November, Marion received an extortion note which read, "If you value your life you will put one thousand $ in small bills in front of the California show [theater]." The small-time hoodlum who wrote the note was caught. Marion, for once, did not think the event was exciting or rattle on about it to her friends. She kept to her rooms at Ocean House and went out rarely.

Christmas was spent in the castle with a few close friends, and then Marion stayed on for the greater part of January and into February. This brush with disaster and her untriumphant departure from films had brought them closer together. They would remain so until his death, spending more and more time together, his own business trips cut way down in number.

In the middle of January 1938, during one of Marion's trips down to Ocean House, she learned of the death of one of her most dedicated fans, Clark Alvord of Nelson, Nevada. Alvord

and Marion had kept up a correspondence since the time of
Show People ten years earlier. Seeing her image on the screen
was the closest he ever got to her, but the experience was the
most significant one of his life. He left her nearly everything he
owned, including his personal effects and 510,000 shares of
South Eastern Mining Company stock—the controlling interest
—and she turned over the legacy to her children's clinic.

On February 7, 1938, the castle was relatively quiet. Marion
likened such moments at San Simeon to living in "a hollow shell."
She and her lone guest, Dorothy Mackaill, were waiting for the
arrival of Lord and Lady Plunket, who were on their way up
from Los Angeles in Hearst's private plane. The ladies were in
the castle office much of that afternoon, calling their bookie in
Hollywood to see if they had won anything at Santa Anita Race
Track. Hearst was working in his study.

Miss Mackaill was a favorite of Hearst's. It was part of Miss
Mackaill's character to be direct, and he found this quality refreshing after so many years of being "yessed" by nearly everyone. He called her "Peck's Bad Boy," and told her that she did
what Marion wanted to do. He might have added that she did
what Marion *used* to do without hesitation, but Marion was mellowing with the years—the playful kitten had become a mild-
mannered tabby with only rare moments of mischief and those
without much conviction.

Dorothy Plunket was the daughter of a great beauty of the
early 1900s, Fanny Ward, described by Anita Loos as once having been a "baby-faced blue-eyed little blonde. . . . She was then
crowding sixty, and the energy she spent on holding back the
clock ought to have aged Fanny beyond her years, but she was
younger in spirit than any of us. (In *Gentlemen Prefer Blondes*
I wrote of Fanny: 'When a girl is cute for fifty years it really gets
to be historic.') . . . She was financially independent through the
generosity of her first husband, so that she and Jack (Jack Dean,
her second husband) could live the rich, full lives of international playboys and girls."

Lady Plunket and her husband had been warned not to attempt to fly if they could not make the flight early in the afternoon and arrive before 3:00 P.M., since after that a killing fog
closed in for half an hour or so and made landing impossible.
The Plunkets were late getting to Hearst's landing strip at Santa
Monica and ignored the warning. An experienced pilot would

have told them that it was too late to make the flight, but Hearst's regular pilot had given in to the co-pilot's pleas to be allowed to take the plane solo in order to get his full license.

By mid-afternoon, fog had moved in from Morro Bay and the entire hilltop was enshrouded. Marion and Miss Mackaill were still preoccupied with the afternoon's race when they were abruptly told to "get off the phone, goddamn it!" by Jack Adams, Hearst's office manager. They learned almost at once that Adams was attempting to guide in the Plunket's plane by telephone to the Santa Maria airstrip.

The ladies ran to the esplanade in front of the great doors to La Casa Grande and peered upward. Suddenly the plane was sighted directly over their heads, the engine roaring as the pilot frantically accelerated his climb to avoid crashing into Hearst's mountain. Then there was an ominous silence. Marion said, "I wonder what's happened? Maybe he's gone back to Santa Maria or San Luis."

When the ladies hurried inside to inform Hearst that the plane was in trouble, he told them, "That's nonsense!" He had a great deal of faith in his regular pilot, and he walked quickly down to secretary Willicombe's office to check on the return flight. As he approached the office, his regular pilot came through the door on his way outside. It was one of the most severe shocks of Hearst's life seeing—at that critical moment—the man in whose hands he had placed the safety of the world's great figures and hearing the man say that the plane was indeed in trouble. It had crashed.

A man in a passing car pulled bobsled champion James Lawrence from the blazing wreckage down the slope. Lawrence had second degree burns over much of his body. The Plunkets and the co-pilot died in the wreck, all burned beyond recognition. When Hearst, Marion, and Miss Mackaill reached the site by car, the fog was already moving away.

Marion began screaming, and she was soon put under sedation by Hearst's doctor. Inconsolable for days, she had disliked flying from the beginning, but she had seldom spoken out against it because Hearst was such an aviation enthusiast. Her hopes for a little distraction from her boredom—"company for dinner"—had been tragically dashed. It was not a new experience for her at San Simeon. During the twelve years she had lived part of her life there, word had been brought to her in 1926 of the death of her pal Rudolph Valentino and then in 1934 of

the suicide of her niece Pepi. The voice of Fanny Ward suddenly
lapsing into silence at the other end of the phone when Marion
called haunted Marion for years, and—for her—life in the castle
was never very gay again.

Despite his enthusiasm, Hearst had been dogged by bad
luck with planes. He had sponsored an entry in the Dole competitive flight to Hawaii in 1927, and the two pilots were lost
over the Pacific. Philip Payne, the managing editor of his *New
York Mirror,* had insisted on going along on yet another trans-
ocean flight which Hearst had sponsored (and nearly canceled
because of the Dole tragedy), and Payne and the two pilots were
lost several hundred miles off the coast of Maine. And then there
was that episode when his own chartered plane would be forced
down by mechanical trouble with Marion, himself, and others
aboard, and they would be reported missing in the headlines of
the world press at the time. Marion was, she told her friends,
"scared silly" of planes. She would not change her views until
the 1950s when most everyone she knew traveled by air, and she
overcame her fears through repeated rides, much as she had
done with the roller coaster at Venice Park years before.

During the spring of 1938, the empire continued to crum-
ble. The elegant magazine, *Pictorial Review,* shut down operations, and a number of Hearst's radio stations were sold. St.
Donat's, which had been Hearst's and Marion's retreat from such
blows as threatened insolvency, was put on the market, but there
were no buyers. In any case, Europe was now more than a pow-
derkeg. It was exploding, and Hitler was lighting the fuses. A
year after their visit to Nazi Germany, Hitler had ordered universal conscription, and the symbolic shovels were thrown down
in favor of real guns. The Rhineland had been occupied, Austria
had been invaded and Nazified, and Czechoslovakia was about
to fall.

Exhausted by his own problems and shaken by Hitler's de-
monic designs on all of Europe, Hearst took Marion off for several weeks in Mexico. Four of his sons and their wives went
along, only George staying home—unusual for George, but it is
believed that he was ill at the time. They went to Acapulco,
where they leased a stone clifftop house, resembling a fortress,
next to the Hotel Los Flamingos and overlooking the Pacific.
They took their meals sometimes at the Hotel and played *besos y*

pesos, a kind of primitive cross between croquet and shuffle-board, there. In photographs taken at the time, Hearst has a haunted look, a slight stoop, and Marion has an anxious strain in her face. They chartered a small boat with a canvas roof against the intense sun for a trip through the Laguna and up the Coyuca River. The sons' wives suffered a bad sunburn, but Marion, who freckled in the sun, remained well away from the rail and wore a turban and long sleeves.

Death seemed to be moving in tandem with financial decline. On April 5, Reine was stricken in her pool at the Lexington Road mansion and died suddenly. Marion was inured to tragedy, after undergoing months of it, and was not as inconsolable as before. She grimly told Marie Glendinning that she was now ready for anything. Sister Rose wrote a few lines addressed to their departed sister, and it was published in Reine's old column in the Los Angeles *Examiner* (Reine had written the gossip column for several years):

> Reine:
> Have courage and be brave. This is our first separation, but not for always. For through eternity, I think we shall parted never be. Though your journey there is the first of the four of us, lead the way, dear, as you did for us here, and remember that we stand by to be united forever more. God bless you, dear.

Services were held at St. Augustine's Church across the street from the Metro studios in Culver City, with Reverend Father John O'Donnell conducting the mass. Father O'Donnell had become close to Marion and her sisters early in their Hollywood stay, and Marion would turn to him for consolation during the agony of her last days. Once again Hearst was an honorary pall-bearer, this time along with his son George.

The future continued looking bleak—except that now the Nazis were giving American newspapers headline after headline and the newspaper business was beginning a boom that would last nearly a decade. In November, Hearst authorized the sale of his silver collection at Sotheby's in London. Christie's in that same city were putting up a number of his art treasures at auction. If that was not enough, in December, Mexican workers urged the government to nationalize Hearst's Babicora ranch land, one of the richest of his land ventures and a source of revenue he was relying upon. They did not succeed, but it was another great worry.

The long hours at the castle and at Wyntoon, which now had taken the place of St. Donat's as their quietest refuge, had to be filled. At Wyntoon, Marion took up quiltmaking. She had little artistic sense, and she usually followed conventional patterns, but some of them turned out to be very attractive and certainly they were all functional. They were given to special friends over the years. Hearst would spend some of his leisure hours writing verse, and one of his poems, which appeared in his newspaper column, suggests the peacefulness of his wooded retreat:

> I am the forest of fire and pine,
> Shadow and silence and peace are mine.
> Mine are the springs and the rills and brooks,
> Which, rising in quiet hidden nooks,
> Join hands with the river and joyously flow
> to the widespread plains which lie below. . . .

He and Marion would take their breakfast in a kitchen and breakfast-room adjoining their private quarters in Bear House, where Hearst could cook up a batch of scrambled eggs and make the coffee, while Marion cleaned up and did the dishes. It was the closest they ever came to domesticity, to playing at keeping house.

Hearst would even manage to look at death with some forthrightness there at Wyntoon, and the swift rushing current of the McCloud River inspired him to write perhaps the most widely circulated of all of his poetic efforts, "The Song of the River," its closing lines reading:

> So don't ask why we live or die, or whither, or
>   when we go,
> Or wonder about the mysteries that only God may
>   know.

Marion and Hearst withdrew during 1939–40 from their larger community of friends as the world became more engulfed by war—by January 1939, the Spanish Falangists under Franco overwhelmed the last battered Loyalists entrenched around Barcelona, and the Spanish Civil War was lost to the Fascists. The last Czech provinces "accepted" a German protectorate and occupation in March, and England and France offered help to Poland, which seemed to be next in line for a *Blitzkrieg* invasion. Hearst followed all of this in the wireless room at the castle and Wyntoon, and Marion saw his face go ashen as huge pieces of Europe fell to the Nazis. He did an about-face over the Germans now and never again spoke of their superiority. They were destroying his beloved Europe. The strain further weakened his heart, and their cross-country trips were infrequent. Picnics at Wyntoon now were small affairs with no more than a dozen intimate friends invited.

In July 1939, the celebrated prodigy of the American theater and radio, Orson Welles, arrived in Hollywood—not quietly and not with the traditional Hollywood fanfare of publicity department trumpets, but with the flashy, awe-inspiring resemblance to fire, water, and thunder so often suggested by Hearst's personality. He came under unusual auspices, a hands-off policy by a major studio, RKO, that would allow him total control over his productions.

All Hollywood was agog. The success of his unorthodox Mercury Theatre stage productions of *Julius Caesar, Heartbreak House,* and *Danton's Death,* not to forget his April Fool's prank on the nation with his pseudo-documentary version of *The War of the Worlds,* together with his extreme youth (he was then twenty-four), gave him the certifiable stamp of a genius. Geniuses were not new to Hollywood—there were Chaplin, Keaton, Griffith—but to have one proclaimed by nearly everyone in advance of his ever having made a picture, that was something new. Marion expressed curiosity and interest, the way she always did when she suspected that a man was capable of some great prank. Charlie Lederer, as he nearly always did, was inclined to dismiss all the hullabaloo, but he doubtless secretly hoped that a few icons would be shattered. And, of course, there were numerous detractors, although Louella Parsons was not as yet one of them.

Contact between Welles and the Hearst-Davies set was

made almost at once. Charlie's friendship with Ben Hecht had brought Herman Mankiewicz and his wife Sara to the castle back in the late 1920s. It should be pointed out that Mankiewicz and Charlie moved in quite a different social set-up than Marion and Hearst did, except for the constant of Charlie's devotion to his aunt. The former two writers were in an exclusive literary circle that included Robert Benchley, Dorothy Parker, and Charlie MacArthur, as well as Hecht and Alexander Woollcott and the George S. Kaufmans in the East. They were astringent, philosophically perverse, and probably only tolerated the more predictable high jinks and literal-mindedness of Hearst and Marion because of their affection for Charlie and their genuine awe of the scale of Hearst's public and private ceremonies. Mankiewicz was writing radio scripts for Welles at his Tower Road house. It was probably there that Charlie Lederer met Virginia Welles, who was having her own difficulties coping with her husband's need to behave like the genius everyone said he was. Welles threw fits as well as handy objects when he did not get his way. He was even better at this than Hearst ever was. Charlie had an appealing, wide-eyed Continental charm, acquired, one suspects, as protective coloration after moving for some years among urbane men and women older than himself who expected him to do something outrageous. Sometimes he did; often he did not. Charlie was becoming better known for his gentleness than for his unpredictable behavior. He was moved to want to help Virginia Welles. She got a divorce early in December 1939, and in the spring of 1940 she married Charlie in rites performed at San Simeon, coming back to the Lederer home on Bedford Drive with her young daughter, Chris, Welles's first-born child. It is one of the ironies of this story that while Charlie was bringing up Welles's little girl, the film *Citizen Kane* was tearing down his aunt's screen reputation.

Something in all of this cross-pollenization triggered a drama in Herman Mankiewicz's brain and doubtless suggested the possibility of one in Welles's. Pauline Kael, in her *New Yorker* Magazine articles on the history of *Citizen Kane*, mentions the similarities between Welles and Hearst's fictional counterpart, Kane. Mankiewicz, with his vivid memories of many weekends at the castle, could scarcely have failed to notice this as he was writing the screenplay. It would be the perfect casting, or rather the perfect vehicle for Mankiewicz's boss, Welles—as perfect as Marion's casting as the Hollywood comedienne of the twenties in

Show People, but several times bolder.

Sara Mankiewicz told the author that her husband had wanted to do something with the Hearst legend for a long time. In all likelihood, however, nothing much had been written on it, except perhaps for some notes on visits to San Simeon, until after a conference with Welles. Welles was having trouble getting his first production launched at RKO for lack of a suitable property. He was all for first doing Joseph Conrad's *Heart of Darkness,* and when that did not work out, his enthusiasm went to a thriller, which, according to *The Hollywood Reporter,* he had hammered out himself into a screenplay called *The Smiler with the Knife* based upon a novel by C. Day Lewis. This latter project was given up when RKO executives would not accept Welles's choice of a second-string leading lady at the studio, Lucille Ball, as its star. Welles met with Mankiewicz in the latter's Tower Road home, where he was recovering from an auto smashup, and they discussed Mankiewicz's idea to do a story about an American tycoon in a prismatic fashion, opening with his death and then flashing back (a decade before *Rashomon* was done by Kurosawa, in which a tragic event is seen from several points of view). Finally, they settled on Hearst as their pattern for the tycoon, which was Mankiewicz's first choice, of course.

Press releases sent out at the time of the movie's first engagements imply that it was all Welles's idea and, when mentioned at all, which was rarely, that Mankiewicz was just a hired hand. Apparently, Mankiewicz *was* offered $10,000 by Welles to keep his name off the credits and, taking Ben Hecht's suggestion, he may have taken the money, which was always in short supply in his household as he was a compulsive gambler. Hecht's advice to him was to take the money *and* the screen credit, too, and "screw Welles." Mankiewicz later successfully petitioned the Screen Writer's Guild to restore to him credit as "co-author" of the film he wrote single-handedly before its release.

Mankiewicz, who was a serious alcoholic, was borne practically on a litter to a remote little town to the east of Hollywood, Victorville, to do the writing (or the dictating—his injuries prohibited his using a typewriter himself, and a secretary, Rita Alexander, accompanied him). Wheels began turning, creating the film that would be hailed by many as the greatest sound film ever made as well as the Juggernaut that would career unfeelingly over Marion Davies, flattening all of her modest triumphs and her three major ones, so that, in future years and until after her death, the chapter on the Davies screen years would be omitted from American movie history, leaving only a patronizing footnote on her fourteen-room bungalow and her role as a Hollywood hostess.

PART SIX

CITIZEN KANE
AND THE
YELLOW
PERIL

I

Very few authors who went up Hearst's mountain failed to write something about it, some, like Aldous Huxley, in a major work (*After Many a Summer Dies the Swan*). Mankiewicz considered Hearst, his barony, and his mistress the perfect components of a screenplay that would have much to say about the tyranny of great power, its principal victim being the man who flaunted it. He entitled his first draft *American*, and its principal settings were a newspaper plant in a large city and a fantastic castle along a semi-tropical coastline somewhere in the United States. He called his publisher Charles Foster Kane and the castle Alhambra (later changed to Xanadu from "Kubla Khan").

The woman for whom Kane leaves his wife is first met on a city street. Mankiewicz knew of Hearst's tender concerns and Susan Alexander's throbbing jaw—she has a toothache—immediately elicits Kane's sympathy. Susan is simple, seemingly guileless, and winsome. She is the uncomplicated listener to Kane's woes and frustrations. When she tells him that she enjoys singing and goes to the piano to perform some sentimental songs, she unwittingly has begun her own humiliation and heartbreak. After Kane divorces his wife and marries Susan (a necessity in 1939–40 demanded by the production code, although Mankiewicz's widow was to tell the author that it was a further device of her husband's to fictionalize Marion), he insists that Susan must *be* something, that she must have a career. When he is washed up in politics through scandal (his dalliance with Susan before his divorce), Kane tells a reporter, "We're going to be a great opera star." The reporter asks Susan, "Are you going to sing at the Metropolitan, Mrs. Kane?" and Susan, already infected with the power virus, tells him, "Charlie said if I didn't, he'd build me an opera house."

Mankiewicz openly discussed his sources for *American* with Welles and apparently told him that he knew Marion Davies to be a talented comedienne. But Mankiewicz knew that a talented Susan Alexander Kane would kill the whole point, that Kane's power must never be seen as benevolent. The screenwriter's perceptions concerning Marion's loneliness while Hearst was absorbed in the management of his publishing empire, about her turning to alcohol to drown her boredom, are among the telling facets of characterization that made the screenplay seem true-to-life. And making Susan woefully inept on the operatic stage would give Welles striking material for the screen. How was he to know, in the event that he cared, that he would be doing grave damage to Marion's completed screen career, to her reputation as an actress?

Welles's genius in films was not too different from Hearst's in publishing. Both men sought quick sensations in their work and enjoyed shocking their audiences. Hearst held the edge financially over Welles by winning vast readership for his publications. None of Welles's movies ever made much money, possibly because they were too literate for the mass movie audience. Welles seemed to realize that he had a flair for sharp satire, but he was unaware that he had a real talent for recreating a lost moment in time. This is as true of *Kane* as it is of *The Magnificent Ambersons,* which followed. Many of the battle scenes in his movie *Macbeth* seem wildly disorganized. They seem this way because quite obviously these confrontations on the battlefield *were* wild and disorganized. In that rich, fertile period of his films from *Kane* to *Macbeth,* Welles saw history as filled with the blinding and confusing smoke around the guns, and the towns destroyed and leaders lost seem almost of casual inconsequence in their context. His approach was existential long before the term itself became fashionable. Susan's addiction to jigsaw puzzles was taken directly from Marion (as was, of course, the alcoholism)—small details that make Susan ring true among the many that give *Citizen Kane* a quality not too different from a documentary that has some added intimacy and dialogue to lend it total credence and a bold satirical edge to keep it stimulating and amusing.

Hearst's aides wasted no time in seeing the film when prints were available and screenings begun. Many years later, Welles said that he and Hearst were together in the same hotel elevator when *Citizen Kane* was opening in San Francisco and that he had invited Hearst to see it. According to Welles, Hearst declined to acknowledge that he had been spoken to. But Hearst biographer John Tebbel writes that if Hearst happened to be away from his home haunts, he would go to a local moviehouse, "and it was in one of these, in San Francisco, that he and Marion sat one night and watched the unfolding of a life remarkably like his own. . . . Contrary to legend, Hearst rather enjoyed seeing himself portrayed on the screen. . . ." Tebbel is probably right on both counts. Hearst never minded being taken for a rascal, in fact, he laughed at such "mistakes." But he was devastated by what they had done to Marion, the more he thought about it, and he began to listen to his legal assistants, who urged that he take sanctions against the film. It had never mattered to Hearst what was said or written about him. He was used to vilification, and he said now that he just was not interested in whether he was Welles's model or not. *Newsweek* Magazine reported in an issue published that fall that "The script of Orson Welles's first movie, *Citizen Kane,* was sent to William Randolph Hearst for perusal after columnists had hinted it dealt with his life. Hearst approved it without comment." But seeing the movie had an entirely different impact upon him. He was an old man trembling with indignation over the way they had handled his mistress in the film. He did not seem to care that they had made her an inept performer in the opera house. His reasoning was probably that Marion had been a screen star, and a famous one at that, so how could anyone confuse Susan Alexander, the singer, with Marion Davies, the movie queen? But the alcoholism was something else. It had been his private cross for fifteen years or more, it had got worse, and now it was being depicted on movie screens around the world—a cheap and sordid sensation, as he saw it. He told Lloyd Pantages that putting that in the film was "cruel and unforgivable." His lawyers began going over the copy of the screenplay passed along to them by Marion's nephew Charlie. Mankiewicz had asked his old friend Charlie to look it over to see if it resembled Hearst too much, but Charlie told him that he didn't think so—that it was more like the life of "Bertie" (Colonel Robert) McCormick and the Pattersons, former publishers of the *Chicago Tribune.* Charlie did not seem to see the danger to his aunt's film reputation, although today he is all too aware of what happened and he is extremely bitter about the movie.

Marion had known for a long time that the story of her years with Hearst was of enormous interest to the public. During her lifetime, she received no less than four offers from publishers for her autobiography, one of them offering her an advance of nearly a million dollars. It angered her that a distorted version would be presented now to untold millions in movie-houses throughout the world. She denied that she had sneaked in to see it and said that she had heard details of the script from both Louella Parsons and Hedda Hopper. A persistent rumor in Hollywood was that Louella had seen *Citizen Kane* in a rough cut at the invitation of Welles and that she had been ecstatic about it. Then Hedda Hopper attended a screening at a more advanced stage, after the musical score had been added, and emerged raging. Hedda made a phone call to Bill Hearst, Jr., telling him that she loved both Hearst and Marion and that something had to be done about the picture. "It's all about their love affair," she began to tell her friends, "only it's all been twisted into something nasty." Louella was embarrassed to have her arch-rival protesting about something that had eluded her. She returned to the screening room at RKO Studios, this time accompanied by two of Hearst's lawyers. Her second look at the film is chronicled in Louella's autobiography, *The Gay Illiterate*, with no mention of Hedda's cue or of a previous viewing. "It was a cruel, dishonest caricature," writes Louella, "The boy genius certainly used all his talents just to do a hatchet job. I walked from the projection room without saying a word to Orson. I have not spoken to him since." Louella was predictably loyal, but, again, she failed to see what the movie might do to Marion's own screen career.

With Louella's wrath aroused and Hearst's legal staff and aides sending out memoranda to newspapers, the crippling forces moved against *Kane*. Much damage had been done with the exposure of the script to the Hearst forces. It is difficult to penetrate Mankiewicz's motive in taking the script to Charlie Lederer, knowing as he did that Lederer was close to Hearst and even closer to Marion. Some believe that Mankiewicz was so embittered by having all credit for his greatest work of screenwriting wrested from him by Welles (before he got half of it back again) that he wanted to wreck Welles.

Mrs. Mankiewicz told the author that her husband based Susan Alexander's disastrous operatic career and her character on composites—on both Mrs. Samuel Insull's career as an actress (her husband built the Chicago Civic Opera) and that of Ganna Walska, an opera star of moderate success married to Harold McCormick, heir to the farm machinery fortune. Quoting Mrs. Mankiewicz: "When Mrs. Samuel Insull gave a performance in New York, my husband as assistant drama critic on *The New York Times* covered it. It was either 1927 or 1928. That

night he was so embarrassed by having to write a review of it—
it was so dreadful—that he failed to complete it in time for the
early edition. They forgave this breach and it ran the following
day." There is a similar episode in *Kane* wherein Leland, Kane's
publishing crony played by Joseph Cotten, is unable to review
Susan Alexander's disastrous appearance on the operatic stage
and falls into a drunken sleep over his typewriter. Kane finished
the review himself, turning in a deadly comment on Susan's
gross ineptitude. In a later interview with Mrs. Mankiewicz, she
conceded that there was much of Marion in Susan Alexander, a
"winsomeness," for example.

Mrs. Mankiewicz believes that Welles and her husband realized that the motivating character in the writing of the script
was Hearst, but that Mankiewicz tried very hard not to make it
biographical. "Hearst wanted terribly to be a great American,"
Mrs. Mankiewicz said, "and leave his mark in many ways. Herman was fascinated by his story. It was glamorous and it was a
great love story. Marion Davies was a captivating minx, witty,
charming and outgoing and loyal. The film was a masterpiece,
but it was considered a calamity by those who cared about American films that the Hearst newspapers' position could have ruined
them [Welles and his staff]. It was only permitted to be shown
in the little places, but Herman was in great demand a few hours
after it had its first screening. The studios heard about its great-
ness and the following year it won him an Academy Award for
the best screenplay, the only award the film received—This in the
face of all the constrictive forces and embargos against it."

Although Welles has said that he began to contribute substantially to the screenplay by the time of the third draft, his
work consisted mainly of suggestions for revision, excisions of
scenes and events, and changing the names of some of the characters. During rewrite sessions with Mankiewicz, the precocious
and solitary nature of the boy Kane began to strongly resemble
that of Welles's own boyhood, far more in fact than it resembled
that of Hearst. Once it went before the cameras under his
masterful direction, the movie was to get the stamp of Welles
that would pervade all of it.

There is a line in *Kane* alluding to Kane's motive for con-
structing Xanadu: "Unhappy with the world he knew, he built
his own." San Simeon was Hearst's world, unique and a little
frightening. Visiting there when Hearst was in residence was a
little like peeking at an analyst's chart. All of his eccentricities

were there to be seen. It was a terribly private world—all those emus and camels and zebras running free and too many dachshunds kept in kennels—far too many for any one man. And Hearst's devotion to Marion was never more obvious than there at the castle. His jealous eye was on her almost constantly. He would try to conceal the extent of his jealousy for it was nearly manic in its intensity. But he simply could not.

Alone in their vast suite at Xanadu, Susan complains to Kane that there is "nobody to talk to—nobody to have any fun with. . . . Forty-nine thousand acres of nothing but scenery and —statues. I'm lonesome." And Kane replies: "I thought you were tired of house guests. Till yesterday morning, we've had no less than fifty of your friends at any one time. As a matter of fact, Susan, if you'll look carefully in the west wing, you'll probably find a dozen vacationists still in residence." Susan tells him: "You make a joke out of everything! Charlie, I want to go back to New York. I'm tired of being a hostess. I wanta have fun. Please, Charlie, please!" Marion had said that she grew weary of "all those people. The strain of the place cards and putting the right people together." Every day was the same—the ritual of who was going to sit next to whom in the baronial dining hall. As official hostess at San Simeon, Marion worked much harder than she ever did in films, shaking hands down on the esplanade steps, filling the days of her guests with little activities—swims, tennis matches, picnics, jigsaw puzzles, not to mention the hours she spent by Hearst's side listening to his views of what was happening in the world, sitting quietly as he phoned an executive in New York or London or wherever there might be major news breaking. If she made a motion toward leaving the room, Hearst would often say, "I want you to hear this, Marion." He seemed to be grooming her as his deputy, but her drinking would become an issue time and again so that even Hearst must have had fears that she never would fill such a role.

Later, Kane tells Susan, "I thought we might have a picnic tomorrow. Invite everybody to the everglades." "*Invite* everybody!" Susan says shrilly. "Order everybody, you mean, and make them sleep in tents! Who wants to sleep in tents when they have a nice room of their own—with their own bath, where they know where everything is?" Susan's tone is humorless, but the comment is almost a verbatim reaction of many of Hearst's guests to his overnight campouts at the ranch. And the shrill tone is

Marion's, in those moments when she can no longer smile as Hearst's gay companion. Most devastating of all is the montage showing Susan's disastrous operatic career. We follow her on a terrible trail through city after city. Banner headlines from the Kane press emblazon her "success" across the screen; then we see the reaction of two backstage crewmen in the fly area, one shaking his head and the other holding his nose and making a thumbs-down gesture.

With such details as these in the minds of the many in Hollywood who flocked to see the early screenings of *Kane*, it was easy for everyone to assume, since it is a community conditioned to think the worst of anyone rather than the best, that they were at last getting at the truth of Marion's erratic career. Word of this reached Marion quickly. Bad news always travels the fastest. She pretended that it didn't bother her. She rather liked Virginia Lederer, the ex-Mrs. Welles. She could not guess how far the film would go toward obliterating her name as a film queen. "Susan Alexander" was an opera singer, as Hearst pointed out. Surely her public—and there were still a few million movie fans who remembered her with fondness—would not confuse the two.

But there was no doubt in anyone's mind once the film was released. It *was* about Hearst, and before many months had passed, people were referring to Susan Alexander as "the Marion Davies part." As for specific legal action, Hearst told Louella Parsons, "I don't believe in lawsuits. Besides, I have no desire to give the picture any more publicity."

Louis B. Mayer, who had reconciled his differences with Hearst and Marion since their abrupt departure from his studio back in 1935, actually wept when he emerged from a screening of the film. That night, Mayer telephoned George J. Schaefer, head of production at the RKO studios and offered to buy the negative of *Kane* so that it might be destroyed. Within a few days, Mayer made Schaefer a firm offer of $800,000, which was roughly the cost of production less advertising, which had not yet begun. Schaefer, loyal to Welles throughout the ordeal, immediately declined, telling Mayer that "*Kane* is an important film and we are proud of it."

Many years after its release, Marion was still sensitive about it. "Years ago," she said, "W. R. gave me some good advice. He said 'Never make anything of an insult or a slap at you. Ignore

it. Make as little of it as possible.' That's what I've done with
Citizen Kane and apparently a lot of people agree with me. It
never made any money."

The film was released exactly ten years before the death of
Hearst. Throughout that decade, Hearst—in his late seventies—
would be in declining health. The parties would have to stop.
Friends of the fair-weather variety would begin drifting away.
The loneliness implicit in the characters of Charles Foster Kane
and wife Susan Alexander living there in the empty halls of
Xanadu more clearly began to parallel that of Marion and Hearst
first alone with only staff and nurses at Wyntoon, where they
would spend the war years, and then in the sprawling Beverly
Hills mansion where he was to die. Coming after the film's production, it was a case of life imitating art, and those few friends
who remained loyal in this period of physical retrenchment no
longer discussed the scandal surrounding *Citizen Kane* even
among themselves. It was simply becoming all too true. Hearst's
great power when his energies seemed boundless, like Charles
Foster Kane's, had been enfeebled by the only enemy he ever
truly feared—old age.

The irony that even her good films would be ignored by film
buffs who had rallied around Gloria Swanson following *Sunset
Boulevard* and Garbo and an entire constellation of silent picture
stars was not lost on Marion over the years. She took it with a
shrug and good humor, and she died before several of her best
films were revived in the 1960s at film festivals and retrospectives—that career, irrepressible apparently, beginning to come
back posthumously and sending startled film scholars back to
their texts to make revisions in judgment.

II

While *Citizen Kane* was being produced and readied for release,
Marion and Hearst both managed to ignore the tempest it was
creating. Although the large parties had been terminated at the
castle (Hearst was then seventy-seven), special friends were
invited to San Simeon and to Wyntoon, which was becoming
increasingly comfortable to Hearst. The withdrawal caused by
invalidism had not yet begun. That summer of 1940, there were
frequent picnics under the benevolent old pines at Wyntoon,

with no special entertainment planned beyond the inevitable nightly movies and the congenial chatter of friends such as Diana Fitzmaurice, who had lost her famed director husband George earlier that year; Eleanor Boardman d'Arrast; Eileen and Harry Ruby; the Pantages; Harry Crocker; and Constance Talmadge Netcher. The pressure was off both Marion and Hearst, even though the teletype and tickertape machines still functioned in Joe Willicombe's office between *Bear House* and *Cinderella* and *Fairy Houses* and Hearst still sat each morning in the big room there with the rushing waters of the river just outside and with half-a-dozen of his newspapers spread out on the Aubusson carpet. He edited them in his instinctive way to keep them exciting, but that strange little dance he used to do in and around them was now a slow shuffle.

Marion, at forty-three, seemed to have forgotten any need ever to be glamorous. She had put on a few additional pounds, and there was a pronounced matronly look to her. Then, once again, their peace was shattered. A phone call came through to Willicombe's office in late July 1940 that something had happened to Marion's favorite sister, Ethel. Marion was put on the line and, in her panic, she thought she had been told that Ethel was "shot." Actually, her sister had choked to death on a piece of steak. Preparations were begun at once to return to Los Angeles nearly six hundred miles away. The urgency of their mission called for them to fly, but, remembering the fiery deaths of the Plunkets, Marion refused, and Hearst was compelled to have her sedated by the residential doctor at the estate in order to get her aboard his private plane. Strong coffee brought her around once she was in the Lexington Road mansion where Ethel had died, and she went upstairs, saying as she climbed the winding staircase, "I can't believe it. It doesn't make any sense." But there on the bed lay Ethel, absurdly strangled, and again Marion's composure broke down and hysteria set in. Counting the dead Plunkets, this was the sixth tragedy Marion had suffered in the past twelve years. Perhaps it was her closeness to Ethel that triggered her intense reaction, but her stoicism during the days following Reine's death was not to be repeated.

She was still recovering from that experience in November when Ambassador Joseph Kennedy, his wife Rose, and two of his sons, John and Robert, came to Wyntoon. Kennedy was back home from England with his large family, and, as is the custom, had tendered his resignation to Roosevelt, who had just won a third term in the White House. But Kennedy, stung by criticism and even rejection in England because of his antiwar feelings, had meant to leave the office, and Roosevelt, for his part, was quite willing to accept the resignation. Perhaps to save face, Kennedy was sent by Roosevelt on an "opinion-molding" trip across the country to talk to Hearst and others opposed to the war—an absurdity, of course, since Kennedy would do nothing but agree with them. He had, in fact, told newspaper columnist Leonard Lyons, "I'm willing to spend all I've got left to keep us out of war." Spartans all, the Kennedys enjoyed the early snowfall at Wyntoon. John went even further by getting into bathing trunks and diving into the icy McCloud River for a swim across and back again.

The Kennedy visit was balm to Marion's injured spirit. She called Joe Kennedy "a good Irishman," admiring and accepting his highly individual opinions much as she did Hearst's. And Joe had paid her the added compliment of bringing his wife and part of his family to sit at her table and sleep in those guest rooms at the Gables, where every bed by now was covered with one of her quilts. The gesture won for the Kennedys a permanent place in Marion's affections. She would follow their many marriages, births, tragedies and triumphs with an avidity she usually reserved for events in the lives of Charlie Lederer and niece Pat Lake. And the Kennedys, for their part, would invite Marion to participate in all of their happy events.

On May 8, 1941, *Citizen Kane* opened at Hollywood's El Capitan Theatre, previously a playhouse, but the ban on the film within the movie circuits remained in effect. Everyone outside Marion's and Hearst's circle attended, and it was a social evening of such excitement that it compared favorably with the premiere performance of Chaplin's *The Gold Rush*. Privately, it was a smashing success, and—while there were some in Hollywood who said it resembled an old Spencer Tracy film, *The Power and the Glory*, a study of a tycoon that also opened with his death and went back into his life—that earlier Preston Sturges film had been clearly a brilliant work of fiction. *Kane* was something else, and its brashness led those who came out of the El Capitan in tingling excitement to make second judgments about it. There was a clannishness in the film community only apparent when one of its members was gratuitously attacked (when attacked for cause, it could be expected that all hands would join the fray and reduce the victim to jelly, leaving such niceties as guilt or innocence to be mulled over later).

But some old hands in Hollywood felt that its origins were unimportant, that it was so fresh in concept and execution it would launch a grand new era of filmmaking in America. W. R. Wilkerson, publisher of *The Hollywood Reporter,* wrote in his column that Hollywood must retract its condemnation and hasty judgments of Welles. The mounting consensus indicated that *Citizen Kane* was the finest film since the advent of sound.

None of Marion's friends would dare discuss even the film's existence. It had become taboo like death itself (and it should not be forgotten that the film's effect upon Marion's long career was murderous). Reaction within the Hollywood hierarchy remained antagonistic, since there were equally fascinating and vulnerable subjects within their group—Cecil B. De Mille, Louis B. Mayer, and Howard Hughes, who was shortly to buy RKO Studios.

Timing was not on RKO's side, however, and the whole episode could be put out of mind by the end of 1941 when the film finally achieved its maximum distribution in a number of independent movie houses and hired auditoriums around the country. Pearl Harbor created shock waves on December 7, 1941, beside which *Kane* was a rather small ripple.

Hearst's dire predictions about "the yellow peril" were coming true on a scale even he never envisaged. To Marion, it was a nightmare made real. Twenty-six years by Hearst's side had made her as paranoid about Orientals as Hearst was. The Japanese, in her tutored view, were not a subspecies of little, evil creatures. They were arch-villains, devious and literate, who had launched a struggle-to-the-death against the white man. As island after island fell to the enemy in the Pacific, for many months "the yellow peril" became as real and as personal a threat to many millions of Americans as it had been for years to Marion and Hearst.

One night in early 1942, Marion said that a Japanese plane was shot down before her "very eyes" a few miles north of Ocean House. Actually, the incident involved a plane of unknown origin, which set off a barrage of anti-aircraft artillery between Santa Monica and Malibu. Hearst climbed to the topmost balcony of the beach house to watch the excitement, while Marion shivered under a table. He seemed at such times to be a man without fear, and certainly if his quest for material pleasures had not called the turns in his life, he would have made a military man of heroic dimensions. But when the incident was over, he was concerned for Marion's safety, and preparations were made to leave Ocean House.

They went to San Simeon, its air of remoteness giving them a sense of security, which proved to be fleeting. They had been there only a few weeks when Hearst called her into his study one evening and, in anxious tones, informed her that the government was urging him to leave the castle, that it was a "sitting duck" for bombardment by the Japanese artillery—presumably affixed to their submarines, and that San Simeon would be singled out by the enemy for such an attack because of his long campaign of vituperation against them—a barrage of propaganda that had begun as early as the Wilson administration. Previous to that, his animosity had been directed against the Chinese, whose hordes of emigrés had glutted the labor market in California for half a century or more. Hearst's prejudice was now shared by even the delicate and sane Garden Club ladies created for *New Yorker* Magazine by Helen Hokinson. One of them told her peers, "Well, there's one good thing about it. We won't have to feel so sorry for Madame Butterfly any more."

Cleveland Amory once said of the magazine *Vanity Fair,* the elegant chronicle of America between two worlds, that it was "not very good at wars and depressions, but between them, in the golden days of the twenties, she was very good indeed." This description fits Marion equally well.

And she managed even now, as the war came so physically close, to retain a childlike naiveté about it. The difference between her attitude toward the First World War and the Second was that now she herself was threatened and the army had taken her favorite kin, Charlie Lederer. He was sent to Officer's Training Camp briefly and, within months, was in India as a Major, fighting the Japanese. Charlie's character and personality did not seem to have been affected much by the discipline of military life. And he was not about to suffer boorishness even in the army. In Calcutta, he dined with an upper-class English lady, who spent most of the evening railing against the Jews, an episode recounted by Ben Hecht in *A Child of the Century.* Charlie had grown up and matured in a community composed mostly of Jews and never had experienced any embarrassment or bias in the company of Marion and Hearst (anti-Semitism was not among Hearst's personal shortcomings even though his newspapers often gave a different impression). When he crossed the lady's parlor to freshen his drink, he noticed that atop the liquor cabinet there was a priceless jade vase. "I am interested in your dislike of Jews," he told his hostess with no special rancor. "Could you tell me just what you've got against them?" "Oh," the lady said, "I've got nothing against the Jews, really," and her eyes widened in horror as Charlie jerked open the liquor cabinet door with such violence, the jade vase crashed to the floor. "You have now," Charlie said.

Still, the true ugliness of war, which Charlie must have experienced out there in the Burma-India theater of operations, never came home to either Marion or Hearst. They would have found Mother Courage's war wagon a quaint relic, Brecht's whole philosophy "foreign and unpatriotic." Marion said that Hearst never was pro-German, "he was pro-American," and sometimes she would say that he was the most patriotic man in the country, wholly innocent as she made the statement that she was spelling out the fact that he was America's most active and consequential jingoist. The Japanese, called "Japs" by Marion and others at the castle, were a far greater threat to life and limb than Hearst's earlier (and later rediscovered) bogeyman, the Bolsheviks.

But unlike Marion's experience during World War I when the war was so remote and invisible to her, this one threatened them rather directly. San Simeon, with its myriad interior lights and its spotlights illuminating its treasures out-of-doors, looked like a Hearstian birthday cake at night. It is entirely possible that the government was fearful that it might be bombarded. When the orders came for their evacuation of the premises, Hearst wanted to stay. He told her that if it blew up, he wanted to stay with it, to go down with the ship, so to speak. "Well, I don't," Marion said, a little shrilly. "I don't want to be blown up for a castle." Then Hearst suggested, probably facetiously, that they could go down in the cellar and hide, but Marion told him, "No thanks."

There was still snow on the ground when Hearst's convoy of mistress, staff, and assorted friends—mostly Marion's—reached Wyntoon. But, nestled among its tall pines, with its dozens of cheery fireplaces, it proved to be a safe haven from the war. It was only later that they learned that an internment camp for Japanese-Americans was located less than an hour's drive from the estate. Then "the yellow peril" seemed closer than ever before, especially when they heard that there had been an escape. Extra guards were posted around the perimeter of the vast estate—50,000 acres of mountain timberland—but freedom appeared the goal of the much-put-upon and humiliated Americans of Japanese descent and not Hearst or his friends.

The biggest excitement of those war years at Wyntoon was the night Marion's bedroom went up in flames. There was near her bed what she called a "Dutch stove," run by electricity. During the night, Marion was awakened by a fiery explosion that ignited her bed, the ceiling, and the attic above. Since her only large window looked over the McCloud River, there was no exit but the door, and flames barred her way. She retreated into a wardrobe and doubtless would have perished, but the door suddenly burst open and Hearst rushed into the room calling her name in the smoky blackness. "We're over here," Marion cried out—she was holding Gandhi in her arms. Hearst found them and threw a wet blanket over her head and his own. A few moments after he got them outside, the entire wing exploded, flames engulfing the roof.

It was the third major fire at Wyntoon in a little over ten years. A second blaze had consumed The Bend, where most of their guests slept, but fortunately that fire had occurred during the day and the chief loss beyond the large Bavarian lodge house itself and its normal supply of European treasures were the clothes owned by their guests. Carmen Pantages Considine and her daughter were left with nothing but their swimsuits, which they had on at the time, but Hearst quickly outfitted them with wardrobes sent up from San Francisco.

Their grim pursuer caught up with them almost immediately when Hearst's favorite dachshund and traveling companion, Helen, died. In answering a letter of sympathy from friend and publisher Frank Barham, Hearst wrote (and published his reply in his column "In the News"):

> You know, Frank, a boy and his dog are no more inseparable companions than an old fellow and his dog. To his dog he is just as good as he ever was—maybe better because he is more appreciative of the dog's devotion. Anyhow, the dog and the old guy understand each other and get along "just swell." So I do miss Helen. I was very fond of her.

William Randolph Hearst in his baronial dining hall at San Simeon, 1937.

BROWN BROTHERS

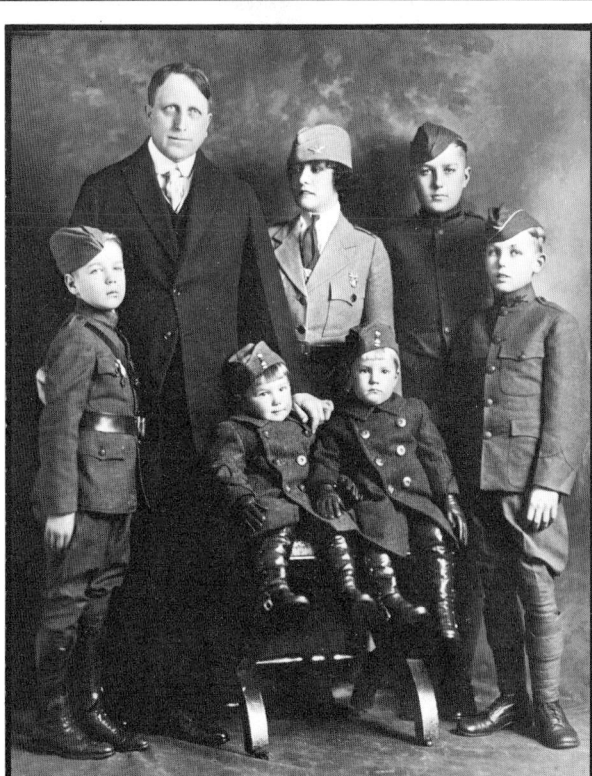

(At left) Millicent and William Randolph Hearst with their five sons: John, the twins Randolph and David, George and Bill, Jr. during World War I, 1917. (Below) Four of the Hearst sons with their father: David, John, George and Bill, Jr. circa 1939. (At right) The castle at San Simeon.

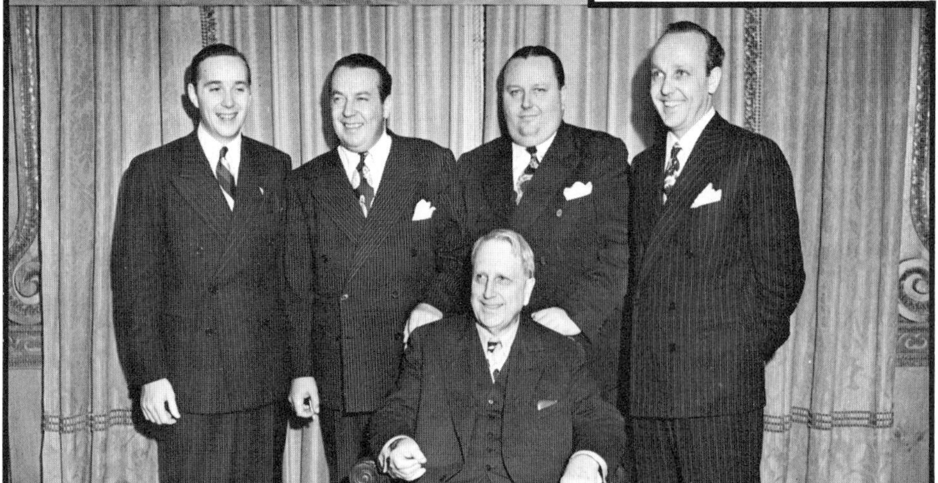

MARION DAVIES ESTATE

(At left) Buffalo graze in a hilly pasture at San Simeon. (Below) Hearst's library at San Simeon.

At right) Marion's beach
ouse at Santa Monica.
Middle) St. Donats' Castle
Wales. (Bottom) The
inderella House at
yntoon, northern California.

HORACE BROWN

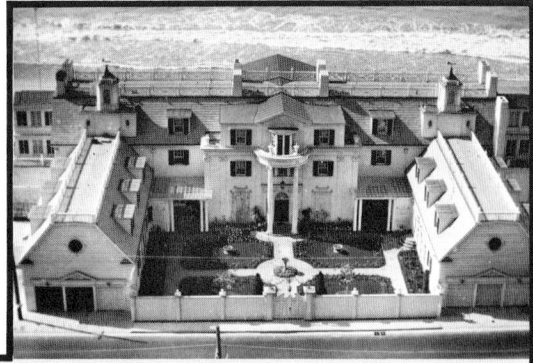

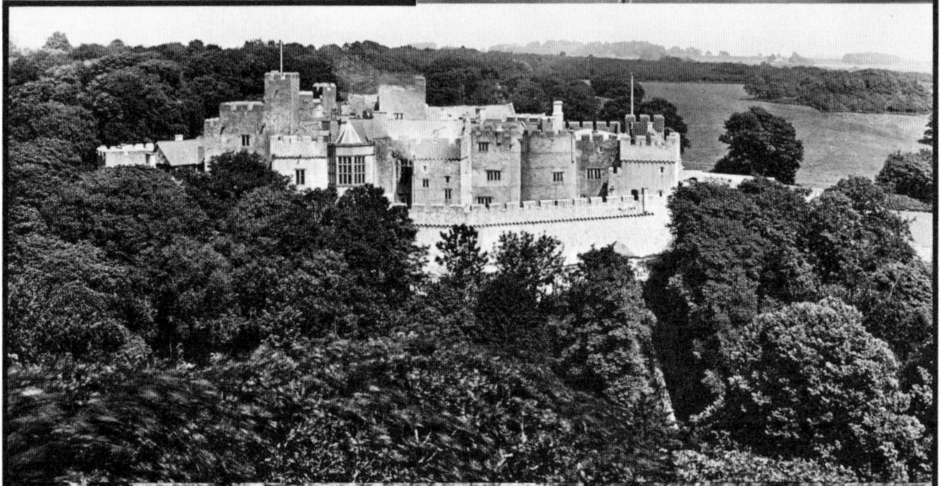

ALICE HEAD

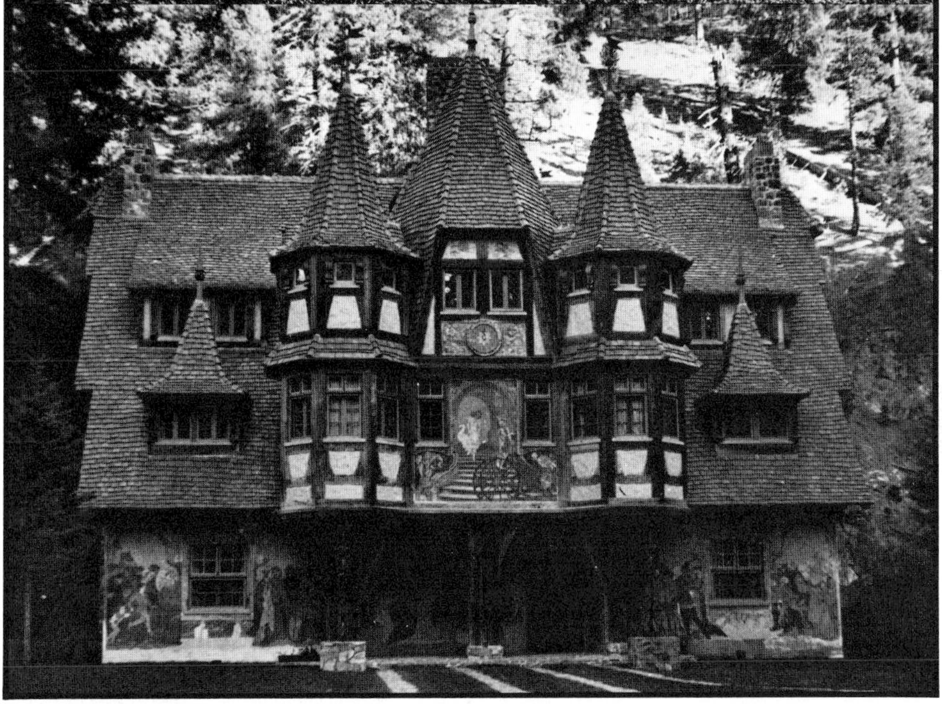

CHARLES LEDERER

(At left, top) Hearst caught with a bite of his birthday cake, 1934. (Middle) Hearst rubs his weary back during a game of croquet with Marion, circa 1938. (Bottom) A wedding at San Simeon. Sister Rose Davies, Doris Duke and Marion are bridesmaids for Mary Grace, 1937. (At right, top) A "Confederate party" at San Simeon. From left: Richard Berlin, Georges Jaumier, Joe Mankiewicz, John Considine, Townsend Netcher, Marion, Irving Thalberg, Arthur Brisbane, Frank Barham, unidentified man, George Fitzmaurice, Raoul Walsh and Bill Hearst, Jr. Buster Collier seated on ground. Man behind Thalberg is unidentified. (Bottom) Four leading ladies at the Tyrolean party; Gloria Swanson, Marion, Constance Bennett and Jean Harlow, 1935.

"Come as Your Favorite Character" party found Marion in a rich boy's suit with a poor-boy cap—the usual mix found in her early films; Harry Ruby as a crazy admiral, and his wife, Eileen Percy, as a cowgirl.

Marion in a trick costume, circa 1932.

Trips abroad: (at left, top) At the Lido in Venice, 1928. "Papa Ben" Douras, Anita Murray, unknown young man, sister Ethel Davies, Lloyd Pantages and Pepi Lederer. (Middle) Marion in a gondola in Venice, 1928. (Bottom) A pause to stretch and refuel. Marion and pet dachshund Gandhi in Spain, 1934. (At right, top) Hearst, a fine photographer, snaps a picture on the beach in Italy, 1934. (Below) The Hearst tour party in Italy: Eileen Percy, Marion, Mrs. William Randolph Hearst, Jr., Bill, Jr., a guide and Hearst, 1934.

(At left, top) Nephew Charlie Lederer and his Aunt Marion in a German square, 1928. (Middle) Buster Collier takes a picture of Il Duce, Rome, 1934. (Bottom) The Hearst caravan lines up in Paris ready for departure, 1934.

(At right, top) Before take-off on a flight to London. Marion, Mrs. George Hearst, Hearst and unidentified man, 1935. (Middle) In Spain: George Hearst, Hearst, Mrs. George Hearst, Dorothy Mackaill, Marion and Eileen Percy. That's Gandhi, again, in the foreground, 1934. (Bottom) Visiting some ancient ruins in Spain: Hearst, Mrs. Bill Hearst, Jr., guide, Eileen Percy, Bill, Jr., Marion, Harry Crocker and Buster Collier.

CHARLES LEDERER

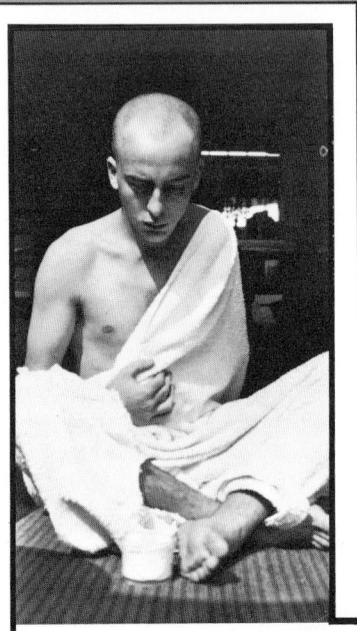

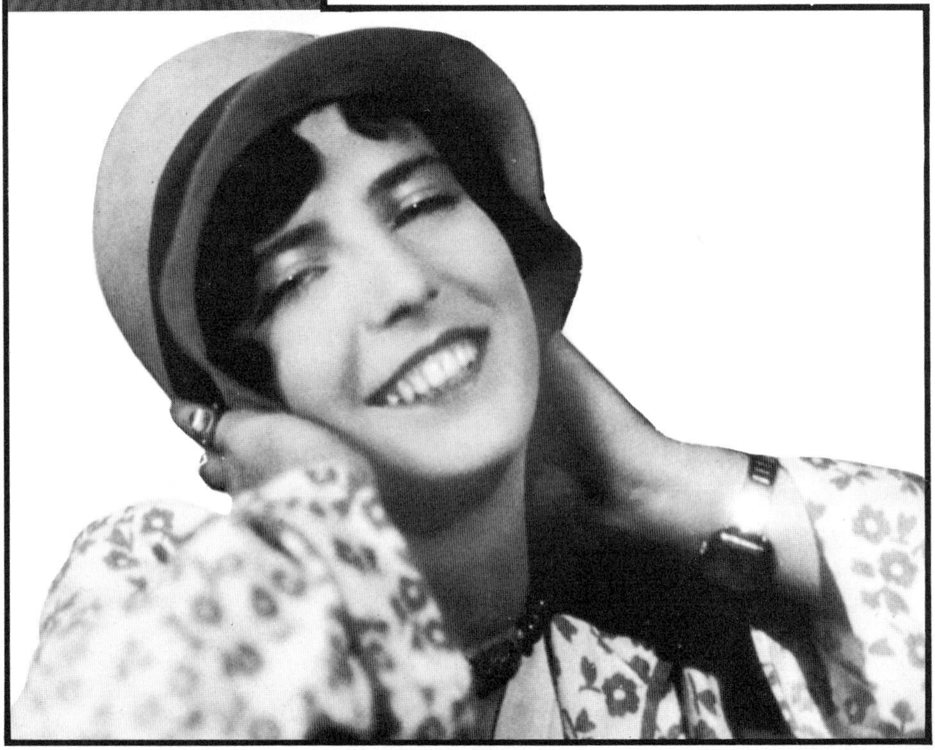

(At left) Charlie Lederer poses as Gandhi, Bad Nauheim, 1928. (Be low) Pepi Lederer at nineteen. (At right, top left) Marion and husband Captain Horace Brown enjoy niece Pat Lake's family: Marion Rose Pat's husband Arthur Lake, Pat and Arthur Patrick, 1957. (Top right) Sister Reine Davies Lederer 1937. (Bottom) A "Lux Radio Thea- ter" program: Mary Astor, Brian Aherne, Aileen Pringle, Marion and the show's producer, Cecil B deMille, 1937.

To my darling
marions devotedly
Reine
1937

ELMER FRYER
HOLLYWOOD

Marion Douras Brown with Captain Horace G. Brown, 1959.

She always slept in a big chair in my room and her solicitous gaze followed me to bed at night and was the first thing to greet me when I woke in the morning. Then when I arose she begged me for the special distinction of being put in my bed, and there she lay in luxurious enjoyment of the proud privilege until I was ready to leave. . . .

Aldous Huxley says: "Every dog thinks its master Napoleon, hence the popularity of dogs." That is not the strict truth. Every dog adores its master notwithstanding the master's imperfections, of which it is probably acutely aware . . . because love creates love, devotion inspires devotion, unselfishness begets unselfishness and self-sacrifice, and that fact is more than a commendable quality in the animal kingdom. It is the eventual hope of humanity.

Helen died in my bed and in my arms. I have buried her on the hillside overlooking the green lawn—where she used to run—and surrounded by the flowers. I will not need a monument to remember her. But I am placing over her little grave a stone with the inscription—"Here lies dearest Helen—my devoted friend."

A love and reverence for animals were qualities Marion and Hearst shared passionately. She remembered his concern for a seal that had scrambled up on the rocks just below San Simeon wharf and for whom Hearst had ordered a shelter constructed; and a castle mouse trapped in a jardiniere carried outside by Hearst, who then carted out bits of cheese and crackers nightly to its special mound—until it vanished, and then he worried for fear one of the larger animals on the place had made a meal of it.

Marion's grief was cushioned by the warm body of her own Gandhi in her lap or in the crook of her arm. They were still inseparable and Hearst had warned her of Gandhi's mortality, but she would only press the dog's head against her cheek and utter some nonsense about Gandhi "never doing a thing like that" to her.

Gandhi's difficulty began that same year that Helen died when he did not want to jump down from Marion's bed, where he usually spent much of the night curled up around her feet—"my hot water bottle," she called him. His head was nodding strangely, and Marion was alarmed, but since he was thirteen years old, she was afraid to call a vet, fearful of being told that something or other had gone bad through old age and having to make *the* decision,

which she found an intolerable thought. One of her nurses volunteered to watch over him that day, but the next evening, Marion
was lonesome for her little dog and phoned the nurse to bring
Gandhi back to Bear House. By this time, the miniature dachshund
had lost control over his bowels and Marion changed her bed linen
several times. She was particularly anxious that Hearst not be
aware of just how ill Gandhi was, as he was stronger than she
was in handling such situations and he might see how bad things
were and talk her into having Gandhi put to sleep.

But that was almost exactly what happened. Hearst came
into her bedroom and wanted to know right away if Gandhi had
"done something" in the room. A vet was summoned, and Marion
began protesting that matters were not as bad as they looked.
"Anybody can get diarrhea," she said. "That doesn't mean he's
going to die. If it did, I'd have been dead ten years ago." Then
Marion was asked to leave the room, and Hearst and the vet had
a conference. Euthanasia was decided upon, of course, but Marion was listening at the door. She came in and told them, "Over
my dead body," but panic made her pass out. She came around
to see them administering the shot to Gandhi and to catch a
glimpse of his eyes staring at her, as she thought, beseechingly.
She somehow found the strength to go into a rage. Bottles and
jars from her makeup table flew against the wall—Hearst quietly
leading the vet away from the scene. A local minister came in
later that day to say a few words over Gandhi's grave and to
console Marion.

A week after Gandhi's death, Bataan in the Philippines fell
to the Japanese after a long and bloody effort to withstand the
invaders. Many American men, officers, and nurses were captured and began a long, deadly march away from that bastion
to internment camps many miles away. The Russians were
mounting a counteroffensive against the Germans that was terribly costly in human lives, the toll being in the hundreds of
thousands. Hearst followed the progress of the Allies, which then
seemed painfully slow, in his office at Wyntoon, which had been
fitted out with telephonic and radio communication equipment.
Marion mourned her dog, and found the dimensions of the war
beyond her grasp. But there were moments when she could
relate to what was happening—when General MacArthur was
placed in command of the South Pacific forces, for example. She
and Hearst spoke of him warmly and thought that he would
make a fine president when the war was over.

All of the lady guests during that period were conscripted into a work force in Marion's sewing room, where she had begun making bandages instead of quilts, which were dispatched in large bundles to the Red Cross. At about the same time, a contingent of medical officers in the California State Guard asked if she would let them use her Children's Clinic grounds and some of its facilities as a medical installation. She immediately agreed and there were meetings to discuss the Medical Corps' needs with some high-ranking officers and one medical administration lieutenant, in command of supplies for the unit. His name was Horace G. Brown; he was from the Tidewater section of Virginia, and there was an ingratiating friendliness about him. Hearst took to him at once, and, through Horace, such amenities as bedspreads for the patients were supplied, although quickly returned when a colonel came through and saw them. But no real social contact was made then between Brown and Marion or between Brown and Hearst. That came later when Horace Brown met Marion's nephew-in-law Arthur Lake.

III

For a few months after the war, both Marion and Hearst made a valiant attempt to resume their old lives. In 1945, Hearst deemed it safe to return to San Simeon when the war began to turn against the Japanese. He was then eighty-two years old and in deteriorating health. Marion would go to Ocean House for days at a time, and, while Hearst must have sensed that she was bored with the empty castle and his numerous doctors and ailments, she pretended not to be. She said she had some things to take care of in Los Angeles and, since many of her real estate holdings were there, it was a credible excuse.

A young fair-haired ex-soldier, Joseph Reith, used to sun himself on some rocks below Ocean House between classes at the University of California. One forenoon, he was roused by a woman's voice shouting at him from above. "Hey, down there!" He looked up and saw the mistress of Ocean House waving at him.

"Come on up for some coffee. I'm having my breakfast and there's nobody to talk to," Marion said plaintively. The blond youth clambered up the slippery stones and in a few moments was seated opposite Marion in a sitting room off her bedroom.

"You're cute," she told him with a kind of tired flirtatiousness. "What's your name?" He told her, as she poured him some
coffee. Then she asked if he wanted something stronger. He
didn't that day, but the next day there was a repeat performance
and he came up and had a vodka stinger with her. It was twelve
noon, her getting-up time, and she said all of her friends had
deserted her. Reith and Marion became rapid friends during a
period of about ten days or two weeks, and once he was treated
to an intimate scene in which Marion chatted with Hearst over
the phone. Her tone was first rather sweet and concerned as she
asked him how he was, but then they apparently got into a discussion over business matters, something Marion wanted to buy,
and she dropped her sweetness, reverting to her sailor's vernacular in upbraiding Hearst. This startled Mr. Reith but scarcely
could have done more to Hearst than to remind him that there
were some things in life that didn't change very much. He may
have taken some satisfaction from that.

When Hearst's heart condition became cause for alarm, his
specialists were concerned about the altitude at the castle and
recommended that he move to the Los Angeles area. There he
would have emergency equipment available if needed. It was
becoming clear to Marion, who tried not to think about it, that
Hearst was not likely to improve very much no matter what was
done, but that the doctors' suggestion might save his life during
a critical moment and might even prolong it. By now, death had
cut down nearly all of those close to her, except sister Rose,
Charlie Lederer, and Pat Lake. Even her cherished dog was gone.
While death was still a forbidden subject around Hearst, Marion
lived with the dread of him dying in his sleep. Every lost pound
on his body was a threat to her, every small tremor made her
quake inside. Sometimes his hands would shake alarmingly as
severe palpitations seized him. Anxiety once again made Marion's drinking a problem and, when it affected her circulation
causing her legs to give way, the nursing staff was supplemented
to include two daily nurses for her.

Hearst finally left his castle headquarters at San Simeon
in 1946, when Marion found a large Mediterranean villa in Beverly Hills. It was the second attempt on her part to find something palatial enough to keep Hearst from fretting about leaving
his "ranch." Earlier that year, she had bought a seven-acre estate
on Lexington Road in Beverly Hills, only two long blocks from

her first mansion in California. The grounds were elaborately landscaped with huge oak trees that had been moved because of their historical value from the busy Wilshire district, where they had stood since the last century. It was two stories tall and consisted of fifteen rooms in the Italian villa style. It had cost nearly a million dollars to build, but Marion paid $250,000 for it in a buyer's market. When she brought down Hearst for a quick inspection, he looked in dismay at its closeness to the street, and then—after barely glancing at its gracefully proportioned interior (a scaled-down palace)—he said dismissively, "Let's go home."

Everything was of a piece in Hearst's life: he ran the newspaper empire with sure genius and enthusiasm, but the newspapers were his principal resource to finance the castle, the acquisition of treasures and lesser palaces. If part of this life structure were removed, there was danger that the man himself would deteriorate rapidly. It was the bitterest of ironies that Marion's ponderous arch-rival remained hunched on its hillside in smug imperviousness to any and all calamities that might befall its creator. The place had taken on a malign character for Marion and she was relieved to be gone from it. But she knew that for Hearst it was a far more serious matter. Whenever they were away from the castle in the past, he would long for it to the point of desperation. One whole new wing at the rear was still unfinished. Marion gave up thinking about what might be best. It was "heads, you lose." Everybody has to die, she decided, and now it was a matter of staving it off by months and days. Most important of all, she didn't want to be isolated during that time of waiting.

Marion watched Hearst's face as they drove down the hill at San Simeon for the last time; she saw a look there of loss and emptiness for which she could find no words of comfort. But she tried anyway. She gripped his arm and said, "We'll come back, W.R. You'll see." And Hearst had shaken his head and great tears rolled down his cheeks when they reached the highway and the towers of the castle were lost in wisps of fog.

The house which Hearst conceded would be satisfactory was located off Benedict Canyon on Beverly Drive and was designed by Gordon Kaufman, one of the most respected architects in the Hollywood area during the boom building period of the twenties. It had been built in 1927 by Milton Goetz at a cost of over a million dollars. Mr. Goetz went broke soon thereafter, and there were several owners before Marion acquired it for only $120,000, a greater bargain than the rejected house on Lexington Road had been. Manicured down to only eight acres, the estate was intensively landscaped except for the hillside brush and bramble visible from the street—a security precaution which Hearst did nothing to change. There were several dozen tall palms in orderly rows flanking a long rectangular swimming pool with a smaller fish pond on a terrace above it just below the house. Tiers of stone steps gave access to the pool and the lower formal gardens. "The Beverly house," as Marion called it, was built of pink stucco with a tiled roof atop its three stories and designed in a U around a cobbled courtyard.

Within six weeks of her purchase, Marion had deeded over the house to Hearst when his doctors informed her that his physical condition would not permit him to return to San Simeon. She told the Hearst sons as well as her friends that she wanted Hearst to spend his last days in his own home.

Marion's days brightened. She always had preferred Hollywood to San Simeon, Wyntoon, or Europe. There was always Romanoff's, where she could meet friends for lunch and watch the other people, a few stars and many anonymous persons who came to the place on a tour of Hollywood's landmarks. Quite a few friends and an occasional fan would remember Marion and come over to say "hello"—until that chilling time a little later when she discovered that she had been forgotten by far too many people, including some she had entertained for weekends or even a week at San Simeon.

In the Beverly house during that first year after the Second World War, Marion entertained often and partied regularly. She sold the beach house since her parties now were scaled down, but she believed that actors were among the most delightful and generous people in the world and needed cheering up more than "civilians" with smaller egos. She could not yet see that they were also notoriously fickle in their affections and friendships.

IV

By 1948, Hearst had lost over forty pounds and his rather small eyes began to look enormous within the deep rings caused by the strain of a failing heart. No longer glacially blue, they seemed permanently haunted—the eyes of a man who stares rather than looks at people and objects, as though he may be seeing them for the last time. But his mind was as sharp as ever and he wrote at least one editorial a week for his newspapers, or, if not, the theme and tone of what it should contain.

William Haines, who had retired from films as a leading man the moment he knew he could make an equally splendid income from interior decorating (and thumbed his nose at Louis B. Mayer, who seemed totally insensitive to male decorators), came by the Beverly house to say hello to Marion and to see Hearst. Hearst came tottering down the long hall of the upstairs to greet him. "What are you up to these days, Billy?" he asked, genuinely pleased to see him.

Haines was doing extremely well, after over twelve years of building a clientele of "the right people" who shared his taste for rococo accents and Empire furnishings. "You know, W.R.," Haines told Hearst, "You got me started in decorating. I didn't know a jardiniere from a peepot until you got me interested in relics." This delighted Hearst and he threw back his head and hee-hawed in that singular way of his.

Marion asked Haines about his companion Jimmy Shields and they sat in the parlor, talking about their days on the Metro lot. They spoke of Jack Gilbert and Garbo, of the time Gilbert believed the great Swede had discarded him and he began walking into the surf in front of Marion's beach house. "I'm really going to do it this time!" he shouted at them, but they only nodded and Haines told him to go right ahead. In disgust, Gilbert stalked out of the water and away from them.

Hearst was still not stepping down from day-to-day control of his newspapers. In 1948 and 1949, he was hoping (and such hopes were life-sustaining to him then) to acquire an existing Los Angeles rival paper through exercising an option acquired by the Hearst Corporation during that period. But Hearst executive Jacob Gortatowsky urged some caution in proceeding with such an acquisition. Profits were diminishing in those years even though income was substantial. Hearst had in mind converting the "option" into a tabloid, but Gortatowsky again dampened this possibility, telling Hearst that it would lose much of its prestige in that form. The project was abandoned.

Since Marion's role in Hearst's life was still an equivocal one to his family, on March 12, 1949, it must have been startling to some to hear Anna Roosevelt Boettiger announce on her mother's daily radio show, that "For her untiring effort in providing a great community service, as well as for her many other charities, Mother and I have chosen Marion Davies as our 'Woman of the Day.'" Other honors would follow—a citation from officers and sailors of the navy ship, U.S.S. *Manchester* making her Honorary Commanding Officer ". . . for her Patriotism, Valor, Fidelity and Abilities"; Los Angeles Sea Scouts awarded her a statuette, their spokesman telling her "44,000 scouts thank you for your good turn" (giving them a ten-meter sailing ship). All of these accolades came to Marion before Hearst's final illness, and he took an enormous amount of pride in her civic recognition. He began to feel that she had to be protected from attack after his death, which he now conceded might be just ahead; she must retain the respect she now commanded. He began what was to become a compelling task for him—his will and Marion's place in it.

As Charlie Lederer remembers it, Hearst believed at one point before his death that someone had been tampering with his will. It was October 1950 when Charlie received a phone call from Hearst asking him to drop by the Beverly house. Hearst asked Charlie to find him an outside attorney, someone having no connection with the Hearst publishing empire or any other publishing firm. Charlie made a few inquiries and then recommended lawyer Gregson Bautzer.

What Hearst wanted specifically was some form of a trust agreement that would insure that after his death Marion would have the same championing and courtesy from the Hearst enterprises that she had enjoyed during his lifetime—the courtesy of listening to her advice on the running of the newspaper empire, no less. In order to guarantee this attitude, certain stocks were to be deposited with Hearst's bank. Although the voting trust agreement pooling Hearst's 170,000 preferred shares in the Hearst Corporation with Marion's 30,000 was signed on November 5, 1950, the stocks were never deposited to guarantee the agreement as Hearst had instructed his staff to do.

V

On April 29, Hearst turned eighty-eight. It seemed improbable that he would reach ninety and there was a certain pitiful *l'envoi* to his remarks about survival.

A cake was carted into one of the rooms on the second floor. Hearst said he didn't want to receive anyone in his bedroom because he was "sick of looking at that ceiling." With his birdlike eyes watching everyone and everything, he sat slightly bent forward, his frail hands gripping the sides of his chair.

Hearst had asked Marion to bring in five of their closest women friends. As weak as he was, he didn't trust his emotions on such an occasion before any man. Among those invited were Marie Glendinning, Eleanor Boardman d'Arrast, Carmen Pantages Considine, Kay Spreckels (later Gable), and Frances Marion, with Marion sitting on the floor at Hearst's feet.

Small remembrances were given Hearst, the largest being an oil painting from Marion—an early photograph of Hearst's mother, Phoebe, holding her son, who wore an infant's long lace gown. Hearst studied the painting for several moments, his eyes beginning to fill with tears. Then sobs shook him and he covered his face, while Marion grabbed him behind the knees, pressing his legs to her body and saying, "It's all right, W.R. It's all right."

His mind still sharp, Hearst could only be desolated as he saw his control over his life being eroded by weakness and old age. His tears on his birthday were not unusual. He was a man of often embarrassing sentimentality. But now he was akin to blind Lear, acutely mistrustful of the sons and Hearst executive fraternity—those now in command who would reshape his precious publishing empire and inevitably exclude Marion from consideration.

Marion's visits to the sickroom, usually lasting about twenty minutes and occurring three times a day, were scrambling, tense affairs with Marion sometimes being given coffee to clear her stumbling tongue before going upstairs.

It is unlikely that Hearst was deceived. No old newspaperman could fail to notice her trembling hands, the reddish eyes, or the overeagerness to make a sober appearance. Perhaps that was why the hierarchy of the Hearst empire—Berlin, Gortatowsky, Huberth, and Bill Hearst, Jr.—appeared just before Hearst began to slide into that night of irreversible collapsing blood channels that led immediately to death. Hearst wished to lay down a policy for the future and he wanted Marion protected.

"We all know of Marion's problem," he would sometimes

say in a moment of candor, and possibly he repeated it to those men who he feared would use her drinking as an excuse to hurt her. He knew what she had thought of Jack Neylan, since retired, and he was pained to see that she had turned against Dick Berlin. Their abilities on the job did not seem to concern her. But Hearst was marvelously clearheaded about the men who made up his staff. If they were good at their jobs, they stayed, regardless of what Marion thought of them.

The summit meeting of the empire rapidly became a death watch and what Hearst had feared was set into motion. The body was taken out of the house with such dispatch while Marion slept—sedated by her doctor—she would babble of murder when awakened and never forgive those who stole from her the privilege, which should have been hers, of saying good-bye to the man who had chosen to live with her for three-and-a-half decades.

Frances Marion had stopped by to see her former movie boss before driving to San Francisco. Hearst had asked her to "stop at San Simeon and look the place over. I want to be sure that everything is all right there." Frances knew as well as anyone that there were two treasures in Hearst's life, and that one of them lived under the same roof with him, but the other was vast and unreachable for him now. Frances reached San Simeon the morning of Hearst's death. Randolph Apperson, kin to Hearst, had lived in the gatehouse for years and now he met Frances there. "We just heard that Cousin Will is dead," he told her. She was stunned and scarcely saw the twin towers of the castle on the distant rise. She knew that he was dying, but Hearst dead was a fact her mind seemed to reject. Then her thoughts turned at once to Marion. "She is going to be lost," she thought, and Marion appeared to her not so much as a mourning mistress as she did an orphan.

There was little that could be done to cheer Marion. Constance Talmadge and Marie Glendinning stayed in the house with her until she rallied enough from her shock to see that their own lives were temporarily in suspension out of their love for her. Marie, who lived in a little Hollywood cottage in retirement, insisted that she had nothing better to do. But Constance had a husband and a home waiting for her return.

Marion's attorneys—headed by Bautzer—believed after Hearst's death that a strong case could be made for Hearst's intention to fulfill the guarantee of depositing his stocks with hers and they were prepared to take the matter to court. On August 26, 1951, Hedda Hopper published a garbled account of the trust agreement "giving complete control of all Hearst enterprises to Miss Marion Davies, the late publisher's friend and confidante. . . . None of the principals in the trust agreement said to give Marion Davies, former actress, control of the widespread Hearst enterprises could be reached last night for comment or amplification of details of the agreement." When the Hearst sons and their attorney, Henry S. MacKay, Jr., read the story, they must have been chilled to the marrow.

On Monday, August 27, attorney MacKay and son Randolph Apperson Hearst, who had been made special administrator of the estate, told reporters that they had known about the "paper" and explained that the "so-called agreement was never executed and for this and many other reasons has no more effect than if it never existed." They referred to Marion as "Miss Douras" and the legal stiffness of this and other statements made by Randolph and his attorney must have given some distressing moments to the Hearst son who had known Marion as a woman of infinite generosity toward himself, his brothers, and his father.

The legal battle for control of the $200-million publishing empire took on some heat when it was reported that Marion's East Coast lawyers would start proceedings to gain control of the Hearst enterprises. Attorneys for the Hearst estate had confirmed already that Hearst had established a trust fund of 30,000 preferred shares of Hearst Corporation stock for Marion. She was to receive a lifetime income from it, the principal reverting upon her death to Hearst's five sons, the principal beneficiaries.

Speculation about the outcome appeared in *Time, Newsweek,* and every newspaper in the country excluding the Hearst chain. *Time* said that "if the opposition tries to prove that Hearst had been incompetent when he made Miss Davies boss, it will have to hurdle the fact that to the very end, all Hearstlings had made a great to do about the clarity of old W.R.'s mind."

Marion hated the prospect of a court fight. She told *Time*: "I would do anything in the world to avoid hurting the boys [Hearst's sons]. After all, they're half of W.R. I'm not the fighting type, but I don't believe in disregarding W.R.'s wishes. He had a reason for having the agreement drawn up. He thought I was the one who understood best what his policies and principles were and that I could see to it that his ideas were carried out. . . . Gosh, I thought I'd have a peaceful time in my old age. Now look at the spot I'm in."

Marion explained then as she would again when questioned about it that she and Hearst sometimes did not care for opinions carried in the Hearst syndicate. She repeated her admiring comments about Eleanor Roosevelt—"She is a great woman. When Westbrook Pegler started hacking at Mrs. Roosevelt time after time, it got boring and annoying. W.R. wired Pegler many times to cut it out; each time Pegler laid it on thicker. I never read his stuff any more." What she was saying was that the Hearst papers were in for some changes, if she took command.

There were prolonged meetings between Marion's attorneys and the lawyers for the estate. A court battle was undesirable to both sides. The estate knew that while Marion was able to make decisions for Hearst and run things whenever he was ailing (she had been immersed in publishing for so many years, she had become Hearst's alter ego, knowing precisely what he would do or say about nearly everything), that day had passed. Even Marion's own attorneys knew that her drinking problem made her highly vulnerable to legal attack and were terrified by the prospect of her making a courtroom appearance with nurses at her elbows to support her in front of strangers knowing nothing of her poor circulation, her chronic "rubber legs." Marion's lawyers knew that much of Hearst's final concern was about her future. There were at least a dozen witnesses—friends and employees who were in the Beverly house—who could attest to this.

It was a unique situation, coming after years of an extraordinary relationship. Hearst had known that Marion drank heavily long before he had drawn up the contested document, and he had known—as had all of her intimates—that drinking rarely affected her wit or her thinking processes. Alcoholism was just a condition that she had, like the chronic poor circulation in her legs, like Hearst's heart problem. Hearst's opinions about Marion's difficulties were well-known and surely would be brought into the courtroom.

But he had referred to her in his will as "my loyal friend, Miss Marion Douras, who came to my aid during the great depression with a million dollars of her own money. . . ." It was the closest he ever came to acknowledging what a good match they had made for over thirty years. She, the girl who had followed him back and forth across the country, the oceans, into pictures and out of them again, whose entire family had been schooled in following his meanderings with their favorite at a specified distance but never far away, she was in the news again and her name was once again being muttered across the Hearst conference tables in New York. What was said of her there is unknown, but it could not have been kind. What was inescapable to all of Hearst's executives was the fact of her closeness to the Chief. Both of them had sought a larger world for a time, a world beyond the bedroom, but in the end, it would come down to that again, a desolated woman at a bedside trying to cheer her dying man.

A compromise was hammered out whereby Marion relinquished all voting rights but would serve the Hearst enterprises as an advisor at a dollar a year, retaining, of course, her 30,000 shares of Hearst stock. She was granted the right to use the Hearst newspapers for publicizing her charitable enterprises, which were extensive, as well as individuals whom she considered worthy. The Hearst Corporation asked for first refusal on Marion's autobiography. She told Hedda Hopper that she did not expect to write one, but changed her mind within a year. Whether pressure from the Hearst family led to her decision to abort this literary attempt is unknown. The night the compromise was signed, Marion wept and said "Thank God it's all over." She thanked nephew Charlie, who had been her deputy at Bautzer's office throughout the ordeal. In a sense, she was set free that night, but as with "lifers" suddenly pardoned or paroled, she didn't know what to do with her freedom. She spoke of going away, but no one believed her.

Charlie Lederer paid his aunt a call nearly every day when he wasn't involved at the studio. There were frequent dinners in the Beverly house with Marion, Charlie, and his wife Annie. Sometimes, she would visit niece Pat Lake and her husband Arthur in their Santa Monica home, where Marion's grandniece and grandnephew, Marion Rose and Arthur Patrick, were affectionate children who enjoyed making a fuss over her. Sister Rose would often stay overnight with Marion and made a genuine effort to avoid the fits of near-paranoid anger that formerly set them to pulling hair. Kay Spreckels, Mary Pickford, and Diana Fitzmau-

rice Cousins, widow of the silent film director George Fitzmaurice
and presently married to an army general, appeared to be in touch
with each other so that there was usually one calling on Marion in
the afternoon every day. Marion's pal from her Metro days, former
star Eleanor Boardman, had moved into the gatehouse of the Beverly place in 1950 and made of the vacant storage area a charming, spacious home in the French style. But Eleanor, recently wid-
owed by the death of director Harry d'Arrast, had inherited a
château in the south of France and was there looking into her
holdings at the time of Marion's own bereavement.

Everyone felt sorry for Marion. "They speak in whispers
and tiptoe around this place like they're in a museum or something," she complained. She knew of one person, however, whose
attitude would not for long be one of condolence for the dead
but would move on quickly to concern for the living. That man
was Horace G. Brown of Virginia, *Captain* Brown now, of the
Maritime Service.

Horace Brown had been a serious suitor to sister Rose until
a year or so earlier. On one of his shore leaves, Marion had
coaxed both of them to the point where she felt it was all right
to phone the papers and announce their imminent marriage.
But then Rose had balked. Horace, who called himself a "Virginia ham," got down on his knees and pleaded with her. "I'll
marry you now or in six weeks or in six years, but I'll wait for
you," he told her. Unimpressed, Rose flounced down the long
gallery of the Beverly house and went home. She had been in
love for years with a married man. Much in the same situation as
Marion had been—unable to marry him. It was a reprise of her
long affair with publisher McLean who was now ten years dead,
the difference being that McLean had been a millionaire. It was
believed by some that Marion paid this married man a salary to
"be good to Rose." Horace said later that Rose's reluctance to go
through with the ceremony was due to her fear of the needle (for
the blood test), but others say that the whole incident had come
about because of a drinking weekend. When Rose sobered up, she
called it off.

It must have been a disappointment to Horace. In her early
fifties, Rose was still an attractive woman. More vain than Marion, she spent more of her time working over her face and figure.
She had a flawless complexion and blue eyes that seemed cold
and austere until she heard or saw something amusing, when
they would become dazzling in their brightness.

Marion, feeling guilty over Rose's change of heart, invited Horace to Sunday suppers at the Beverly house. He met Hearst upstairs in his room, where illness confined him, and learned that Marion already had briefed her companion about Horace's abilities as a slightly off-color story teller, sailor's jokes he had brought back from his voyages which broke up Marion and sent her into giggling fits. Hearst seemed pleased that there was someone around to lift her spirits during that prolonged crisis of his final illness. On one occasion, Horace was invited to spend a few days in the guest house and would go up evenings to play cribbage with Hearst, who would ask him to tell "some of those great stories Marion finds so funny." Horace would carefully edit himself, fearful that the old man would throw him out for being profane, and Hearst would laugh anyway, holding his hands over his chest as though such a precaution might spare his heart the strain of more robust laughter.

Seeing them together perhaps Marion noticed what others did later. Horace was a big man with the same long sloping nose that Hearst had, the same narrow-set blue eyes. His resemblance to Hearst was sufficient to make visitors to the Beverly house look twice following Hearst's death, and some felt a chill whenever Horace approached from a distance, since on October 31, 1951, ten weeks after Hearst's death, Horace Brown and Marion were married at Las Vegas, Nevada. She was fifty-four years old, but that was not given out for publication—in the newspapers, she was forty-five, but all other details were correct, and it was, as all of the press pointed out, her first marriage.

VI

The marriage was sensational page-one news throughout the country. The sensation lay in the fact that she had married so very soon after the death of her companion in that relationship which had been called by many, including some of her closest friends, "the romance of the century."

But there were reasons why it happened when it did. Marion bitterly resented the breaches of courtesy, too numerous to mention, by four of the Hearst sons and the Corporation itself that had occurred since the day of Hearst's death. They were treating her as though she had been only a paid companion.

She began dwelling on marriage as an instant way to respectability, to an answer to this shabby dismissal. And she was far more lonely than she ever dreamed she could be. Nothing seemed to cheer her. The tone in the voices of her friends bothered her —so unnatural, she thought, so fearful of saying the wrong thing, they might still be standing around her parlor on that day he was stolen from her. She was being treated like a pariah by the Hearst faction and like a widow by her friends. She objected rather strenuously to both attitudes. With Horace Brown, at least there would be some action in her life.

Horace was forceful and direct, but this force and his directness were channeled in a direction with no visible goal. He resembled Virginia Woolf's Jack Mytton, who once seized a candle and set fire to his nightshirt, staggering burning from his house just to show everyone how he cured the hiccoughs. Horace wanted to be liked nearly as desperately as Hearst had, and he would go to almost any lengths to win approval. But he had an active contempt for "phonies."

Marion shared a Douras trait of admiring the outrageous. Some Hollywood folk who enjoyed seeing pretentiousness pricked were often delighted to see Marion and her sisters gathered in a corner of one of their houses exploding with mirth over some social assault by Eddie Kane or Harry Crocker or perhaps their own nephew Charlie Lederer.

Horace had a serious side as well. His first wife Virginia was killed in a car wreck and he had felt responsible for her death. Taped up for injuries sustained in the same crash when their car failed to make a hairpin turn in the mountains and plunged over a cliff, he was a forlorn creature on the fringes of the film colony long before Marion met him. The Lakes, Arthur and Pat, felt sorry for Horace and invited him to come to their house to convalesce. Pat was by then a woman of some sophistication earned through years of European travel with Aunt Marion. She anticipated the punchlines of nearly all of his jokes and his long stories of his life as a Hollywood extra drove her quickly to take a stronger martini. She was perhaps inured to such tales of Hollywood. Later, Horace would sell his memoir of "Extra Life" to a Richmond newspaper. But she endured Horace's obsessional need to be liked and, in time, began calling him "Uncle Horace" even before he married her aunt.

Some of Marion's friends were quick to call him a fortune-hunter and recalled that he had been married to Grace Tibbett, who once had been the wife of opera star Lawrence Tibbett. But there is no evidence that Horace profited especially from that mismatch except that Grace Brown sent him off to the Merchant Marine Academy in New England to learn to be a sailor and equip him for a new career. He never tired of saying how much he loved the sea, so when that marriage began going sour, his wife was generous enough to send him in a direction that might take him to some prosperity and fulfillment on his own.

Horace's return and retirement from active duty as a Merchant Marine off Korea was accomplished within days with Marion's friends in Washington handling most of it. Marion even seemed a little desperate to get Horace back next to her. Probably he had told her that if she were ever free, he would like to marry her. Marriage with a passably handsome man of her own generation who looked enough like Hearst to be his brother was her motivation, of that no one close to her had any doubt.

But her rational self had to be put down. *Marry* Horace? Marry a roustabout stunt-man, a wandering sea captain? Even Horace had thought such an eventuality unlikely as late as the spring of that year when he had been invited to move into the guest house. "Marion was very gracious," he recalled. "I had no romantic aspirations. It wasn't my territory. And Mr. Hearst was very kind to me. Of course, a man of his intelligence and me don't have very much in common." But he did have the title— Captain—won at sea through his gruff but friendly way of handling men, and that was something socially elevating in Hollywood where titles of any kind impress, or, as Marion once said, "[His Captaincy]'s even better than being a Prince from some country nobody ever heard of." Cold sober, this still did not convince her, and it is said that Horace had to get her tight before she would agree to run off to Las Vegas—*kidnap* her, some said. But that does not seem very likely when she wanted marriage so badly and here was someone who both courted respectability and punctured it when it turned out to be empty or false, just as she had for years. Horace and Marion had far more in common than many of her friends would concede. He had fought his way up from his lower-middle-class origins through some hard work and not a little charm. He was terribly insecure about new acquaintances, and constantly alert to any tinge of dislike or, he hoped, any evidence of pleasure at being in his company.

Alcohol was Marion's maid of honor on her wedding night

—it encouraged and sustained her. It dissolved the differences between herself and Horace that remained—and there were some, enough to make the next ten years an up-and-down affair. One of her nurses was so disturbed by the quantities of whiskey she was taking in on that day before her "elopement," she phoned Dr. Corday and asked what might be done. It apparently seemed immediately clear to the doctor that Marion was attempting to work up her courage in order to take some bold step in her life. This was confirmed when Marion herself phoned Corday to ask if he would accompany Horace and her to Las Vegas for their wedding. According to Horace, Corday even got as far as the airport with them before being called back by an airport page to a seriously ill patient. But Horace's handsome son Gates went with them, and Arthur and Pat Lake drove over to Palm Springs to meet them on their way back from the ceremony. Arthur was something of a celebrity again after his film career had begun to wane. He was repeating his film role of Dagwood in the television version of the comic-strip, *Blondie*. The slenderness required by his role and his high-pitched voice (in the same range as Hearst's had been) made Arthur seem in constant need of protection as a TV character, but in life he was a big man, as tall as Horace, constantly battling his weight.

Charlie Farrell, who ran the famed Palm Springs spa, the Racquet Club, threw a reception for the newlyweds there. Marion was badly hung over and still wearing slacks and dark glasses, but she was delighted to embrace her niece Pat and feel that there was some family in attendance. Although Charlie Lederer was not there on that last day of October—it was Halloween—she had his indirect blessing. He and her lawyer, Gregson Bautzer, had decided that Horace might be less inclined to plunder her fortune than one or two others among the men who had begun courting Marion two or three weeks after Hearst's death. One of them, possibly more handsome than the others and therefore more dangerous, had had some difficulty with the government several years earlier and had gone to Mexico until it had all blown over. He was a man constantly in need of huge sums of money for his various ventures and the banks may have become less cooperative after his trouble. While Horace had some difficulty fitting into Marion's assorted groups of friends, excepting that with former naval officer Dr. Frank Nolan, Buddy Rogers, and Mary Pickford, and certain rotarians of the Hollywood community, Charlie's judgment about Horace turned out to be correct. And Charlie and Horace were to share the final gesture of holding Marion by the hand as she lay dying or—when she was wasted by illness—carrying her from her bed to a chair.

The Shindler private police guards were still on duty when Horace and Marion returned to the Beverly house. They had been hired by Marion's lawyers soon after Hearst's death to protect the property. Within a few months of the marriage, nearly all of them would be dismissed as Horace cultivated friendships among the Beverly Hills police force—he once had been a policeman in Richmond—and invited them up to the house for hot coffee on their patrols. Any prospective burglars, if their stay within the grounds of the Beverly house were prolonged beyond a half hour or so, would be certain to be intercepted by a cruising police car coming up the hill for a coffee break. Already Horace was saving Marion money, a token perhaps, but it did a great deal for his ego.

Horace spoke later of there being thousands of telegrams awaiting Marion upon their return to the mansion. Probably this is an exaggeration. Those wires that did come were mostly from far away and from friends to whom Captain Horace Brown was a mystery. Marion herself was in a gay mood once she was home again with a ring on her finger. She kidded Horace about the event having fallen on Halloween, wondering if it was "a trick or a treat." There were phone calls from Hedda Hopper and Cobina Wright wishing her happiness, and Marion believed on her wedding morning that she had done something brilliant—she had achieved the goal of a lifetime and banished her loneliness with one stroke.

In the weeks ahead, Marion's life *did* brighten perceptibly. Charlie continued to drop around often, and the Lakes were seen more regularly than ever at the Beverly house. Horace had a sister who visited frequently; and he had three sons. There was family surrounding Marion again to step into the vacant spaces in that long, long trail of the dead and vanished in her life: Mama Rose, Pepi, Papa Ben, Ethel, Reine, and Hearst. And Horace made things happen around himself. He craved action and excitement the way Marion had when she was just emerging from the chorus or when she was becoming bored at the castle. Unfortunately, there wasn't very much in their vicinity. In truth, life had been more eventful for him when he was an extra in such movies as *High, Wide and Handsome* (1937), a film concerned with the bringing in of wildcat oil wells. In that, Horace was cast as an oil line worker fighting off some marauding teamsters. He was beaten with whips and thrown into a muddy lake, but he was game about it and any violence done to one's body while working as an extra usually doubled or tripled your pay for the day. He had been in quick succession a nobleman in the background of Garbo's *Conquest;* a fireman helping to put out the fire in *In Old Chicago;* a pirate in De Mille's *The Buccaneer;* an ice skater who couldn't skate in *There Goes My Heart;* one of an army of "happy peasants" in *Rosalie;* and Frank Morgan's stand-in for *The Crowd Roars.* His work in films even won him a certain celebrity in his home town back in Virginia.

Horace soon discovered that Marion had fallen into limbo with Hearst's death; nothing very much was happening around her, and action had to be invented. He managed this sometimes in a spectacular fashion. When Marion complained of sister Rose's "martini storms," which she actually feared, Horace contrived to have Marion present by Rose's poolside when he shoved her—wheelchair and all, in her Sunday best—into the pool. On another occasion, he shot out all of the lights in Rose's driveway, "never missing a single damn one." Horace was not drunk at the time; he was not a drinker in any serious way as Marion was.

Marion became alarmed and thought Horace needed some constructive activity even though there was no need for him to have any kind of gainful employment. She attempted to make him an executive in a television company in which she held the principal interest, but that did not work out. Horace was an outdoors type, a seaman, a man who liked to go into the hills and shoot. He was not at home in the role of television producer even with fancy stationery bearing his name as a company executive, his own office, and painstaking coaching by experts in his duties. Perhaps to regain some of the respect he feared he had lost in the TV debacle, he took Marion back East to visit his family—his brothers and sisters living in the Tidewater section of Virginia. It was there that he got the notion that some of the sights and sounds of the bay waters of Virginia could be exported to the Beverly house. He dug up several dozen oysters and captured a number of bull frogs, carrying them back to California in a station wagon. He dumped the oysters in one of the reflecting pools, along with several buckets of Tidewater mud. He planned, he said, to operate on them a little later in order to induce the formation of pearls. The bull frogs leaped about the gardens in the vicinity of the pools and could be heard splashing into the water and croaking through the night. In a sense, this effort was no more absurd than that of others, who had "authentic" New England farmhouses built for them on an acre or two of Beverly Hills with a few barnyard animals to make the attempt convincing. Marion, in some despair, told Horace that she thought he was crazy. He agreed with her and calmed down for a while.

Actually, Horace was quite sane. He was simply restless. And Marion was suffering from the same complaint. The warm and supportive chatter of a dozen friends or more lolling about her house was over. She knew that they were; many of her friends were gone, her films forgotten. It was far worse ignominy than Hearst ever could have imagined would descend upon her.

PART SEVEN

THE
MOOD
IS BLUE

I

Perhaps for Marion's sake alone or perhaps because at times his desperate friendliness made its point, beginning in 1952, there was a patchwork kind of social life for the Captain Horace Browns. Mr. and Mrs. Alexander Saunderson of Pasadena, who had been brought to Marion's house by Eleanor Boardman d'Arrast, came over often. Saunderson was a hearty Scotsman and his wife was a Van Allen from the East Coast—members of legitimate society. Sonja Henie, whose career in films had begun with Marion's help, came whenever she could manage it. The Martin von Dehns of Bel Air and Palm Springs nearly always included the Browns whenever they entertained. Some neighbors, the Anthony Norvells, held a dinner dance in honor of Thelma Viscountess Furness and Mrs. Reginald C. Vanderbilt, and Marion and Horace were invited. Marion wore a black evening gown and a silk wrap, two emerald and diamond bracelets, her large emerald brooch pin encrusted with diamonds, her choker necklace of emeralds and pearls, and her twin-crescent earrings of emeralds. No one ever got very far in cautioning her about excessive use of her jewelry on such occasions. "I earned every damned one of these," she would say, a little defiantly, as she secured an earring valued at about $12,000. The occasion was notable chiefly because Lady Lawford's actor son Peter met Patricia Kennedy there. Marion later lost the $15,000 diamond and emerald bracelet while attending friend Sonja Henie's ice show at the Shrine Auditorium—the least valuable item of the $200,-000 collection she was wearing that night. At still another party, this one in Tallulah Bankhead's honor, Tallulah told Marion, "If you hadn't been so stinking rich, you would have become the screen's number-one comedienne." Marion was pleased but she said, not surprisingly, that it was nice to hear but not true. "With me, it was 5 percent talent and 95 percent publicity." And by this time, approximately fifteen years after *Citizen Kane,* she probably believed what she was saying.

The house staff remained unchanged. Tom Kennington, who had worked as secretary to Hearst, relieving regular secretary Richard Stanley, was kept on in the same position for Marion. Cleo Washburn, a maintenance man and gardener at the beach house was retained. One new employee, Faith Grant, was brought in less than three weeks after Hearst's death. Miss Grant had been a victim of the Hearst empire's ungallant day of retribution against Marion. She had been working as assistant librarian at the Los Angeles *Examiner,* but she had been guilty of visiting the Beverly house frequently, since she was Tom Kennington's girlfriend, and being asked in for a drink with Marion. Her life at the newspaper library become one of nearly total harassment and humiliation the week of Hearst's death and burial. Marion told her, "The hell with those bastards. We'll find something for you to do here." And she did. Marion's nurse Floretta Mouser was becoming her nearly constant companion on excursions away from the Beverly house. Often dressed in simple civilian gowns, Mrs. Mouser would attend charity luncheons and support her at the elbow. When Marion made the rounds of a social affair, shaking hands with old friends and exchanging light conversation, the sight of two employees—Mrs. Mouser and a male attendant—soberly blank-faced or with fixed smiles at either side of her began to give Marion a reputation as a hopeless alcoholic. Her drinking *was* an increasing problem since she was still as allergic to alcohol as ever, but she was not falling-down drunk; her poor coordination would plague her until very near the end of her life. When he was not out in a police prowl car with his cronies on the force, Horace was her escort of choice. His physical help in getting her around was done with enough grace as to make it practically invisible, and he was not to be passed over quickly as was Marion's staff. Horace always saw to that.

Christmases were the most difficult times for Marion to get through. Everyone who mattered to her except for Charlie, Pat, and now Horace, was dead, and Charlie was not an avid celebrant of Christmas. In former years, she and Hearst would receive mountains of presents and there were trees in all of the houses—Wyntoon, San Simeon, Ocean House, the Lexington Road place, and the staff at St. Donat's often would send pictures of the castle at Christmastime garlanded with holly. Marion took one look at the small pile of presents and said to Horace, "Let's get out of here."

They went over to visit nurse-companion Mrs. Mouser and her ailing husband in their Hollywood cottage. Marion sat close to Horace as he squeezed one arm about her. Their excursions out of the house began a new ritual for Marion in her last years each and every Christmas and on one of them, they would visit Kay Spreckels and her children, with Horace playing Santa Claus. After lots of "Ho! Ho! Ho!"-ing with the kiddies and patting them on their heads and bottoms, Horace lifted his beard to ask Kay for a drink.

"He isn't Santa Claus!" declared one of the youngsters, who caught the gesture.

Marion and Horace were often two lost souls, and a sense of a rather hopeless desolation began to pervade the Beverly house. It might have been expected that there was a reservoir of goodwill toward Marion built up through the years of her lavish party-giving, her charities which were still going on, her camaraderie with the hundreds of relatively obscure workers and technicians in the film industry, and that Horace might be excused any number of breaches of decorum because he was married to Marion. But Hollywood, like any small town, began thinking of Marion in terms of pity rather than regard. A few hostesses—Cobina Wright, Kay Spreckels, Zsa Zsa Gabor, Sonia Henie, Eleanor Boardman d'Arrast, and the Samuel Goldwyns—usually attempted to include the Browns at their parties. Frances Goldwyn was a particular friend and remained loyal to the last. But there were far too many who forgot the hundreds of times they were invited to Ocean House and San Simeon, far too many actors who forgot the parts they had been given at a word from Marion to a producer or a director.

Marion did not remain silent in the face of this ostracism. She complained to Horace, to Charlie, to visiting friends. And Horace, naively perhaps, attempted to ignore the social abuse, sometimes telling a guest at the Beverly house, "I don't know why Marion married me. She's one of the greatest women in the world and I'm nobody. I was just plain lucky, I guess."

To fill the void and give them a lively companion, Horace went to an animal farm in the San Fernando Valley and bought a monkey. Marion did not appreciate this effort, but by now she

decided that Horace was slightly eccentric and it did give her
something to talk about with the staff. She was distressed though
to see Horace coddling the simian, whom he had named "Junior," and carrying him around like a baby. She never had been
able to have a child of her own, felt she was too old to begin
now, and this was simply too much.

For months, Junior had the run of the Beverly house,
swinging from the brocade draperies and rubbing his milk-cov-
ered lips over the windows when he wasn't leaping onto the head
or shoulder of a startled guest. Perhaps it gave a convenient
excuse to some, but Marion thought a few of her prospective
guests were a bit too quick in telling her that they were allergic
to monkeys.

Monkeys are affectionate and usually intelligent creatures.
Their craving for human attention is often insatiable. When
Junior jumped into Marion's arms or tugged at her dress or
peignoir, she would scream for help. Her bedroom door was
permanently shut to Junior and became a retreat from the bed-
lam of his presence—broken Meissen and Dresden china, torn
draperies, smeared walls and windowpanes. She confided to Marie Glendinning that she lived in fear of Junior leaping into her
hair "like a bat and getting stuck there."

One afternoon, Horace discovered his little friend missing,
but Marion would not allow her hopes to rise too much. He had
been missing before, his notoriety in the neighborhood widening
as he became known as "the little terror of Beverly Hills." On
this occasion, Junior was discovered tying up traffic in Benedict
Canyon, standing in the center of an intersection and refusing
to be intimidated by the honking of cars surrounding him. Horace said that an eyewitness told him that Junior was "directing
traffic." He was also collecting refuse from the street and Marion
was convinced he was a germ-carrier. With a half-eaten apple
in one hand and a squashed orange in the other, he juggled
both while he picked up a half-rotten banana. Other times, he
enjoyed a swim in the pool—which kept nearly everyone but Horace out of it.

Horace wept a little on the way from Jungleland, where he
finally took his "baby." "These little devils can weasel their way
right into your heart," he said, but Marion did not agree. Dogs
were another matter—her love for Gandhi was well-known and
his death still could evoke a tear now and then—but "wild animals," as she deemed Junior, never.

In one area, there was no doubt. Horace was an impressive male, tall and commanding, with a healthy interest in women and in keeping Marion content on a physical level. There was something engaging about their eagerness to be together. Marion liked to be embraced and kissed. "Give me a big sloppy kiss, Horace," she would say, and he would oblige wherever they happened to be. Marion always had needed to establish some claim, however small, upon the emotions of the men around her. She was very feminine in this, although it is a characteristic of leading actresses to do so. With Hearst, she always had known where she stood. And with Horace, she early decided that he intended to earn his keep.

Marion needed that intimate contact; she always had— more than the company of friends. Those who deplored the steady erosion of her friends over that final decade had to concede that "a big sloppy kiss" was something she needed more. And some of the friends had not abandoned her through choice; a number of them had moved away: Anita Loos, who had settled permanently in New York, Charlie Chaplin, who had chosen a kind of exile in Switzerland, Dorothy Mackaill, who had moved first to New York, then to Hawaii, and Aileen Pringle, who also had settled in New York. And Horace was witness, of course, to acts of charity by Marion beyond number. When she visited ex-policeman Brown's old Precinct House in Richmond, she wanted to pay the fines of about thirty petty crooks and drunks sleeping it off. The Judge allowed her to ante up the fines for two who were sober enough to be released, giving them some pocket money and her autograph. A few weeks later Horace appeared in the West Los Angeles Municipal Court to pay a traffic fine and observed a fellow sailor temporarily out of funds. He paid the sailor's fine, telling the judge, "I just don't like to see sailors in trouble."

For a few of those remaining in Hollywood who dropped her, the gesture had its point. Marion always had been uncomfortably genuine, had been her very natural self even in the most artificial and hothouse of environments. This rare virtue, nearly unknown in the film colony, had been tolerated earlier because of her wit, her vitality, her closeness to the great power that was Hearst's, and her extraordinary gift for seeing to others' pleasures. But now she seemed to have no mind of her own. Even during the many years with Hearst, though dominated, she had been frequently rebellious. Now she allowed Horace to be more than her protector; he was a sometimes graceless "social secretary" fending off "phonies" by turning a garden hose on them as they came up the drive from their cars. Marion told them that Horace was "terrible," but she made few apologies. But there were a select few whom Horace accepted: Mary Pickford, who did not return the favor in those first months, Fifi D'Orsay, whose outspokenness in that less permissive era appealed to him, Eleanor Boardman d'Arrast, whose air of gentility seemed real to him, Connie Talmadge and Eileen Percy Ruby, Marion's oldest pals no matter what, Marie Glendinning, who thought him "awful," but conceded that "he was a man and a husband and he was *there*," and Speed Lamkin, whose gay wit seemed to be something that Marion needed. In addition, of course, there was Marion's surviving family. Charlie Lederer and Horace struck up an odd sort of friendship, odd because they could not have been more opposite in their minds, likes, and personalities. Horace bought Charlie a little MG sports car along with one for himself, and Charlie's MG survived Horace's. Sister Rose was around far too often to suit Horace, who had changed his earlier high opinion of her after witnessing actual hair-pulling fights between the sisters. Once, at a small dinner party with just Rose, Fifi D'Orsay, and an unidentified English girl visiting the Browns, Rose was staggeringly drunk and nagging Marion about an estate in Palm Springs she wanted Marion to buy for her. When Marion looked embarrassed and said tersely, "You'll get it so let's drop it," Rose turned to Fifi and asked, "What do you want from Marion?" Fifi told her, "I just wanted to have a quiet dinner with my friend." At this, Marion quickly wound up the dinner and took Fifi off to a corner of the library where they could chat.

Marion rarely spoke of Hearst once she had got over the shock of his death and its bitter aftermath. She had to feel her drinks before she could discuss his part in her life with journalist Flink and, of course, it was concern over that phase of her past that prompted her to terminate that book project. She kept Hearst's poetry, his letters to her, and the telegrams locked in a trunk along with informal photos of the two of them taken in Europe and at San Simeon and Wyntoon. Even the sight of that trunk could bring her to the verge of tears, and it was kept out of sight.

II

On July 17, 1952, after only eight months of marriage, Marion filed a suit for divorce from Horace Brown in Santa Monica. The action surprised none of her friends. Marie Glendinning, Kay Spreckels, and Eleanor Boardman had expected it much earlier. Even Mary Pickford had imperiled a friendship with Marion going back over thirty years when she rushed up to Horace at a party and struck him repeatedly on the chest crying, "You're all wrong for Marion! Wrong! Wrong!" Finally Mary accepted him after her husband Buddy Rogers convinced her that he was "all right," her friendship with Horace surviving Marion's death.

Horace was in his car heading toward the Bay Bridge near San Francisco when he heard Hedda Hopper broadcast the news of Marion's move. So intense was the rivalry in the film columnist's profession that spouses would often learn that their marriage had gone on the rocks before even a phone call had come from their mates. One actress read in the paper that she was expecting before she could break the news to her husband. You either "told it to Louella or to Hedda," and Marion had phoned Hedda, giving those who noticed a hint that the friendship between Louella and herself was over. Horace had left the Beverly house early that afternoon "to cool off." He and Marion had engaged in a shouting match that had lasted all night.

What had pushed Marion to this point after putting up with Horace's pranks for months was not too clear. A point of crisis appeared to have been reached following an episode involving the telephones in the Beverly house and a member of her family as well as two of her intimate friends urged her to leave him. Of course, these well-intentioned parties had only heard Marion's side of the story.

Early one morning—it was two or three o'clock—while Marion was talking with a reporter on the night desk at the Los Angeles *Herald and Express*, Horace entered the room and ripped out the telephone wires. "For Christ's sake, Horace," Marion asked him, "Have you gone nuts?"

"Call me crazy. Call me anything you like, but I'm going to stop those calls," and he ran from room to room ripping out every extension in the place—thirteen in all. In Marion's condition, suffering from poor coordination in her legs and about seven hours of nonstop pink ladies, it was impossible for her to catch up with him. She stumbled after him, dazed by his actions, shouting "*Idiot! Idiot!*"

But again Horace was protecting Marion. After her death, he confessed that he was forced to "disconnect her" because she was getting drunk and phoning the Hearst paper in Los Angeles every night "just to talk nonsense." "She would be on the phone with the night editor sometimes for an hour or two giving her views on what was wrong with the world and how the newspaper should be run." Since one of the provisions of the release she had signed giving up her control over the Hearst empire stated clearly that she was to be given any editorial cooperation requested for herself, her charities, or her friends, the night man could not hang up. In a chilling communication from an old-timer on the newspaper still loyal to Marion, Horace was informed that the staff was tape-recording her rambling monologues to be played back later by Hearst executives "just for laughs."

Horace turned his car around and headed south. He hurried through the Beverly house until he found Marion sniffling on a sofa. "What's Hedda talking about?" he asked. "A fine thing to do to a guy when his back is turned."

By late afternoon, Marion's secretary, Tom Kennington, was on the phone with Paul Coates of the Los Angeles *Mirror* telling him that "Captain and Mrs. Brown have not come down from their rooms yet." In his column the next day, Coates wrote that

> An hour or so later, Captain Brown climbed out of the sack and returned my call. "You want a statement," he told me. "You can say I said I love Marion more than anything in life. She means everything to me."
> "About the hose——" I said.
> "What hose?"
> "The one you turned on Marion's friends," I explained.
> Horace laughed heartily. "Oh," he said, "that one."

Hedda Hopper followed up her broadcast with a lead item in her column saying, "I have just talked to Marion Davies and Captain Horace Brown. They have reconciled.

"Said the captain, 'I don't know why she took me back because I'm a beast. I bought her a monkey as a pet and then the monkey bit her. I pulled the phones out by the roots. . . . I went down to her sister Rose's house and shot out all the lights in her driveway. I pushed her [meaning Rose, although Horace was imprecise and Hedda's failure to clarify the remark led nearly everyone to believe that Marion had been pushed] in the swimming pool when she was in the wheelchair. I'm a beast.' "

"I said," continued Hedda, suddenly assuming her familiar role of public scold, "I know it, and you ought to beat your head against a stone wall every day for me."

Then Marion got on the phone and told Hedda, "I took him back. I don't know why. I guess because he's standing right beside me, crying."

"And," Hedda wrote, "we all laughed like a bunch of hyenas, and Marion said, 'Thank God we all have a sense of humor.' "

It is puzzling when studying Horace's life before he married Marion to see how barren it is of the wild blows at convention and civil behavior he delivered after the marriage. True, he was volatile and quick to anger. There were scuffles a-plenty in his life as a soldier and at sea. While he was married to Virginia Powell, a neighbor killed his son's pet duck with a rifle and he posted a notice on the nearest telephone pole daring the culprit to come forward with his weapon "and I'll make him eat it." But in every case, he was reacting to something someone had done to him or to his loved ones. When he pushed sister-in-law Rose Davies into her swimming pool, he explained that he had done so because a photographer in a helicopter had been buzzing overhead trying to get an interesting shot of Marion and Rose. "I decided to give him a surprise. Rose wasn't hurt. She wasn't a cripple. She just had this game leg that would go out of joint every so often. But I wouldn't want to repeat what she called me as she climbed out."

Even Marion had laughed at the incident. She had always resented Rose a little ("My favorite sister was Ethel. Don't tell Rose. She'll kill me.") and, like Hearst, knew that she used her "game" leg for dramatic purposes whenever she needed something. Marion probably resented having to pay Rose's last lover an allowance over the years. And then to see Rose—the woman Horace once had kneeled before begging her to marry him—pushed into her own swimming pool really broke up Marion.

He confessed to enjoy "getting a rise out of Rose." When he assaulted her sensibilities with some outrage, the air would be blue with her profanities. There seemed to be not so much mal-

ice in his mischief as a target for it. And when he turned a hose
on a clutch of film actors, he was putting in place a group of
superficial, egocentric operators who really didn't care about
Marion. They had come because they had heard that her husband was the barbarian of all time, the lout of the ages, and that
she put up with him because she was falling-down drunk nearly
all of her waking hours. Well, reasoned Horace, he would show
them that at least half of what they had heard was true. There
was a boldness about his behavior that fairly took one's breath
away. Marion had to concede that if she ever had the courage to
leave Horace for good, she would never forget the impact he had
made upon her life. She always had gravitated toward any excitement and Horace enjoyed creating it. It didn't matter so
much that sometimes it resembled a car crash. The victims were
always able to walk away. Around Horace, there was some of the
throb of sensation she had felt when Hearst was putting together a major news story. "Gee whiz!" was a phrase Marion frequently used when thrilled and a Hearst editor declared that it
was Hearst's simple intention to make every reader similarly
goggle-eyed. As *Life* Magazine had editorialized following his
death:

> He slashed up the front page with scare headlines. . . . He
> filled up the paper with cartoons and photographs, mostly
> of actresses in bathing suits. . . . The best sob stories that
> ever appeared in the Hearst papers were written about
> orphans who never existed. . . . Hearst Journalism, in its
> oldest and yellowest days, may have struck some readers
> as undignified and phony, but it never struck any reader as
> dull. Like it or not, no one could ignore it.

And like him or not, no one could ignore Captain Horace Brown.
Marion and Horace would have many a private laugh about that.
"You're awful, Horace," Marion would say, "just plain awful,"
and there was more than a hint of awe in her voice to back it up.

III

Soon after Eleanor Boardman d'Arrast's return to America and
her move into Marion's gatehouse, Eleanor asked Marion if she
would enjoy a small cocktail party. Marion thought that a splendid idea, and Eleanor invited former chorus boy Roger Davis,
who called himself "the oldest living chorus boy in the country"

and who had traveled for many years with Fannie Brice. Other close friends who came were Orry-Kelly, the dress designer from Warner Brothers, one of several durable relationships Marion took away from her three years at Warners, Carmen Pantages Considine, William Haines, and Jimmy Shields.

Marion appeared only a little late with Horace at her elbow. He was wearing his navy uniform, which he reserved for special occasions (he had become an officer in the Navy League, the Beverly Hills branch), and Roger Davis rather unkindly said, "I didn't know it was a costume party." This broke up everyone, and Marion laughed and gave Horace an affectionate squeeze of the hand. She had accepted Horace's need to be in and around uniforms. The Navy League and its accouterments gave Horace the same feeling of respectability and dignity that her own Foundation had given her.

By tacit agreement, most of the small group ignored Horace, one or two of them pretending that he wasn't there, and Horace reacted in kind by going off to Eleanor's dressing room and falling asleep. A couple of hours later when Marion was ready to go back up the hill to her home, she seemed to have forgotten that she had come with Horace and started out the door alone. Eleanor then became a little frantic and told her, "Get Horace out of my dressing room. I don't want him left here. I don't trust him." Marion looked at her old friend with a tinge of disappointment, and it was difficult to know for certain whether she was disappointed to see such a lack of understanding of Horace's behavior or to have to endure such a reversal. As Horace saw it, Hearst had gone along with the "phonies" of Hollywood because he had to, because much of the time he was in the business himself and Marion was an important member of the community. But Horace had small patience with the "tinsel" world of movie people. He believed that they were being two-faced toward Marion, ridiculing her and himself behind their backs— and perhaps he was right. Hollywood is not a place of eternal loyalties or charitable consideration for one's weaknesses. You fall in Hollywood, and you are devoured. Rather bestial, grown children run amuck there, and you must be nimble and have your wits about you to survive.

Sometime in September 1952 Charlie Morrison, owner of the Mocambo Night Club in Hollywood and a close friend of Marion's, came to the Beverly house seeking a favor. His daughter Marilyn recently had married the fantastically successful singer of popular songs, Johnny Ray. Marion had never met the singer, but she had heard his record hit, *The Little White Cloud That Cried,* and she had read that teenaged girls had screamed and a few had fainted when he appeared in person at the New York Paramount Theatre—Marion kept up with what was happening in show business. Now Johnny Ray's new father-in-law proposed that Marion give a bang-up party for him on his first trip to Hollywood. Ray was coming in town to appear at a rival nightclub, Ciro's. Marion suggested that a slightly smaller estate she owned in Beverly Hills be used, but Morrison insisted upon the mansion on Beverly Drive. Who said what became important a few months later when Marion was sued by Charlie Morrison for failure to pay his own catering company for champagne, chicken, and carnival tents supplied by him when she entertained his daughter and her husband along with seven hundred guests from the film colony.

Mr. Morrison insisted upon the Beverly house and finally Marion agreed. "My firm will supply everything," he told her. What he didn't say was that he expected her to pay for it. Her secretary was kept busy for the next couple of weeks coordinating the plans which daily became more grandiose as Marion got caught up in it. The garden paths were carpeted with synthetic grass, a circus tent was erected next to the fishpond, and three of the rooms in the mansion were redecorated to resemble New York's El Morocco, the Stork Club, and Twenty One.

Marion stayed in her rooms for nearly an hour after the first guests had arrived. She wanted to make a good impression on everyone and beyond that to reassert her identity as a social creature. Designer Don Loper had created a black gown for the evening but Marion had gained several pounds between her last fitting and the night of the party and could not get into it. She settled for a white satin strapless design also by Mr. Loper. From her safe, she extracted three quarters of a million dollars worth of her jewelry to set off the simple gown: diamond teardrop earrings, two bracelets encrusted with rubies and diamonds, her diamond necklace and another one fashioned of two strands of rubies, and along with her wedding band she wore a huge ruby ring she prized. The treasure was excessive by at least a bracelet, a necklace, and a ring, but she was looking very much her old self when she was ready to go downstairs to join the receiving line next to Horace and Mr. and Mrs. Johnny Ray.

Columnist Sheilah Graham sagely commented that what

was missing were the lively ones since left for the other world or
other shores—Clara Bow, John Gilbert, Douglas Fairbanks, Sr.,
Norma Talmadge, Mabel Normand, Fatty Arbuckle, and young
Charlie Chaplin, and, she should have added, young Marion
Davies. No one could excel Marion in lifting a huge party's spirits
when she was the acknowledged Queen of Hollywood society.

Nearly everyone of any standing in the film colony had
been invited, and they came in such hordes of Cadillacs, it required an entire platoon of policemen to handle the traffic along
Beverly Drive. There were the leading ladies—Crawford, Gardner, Simmons—and men—Heston, Cooper, and Curtis, comics
Skelton, Lewis, Benny, and Durante—and singers Shore, Horne,
Davis, and Sumac—and the men who created films—Frankovitch, Brackett, Donen, and Farrow. There were some conspicu-
ous absences, too. Marilyn Monroe, who was exciting far more
audiences around the world by that time than Mr. Ray was, did
not attend, and sister Rose Davies was not listed among the
guests. Louella Parsons came, but not Hedda Hopper, perhaps
for that reason. Nearly all of Marion's close friends were there:
Eleanor Boardman, Lloyd Pantages and his sister Carmen, Kay
Spreckels, the Harry Rubys, nephew Charlie Lederer and Annie,
niece Pat Lake and Arthur, and lawyer Gregson Bautzer. It was
—nearly all of them sensed—a farewell appearance by Marion
in the setting most appropriate to her. Among the numerous
reporters and photographers were some from *Life,* which would
cover the affair in its regular feature, "*Life* Goes to a Party."

Marion would have agreed with Miss Graham. Something
was missing. Only Brod Crawford attempted to recall the foolishness of the past by putting salt on the tail of a marble bird in
the hand of one of Hearst's nubile garden figures. Most of the
film people behaved as though they were in a nightclub—or a
museum. The young lady who "fell" into the fishpond made sure
that her accident was recorded by a news photographer. Some
guests toured the house and inspected the slick oil portraits of
Marion in her film roles as intently as the Greuzes and the Fragonards. More than half of them were strangers to Marion and
nearly all of them to Horace. Although Horace went up to people
and introduced himself and it must have been the most exciting
evening in the years of his marriage to Marion, Marion did not
seem to be enjoying herself. There were numerous gate-crashers,
and she tolerated it, saying that if they wanted to visit her home
that badly, let them stay. But she felt no sense of belonging with

her guests. The zaniness of the twenties had died and in its place had come a cool professionalism. Still, she was gracious and met nearly everyone and stood for an hour posing for the news photographers with group after group. She told the reporters that she had merely wanted "to have a little fun before I die," a remark that could only be understood by those who knew her mood that evening—she was a survivor from another age and she felt every minute of her years that night. The days of the free spenders were long since over, and she knew that they were.

IV

Marion was never an intellectual, although she had a shrewd and canny instinct for seeing the absurd in life. She seldom read anything heavier than a mystery novel. But she had known as friends Churchill, Shaw, and other first-rate thinkers of our time. She ranked Hearst among those with the finest minds. Now she was entering a time in her life she called "my no-mind days." She knew there was no going back for many of the "thinkers" in her life were now dead. "I've lived too long," she would say to Horace.

Marion went into a period of deep depression. She had been seeing the *Time* reporter, Stanley Flink, for months in an effort to get her life story into some kind of shape for publication. Flink had a tape recorder permanently at the Beverly house for sessions that lasted for hours when Marion was in an especially reflective mood. But now she was no longer certain that she wanted the truth about her years with Hearst committed to print.

As Cobina Wright, Sr., remembers it, Flink had been brought to Marion by the Southern novelist Speed Lamkin whose writing career after one or two small successes seemed to be in limbo. The novelist was one of a group of young men with a taste for brittle parlor wit who had gathered about Cobina, the only one in Hearst's stable of columnists who knew society as an insider. Cobina told Marion that the novelist wanted "desperately" to meet Marion, and an afternoon cocktail party was planned to bring them together. Lamkin eventually would attempt to recreate something of Marion's world in a novel, *The Easter Egg Hunt,* a book that evoked something of the spiritual undernourishment of the film colony and the ruthlessness of certain Hollywood types. It fails as a portrait of Marion, however—if that was his intention—since his heroine is perhaps the dullest character in the book.

Horace was usually a quiet spectator whenever the young writer Lamkin was "camping it up" to Marion's delight. Horace said later that Marion "got a few laughs out of him. It just wasn't the kind of thing I found funny."

But in 1952 a more important literary possibility was Flink's project of setting down all of that nearly incredible past. When doubts began besetting Marion, all the hours of tape, all the days of patiently waiting for her to dredge up from her past just when she had met Mr. Hearst, what her childhood had been like, what really had happened on that yachting weekend when Thomas Ince died, all seemed to be lost. She began talking to nephew Charlie about buying back the tapes. Rather mysteriously, the project was abandoned and Hedda Hopper rushed into print with word that "Marion Davies' life story will not be published."

Marion had been reluctant to permit Horace to sleep in the main house during the first days of their marriage. It seemed to her a sacrilege of some kind. But this proved awkward. She would come down to the guest house for a connubial night like Marie Antoinette escaping to her country hideaway for her amours. She soon saw the absurdity and Horace moved into the villa which he would inherit one day.

Marion closed down Hearst's suite and it was kept exactly as it was when he died. With that done, she attempted to live at least a part of her life in the present. She took Horace along whenever she visited the Children's Clinic, which she had endowed. They bought a large farm near Gloucester, Virginia, and there were frequent trips East. But pressures continued to build, nearly all from outside. "People are trying to break us up, Horace," she would say sometimes after a few gin fizzes.

"Yeah, honey," Horace would answer. "I know that, but we won't let 'em."

When Horace would tell almost total strangers that he was "Marion Davies' husband," he was not bragging, as many of her friends who heard about it believed. Actresses, as a breed, like to think they are always remembered, that when they retire from the stage or the screen their fans will not forget them. But people do forget, and by Horace's decade of life with Marion an entire generation had gone by since Marion's last movie. Some of her contemporaries and a few of their children knew of her. "She lived in that castle with Hearst and she made movies," was the gist of their recollection. Like other leading ladies who had not become symbols of their eras, as had Clara Bow in Marion's screen days and Marilyn Monroe during Marion's years with Horace, Marion Davies might have faded into the film history books along with her friends Eleanor Boardman, Dorothy Mackaill, and Billie Dove, as well as Renee Adoree, Corinne Griffith, Clair Windsor, Ruth Chatterton, Estelle Taylor, Anita Page, Bessie Love, and Alice White. These were all big marquee names at one time or another in the twenties and early thirties.

When Horace Brown told an unamazed gas station attendant or a waitress that he was married to Marion Davies, he was at the time attempting to turn on some marquee lights for a shuttered theater. But he was tireless in his efforts to revive this faded glory. He had been witness to several encounters with old fans who not only remembered the name of Marion Davies but also recognized the bright smile, the eyes that once had been as expressive as were those of Bette Davis a decade later. "You're Marion Davies, aren't you?" they would ask, and Marion would nod happily and it would keep her in good spirits for a week.

She was even more delighted when an old friend or acquaintance would come up to her in a restaurant or hotel lobby and embrace her. She never forgot a face among the thousands she had seen as a Broadway showgirl and then film star and mistress of the castles at San Simeon, Wyntoon, and St. Donat's. "It's nice to be remembered," she would tell Horace, who responded with a squeeze or a kiss on the cheek. Horace shared her happiness at those moments.

It was easy for Marion to forget the bad times with Horace at such moments as these, but whenever Horace would misbehave, the Greek chorus of her family and friends would all begin rending the air with their cries for Horace's banishment.

On the night of November 11, 1952, Marion learned that, for some of her former friends, there was no going back to the old closeness and that to them she was as good as dead. She was sitting in Romanoff's Restaurant in Beverly Hills with Horace, Kay Spreckels, and Mr. and Mrs. Messmore Kendall (Kendall was a New York art dealer from whom Hearst had bought paintings and antiques over the years). Kay suddenly looked toward the lobby entrance and waved a hello to a man standing there talking with a waiter. The man was William Randolph Hearst,

Jr., and he was having a conversation with the waiter who had just told him that his friend, owner "Prince" Mike Romanoff, had gone home. It was shortly after ten o'clock.

Marion wondered if Hearst's son and heir to the throne still resented her. It had been over fifteen months since his father had died, and Marion hadn't heard a word from any of the Hearst boys except from George, who was still in close touch.

"I don't see why he should," Horace told her, and promptly signaled the captain of waiters. A message was conveyed to Bill Hearst by the captain that Mr. and Mrs. Brown and Mrs. Spreckels would like him to come to their table.

"No thanks," Bill instructed the captain to reply. "I'm too tired." He explained to a reporter later that he wanted "nothing to do with that gal [whom he called "M.D."] any more. I had it too long while Father was alive. Besides, Mother is in town and it would have been murder."

Bill left the restaurant and as the group at the table watched him go, Horace noticed Marion shudder and put her hand to her mouth. He knew she was distraught and it enraged him. Rushing across the room and out to the street, he managed to overtake Hearst. "That's no way to treat my wife," Horace began. "Your brother George doesn't feel that way about her."

"I'm not interested in your so-called wife," Bill Hearst said tensely. Horace, easily roused to anger, was enraged that Bill should speak so dimissively of the woman who had extended him nothing but good will for years, the woman who was "Daisy" to him and his brothers when their father lived. Without hesitation or further comment, Horace took a swing at the slightly younger man, who blocked the blow with his left fist. Both men were in good trim—Horace perhaps about twenty pounds heavier —and both were men who believed in keeping fit. After Horace attempted two more wild swings, William Randolph Hearst, Jr., in his forty-fourth year of life, knocked to the pavement the husband of the woman who had been his father's mistress through three-quarters of his span of life.

At that moment, the parking attendant, who recognized Horace as a man who tipped handsomely and who somehow failed to recognize Bill Hearst, Jr., intervened. Shoving himself in front of Horace, the boy told Bill, "Don't hurt this man!"

Bill Hearst walked across the street toward his car, but Horace, predictably, brushed himself off and followed. Horace asked if they shouldn't shake hands: "Forget this whole thing and come in and have a drink."

Bill said, "Nope," and studied Horace for a moment. Was it a likeness to his father that he suddenly saw or was he comparing the two men—his father abhorring violence and trying to calm everybody down whenever it threatened to break out while this Captain Horace Brown ran amuck like an enraged bear and then, defeated, had his paw on the car and an uncertain smile on his face? According to the story that appeared the following day in the *Los Angeles Times*, Bill said that "Captain Brown has pestered me many times. I never met him face to face before, but he has phoned me at 3 o'clock in the morning and demanded that I come to see her. But I'm never going to."

It was the first public view of the freeze-out of Marion by the Hearst family and it made every front page in the United States and banner headlines in New York and Los Angeles: "HEARST SLUGS MARION'S CAPT."

Horace did his best to recoup. He told reporters that he had lost his balance when the blow connected and that it had required several men to separate the two combatants, and then added with a shrug, "Funny thing. I've been in dozens of brawls before, during my seagoing days, but this is the first time anybody thought it was important." He considered what he had done an act of Southern chivalry and said he would do it again under similar circumstances.

Marion was ambivalent about the affair. She confided to her friends that she regretted the notoriety—the first headline scandal in which she had been involved since the death of Thomas Ince. "I've tried to be a good girl," she said, "and Horace meant well. I guess he always means well."

V

There was little incentive for Marion to entertain in the Beverly house. What few friends survived would come in small groups or singly: Clark Gable would go hunting with Horace and spend time on the golf course with him, then come back to the Beverly house to recall moments of hilarity from the past with Marion— she was living more and more in the past now; Frank Sinatra came up to pay his respects out of loyalty to her kindnesses to him but the big empty house probably spooked him. A Palm Springs neighbor and former suitor of Marion's, Hyatt von Dehn, became a crony of Horace's, as did Buddy Rogers, who had his own cross with Mary Pickford's illness. Buddy would come close to giving up on his new friend when Horace came up to Pickfair to show off a new gun he had bought and, while demonstrating it, slipped on a spot of grease in the driveway and the gun went off, the bullet ricocheting back and putting a crease in Mary's scalp. Mary promptly thanked the Lord for sparing her and her religious preoccupation was pursued with even greater zeal than before.

And Marion was trying to do something about her own weaknesses. She would go on the wagon for months at a time, and, as a splendid bonus, the weight would go off and she would look very much as she had during all those years on the screen. They made an attractive couple with Marion decked out in a Don Loper gown and all of her "trinkets" from Tiffany's. When she was not on the wagon, her staff conspired to keep her drinking down anyway. They mastered the delicate art of floating liquor atop a glass of soda or tonic so that Marion would take a taste and get the sensation of a strong drink without the debilitating effects of a long day with the bottle.

The Kennedy family had been encouraged by Joseph, Sr., to look upon Marion as kin. This kindness meant as much to Marion during her last years as anything else for she knew that it was not an act of charity. "Big Joe," as she called him, genuinely admired her as a human being and the feeling was reciprocated. In 1953, Marion and Horace attended the wedding of Eunice Kennedy to Sargent Shriver and that of John Kennedy to Jacqueline Bouvier in Newport. The Browns then discreetly remained East so that the newlywed John Kennedys could honeymoon in Marion's Beverly house. The following year, there was daughter Patricia Kennedy's marriage to actor Peter Lawford, a social event marked by a rare meeting when Marion said a polite "hello" to Hearst executive Richard Berlin and his wife. Marion and Horace arrived at the Church of St. Thomas More in a green Rolls Royce which she had acquired for their use in the East. While they were in New York, Marion persuaded her old friend Liz Whitney Payson to have an operation which some believe saved Mrs. Payson's life.

Just before their third anniversary, Marion again filed suit for divorce from Horace. This time, her decision seemed altogether engineered from outside—friends insisting that she didn't "need" troublesome Horace. But she did, of course. She needed his comforting presence, his laughter, more desperately than her well-intentioned friends could ever fathom, and in ten days' time they were reconciled, this time for keeps.

Right after they had got back together again, a musical written by Charlie Lederer and Luther Davis opened in New York. *Kismet* was fashioned out of rather old-fashioned materials, its book based upon the 1912 Edward Knoblock play, but, to the surprise of many in show business, it was a dazzling success, and over a year later was still playing to capacity audiences at the Ziegfeld Theatre. It was opulent and even garish, but audiences responded to its naive *Arabian Nights* tale and to the lush music fashioned out of Borodin's—*Stranger in Paradise, Baubles, Bangles and Beads,* and *This Is My Beloved* were not only great hits of the day, they became popular standards just as most of Marion's movie hits had done. The script for the show won Charlie Lederer a "Tony," the highest accolade on Broadway.

Marion had invested $180,000 of her own money in the show and had bought an additional five percent in the name of the Damon Runyon Cancer Foundation. This latter, perhaps, was a prophetic gift since she would be stricken herself within five years. Her personal investment would continue paying dividends to her throughout her remaining lifetime, tripling the amount she had put into it.

And her real estate ventures were prospering. In July 1954, she had had a twenty-two-story office building erected in New York on Park Avenue at 57th Street to be known as the "Davies Building." Sixty-one workmen had installed its prefabricated exterior walls of aluminum in a single day and there was extensive photo coverage of the event. The building cost Marion $9 million. Then in 1955, she bought the popular Desert Inn in Palm Springs for $1,750,000. The Spanish-style resort hotel and its numerous guest bungalows was a faint reminder of San Simeon, and Marion and Horace made frequent trips to inspect the property and enjoy its several comforts. She had plans to more than double her investment there, creating what she described as being a "miniature Rockefeller Center." Within a few months, still another New York project, the seventeen-story Douras Building at Madison and 55th, named in honor of her father the judge, was ready for occupancy. But in June 1956 Marion's old and cherished beach house was pounded into rubble because its new owner, Joseph Drown, wanted to erect a motel on the site. Marion tried to ignore the occasion, but she could not. In less than a month, she suffered "a slight cerebral stroke" and was admitted to Cedars of Lebanon Hospital. She told Hedda Hopper, "We blondes seem to be falling apart." (Marilyn Monroe had been having a series of much publicized maladies at the time.) Horace spent the night in the room next to hers and would leave only when her doctors assured him that her illness was not grave.

After about two weeks' stay, Marion returned to the Beverly house, told by her doctors to take it easy. But the stroke had frightened her. She never had been truly ill before, nothing except the debilitating effects of more than forty years of drinking, and she had stood up to that abuse far better than the average drinker. Much of her old spirit and fire were gone and she seemed much closer to both Horace, and rather astonishingly, to her church. Father John O'Donnell became a frequent visitor to the Beverly house and she tried to become a regular communicant in her faith, although it seemed alien to her character. Possibly some of the incentive for her return to the fold was her growing sense that her time was running out. Since her stroke, she had a dread of dying in her sleep. She was not afraid of death, but she wanted to be prepared for it. All of this was underscored when Louis B. Mayer died in November 1957 of leukemia. An era had ended, the newspapers said, but she realized that it was *her* era. Then her old friend Norma Talmadge died of a stroke that Christmas Eve while visiting Las Vegas. Marion appeared near collapse at her friend's bier and she was supported by Horace and George Jessel, who once had been married to Norma. Less than six months later Harry Crocker died after an illness of three years. Harry, who had been her foil in many a gag, was gone. Marion, with something of a chill, told Mary Pickford at the viewing, "There aren't many of us left."

Marion felt an urgency to settle a number of matters. She and Horace had become friendly with Dean Warren of the University of California Medical Center in Los Angeles and it was decided among them that her Children's Clinic could better serve the community if it became a part of the University. Marion and the Dean's advisors went over the cost of adding a wing to the Medical Center to be known as the Marion Davies Children's Clinic and, informed that cost of such an addition would come to nearly two million dollars, she immediately wrote a check for that amount.

In February 1959 Marion had a back tooth extracted. There were complications and she was admitted that same week at Huntington Memorial Hospital for observation. The most distressing complication was that there was a small growth in her jaw that might be malignant. A conference was held by her doctors and they urged that she undergo surgery. "Oh, no, you don't!" Marion told them. "Not the knife." She simply could not bear the thought that she might be even slightly disfigured. Then she recalled a doctor from Pasadena who had removed a growth from Hearst's cheek without surgery. She left her own doctors and went to the Pasadena man.

Some of her friends believe that this was a mistake, that if she had remained in the hands of her specialists and had the surgery performed, she would still be alive today. Perhaps. As Billy Wilder once said, "Hindsight is always 20–20."

Later that year Kay and Clark Gable were in Naples, where he was making a film with Sophia Loren. Kay, upset by news of Marion's failing health, urged Marion and Horace to join them there, but Marion told her that she had done enough traveling in her life even though she would love to see them. She said that she loved her home too much to leave it and she began an extensive remodeling job that would take her into the spring of 1960.

She sold the Desert Inn in Palm Springs in early 1960 for $2,500,000, making a considerable profit on the deal, as she usually did in real estate ventures. But she still had the Davies, Douras, and Squibb buildings in New York, the Warwick Hotel there, an apartment house on Sutton Place, five houses in the Los Angeles area, one in Palm Springs, and many thousands of acres of ranch and undeveloped land in the United States and Mexico. Her fortune by this time probably exceeded $20 million.

In the late spring of 1960, Marion wrote Joe Kennedy urging him to use her home in Beverly Hills as his "headquarters" during the Democratic Convention to be held in Los Angeles that summer. Kennedy accepted and Marion began searching for a home to rent for herself and Horace. The staff would remain behind to serve the Kennedys except for three or four, including two of Marion's nurses. She and Horace took a summer rental at the beach and moved into the home of "Teddy" Lynch, the former Mrs. J. Paul Getty. Rose did the same with her house in Bel Air, turning it over to Robert Kennedy and his family, while she stayed at a rented home in Santa Monica.

The nomination of John Kennedy that summer was the hap-

piest political turn of events in Marion's entire life. The lady who
had urged the nomination of General MacArthur on the Republicans in 1948 now was as delighted with the liberal choice of the
Democrats as the Kennedys themselves. That fall, she would
open her Beverly house more than once for political rallies in
Kennedy's behalf.

Honors were heaped upon her when word seeped through
the film colony that she was dying of cancer. She and Mary Pickford were given the Award of Merit by the Navy League, with old
friend Dick Powell standing at her elbow for support. The Boy
Scouts, whose benefactress she had been on numerous occasions,
made her an honorary member of the troop. An organization of
wounded soldiers at the Veterans Hospital gave her a citation for
her encouragement and philanthropies.

And she *was* dying. Cobalt treatments were not able to halt
the growth that was giving her nearly constant pain. And the
treatment itself was nearly as disfiguring (in discoloring her
cheek) as the dreaded "knife" might have been. She dabbed a
piece of cotton into a mixture of laudanum and some other po-
tent drug and patted her sore jaw with it almost constantly. She
wore a white silk kerchief to hide her disfigurement.

There were some moments of pleasure remaining, however.
Joe Kennedy, now the father of the President, flew into Palm
Springs for two weeks as Marion's house guest. Knowing that
Marion probably would never get to see them again, he brought
along three of his preschool grandchildren with their nurse. It
was in January at his son's Inauguration that Joe Kennedy had
seen the inroads of the illness in Marion's face and physique.
Marion and Horace had been honored guests and had stood just
behind the family at the swearing-in ceremonies. The Kennedys
had seen to it that she and Horace were given the Presidential
Suite at Washington's Sheraton-Park Hotel. Possibly she knew
that some of this extraordinary attention stemmed from an
awareness in others that she was dying. One member of her
family said that she sensed it and even had said that she was
going to see John Kennedy into office "if it's the last thing I do."

By early spring 1961, Marion was in need of ever heavier
sedation to keep back the pain. She was forced to enter Cedars
of Lebanon Hospital. Horace had a bed moved into her suite so
he could be with her during the bad times. Old friend Doris Duke
cooked up dishes she knew Marion liked and brought them in.
When Eleanor Boardman d'Arrast came to see her, she told Elea-

nor that she had had a wonderful life, "but I'm paying for it now."

Back in Hyannis Port, Joe Kennedy phoned Marion's doctors, and when he learned that there was nothing more that they could do, he had three cancer specialists flown out—two from New York and one from Illinois. The doctors spent the day at her bedside. On the following day, Marion underwent surgery for malignant osteomyelitis. She believed that the operation was a success; her morale zoomed skyward, and within ten days, she attempted to walk. But her poor coordination and weakened state combined to do her in—she fell and broke her leg. With her jaw in bandages, her leg in traction, and bottles of supportive fluids entering her body through tubes, she still did not give up. Her gallantry at Cedars of Lebanon impressed everyone she knew and all of the staff there.

She failed rapidly in August; she seemed to be going out with summer. On September 22, 1961, a Friday night, Marion died. At her bedside were Horace, Charlie, niece Pat Lake, and sister Rose. Father O'Donnell conducted the Requiem Mass at the Immaculate Heart of Mary Church, following a Recitation of the Rosary the night before at Pierce Brothers Mortuary. Mary Pickford earlier had accompanied Horace there to determine whether the solid bronze casket should be open or not. It was closed throughout the various Catholic rites.

Telegrams of condolences to Horace and to "the family of Marion Davies" came to the Beverly house from Richard Nixon, Robert Kennedy, Henry Cabot Lodge, Harry Truman, Barry Goldwater, Herbert Hoover, General Douglas MacArthur, Earl Warren, and John Nance Garner.

Something over a hundred people attended the funeral services—about the number of guests filtering through her beach house on an average weekend. The honorary pallbearers included Joseph Kennedy, Bing Crosby, Lawrence Gray, director Mervyn LeRoy, and perhaps most significantly, Hearst executive Richard Berlin. Active pallbearers were director Raoul Walsh, Dick Powell, Howard Strickling, Buddy Rogers, Gregson Bautzer, George Hearst, Glenn Ford, and Ed Pauley, but this task was turned over at the last moment to sixteen members of the Naval ROTC from two campuses in the Los Angeles area. Sister Rose was too overcome with grief to leave her limousine, either for the mass or the graveside ceremonies.

By the time of her death, Marion had been declassed by a

number of small and large-scale revolutions, among them that same television which she had insisted was taking the place of the movies. TV had given the public star *characters*—"Lucy," "Matt Dillon," "Peter Gunn," "the Beverly Hillbillies," and the old, flamboyant individual star no longer prevailed. She had been made to seem passé too, by the drastically altered life style of the wealthy; few could afford a domestic staff of thirty or more and, at the end, Marion was living in a manner that seemed decadent to many and excessive to some, but was simply the way she had lived for three-and-a-half decades.

But she was to die too soon. No more than three years after her death film critics rediscovered Marion. Pauline Kael in her 1971 *New Yorker* articles on the making of *Citizen Kane* stated unequivocally that Marion Davies had been a major leading lady who had not needed the drum-beaters of the Hearst empire to remain in the movies. The adjectives used by dozens of non-Hearst critics during her screen career—"delightful," "enchanting"—were being used again. Existing prints of her films are in rather brisk circulation as of this moment, and, unlike the reaction to those of her friend Rudolph Valentino, audiences do not come to laugh at their unintentional humor, but at the genuine comedy of a lady who learned her craft by the side of a master (Chaplin) and became as natural a performer before the camera as anyone before or since.

Perhaps all of the earlier critical misjudgments in our day cannot be ascribed to the impact of *Citizen Kane* but at least partially to the paradoxes in the lady herself. She spent most of her life surrounded by servants; her social appearances saw her bedecked with jewels; her wealth was sufficiently huge and far-flung to keep her heirs and executors at odds, but the fortune still not consumed by stiff and continuing legal fees even a decade after her death. Yet she was certainly the most human millionairess of our time. She remained mentally fixed to that turf she had known as a brawling youngster in Brooklyn, Chicago, and Manhattan—one of the kids on the block. And even while dying, she had managed to glance backward and see that she had had an extraordinary life. Shortly before her final coma, and while she still had a voice, she had called over Horace to tell him that she had no regrets.

The End

APPENDIX

THE FILMS OF MARION DAVIES

THE SILENTS

RUNAWAY, ROMANY
Produced by George Lederer for Ardsley-Pathé
Directed by George Lederer
Story by Marion Davies from an idea by Clarence Lindner

Cast

Romany	Marion Davies	Anitra St. Clair	Ormi Hawley
Theodore True	Joseph Kilgour	"Inky" Ames	Gladden James
Zinga	Pedro de Cordoba	Hobart	Boyce Combe
Bud Haskell	Matt Moore	Zelaya, Chief of the Gypsies	W. W. Bitner

Story: The daughter of a wealthy father strays from home with a band of gypsies. He dedicates his life and part of his fortune to her recovery. The daughter, now called "Romany," has one friend outside the gypsy camp, manly Bud Haskell. She flees to him when the gypsy chief commands her to marry his son, the swarthy Zinga. True, the tycoon, believes for a time that Anitra St. Clair is his daughter and she comes to live with him. But this young impostor is exposed and Romany returns escorted by Bud, her identity confirmed and the True family reunited.
Released December 23, 1917

BEATRICE FAIRFAX
A serial produced by Hearst-International for Pathé starring Marion Davies in the title role. There are 27 chapters surviving in the Davies archive and there may have been 30 chapters in all.
Released throughout 1918

CECILIA OF THE PINK ROSES
Produced by Cosmopolitan Pictures for Graphic Films
Directed by Julius Steeger
Screenplay by Sam Weller from a story by Katharine Haviland Taylor
Camera work by Andre Barlaiter

Cast

Cecilia	Marion Davies	Mary, Jeremiah's wife	Willette Kershaw
Jeremiah Madden	Edward O'Connor	Dolly Vernon	Eva Campbell
Harry Twombly	Harry Benham	Father McGowan	Daniel L. Sullivan
Johnny as a boy	George Le Guere	George Dickson	John Charles
Johnny as a young man	Charles Jackson	Dr. McNeil	Joseph Burke

Story: A new brick is invented by Jeremiah Madden, a poor bricklayer. His wife is dangerously ill and he fears that she will not live to enjoy the fruits of his invention. Under the kindly, watchful eye of Father McGowan, daughter Cecilia (Marion Davies) takes care of mother, runs the house, and looks after little Johnny, her brother. The aid of a noted physician is denied the mother when the doctor is afraid the bill will not be paid, and the mother dies. The family suddenly becomes immensely rich following her death as the patent on the brick is sold and royalties begin flowing in to Jeremiah. This sudden transition changes little in the Madden household except for Cecilia, who is thrown into "high society," where she knows only humiliation and heartbreak. She then realizes that they were happier when poor.

Released May 5, 1918

Comment: New York American—". . . there were few dry eyes at the Rivoli Theater yesterday when the vision of Marion Davies faded on the screen." *New York Times*—"There is no objection to Miss Davies. She is by no means a sensational screen actress, but she fills the requirements of her part, as do the others in the cast in their parts."

THE BURDEN OF PROOF

Produced by Cosmopolitan Productions for Select
Directed by Julius Steeger
Screenplay by Sam Weller, derived from Sardou's play, *Diplomacy*
Camera work by Andre Barlaiter

Cast

Elaine Brooks	Marion Davies	George Blair	L. Rogers Lytton
Mrs. Brooks, her		Frank Raymond	Willard Cooley
mother	Mary Richards	William Kemp	Fred Hearn
Mrs. Durand	Eloise Clement	Butler	Fred Lenox
Robert Ames	John Merkyl	Maid	Maude Lowe

Story: The locale of Sardou's play has been shifted to Washington, D.C., and this time the spies are Germans plotting against the United States. Elaine Brooks is in love with Robert Ames, a young member of the United States Department of Justice. Her mother, once prominent in society, has lost her fortune and is obliged to write social gossip for a paper owned by a certain Dr. Kemp. Kemp is in reality in the employ of the German government. He commissions one of his aides, Mrs. Durand, to get close to Elaine Brooks and so meet Ames.

In a short time, Elaine and Ames are married. Before they leave on their honeymoon, Mrs. Durand visits them and succeeds in securing important papers from Ames's desk, sending them to Dr. Kemp and establishing "evidence" that will point to Elaine as the guilty party if her work is discovered. As they are leaving town, Frank Raymond, a friend of Elaine's, returns from abroad. Before sailing, he had given Elaine a picture of himself. Of course, Mrs. Durand has got her hands on this and as a result, Raymond has fallen into the hands of German spies on his arrival in Europe and important government papers are taken from him. He accuses Elaine of being a traitor. So when the next moment Ames discovers the loss of his documents, he is convinced that she is the guilty party.

It remains for George Blair, one of the heads of the Department of Justice, to solve the problem and at the same time restore the domestic happiness of Ames and his wife. Mrs. Durand, Kemp, and the other spies are captured, Elaine's name is cleared and Ames asks her forgiveness.

Released September 21, 1918

Comment: Motion Picture News (New York City)—"Miss Davies is no dramatic actress and lacks poise and grace while facing the camera. The whole cast, with the exception of L. Rogers Lytton and Fred Hearn, is rather ill-at-ease, probably because of over-direction."
Sacramento Union—"One of the most thrilling stories of love and intrigue ever shown in the city is Marion Davies' latest Select picture, 'The Burden of Proof.'"

THE BELLE OF NEW YORK

Produced by Select Pictures Corporation
Directed by Julius Steeger

Cast

Violet Gray . . . . Marion Davies	Amos Gray . . . . L. Lytton Rogers
Jack Bronson . . . Raymond Bloomer	William Bronson . . Etienne Girardot
	and Christian Rub

Story: Violet Gray is the daughter of an inventor whose invention is stolen by a capitalist named Bronson, who has a handsome son, Jack. The shock of the theft kills Gray and Violet goes off to New York, where she becomes a cabaret singer. She falls in love with Jack Bronson, who has become a constant patron, but when she discovers that he is the son of the man who killed her father, she flees from his side and becomes a Salvation Army lassie. On her rounds of the Tenderloin, she comes upon Jack, drunk and injured. She nurses him back to health and undertakes his regeneration from the life of a spendthrift and wastrel. He has been cut off from his family and friends and Violet recognizes the finer qualities underlying his perversity. Heroic measures are necessary to accomplish this redemption and, in the wind-up, Violet not only becomes the belle of the town but loses her heart to the subject of her solicitude. Jack and Violet are married after his father confesses.

Released March 27, 1919

Comment: Utica (N.Y.) *Observer*—"Marion Davies is as beautiful as she is talented."

GETTING MARY MARRIED

Produced by Cosmopolitan Productions for Select
Directed by Allan Dwan
Screenplay by Anita Loos and John Emerson

Cast

Mary . . . . Marion Davies	Mrs. Bussard . . Amelia Summerville
James Winthrop . . . . Norman Kerry	Matilda
Amos Bussard . . . . Frederick Burton	Bussard . . . . Constance Beaumar
Ted Barnacle . . . . Matt Moore	John Bussard . . . . . . Elmer Grandin

Story: Getting Mary to the altar becomes not only the main object of her suitors but that of the family who will profit by it since she loses her inheritance the moment she is wed.

Released April 19, 1919

Comment: Allan Dwan—"Marion Davies was lots of fun. She stuttered and stammered and it was a little difficult for her to speak at times, but she was fine . . . she had a sense of humour and if you gave her anything funny to do, she'd do it funny. She had a great smile."

THE DARK STAR

Produced by Cosmopolitan for Paramount-Artcraft, presented by Famous
    Players-Lasky
Directed by Allan Dwan
Adapted from the novel by Robert W. Chambers

Cast

Rue Carew . . . . Marion Davies	Mr. Stull . . . . Arthur Earle
Jim Neeland . . . . Norman Kerry	German spies . . . . Butler Conblough
Princess Naia . . . . . . Dorothy Green	*and* Emil Hoch
Prince Alik . . . . Matt Moore	Ship captain . . . . James Laffey
French secret agent . . . Ward Crane	Steward . . . . . William Brotherhood
Mr. Brandes . . . . George Cooper	Reverend
	William Carew . . . . . . Fred Hearn

Story: A fabulous jewel known as "the Dark Star" is stolen; a pastor's daughter gets involved, falling into the depths of a spy plot concerning war plans and fortifications, but a handsome prince saves her life and the gem is recovered.

Released August 16, 1919

Comment: Kansas City (Mo.) *Post*—"A picture not equalled by any other seen here for some time. . . . She [Marion Davies] is especially charming in her love scenes."

THE CINEMA MURDER

Produced by Cosmopolitan for Paramount-Artcraft
Directed by George D. Baker
Screenplay by Frances Marion, based on a story by E. Phillips Oppenheim

Cast

Elizabeth Dalston . . . Marion Davies	Douglas Romilly . . . W. Scott Moore
The Fiancée . . . . Peggy Parry	Sylvanus Power . . Anders Randolph
Mrs. Power . . . . Eulalie Jensen	Power's "Man
Philip Romilly . . . . Nigel Barrie	Friday" . . . . Reginald Barlow

Story: A young actress is a witness to a supposed murder and later falls in love with the supposed murderer. She finally gives up her career for the man and there is a surprise ending in which the mystery of "the murder" is cleared up.

Released December 10, 1919

Comment: Providence (R.I.) *Evening News*—" 'The Cinema Murder' represents her [Marion Davies] as a vivacious, high-spirited actress, a role in which she is, of course, thoroughly at home. Her dancing skill and her graceful appearance in lavish costumes in the latest mode are pleasing features."

APRIL FOLLY

Produced by Cosmopolitan for Paramount-Artcraft, presented by Famous Players-Lasky
Directed by Robert Z. Leenard
Screenplay by Adrian Johnson from a story by Cynthia Stockley

Cast

April Poole . . . . Marion Davies	Ronald Kenna . . . . . . Herbert Frank
Kerry Sarle . . . . Conway Tearle	Olive Connal . . Amelie Summerville
Mrs. Stanislaw . . . . . Hattie de Laro	Butler . . . . Charles Peyton
Lady Diana	Dobbs . . . . Spencer Charters
Mannister . . . . Madeline Marshall	Earle of Mannister . . Warren Cooke

Story: Kerry Sarle is head of a publishing firm whose magazines have been made highly successful by the stories of a young and clever author, April Poole. April writes a story which she reads to Kerry Sarle filled with romance and adventure, which carries the reader from the dreary library of an English mansion to a costume ball in Greenwich Village and on, by ocean liner, to a dramatic moment in a hut in Capetown, South Africa.

As the tale is spun by April, she borrows Kerry Sarle's name for her hero, a South African millionaire. The heroine is given her own name. There are moments of threatened tragedy and scandal, and death even lurks in the background. As the real April, Kerry Sarle thinks her a fine little pal but takes her charms for granted and never notices the depth of her feelings for him. Finally he does and April gives up fantasy for a much sweeter reality.

Released March 26, 1920

Comment: New York *American*—"Marion Davies is beautiful. She is like a shower of sunshine after a bleak and slate-gray morning."

THE RESTLESS SEX

Produced by Cosmopolitan for Paramount
Directed by Robert Z. Leonard and Leo D'Usseau
Screenplay by Frances Marion from a story by Robert W. Chambers
Settings by Joseph Urban

Cast

Stephanie Cleland . . Marion Davies	Stephanie as a child . . . . Etna Ross
Jim Cleland . . . . Ralph Kellard	Jim as a boy . . . . Stephen Carr
Oswald Grismer . . Carlyle Blackwell	Marie Cliff . . . . Vivian Osborne
John Cleland . . . . Charles Lane	Helen Davis . . . . Corinne Barker
Chilsmer Grismer . . . Robert Vivian	

Story: This is the story of restlessness among rich New Yorkers—the orchid in the limousine. There is a masquerade ball and lots of lush settings. Stephanie Cleland grows up wistfully hoping to find fulfillment in life in maturity, but she encounters only boredom until she meets the right man.
Released September 13, 1920

Comment: Movie Story—"Miss Davies, as usual, acts just like Marion Davies. But then most Robert W. Chambers heroines act like Marion Davies. The part, therefore, suits her perfectly."
New York Times—"The story is long and complicated and does not particularly emphasize the supposed restlessness of either sex but is full of such loving and longing and lingering as usually fill a Chambers novel. The restlessness noticed yesterday afternoon was felt by those spectators who like more life and less length than the picture has. Miss Davies does little in the way of acting, and Ralph Kellard and Carlyle Blackwell, as her heroes, do too much."

BURIED TREASURE

Produced by Cosmopolitan for Paramount
Directed by George D. Baker
Settings by Joseph Urban

Cast

Marion Davies *and* Norman Kerry

Story: Strung around the idea of reincarnation, this film goes back in time to the days of the Spanish galleons and pirates burying their treasure—to be found centuries later.
Released February 13, 1921

Comment: New York Times—"It often seems to be offering its incredible plot seriously, and is entirely humorless except when unintentionally humorous. The acting of its players is well below the screen's average, and the subtitles are numerous and pompously inappropriate."

ENCHANTMENT

Produced by Cosmopolitan for Paramount
Directed by Robert G. Vignola
Written by Frank R. Adams
Settings by Joseph Urban

Cast

Marion Davies *and* Forrest Stanley

Story: The frothy experiences of a vain little flapper. Her father induces an actor friend to become a gentlemanly cave man and the film becomes another variation of "The Taming of the Shrew" theme.
Released 1921

Comment: Photoplay—"Exquisite offering! Story is not particularly strong but if you want to rest your eyes for an hour, and let your mind forget the black and white everyday realities—see this Marion Davies production. Miss Davies proves one of our most adorable heroines. She more than proves her place among the stars."

BEAUTY'S WORTH

Produced by Cosmopolitan for Paramount
Directed by Robert G. Vignola
Screenplay by Luther Reed from a story by Sophie Kerr
Settings by Joseph Urban

Cast

Prudence Cole ......Marion Davies	Aunt Elizabeth
Cheyne Rovein ....Forrest Stanley	Whitney ....Martha Mattox
Amy Tillson ....June Elvidge	Aunt Cynthia
Mrs. Garrison ......Truly Shattuck	Whitney ....Aileen Manning
Jane ....Lydia Yeamans Titus	Soldier (in charade
Henry Garrison .....Halam Cooley	scene) ....John Dooley
Tommy ....Antrim Short	Doll (in charade
Peter ....Thomas Jefferson	scene) ....Gordon Dooley

Story: Quaker maid is induced to become a society butterfly by an artist moving in high society circles in order to win the attentions of a childhood sweetheart. The artist designs beautiful gowns for her, stages a charade in which she carries away the honors, and finally the man she has wanted to marry proposes. It is then that she decides that she hasn't been in love with him but does care for the artist who has been responsible for her success.

Released March 26, 1922

Comment: New York Times—"For about five or ten minutes 'Beauty's Worth,' at the Rivoli this week, is a thing of beauty and of joy. In the course of an incredibly artificial and tediously labored story, the film finally reaches the point where a charade in three scenes is introduced ... they are altogether delightful. Fantastic in design, simple in theme and carefully executed to the last detail, they are a treat to the eye and at the same time diverting."

WHEN KNIGHTHOOD WAS IN FLOWER

Produced for Cosmopolitan for Paramount
A William Randolph Hearst Production
Directed by Robert G. Vignola
Screenplay by Luther Reed from the novel by Charles Major
Production design by Joseph Urban

Cast

King Henry VIII ......Lyn Harding	Grammont, the sooth-
King Louis XII .....William Norris	sayer .....Gustav von Seyffertitz
Charles Brandon ...Forrest Stanley	Sir Adam Judson ..Charles Gerrard
Duke of	An Adventurer ......George Nash
Buckingham ..Pedro de Cordoba	Sir William
Sir Edwin	Brandon .....Arthur Donaldson
Caskoden ...Ernest Glendinning	Queen
Francis Duc	Catherine ..Theresa M. Conover
d'Angoulême ....William Powell	A French lady-in-
Cardinal Wolsey ....Arthur Forrest	waiting ....Flora Finch
Duc de Longueville .Macey Harlam	Lady Jane
The King's Jester ...Johnny Dooley	Bolingbroke ......Ruth Shepley
The King's Tailor ....William Kent	*and as* Mary Tudor, Sister of
	Henry VIII ....Marion Davies

Story: We first see Mary Tudor, younger sister of King Henry VIII, floating in a barge on her way to a tournament. There, one of the jousters is Charles Brandon, a handsome soldier and a commoner. Brandon wins the joust and Mary Tudor rewards him with a gold necklace and a glance that plainly shows she is taken with him. He returns the glance and sets the drama in motion.

The Duke of Buckingham and others resent the sudden rise of Charles Brandon as Mary Tudor's favorite. Tottering old King Louis XII of France, half-blind and suffering from other ills of advanced years, has already sent an ambassador to Henry's court to seek the hand of Mary Tudor for himself in marriage—and, of course, an alliance between the countries. When it appears that Mary Tudor will have none of this (she even makes a face at the French ambassador), the Duke of Buckingham's hooligans set upon her and her lady-in-waiting, hoping that Brandon will come to their rescue and be finished off. He comes, but he finishes off the hooligans. For this, he is arrested for murder and Mary Tudor is forced to confess her strong feelings for him to her brother, the King, in an attempt to save his life. But Henry's hands seem to be tied and Brandon is taken away.

Mary asks that the jailed Brandon be brought to her through a secret passage and they run away together, she disguised as a boy. When they reach an inn in Bristol, a half-drunk adventurer approaches her while Brandon is gone for a moment and swears that "she is the most attractive woman any man has ever claimed to be." She engages him in a duel and soldiers outside prevent Brandon from returning to help her. Meanwhile, pursuers sent by the Duke and the King arrive and Mary whips off her boy's hat and shows her curls, declaring that Brandon is her lover and that King Henry is determined to send her off as bride to a decrepit French king. The adventurer and all of his cronies swear allegiance and help, and there is a wild sword fight when Buckingham arrives, but it all ends when Henry himself makes an entrance. Everyone drops to his knees and Brandon is turned over to face execution in the Tower. It is Cardinal Wolsey's suggestion that Mary, who seems to be pining away, be given the chance to agree to her marriage to Louis XII if Brandon's life is spared. Finally, Mary Tudor agrees to the marriage if Brandon is freed. Henry has Brandon released and sent into exile in "New Spain."

In France, the enfeebled King attempts to show how young he is and plays blind man's bluff with Mary, his bride, and other courtiers. When he climbs out of bed and swears that he is going to dance with Mary "if it is the last deed of the King of France," he drops dead. His nephew Francis (William Powell in his first major film role) is taken with Mary Tudor and whispers to her that she will become *his* bride when he is King of France. This so alarms Mary that she gets in touch with Brandon in "New Spain" since her brother Henry has faithfully promised that she may choose her own second husband. King Francis, right after his ascension to the monarchy, attempts to seduce Mary in her own apartments just as Brandon and his friend Caskoden arrive to take her away. Brandon subdues Francis and they make their getaway.

While a courtier from King Francis makes his bid for Mary's hand to Henry, Mary Tudor enters the castle and embraces her brother. Henry tells her that she is just in time to hear that she must return to France as the new King's bride. "How can that be, brother," she asks, "when I already have a second husband?" and she brings in Brandon to an astonished Henry VIII, who has to concede that she is a determined young lady. "I might as well have consented in the first place," he says, "and saved us all this trouble."

Released September 15, 1922

Comment: Photoplay—"Marion Davies is the petulant *Mary Tudor*, the role once done behind the footlights by the glorious Julia Marlowe. Miss Davies puts more variety into the role than in anything she has heretofore contributed to the silversheet."

Berkeley (Calif.) *Gazette*—"Excellent . . . a super play. The scenery and acting are excellent, especially the characterizations of King Henry VIII and Mary Tudor (Marion Davies)."

ZITS Weekly, New York—"Not in years has an actress received such glowing criticism as did Marion Davies when she opened in 'When Knighthood Was in Flower.'"

New York Review—"The greatest triumph, however, is that of Marion Davies in her role of Mary Tudor. . . . Miss Davies's persistence in pursuit of her ambition has at last borne genuine fruit—she does not rely mainly on her beauty in this picture but really acts. She agreeably astonished her first night audience with a carefully-wrought and easily-expressed characterization. It looks as if Miss Davies will have to be reckoned with for herself alone hereafter."

Washington Times—"What a picture! . . . Miss Davies is a revelation to her warmest admirers. Two scenes stand out by which her repute as a consummate 'emoter' will stand for a long, long time."

THE BRIDE'S PLAY

Produced by Cosmopolitan for Paramount
Directed by George Terwilliger
Story by Donn Byrne
Settings by Joseph Urban
Photographed by Ira H. Morgan

Cast

Marion Davies, Wyndham Standing, Carlton Miller, Jack O'Brien, Richard Cummings, and Eleanor Middleton

Story: Marion Davies plays two characters—a modern young bride and a bride of many centuries ago. The story is based on an ancient Irish legend about a bride who is snatched away by a young Lochinvar at her wedding.

Released 1922

Comment: New York Evening Telegram—"Miss Marion Davies appears in one of the most beautiful and charming pictures of her screen career."

Photoplay—"It is not an effective picture. Davies does not fulfill her promise."

THE YOUNG DIANA

Produced by Cosmopolitan for Paramount
Directed by Albert Capellani and Robert C. Vignola
Screenplay by Luther Reed from a story by Marie Corelli
Settings by Joseph Urban

Cast

Marion Davies, Clara Kimball Young, Forrest Stanley, Gypsy O'Brien, Maclyn Arbuckle, Pedro de Cordoba
Story line unavailable.

Released August 27, 1922

Comment: Photoplay—". . . a style show, perhaps, but not a good motion picture. Beautiful sets, but along about the third reel, one begins to wonder if a little honest emotion wouldn't help."

ADAM AND EVA

Produced by Cosmopolitan for Paramount
Directed by Robert G. Vignola
Written by Guy Bolton and George Middleton, adapted from Mr. Bolton's play
Photographed by Harold Wenstrom
Settings by Joseph Urban

Cast

Marion Davies, Tom Lewis, William Norris, Percy Ames, Luella Gear, *and* T. Roy Barnes (*as the salesman-hero*)

Story: The breezy story of the way a distraught father flees from his parasitical household and leaves the curing of the family to a resourceful young salesman. The spoiled daughter falls in love with the salesman and is tamed by him.

Released 1922

Comment: Photoplay—"Her [Marion Davies's] work here makes us think her forte is light comedy. Marion Davies gives a graceful performance as the daughter of the house, as graceful as her gowns."

LITTLE OLD NEW YORK

Produced by Cosmopolitan and distributed by the Goldwyn Corporation
Directed by Sidney Olcott
Screenplay by Luther Reed, based upon the play by Rida Johnson Young
Photographed by Ira H. Morgan and Gilbert Warrenton
Designed by Joseph Urban
Special music by Victor Herbert

Cast

Larry Delevan ......Harrison Ford	Delmonico ....Charles Judels
Robert Fulton .....Courtenay Foote	Bully Boy Brewster .Harry Watson
Washington	Bunny ....Spencer Charers
Irving ....Mahlon Hamilton	The Hoboken
Cornelius Vanderbilt ..Sam Hardy	Terror ....Louis Wolheim
John Jacob Astor ....Andrew Dillon	John O'Day ....J. M. Kerrigan
Henry Brevoort ....George Barraud	Patrick O'Day ....Stephen Carr
Fitz Greene	Mrs. Schuyler .....Marie R. Burke
Halleck ....Norval Keedwell	Betty Schuyler ......Mary Kennedy
Philip Schuyler ....Riley Hatch	Rachel Brewster ..Elizabeth Murray
Reilly ....Charles Kennedy	Ariana du Puyster ..Gypsy O'Brien
Chancellor	*and as*
Livingston .....Thomas Findlay	Patricia O'Day ...Marion Davies

Story: "The early years of the century find Bowling Green the center of the activities of little old New York." Thus opens this fast-moving story of New York of the early nineteenth century when Robert Fulton was attempting to get his steamboat project financed. Marion Davies as Pat O'Day is a member of a small Irish family, the only other survivors being a father and her brother Patrick. Patrick falls heir to a fortune in New York, which, if he does not appear to claim it, will go to a New Yorker, Larry Delevan. The O'Days leave Ireland for the long voyage to America, but ailing Patrick dies on the way and father John O'Day decides to claim the fortune anyway by disguising daughter Pat as a boy.

Delevan does not expect the O'Days to show up and he is celebrating the final day of his year of waiting and talking of investing some of the fortune in the *Clermont*, his friend Robert Fulton's steamship, when the O'Days arrive. Delevan takes this blow moderately well and the "boy" and his father are more or less made to seem welcome.

Pat, wearing a boy's tight trousers and a white shirt and dark jacket, falls in love with cousin Larry, but he is very proper and tells "him" not to act like a girl. His fiancée is snobbish Ariana du Puyster, who thinks she is a singer, and there is an amusing sequence wherein Pat O'Day plays the harp and sings an Irish ballad in counterpoint to Ariana's parlor cater-wauling, much to the latter's indignation.

Finally, the *Clermont* is launched with Pat and Larry aboard. John Jacob Astor is offered the last share in the venture, but Larry wants it and Pat gives him a check to cover his purchase.

An inveterate gambler, Larry puts up his house as a wager on a fight between Bully Boy Brewster and the Hoboken Terror. The fight takes place in a firehouse and when it looks very much as though the Terror is going to annihilate Bully Boy, on whom Larry has wagered everything, Pat rings a false alarm and the fight breaks up. Larry is blamed and a mob surrounds his house, angry and calling for his appearance. Pat emerges and confesses that she turned in the alarm, and the mob, still thinking her a boy, drags her off to a whipping post. After undergoing several lashes from the Hoboken Terror, she cries out for him to stop. "I'm a girl!" she wails. Then she confesses to Larry, who smiles in relief as he has become overly fond of his cousin.

Released August 1, 1923

Comment: New York Times—"For costumes and settings and photography, 'Little Old New York' is one of the most exquisite productions ever thrown upon a screen. In spite of the moderate thrill of the narrative one envies the days of long ago even with the lack of speed and electric light. The story is sweet and appealing and runs along without a single hurtful halt, and Sidney Olcott, the director, has shown excellent taste in refraining from any of the usual motion picture gymnastics. The acting is quiet and natural and the characterization is good, although Marion Davies is far too feminine ever to be mistaken for a boy. But as the picture rolls along the illusion gains headway and one lives with the picture."

YOLANDA

Produced by Cosmopolitan for Metro-Goldwyn-Mayer release
Directed by Robert G. Vignola
Screenplay by Luther Reed, adapted from the story by Charles Major
Photographed by Ira H. Morgan
Settings by Joseph Urban
Special musical score by William Frederick Peters
Overture composed by Victor Herbert

Cast

Princess Mary of Burgundy *and* Yolanda, the burgher maid . . . . Marion Davies	Campo Basse . . . . Ian MacLaren
King Louis XI of France . . . . Holbrook Blinn	Oliver de Daim . . . . . Gustav von Seyffertitz
Charles, Duke of Burgundy . . . . Lyn Harding	The Dauphin . . . . . . Johnny Dooley
Maximilian of Styria . Ralph Graves	Jules d'Hymbercourt . . Paul McAllister
Queen Margaret . . . Theresa M. Conover	Antoinette Castleman . . . . Mary Kennedy
Bishop La Balue . . Maclyn Arbuckle	Antoinette's Father . . . . Thomas Findlay
Innkeeper . . . . Leon Errol	Count Galli . . . . Martin Faust
Sir Karl Pitti . . . . Roy Applegate	Lord Bishop . . . . . Arthur Donaldson

Story: Disguised as a burgher maid, Princess Mary goes to the silk fair with her close friend Antoinette Castleman. Here, as "Yolanda," she is a fun-loving girl, out for a good time. Dressed in her becoming peasant frock with a cap set demurely on her head, she captivates Maximilian of Styria, who believes her to be a commoner. Her father, Charles, the Duke of Burgundy, has made plans for her to marry the idiot Dauphin of France. She escapes in her disguise and goes to Switzerland. The Prince (Maximilian) is also incognito and there is a little romance. Finally, she is caught and turned over for her marriage, but Maximilian charges in and rescues her.

Released February 20, 1924

Comment: New York Times—"Miss Davies's acting is effective throughout." Robert E. Sherwood in the *New York Herald*—"Marion Davies looks lovely. . . . Undoubtedly the loveliest and most convincing scenes that have ever been built in an American studio . . . 'Yolanda' is gorgeous to behold."

JANICE MEREDITH

Produced by Cosmopolitan for Metro-Goldwyn-Mayer release
Directed by E. Mason Hopper
Screenplay by Lillie Hayward from the story by Paul Leicester Ford

Photographed by Ira A. Morgan and George Barnes
Settings by Joseph Urban
Special musical score by Deems Taylor

Cast

Janice Meredith . . . . . Marion Davies	Marie Antoinette . . . . Princess
Squire Meredith . . Maclyn Arbuckle	Marie de Bourbon
Patrick Henry . . . . . . Robert Thorne	Mrs. Loring . . . Helen Lee Worthing
Charles Fownes . . . . Harrison Ford	Benjamin Franklin . . . . . . Lee Beggs
Mrs. Meredith . . . . . . Hattie De Laro	Lord Cornwallis . . . . . Tyrone Power
Tabitha Larkin . . . . . Mildred Arden	Martha Washington . . Mrs. Maclyn
General Charles Lee . . . Walter Law	Arbuckle
Lord Clowes . . . . Holbrook Blinn	Dr. Joseph Warren . . . . Wilfred Noy
Thomas Jefferson . . . . Lionel Adams	Paul Revere . . . . Ken Maynard
George Washington . Joseph Kilgour	Squire Hennion . . Spencer Charters
LaFayette . . . . Nicolai Koesberg	Susie . . . . May Vokes
Col. Rahl . . . . George Siegmann	Charles Mobray . Douglas Stevenson
A British sergeant . . . . . W. C. Fields	Theodore Larkin . . . . Harlin Knight
Philemon Hennion . . Olin Howland	Arthur Lee . . . . Joe Raleigh
Louis XVI . . . . Edwin Argus	Parson McClare . . Wilson Reynolds
Lord Howe . . . . George Nash	Cato . . . . Jerry Paterson

Story: Of epic scope, encompassing all of the American Revolution's drama and principal characters, it is difficult to compress the details of *Janice Meredith*. In essence, it is a love story with Janice, daughter of a wealthy New Jersey landowner, falling in love with her father's handsome English bond servant, Fownes (Harrison Ford). Alarmed by this development, her father ships her north for a long visit with her cousin in Boston. There, the countryside is seething with rebellion (the Boston Tea Party, etc.) and Janice meets Lord Clowes, learning of the plan to march the British troops on Concord. She alerts the rebels, sending Paul Revere scurrying on his heroic night ride.

Back in New Jersey, she finds that Fownes, the man she loves, has joined rebel forces on Washington's staff. He comes back briefly and appropriates her favorite mount in the stable, but she keeps silent. At their next rendezvous, also in the stable, they are surprised by Lord Clowes, her father and some British troops. Fownes thinks Janice has betrayed him, but later he escapes with Janice's help. Then Lord Clowes arrests Janice for aiding the prisoner and brings her to Trenton. There, at the Hessian headquarters, Janice sees Fownes disguised as a Hessian. He receives papers from the Hessian Colonel giving the disposition of the British forces. Suddenly, Fownes is unmasked and ordered shot, but before he is taken off, he slips the important papers to Janice and whispers that Washington must be told and prepared to attack. Janice is freed by the Hessian Colonel with a gentle admonition and she goes through a snow storm to deliver the news to Gen. Washington. The heroic crossing of the Delaware follows, perhaps the pictorial highlight of the film.

At dawn, Fownes is about to be shot, but he is saved by a bomb explosion, shattering the house where he is jailed. Colonial forces rush the house following the explosion and seize Lord Clowes, who is about to murder Fownes. Fownes tells Janice that she must now give up all Tory associates, including her father. This last is too much and they part in anger.

Janice and her father return home, where she agrees to marry Philemon Hennion, a rich young man of her father's choice, but the wedding is interrupted by a rebel raid led by Fownes. Philemon is arrested for aiding the British and the Meredith lands are confiscated. The Squire and his family flee to British-held Philadelphia, where the British troops are partying and living in luxury while just outside in the country Washington and his troops are suffering their worst winter at Valley Forge. There is a brief and unhappy meeting in Philadelphia between Janice and Fownes—he has penetrated British lines just to see her.

With Washington's forces strengthened by French aid, the battle of Yorktown proceeds and the British are defeated. While the battle rages, Lord Clowes seizes Janice and carries her off in a coach, but Fowns rescues her after a furious chase and kills Clowes.

With peace restored, Janice and Fownes are married at Mount Vernon.

Released August 5, 1924

Comment: New York Times—"No more brilliant achievement in ambitious motion pictures dealing with historical romances has ever been exhibited than Marion Davies's latest production, 'Janice Meredith,' which was presented last night before a notable and enthusiastic gathering in the Cosmopolitan Theatre. . . . Mr. Hopper has taken full advantage of the opening left to him by Mr. Griffith (in 'America'). It is the unforgettable crossing of the Delaware by Washington. This sequence is to 'Janice Meredith' what Paul Revere's ride was to 'America.' It is something in moving picture photography which will be remembered for years by all those who see it, even if they behold it but once. . . . Miss Davies proved her histrionic ability in 'When Knighthood Was in Flower,' and also in 'Little Old New York,' but in many scenes of 'Janice Meredith' she gives even a better performance. . . . She is enthusiastic, loving, mischievous, petulant, fiery and imperious."

LIGHTS OF OLD BROADWAY

A Monta Bell Production produced by Cosmopolitan for Metro-Goldwyn-Mayer

Directed by Monta Bell

Screenplay by Carey Wilson from Lawrence Eyre's play "Merry Wives of Gotham"

Titles by Joseph W. Farnham

Photographed by Ira Morgan

Settings by Cedric Gibbons and Ben Carré

Wardrobe by Ethel Chaffin

Film Editor: Blanche Sewell

Cast

Fely } Anne } . . . . Marion Davies	Lambert de Rhonde . . Frank Currier
	Mrs. de Rhonde . . . . . . Julia Swayne Gordon
Shamus O'Tandy . . Charles McHugh	
Mrs. O'Tandy . . . . . Eleanor Lawson	Tony Pastor . . . . George Bunny
"Red" Hawkes . . . . Mathew Betz	Andy . . . . George K. Arthur
Fowler . . . . Wilbur Higbee	Thomas A. Edison . . Frank Glendon
Dirk de Rhonde . . . . . Conrad Nagel	

Story: The O'Tandys are poor Irish immigrants living in a Shanty-town on the edge of New York. Driven to desperation, they allow their daughter Anne to live with the wealthy de Rhonde family, where she can be educated and given decent clothing and some refinement. Fely gets a job singing at Tony Pastor's.

During an Irish uprising in Shanty-town, Fely encounters handsome Dirk de Rhonde being attacked by the mob, his coat torn off his back. She rescues him and finds some tattered clothes for him to wear in order to pass through the mob of Orangemen. They fall in love and he visits her hovel of a home, but is very democratic and not obviously offended by the mean surroundings.

Eventually the de Rhondes are made to accept Fely because of Dirk's strong feelings for her and they return to Shanty-town to rescue her father from poverty. As they leave downtown, all the lights in New York City are turned on for the first time.

Note: During the riot, an early form of Technicolor was used for a five-minute sequence. It is ungarish and quite satisfactory. Also, the police turn fire hoses on the Irish mobs, anticipating by thirty years the repressive measures taken against the crowds in Birmingham, Alabama.

Released January 24, 1925

Comment: Chicago American—". . . not only is Marion Davies's 'Lights of Old Broadway' the finest cinema achievement of the month; it is also a safe bet for a place among the best of the year."
Chicago Tribune—"Marion Davies is adorable . . . if I know you at all, you're going to come out of the theater mightily satisfied."
Baltimore (Md.) *News*—"In 'Lights of Old Broadway' Marion Davies returns to the field in which she has proved herself—the bright, particular light-historical and romantic comedy drama . . . Miss Davies is superb as Fely."

ZANDER THE GREAT

Produced by Cosmopolitan for Metro-Goldwyn-Mayer release, copyright 1925 by William Randolph Hearst
Directed by George Hill
Screenplay by Frances Marion and Lillie Hayward from the play by Salisbury Field
Photographed by George Barnes and Harold Wenstrom
Assistant director: Frank O'Neil
Film editor: James McKay
Settings by Joseph Urban
Costumes by Gretl Urban

Cast

Juan Fernandez	....Holbrook Blinn	The Sheriff	.....Hobart Bosworth
Dan Murchinson	....Harrison Ford	Mr. Pepper	.........Richard Carle
Good News	.........Harry Watson	Mrs. Caldwell	......Hedda Hopper
Texas	..............Harry Myers	Elmer Lovejoy	......Olin Howland
Black Bart	......George Seigmann	Zander	.........Master John Huff
The Matron	.........Emily Fitzroy	*and as* Mamie Smith	.Marion Davies

Story: From the time Mamie Smith is fourteen years of age, a lonely orphan girl with an eager, imaginative face, she searches for some family, anyone, who can be the recipient of all the love she has in her heart. Finally, she finds a happy home with a kindly woman and her baby boy. Mamie is an amusing youngster who manages to achieve a degree of happiness even in the most forbidding and austere surroundings.

Grown to young womanhood, Mamie's foster mother is struck by a fatal illness and, as she is dying, Mamie promises to see that Zander, the boy, is taken to his father somewhere in Arizona. With her responsibility weighing heavily on her young shoulders, Mamie drives a rickety Ford from New Jersey to the far West with Zander and his pet rabbits. Once there along the border between Mexico and Arizona, she becomes a housekeeper, quite innocently, for a band of bootleggers. When the Sheriff comes around to investigate the presence of the little boy in such surroundings. Murchison, the handsome chief bootlegger, pretends to be Zander's father. When Mamie learns the truth about Murchison's occupation, she is so visibly distressed that Murchison takes the boy away and locks her up, fearful of having his business exposed. Mamie escapes to the desert, falls into the clutches of Black Bart and his bandits, but escapes again in a sandstorm. There ensues a wild gunfight in which Murchison rescues her. He then explains that he knew Zander's father but that the man died in his arms. He forsakes his wild companions and, as the picture fades, there is every indication that he and Mamie will provide Zander with suitable parents by proxy.

Released May 2, 1925

Comment: Joseph M. Schenck—"Miss Marion Davies shows herself an actress who is capable of great pathos, tenderness and comedy. 'Zander the Great' is not a spectacular picture, with thousands of people in the cast or lavish sets, but a simple love story, charmingly told and acted. It is a triumph for Miss Davies, the director, cast and producer."
St. Louis Globe-Democrat—"It is a better movie than a play."

Boston Traveler—" 'Zander the Great' is the best Marion Davies has appeared in. . . . Let us hope she continues in this type of film, now that she has learned the difference between slapstick and straight comedy. It fits her better than her 'super-productions.' "

Hearst Syndicate—"In this role, Miss Davies presents two entirely new facets to her screen characterization—a light comedy touch and a quaint whimsical sweetness.

"She has all the essentials for comedy—a keen sense of humor, the capacity to throw herself entirely into the part she is playing, the youth, the gaiety of spirit, vitality and dash that are such necessary factors for getting this particular form of acting over on the screen."

BEVERLY OF GRAUSTARK

A Cosmopolitan Production for Metro-Goldwyn-Mayer
Directed by Sidney Franklin
Screenplay by Agnes Christine Johnston from the novel by George Barr McCutcheon
Titles by Joe Farnham
Photographed by Percy Hilburn
Settings by Cedric Gibbons and Richard Day
Costumes by Kathleen Kay, Maude Marsh, and Andre-Ani
Film editor: Frank Hull

Cast

Beverly Calhoun	Marion Davies	Duke Travina	Albert Gran
Dantan	Antonio Moreno	Carlotta	Paulette Duval
Prince Oscar	Creighton Hale	Saranoff	Max Barwin
General Marlanax	Roy D'Arcy	Mr. Calhoun	Charles Clary

Story: Beverly Calhoun returns unexpectedly from finishing school. There is the suggestion that she has been expelled. In any case, her wealthy father thinks it best that she leave the country for a while and he suggests that she visit a distant cousin in Graustark who happens to be the Prince.

She arrives in Graustark smack in the middle of a court plot to prevent Prince Oscar from taking over as monarch. General Marlanax is behind the conspiracy. The Prince himself is indisposed at a critical moment and it is decided that Beverly should impersonate him, which she does by concealing her golden hair under an officer's cap (and then having it cut for a later appearance). The General insists that the "prince" preside at a dinner in the officer's mess at which the "prince" must drink three toasts, the last one calling for draining a tankard the size of an umbrella stand. Beverly trickily spills most of her wine but the General sees this and refills the tankard. Reeling drunk, the "prince" is helped to "his" rooms by Dantan, a handsome aide. From then on, she is constantly shielded by "Dantan," who pretends not to penetrate her disguise. Out in the countryside, they are set upon by hired killers sent by the General but Dantan fends them off. Eventually, they get back to the capitol, restore the real Prince to his position and Beverly reveals her true sex to Dantan, who, of course, has fallen in love with her.

Released April 19, 1926

Comment: New York Times—"In the part of Beverly Calhoun, Miss Davies is in her element, and she displays no mean ability in the handling of her role. She looks petulant, shocked, and mildly frightened in turn. . . ."

THE RED MILL

A Cosmopolitan Production for Metro-Goldwyn-Mayer
Directed by William Goodrich
Adaptation and scenario by Frances Marion from the musical comedy by Victor Herbert and Henry Blossom
Titles by Joe Farnham

Photographed by Henry Sartov
Settings by Cedric Gibbons and Merrill Pye
Costumes by Andre-Ani
Film editor: Daniel J. Gray

Cast

Tina	Marion Davies	Timothy	Snitz Edwards
Dennis	Owen Moore	Governor	William Orlamond
Willem	George Seigmann	Innkeeper	Fred Gambold
Captain Jacop Edam	Karl Dane	Gretchen	Louise Fazenda
Burgomaster	J. Russell Powell		

Story: Tina is a little Dutch slavy who longs to have a beau all to herself. She washes mountains of dishes, scrubs the floor, and makes the beds. In an upper bedroom, she glimpses a gentleman from Ireland, a stranger to the town. He sees her and smiles and soon it is evident that all Tina can think of is the Irishman Dennis. Her employer beats her and she gets caught after dark in a haunted windmill. She also wins a skating race by dint of a huge St. Bernard chasing a cat across the ice and snagging her costume as he runs between her bowed legs. But all's well in the end with Dennis assuring her that he will be happy to see her again; and Gretchen, the boss's homely daughter, has been saved from a forced marriage to marry her gawky soldier lover, Captain Edam.

Released February 12, 1927

Comment: New York American—"Joy is unconfined."
New York Evening World—"Rather tepid romance."

TILLIE THE TOILER

A Cosmopolitan Production for Metro-Goldwyn-Mayer
Directed by Hobart Henley
An original scenario by A. P. Younger based on the comic strip by Russ Westover

Cast

Tillie Jones	Marion Davies	Sadie	Estelle Clark
Mac	Matt Moore	Bill	Bert Roach
Pennington Fish	Harry Crocker	Bubbles	Gertrude Short
Mr. Simpkins	George Fawcett	Mr. Smythe	Arthur Hoyt
Mr. Whipple	George K. Arthur	Ma Jones	Claire McDowell

Story: Tillie is a stenographer in Mr. Simpkins' office and her steady beau is Mr. Whipple, who also works there. But the truth is that Whipple bores her as does her situation. She really likes another office worker, Mac, much more, but his office prospects are dim. She aspires to higher things and thinks she has latched onto a way to get there when she meets Pennington Fish, who is fabulously wealthy. After just a dinner and an evening in Fish's apartment, she becomes engaged to Fish, an alliance which she says will "make things easier for mother." But Tillie goes back to Mac and he gets a promotion at the office.

Released June 5, 1927

Comment: New York Herald-Tribune—"Miss Davies . . . plays with the keenest appreciation of the comedy situation and delivers the wisecracks in the manner of a girl whose daily communications are 'Get the wringer—he's all wet.'

"We found 'Tillie the Toiler' 7 reels of unadulterated joy."
New York Daily News—"Marion Davies, ever improving her picture prowess, makes the most of the funny stuff."

Note: "Tillie the Toiler" was reported in the *Exhibitors Herald* issue of December 24, 1927, as among the top twenty-five money-making films from all studios of the year.

THE FAIR COED

A Sam Wood Production for Cosmopolitan, released by Metro-Goldwyn-Mayer
Directed by Sam Wood
Adaptation and continuity by Byron Morgan; suggested by George Ade's play
Titles by Joe Farnham
Photographed by John Seitz
Settings by Cedric Gibbons and Arnold Gillespie
Costumes by Gilbert Clark
Film editor: Conrad A. Nervig

Cast

Marion	Marion Davies	Rose	Thelma Hill
Bob	Johnny Mack Brown	Housekeeper	Lillianne Leighton
Betty	Jane Winton	Herbert	Gene Stone

Story: Marion arrives at Bingham College in her car, a rare possession at that school. She is particularly impressed by handsome Bob, the school athletic coach, who is poor and car-less. Her dormitory mate Betty also has her eye on Bob and it would seem that she is his girlfriend until Marion humiliates Betty on the basketball court, then, about to be caught red-handed, faints. She is carried off to her room by Bob as Betty fumes. Bob resents her trickery but is nevertheless trapped in the end and they become sweethearts.

Released October 23, 1927

Comment: New York Times—"Marion Davies prances through the part of the saucy Bingham College blond. . . . Miss Davies is vivacious and attractive as the girl . . . sometimes her gestures and droll expressions are slightly reminiscent of Chaplin and Beatrice Lillie."

Photoplay—"Marion Davies is a natural born comedienne, no mistaking. . . . Joe Farnham should have a raise in pay for the rip-roaring titles."

QUALITY STREET

A Marion Davies Production for Metro-Goldwyn-Mayer
Directed by Sidney Franklin
Scenario by Albert Lewin and Hans Kraly, adapted by Hans Kraly and Albert Lewin from the play by Sir James M. Barrie
Titles by Marian Ainslee and Ruth Cummings
Photographed by Henry Sartov
Settings by Cedric Gibbons and Allen Ruoff
Costumes by René Hubert
Film editor: Ben Lewis

Cast

Phoebe Throssel	Marion Davies	Nancy Willoughby	Margaret Seddon
Dr. Valentine Brown	Conrad Nagel	Henrietta Turnbull	Marcelle Corday
Susan Throssel	Helen Jerome Eddy	Patty	Kate Price
Mary Willoughby	Flora Finch		

Story: At the time of the Napoleonic wars, Dr. Valentine Brown kisses Miss Phoebe Throssel's cheek when they are walking in the rain (her cheek is wet and he cannot resist). It makes a profound impression upon her, although he shows no special interest in her immediately after that and he soon goes off to war.

During the war, Phoebe and sister Susan open a private school, which is successful. The war ends and Valentine returns to Green Willow Village, England, and to Quality Street to find Miss Phoebe grown older—hard work and strain have etched fine lines into her face and there is a pathetic sadness to her mouth. So Valentine turns away politely and Miss Phoebe invents a niece for herself, Miss Livvy.

With the help of lots of ringlets and a little face powder, Miss Livvy is a youthful, outrageous flirt. She is what Miss Phoebe wishes she had been in her younger days. Valentine seems to succumb to her obvious charms and there are several encounters between them, but it turns out that it is Miss Phoebe whom he loves.

Released November 1, 1927

Comment: New York Evening World—"Marion Davies plumbed unsuspected wells at the intimate little Embassy Theatre and brought up a startling realistic bag of emotion to make 'Quality Street' a poignant, living thing.

"By so doing, she took one colossal leap from the leading ranks of comediennes to the front rank of the screen's dramatic stars. She gives a performance whose quaint wistfulness, poignancy, and power make it the most surprising event of the season."

Comment: Mordaunt Hall in the *New York Times*—"Gentle and refreshing is the screen translation of Sir James M. Barrie's old play 'Quality Street,' in which Marion Davies, as Phoebe Throssel, gives the most conscientious performance of her film career. . . . It is a production with no little charm. Sidney Franklin is to be congratulated on this production of a sort of English Pomander Walk romance of the Napoleonic days."

New York Herald-Tribune—"Here is youth, romantic, innocent youth. Just a sight of Marion Davies and Conrad Nagel dancing on the green imbued us with the joy of living, and Miss Davies is exquisitely lovely as the belle of 'Quality Street.' Her playing of the youthful Phoebe is a beautiful thing, and it seemed quite remarkable to us that she could so markedly differentiate between the gay Miss Phoebe and the coy Miss Livvy."

The New Yorker—"Sir James M. Barrie's 'Quality Street' has come to the movies nicely conceived and nicely directed."

THE PATSY

A King Vidor Production for Metro-Goldwyn-Mayer
Directed by King Vidor
Screenplay by Agnes Christine Johnston based on the play by Harry Conners
Titles by Ralph Spence
Photographed by John Seitz
Settings by Cedric Gibbons
Costumes by Gilbert Clark
Film editor: Hugh Wynn

Cast

Patricia Harrington	..Marion Davies	Pa Harrington	.....Dell Henderson
Tony Anderson	...Orville Caldwell	Billy	.............Lawrence Gray
Ma Harrington	.....Marie Dressler	Grace Harrington	....Jane Winton

Story: In a middle-class family, two sisters constantly battle over boyfriends—usually belonging to the older brunette sister Grace. Their mother sides with Grace, and Patricia winds up the Patsy, even having to lend her sister a beautiful coat to wear at the Yacht Club dance, a possession for which she has sacrificed much. She skips into the Yacht Club in a hand-me-down shawl and when there is no one to dance with, does a tango with her fingers on the tablecloth. Eventually she manages to get alone with one suitor, an alcoholic, but he is too drunk to really appreciate her hilarious parodies of Mae Murray and Pola Negri. In the end, one of them prefers her to sister Grace and all ends happily.

Released April 22, 1928

Comment: Photoplay—"After two or three reels of this one the director tossed away his script—maybe his megaphone, too—and turned the picture over to Marion Davies. Which was a very smart thing to do, for when

Marion cuts loose with clowning the result is that sort of comedy which reflects its results in crowded theaters."
Mordaunt Hall in the *New York Times*—"Of all the varied Cinderellas who have from time to time graced the screen, Marion Davies, in an adaptation of Barry Conners stage comedy, 'The Patsy,' not only holds her own in the matter of vivacity and appearance, but she also elicits more fun than one would suppose could be generated from even a modern conception of the undying role."

HER CARDBOARD LOVER

A Cosmopolitan Production for Metro-Goldwyn-Mayer
Directed by Robert Z. Leonard
Suggested by the play of the same name

Cast

Sally . . . . Marion Davies	The baritone . . . Andres de Segurola
Simone . . . . Jetta Goudal	Argine . . . . Tenin Holtz
André . . . . Nils Asther	*and* Pepi Lederer

Story: Sally is an indefatigable schoolgirl visiting Monte Carlo who has a longing for autographs. Sometimes she wants these signatures because the men are great, but in the case of André, it is because he is "beautiful."

The characters are reversed in this very free screen translation of the play. If there is any cardboard lover, it is Sally. She is rather a persistent blonde running after a handsome, dark-haired man. To carry out her purpose, she goes so far as to dress herself in a bell-boy's uniform. The first man she accosts for an autograph is the baritone, Andres de Segurola, who is not blind to feminine beauty, but what he writes in her autograph book sends Sally away indignant.

André attempts to explain these strange matters to his dark-eyed girlfriend Simone. Sally decides that his interest in Simone is so serious, she must "save" him from this predatory female. In doing so, she misses her target and socks André in the jaw. But all ends happily and her visit to Monte Carlo helps her to grow up a little.

Released September 2, 1928

Comment: New York Times—". . . contains the merest suggestion of the play of the same name. Although the comedy is frequently far too fractious, this production is so expensively staged and costumed that its interest is unfailing. It aroused many an outburst of laughter yesterday afternoon, but it is nevertheless a pity that Miss Davies, who has proved herself such an excellent comedienne, does not act with more restraint. . . . Miss Davies's impersonation of Miss Goudal is so remarkable that one can hardly be quite certain that she is not Miss Goudal."
New York Sunday News (Irene Thirer)—"It is Miss Davies's most inferior offering in some seasons of cinema. . . . Marion depends too much on her slapstick ability—which we admit is grand—and the story isn't big enough to carry it."
New York Morning Telegraph—"The plot has been wholly altered for the appeasement of the morality squad. . . . Despite these enforced changes, we nevertheless recommend the picture for Marion Davies's performance. Here is the finest comedienne on the screen today, and therefore deserving of your attention, no matter what her vehicle."

SHOW PEOPLE

Produced by Cosmopolitan for Metro-Goldwyn-Mayer
Directed by King Vidor
Screenplay by Laurence Stallings and Agnes Christine Johnston from a scenario by Wanda Tushock
Titles by Ralph Spence
Photographed by John Arnold
Film editor: Hugh Wynn

Cast

Peggy Pepper ......Marion Davies
Billy Boone ....William Haines
Colonel Pepper ....Dell Henderson
and Paul Ralli, Tenin Holtz, Harry
Gibbon, Sidney Bracy, Albert Conti
Walk-ons: Renee Adoree, George K.
Arthur, Charlie Chaplin, Karl Dane,

Marion Davies *as herself*, Douglas
Fairbanks, Sr., John Gilbert, William
S. Hart, Leatrice Joy, Rod La Roque,
Polly Moran, Mae Murray, Louella
Parsons, Aileen Pringle, Dorothy Se-
bastian, Norma Talmadge, Estelle
Taylor, *and* Claire Windsor

Story: Peggy Pepper reaches Hollywood in a battered Model-T Ford driven
by her Georgia-Colonel father. The Colonel drives his overdressed daughter,
who is done up in ribbons and bows, to the gate at Metro-Goldwyn-Mayer
only to be turned away. The early scenes of 1928 Hollywood have a tingling
excitement and wry humor, almost a satirical documentary quality.

The Colonel and his daughter meet an outgoing Mack Sennett–type
comedy actor in a studio commissary. Billy Boone, as the actor calls himself, agrees to take her to his boss, a comedy director whose mind is perilously close to insanity. Peggy wears her finest party dress for the test scene,
unaware that she is going to be soaked by a squirting seltzer bottle. Her
shock gives way to tears and, back in the dressing room, she is nearly
inconsolable as Billy tells her she has to learn to "take it on the chin."

Peggy and Billy have a romance, but her rise to prominence as a comedienne is fast, and when she is cast in her first dramatic role, her leading
man, a phony count who used to wait tables in a spaghetti joint, tells her
that she is now too important to bother with the old Mack Sennett crowd;
she must move with the "best" of Hollywood society since she has an image
to live up to. She changes her name to Patricia Pepoire, exposes her upper
teeth like a rabbit (in a parody of Gloria Swanson), buys an expensive
foreign limousine, a house with a foyer resembling Grand Central Station,
and gets herself a droll maid. She no longer returns Billy's phone calls and
gets herself engaged to the phony count. At a dinner in Billy's modest home,
the perplexed old Colonel wonders what Hollywood has done to his innocent
daughter.

Letters come in from exhibitors complaining, asking the studio to please
not send any more Patricia Pepoire features, saying "the public is tired of
her." When the studio head tells her to "come down to earth and be old
Peggy Pepper," she flounces out of his office and soon is in a wedding gown
about to be married to her phony count (the publicity, he tells her, will put
her on the top again). Billy comes to her home just before the wedding and,
denied entry by a guard, goes in through the back door with a laundry
basket. He demands to see Peggy who is upstairs dressing. Peggy, in her
wedding gown, goes down to the dining room where Billy waits (among
the custard pies) and Billy tells her that she must wake up before it is too
late, that she is ruining her life and career through her pretensions. She is
furious and picks up a custard pie to heave it at Billy, but the door opens
just at that moment and the phony count, who is searching for his bride,
gets the pie full in the face. Peggy suddenly sees the absurdity of it all,
doubling up with laughter as her phony count gravely insists on going
ahead with the ceremony, whitened face and all. Peggy flees the chaos with
Billy.

Released November 11, 1928

Comment: New York Times (Mordaunt Hall)—"So clever is the comedy in
'Show People', the current film at the Capitol, that it would not be at all
surprising to hear that many in the audiences had sat through it twice. It
is a hardy satire on Hollywood life, directed by King Vidor . . . but he is not
alone responsible for the gaiety in this picture, for Marion Davies shares
honors with him through her unusually clever acting."

Note: This film is generally conceded to be Marion Davies's finest: it was
the New York Film Festival Retrospective Choice, 1967, and the opening
night feature at the King Vidor Retrospective, Los Angeles, 1971.

THE TALKIES

THE HOLLYWOOD REVUE OF 1929

A Cosmopolitan Production for Metro-Goldwyn-Mayer
Directed by Charles Reisner
Production numbers staged by Sammy Lee
Music by Nacio Herb Brown and Arthur Freed
Settings by Cedric Gibbons

Cast

Marion Davies, John Gilbert, Norma Shearer, William Haines, Joan Crawford, Laurel and Hardy, Lionel Barrymore, Gus Edwards, Buster Keaton, Polly Moran, Gwen Lee, Karl Dane, George K. Arthur, Marie Dressler, Conrad Nagel, Anita Page, Bessie Love, and Charles King; *and featuring* Cliff (Ukulele Ike) Edwards, Natacha Natova, Jack Benny, the Brox Sisters, the Rounders, the Albertina Rasch ballet, *and a chorus of 125 girls*

Story: There is no plot—this is an adaptation of the theories and practice of Florenz Ziegfeld, Earl Carroll, and George White. It is a collection of skits, blackouts, tableaux, dances and songs. Conrad Nagel narrates, adding a humorous element to the action. Among its best moments are the songs, "Singin' in the Rain," with Marion Davies, Joan Crawford, and the Brox Sisters wearing yellow slickers under a downpour; "Low Down Rhythm"; and "Orange Blossom Time," the latter done with the actual aroma of orange blossoms being wafted over the audience during its New York and Hollywood runs. Two of the sequences are in Technicolor.

Released August 14, 1929

Comment: Mordaunt Hall in *The New York Times*—"Brimming over with good fun and catchy music, Metro-Goldwyn-Mayer's ambitious audible picture, 'The Hollywood Revue,' which was launched at the Astor Theatre, won frequent outbursts of genuine applause. It is a talking and singing film free from irritating outpourings of coarse slang or a tedious, sobbing romance. . . . It trots gayly along from beginning to end with a wonderful fund of amusement and its clever and lavish staging is enhanced by imaginative camera work."

MARIANNE

A Marion Davies Production for Cosmopolitan Productions, released by Metro-Goldwyn-Mayer
Dialogue by Laurence Stallings and Gladys Unger
Music and lyrics by Roy Turk and Fred E. Ahlert and Raymond Klages and Jesse Greer
Additional music by Nacio Herb Brown and Arthur Freed
Art director: Cedric Gibbons
Costumes by Adrian
Photographed by Oliver Marsh
Recording engineer: Douglas Shearer
Film editor: James McKay

Cast

Marianne	Marion Davies	Sam	Benny Rubin
André	George Baxter	Lieutenant Frane	Scott Kolk
Stagg	Lawrence Gray	The General	Robert Edeson
Soapy	Cliff (Ukulele Ike) Edwards	Pere Joseph	Emil Chautard

Story: Marianne, who lives in a rural village of France along the battlefront in the First World War, has promised her love to a French soldier, but, almost against her will, she loses her heart to a rough-talking American, Stagg. She raises a few pigs, one of them being a pet, but a smooth-talking lieutenant talks her into cooking him for the General and his companions. She kills her pet pig and Stagg steals the porker before she has a chance to serve it. Her French lover returns sightless from the front and she feels she must renounce Stagg and stick by André. Stagg goes home. Meanwhile, André sees that Marianne really loves the American and pines for him, so he enters the church as a novice priest. When back in New York, Stagg learns that Marianne is again alone, he sends for her and she comes to America to be his bride.

Released October 18, 1929

Comment: Mordaunt Hall in *The New York Times*—". . . Marion Davies gracefully and charmingly attempts the difficult feat of impersonating a French peasant girl during the World War. In quite a number of instances, she succeeds with her French and she does especially well when speaking English with a French accent.

New York Herald-Tribune (Marguerite Tazelaar)—"Miss Davies gives an emotional performance of such genuineness and yet restraint that it turns the prankish comedy for a moment into tragedy—heart-breaking, lyrical tragedy."

New York Daily News (Irene Thirer)—"The dialogue prepared for her [Marion Davies] is screamingly funny . . . dandy entertainment."

NOT SO DUMB

A Marion Davies Production for Cosmopolitan, released by Metro-Goldwyn-Mayer
Dialogue by Justin Mayer, based on "Dulcy," a play by Marc Connelly and George S. Kaufman
Photographed by Oliver Marsh

Cast

Dulcy	Marion Davies	Mr. Forbes	William Holden
Gordon	Elliott Nugent	Van Dyck	Donald Ogden Stewart
Bill	Raymond Hackett	Angela	Sally Starr
Leach	Franklin Pangborn	Perkins	George Davis
Mrs. Forbes	Julia Faye		

Story: Dulcy is an exasperating dumbbell, full of Pollyanna bromides and a fearful determination to run the party and her guests. Her idea of "helping" her hardworking fiancé is to interfere in his business deals, annoy his guests, and otherwise behave moronically, all with the best intentions. She also has an irresistible impulse to broadcast information given her in confidence by friends and fiancé. But in the end her dumb intrusiveness unexpectedly pays a dividend and all is well.

Released February 7, 1930

Comment: Mordaunt Hall in *The New York Times*—"Marion Davies, who is always at her best under the direction of King Vidor, shines in the role of Dulcy, a girl that might be described as a 'Miss Malaprop' of today. . . ."
Motion Picture Magazine—"If Marion is a dumb-bell I wish more movie stars were dumb . . . as Marion plays her, and it's her most difficult role, you like Dulcy so well that you wish she'd keep on being a nuisance."

THE FLORADORA GIRL

A Marion Davies Production for Metro-Goldwyn-Mayer
Directed by Harry Beaumont
Screenplay by Gene Markey, with additional dialogue by Ralph Spence, Al Boasberg, and Robert Hopkins
Photographed by Oliver T. Marsh
Settings by Cedric Gibbons

Cast

Daisy . . . . Marion Davies   Lord Rumblesham . . Claude Allister
Jack Vibart . . . . Lawrence Gray   Fontaine . . . . Sam Hardy
and Ilka Chase, Louis John Bartels, Vivian Oakland, Jed Prouty, Nance
O'Neil, Robert Bolder, Jane Keithly, *and* Maude Turner Gordon

Story: Daisy Dell is one of the famous Floradora Sextette of the Gay
Nineties—the last, in fact, as all the others are either married or engaged.
She falls in love with a society man named Jack Vibart. At first Jack's intentions are strictly dishonorable, but he later realizes Daisy's true worth
and they become engaged.

However, Jack loses all of the family money on a crooked horse race in
which a scoundrel by the name of Fontaine is involved. Jack's mother tells
Daisy that the only way the family can be saved from complete ruin is for
Daisy to give up Jack so that he can marry a wealthy debutante. This she
does, but in the end Jack recoups the family fortune by going into the horse-
less carriage business and he and Daisy are happily married.

Released May 30, 1930

Comment: New York Telegram—"Marion Davies is ideally suited to the part
of Daisy and makes the most of it."
New York Review—"Those almost legendary characters of the oft-lamented
'gay nineties' sing and dance again with all their old accustomed charm in
'The Floradora Girl.'"
Mordaunt Hall in *The New York Times*—". . . virtually a travesty, but one
that is shrewdly directed with a good sense of humor. Marion Davies, the
stellar performer, is seen to excellent advantage as Daisy, one of the famous
Floradora sextette. . . ."

THE BACHELOR FATHER

A Marion Davies Production for Metro-Goldwyn-Mayer
Directed by Robert Z. Leonard
Based on a play by Edward Childs Carpenter
Settings by Cedric Gibbons

Cast

Tony . . . . Marion Davies   Ashley . . . . Ralph Forbes
Sir Basil Winterton. .C. Aubrey Smith   Butler . . . . Halliwell Hobbes
and Ray Milland, Guinn Williams, David Torrence, Doris Lloyd, Edgar
Norton, Nena Quartaro, Elizabeth Murray, *and* James Gordon

Story: A gay old blade, rusted a bit by age, is lonesome in his declining
years, so he summons the children of his youth to share the luxuries of his
broad English acres. One is the daughter of a fiery Italian prima donna,
another the son of a girl long-forgotten, and the third a fascinating hoyden,
Antoinette or "Tony," whose mother was once a headliner of the New York
stage.

The children find their crotchety old bachelor daddy not really to their
liking, but agree to accept him on approval. Shadows fall, however, when
the Italian daughter and the son leave again to pursue their careers. The
old man misses them, but his sadness is dissipated by the presence of Tony
for the slangy sprite is his favorite. Meanwhile, young love blooms and
Tony reaches a very satisfactory understanding with the son of her father's
lifelong friend.

Released February 1, 1931

Comment: Mordaunt Hall in *The New York Times*—"The mills of Hollywood have ground out a good pictorial adaptation of 'The Bachelor Father.'
. . . Miss Davies does quite well in her role."
William Boehnel in the *New York World Telegram*—"Marion Davies, who
has come to be regarded, and not without some justification either, as the
screen's leading comedienne, has returned to the Capitol, where she offers
an altogether delightful, engaging and humorous performance. . . . It is
first rate entertainment from every angle."

New York American (Regine Crewe)—"Bubbling over with fun and salted to taste by a tear or two, an adroit adaptation of 'The Bachelor Father' brings the sparkling Marion Davies to the screen of the Capitol this week. The picture is reaping a harvest of hilarity. Yet its pathos wins the tribute of a sigh. That star's artistry so completely captivates her audience that it shares all her joys and sorrows."

IT'S A WISE CHILD

A Marion Davies Production for Metro-Goldwyn-Mayer
Directed by Robert Z. Leonard
Adapted from the play by Laurence E. Johnson
Settings by Cedric Gibbons

Cast

Joyce	Marion Davies	Mrs. Stanton	Clara Blandick
Steve	Sidney Blackmer	G. A. Appleby	Robert McWade
Cool Kelly	James Gleason	Otho	Johnny Arthur
Bertha	Polly Moran	Alice	Hilda Vaughn
Roger	Lester Vail	Bill	Ben Alexander
Annie	Marie Prevost	Jane Appleby	Emily Fitzroy

Story: A slight tale involving a misunderstanding about an impending baby, with Marion Davies as the innocent victim. Marion is a well-meaning fixer.

Released May 15, 1931

Comment: New York Times—"It is smooth, well-timed and occasionally tremendously funny, and yesterday's audiences found it hugely to their liking. . . . Marion Davies performs in her best manner."

FIVE AND TEN

A Marion Davies Production, released by Metro-Goldwyn-Mayer
Directed by Robert Z. Leonard
Adapted from a story by Fannie Hurst
Settings by Cedric Gibbons

Cast

Jennifer Rarick	Marion Davies	Ramon	Lee Beranger
Bertram "Berry"		Piggy	Arthur Housman
Rhodes	Leslie Howard	Brooks	George Irving
John Rarick	Richard Bennett	Hopkins	Halliwell Hobbes
Jenny Rarick	Irene Rich	Dennison	Charles Giblyn
Avery Rarick	Douglass Montgomery	Taxi driver	Henry Armetta
(then known as "Kent Douglas")		Midge	Ruth Selwyn
Muriel	Mary Duncan		

Story: Jennifer Rarick, daughter of a rich dime store merchant who has left Kansas City to make his home on Fifth Avenue, agrees to sell kisses at a charity booth and meets architect Berry Rhodes, who is the fiancé of the bazaar's head, a determined lass named Muriel. Jennifer talks her way into Berry's apartment, where she encourages him to seduce her. Muriel, aware of what has happened, tells Jennifer that she cannot buy Berry away from her, that she is "nouveau riche" and cheap and not Berry's social type at all. Jennifer runs home to brother Avery, who is getting drunk because he has learned that their mother, in her loneliness, has taken a lover.

Avery tries to warn his father that the family riches are making a wreck of all their lives, but the father dismisses this, whereupon Avery gets in a private plane and crashes deliberately, mortally hurt.

The grieving family members realize they must do something with their lives, and they decide to go to Europe. Before their ship departs, Berry rushes to dockside, disenchanted with his wife of ten months—who has attempted to "sell" him to Jennifer for $100,000—and swears that he will follow her to Europe.

Released July 10, 1931

Comment: New York Times—". . . far beyond the glum outlook of the economic lords is the fact that the picture is enjoyable. Marion Davies has a part in it—that of the merchant's daughter; and also there is Leslie Howard. He glides gently along his way, making love in that bland way best known to young architects and playwrights on the Riviera."

POLLY OF THE CIRCUS

A Marion Davies Production, released by Metro-Goldwyn-Mayer
Directed by Alfred Santell
Adaptation by Carey Wilson of the play by Margaret Mayo
Dialogue by Laurence E. Johnson
Photographed by George Barnes
Recording director: Douglas Shearer
Art director—Cedric Gibbons
Gowns by Adrian
Film editor: George Hively

Cast

Polly	Marion Davies	Don	Clark Marshall
Reverend John Hartley	Clark Gable	Mrs. McNamara	Lillian Elliott
Reverend James Northcott	C. Aubrey Smith	Eric	Guinn Williams
		Beef	David Landau
Downey	Raymond Hatton	Half-Pint	Little Billy
Mrs. Jennings	Maude Eburne	Usher	Ray Milland
Mitzi	Ruth Selwyn		

Story: Polly, an aerialist in the circus, is injured in a fall and is taken to the house of a young minister, the Reverend John Hartley. During her recovery, they fall in love, but he has to renounce his successful parish when they will not accept Polly's vulgarisms. When Polly sees how desparately unhappy her husband is without any parish, she returns to the circus.

Old Uncle James, who has once told Polly that she stood in John's way, sees through her sacrifice that she deserves her chance with John and he and John race to the big top to reassure her before her nightly triple somersault fifty feet above the ground without a net. "It's *okay,*" says gruff Uncle James, using Polly's vernacular.

Released March 18, 1932

Comments: New York Times—"Miss Davies gives quite a good performance as Polly."

BLONDIE OF THE FOLLIES

A Marion Davies Production for Metro-Goldwyn-Mayer release
Directed by Edmund Goulding
Scenario by Frances Marion
Dialogue by Anita Loos
Photographed by George Barnes
Recording director: Douglas Shearer
Art director: Cedric Gibbons
Gowns by Adrian
Musical score by Dr. William Axt
Film editor: George Hively

Cast

Blondie McClune	Marion Davies	Pop McClune	James Gleason
Larry Belmont	Robert Montgomery	Gertie	Zasu Pitts
Lottie *or* Lurlene	Billie Dove	Jimmy	Jimmy Durante

and Sidney Toler, Douglas Dumbrille, Sarah Padden, *and* Clyde Cook

Story: Blondie and her best girlfriend Molly live in the same slum building in New York. Molly is going out with older men, hopeful of a break that will make her an actress and take her out of the slums. Molly succeeds and comes back to visit the slum and her weary mother as well as Blondie and the McClunes. Pop resents Molly's sudden affluence, thinking it immoral, and will have none of her. But Blondie is impressed and goes back to Molly's penthouse for a visit. There, she meets Larry Belmont, a wealthy playboy. They are mutually attracted, much to Molly's displeasure.

Meanwhile, Larry persuades one of the producers of the Follies to take on Blondie as a member of the chorus. Molly gets into a hair-pulling fight with Blondie for "stealing" her boyfriend. Blondie breaks with Larry because she doesn't want to hurt her old friend Molly. During a "crack-the-whip" routine on stage, Molly allows Blondie to slip from her grasp and tumble into the orchestra pit. Her leg fractured in several places, Blondie is forced to leave the theater for good and gamely gives a farewell party for herself, but Larry, still loving her, goes out and brings to her home three or four specialists "who have studied her X-rays" and insist that after re-setting the fractures she will be able to walk and dance again.

Released September 1, 1932

Comment: New York Times—"The assumption in 'Blondie of the Follies,' which was jamming the auditorium of the Capitol yesterday, is that there is something to record about the life of a Follies girl. Whether one accepts this premise or not, the film does offer a number of good features. . . . Marion Davies and Robert Montgomery are completely satisfactory in the leads. Both are light comedians and as seriously disturbed and frustrated lovers the two players are admirable."

PEG O' MY HEART

A Robert Z. Leonard Production for Cosmopolitan, released by Metro-Goldwyn-Mayer
Directed by Robert Z. Leonard
Screenplay by Frank R. Adams, adapted by Frances Marion the play by J. Hartley Manners
Musical score by Herbert Stothart
Photographed by George Barnes
Art director: Cedric Gibbons
Recording director: Douglas Shearer
Film editor: Margaret Booth

Cast

Peg	Marion Davies	Mrs. Brent	Doris Lloyd
Pat	J. Farrell MacDonald	Smythe	Nora Cecil
Ethel	Juliette Compton	Terance	Geoffrey Gill
Jerry	Onslow Stevens	Jarvis	Robert Greig
Alaric	Tyrrell Davis	Michael	Mutt
Mrs. Chichester	Irene Browne		

Story: Peg, a poor Irish daughter of a fisherman, comes into a fortune, the catch being that she must live in the Chichester mansion in England in order to claim the money. Her father Pat persuades her to go and he even agrees to stay out of his daughter's life, a further condition. She falls in love with Jerry, one of the Chichester friends, but she renounces this possibility when she sees how unhappy and treacherous the snobbish Chichesters are (they are only keeping her with them because the money will continue to come in as long as she is under their roof). She returns to her Irish village and her father with her dog Mike, who also has been abused by the Chichesters. Jerry goes all the way to Ireland to declare his love and intention to marry Peg.

Released May 19, 1933

Comment: New York Herald Tribune (Marguerite Tazelaar)—"Years have not dimmed the dewey appeal of J. Hartley Manners' sentimental little epic,

'Peg o' My Heart,' now showing at the Capitol, with Marion Davies as comically wistful a Peg as you could wish."

Mordaunt Hall in *The New York Times*—"Marion Davies is entrusted with the role of the buoyant colleen and the mirth and sympathy of an audience yesterday afternoon was a sure testimonial to her successful performance . . . she gives a whole-souled portrayal, always devoting more thought to Peg than to any idea of making herself especially attractive."

GOING HOLLYWOOD

A Marion Davies Production for Metro-Goldwyn-Mayer
Directed by Raoul Walsh
Screenplay by Donald Ogden Stewart from a story by Frances Marion.
Music and lyrics by Nacio Brown and Arthur Freed

Cast

Sylvia Bruce	Marion Davies	Ernest B. Baker	Stuart Erwin
Bill Williams	Bing Crosby	Bert Conroy	Ned Sparks
Lili Yvonne	Fifi D'Orsay	Jack Thompson	Bobby Watson
Jill Barker	Patsy Kelly		

Story: A big singing movie star and his actress girlfriend, who is French and combustible, are on their way to Hollywood to make a picture together, when a school teacher and a super-fan of the singing star spots them and follows them all the way across the country. The singing star succumbs to the schoolmarm's persistence and good looks, and the young lady replaces the flighty actress both in his affections and in his movie as leading lady.

Released December 23, 1933

Comment: New York Times—"The overwhelming magnitude of the latter-day musical pictures is gratefully absent from this one. It is warm, modest and good-humored. Bing Crosby has a manner and a voice, both pleasant."

OPERATOR 13

A Cosmopolitan Production for Metro-Goldwyn-Mayer
Produced by Lucien Hubbard
Directed by Richard Boleslavsky
Screenplay by Harvey Thew, Zelda Sears, and Eve Greene from the stories of Robert W. Chambers
Songs by Walter Donaldson and Gus Kahn as arranged by Dr. William Axt
Photographed by George Folsey, ASC
Recording director: Douglas Shearer
Art director: Cedric Gibbons
Costumes by Adrian
Film editor: Frank Sullivan

Cast

Gale Loveless	Marion Davies	Captain	
Captain John Galliard	Gary Cooper	Channing	Willard Robertson
Eleanor	Jean Parker	Sweeney	Fuzzy Knight
Pauline	Katharine Alexander	Major Allen	Sidney Toler
Dr. Hitchcock	Ted Healy	Colonel Sharpe	Robert McWade
Littledale	Russell Hardie	Mrs. Shackleford	Marjorie Gateson
John Pelham	Henry Wadsworth	Gaston	Wade Boteler
General Stuart	Douglas Dumbrille	Operator 55	Walter Long
		and the Four Mills Brothers	

Story: During the Civil War, Gale Loveless is an actress on a tour of the front lines entertaining the Union Army troops. She is approached by an old actress friend, Pauline, to join her in espionage work for the Union cause. Gale quickly agrees.

The two ladies are sent into the Deep South where Pauline, in the guise of Mrs. Vail, leases an old mansion and pretends to be an ardent Confederate. Gale, disguised as a mulatto laundress, works on Mrs. Vail's rented plantation and eavesdrops on soldiers and officers. Anything she hears about troop movements she passes along to Pauline.

A handsome cavalry officer, Captain Galliard, rides onto the property; he notices the beautiful mulatto but goes on. He is a Confederate spy or at least working in their intelligence branch. "Mrs. Vail" is soon caught by the Confederates and gallantly declines to name her assistant, but then, with Gail's help, she escapes to the north. Pauline is too well-known to be of any further use, but Gale is sent to Richmond as a "Miss Anne Clairborne." Captain Galliard turns up at an officers' dance and seems to recognize something about Anne. She says she is a common type, but he is wildly attracted to her and she to him, and soon they are hopelessly in love.

Anne is warned by another agent that they are coming to arrest her so she changes into a Confederate uniform and attempts to ride north. Captain Galliard tries to stop her and she strikes him with her riding crop. She finds sanctuary in an abandoned house. There Galliard, his head wound bandaged, catches up with her and tells her what a traitor she is. But when a battle rages outside the house, she manages to keep him from joining the fray and probably saves his life. At the end of the war they meet again, no longer enemies.

Released June 22, 1934

Comment: New York Herald Tribune (Marguerite Tazelaar)—"A Civil War drama with a spy angle, 'Operator 13' offers Marion Davies a vehicle for a straight dramatic performance in which she exhibits far more talent than one might expect . . . she brings to the picture a characterization believable, and at the same time surprising, for the awareness with which she imbues her 'Operator 13.' "

Mordaunt Hall in *The New York Times*—"In its own peculiar fashion it is entertaining and besides the capable work of Miss Davies there are splendid performances by Jean Parker and Gary Cooper. . . . Miss Davies is highly amusing as the girl who is constantly carrying laundry in baskets but who is really Operator 13."

PAGE MISS GLORY

A Marion Davies Production for Warner Brothers release
Directed by Mervyn LeRoy
Screenplay by Delmer Daves and Robert Lord from the play by Joseph Schrank and Philip Donning
Music and lyrics by Harry Warren and Al Dubin
Musical director: Leo Forbstein
Photographed by George Folsey
Gowns by Orry-Kelly
Film editor: William Clemons

Cast

Loretta	Marion Davies	Joe Bonner	Hobart Cavanaugh
Click Wiley	Pat O'Brien	Mr. Frelschultz	Joseph Cawthorn
Bingo Nelson	Dick Powell	Mr. Hansburger	Al Shean
Gladys	Mary Astor	Yates	Berton Churchill
Ed Olsen	Frank McHugh	Loretta's Mother	Helen Lowell
Slattery	Lyle Talbot		
Betty	Patsy Kelly	*and* Mary Treen, Harry Beresford,
Petey	Allen Jenkins	Gavin Gordon, Lionel Stander, and
Blackie	Barton MacLane	Joseph Crehan

Story: Loretta, from the backwoods, gets a job as a chambermaid in a swanky Park Avenue Hotel. In the hotel but unable to pay the stiff rent is Click Wiley, a promoter, and his pal Ed Olsen, as well as Ed's girlfriend Gladys.

A yeast company offers $2500 for a photograph of America's most beautiful girl. Olsen makes a composite, christens her "Dawn Glory," and the photo wins the prize, the whole nation becoming "Miss Glory" conscious.

A daredevil flyer comes in town to visit them, and Bingo Nelson, the flyer, falls in love with Dawn Glory's photo. Meanwhile, Loretta has fallen in love with Nelson, from seeing him in the newspaper and then in the hotel.

Gladys accidentaly sees Loretta attired in Dawn Glory's dress. Immediately the three con artists introduce Loretta as "Dawn Glory" to get themselves off the hook.

Loretta is first kidnapped and then exposed but Bingo loves her anyway.

Released August 29, 1935

Comment: New York Herald Tribune (Richard Watts, Jr.)—". . . her [Marion Davies'] gift for low comedy merriment disappears and, amid a despairing attempt to be both alluring and whimsical in one wholesale effort, her performance becomes completely routine and lacking in every trace of distinction."

New York Times (Andre Sennwald)—"To Miss Marion Davies (who comes out of retirement for the occasion) the producers entrust the considerable task of being the most beautiful girl in the country without realizing it."

HEARTS DIVIDED

A Marion Davies Production for Warner Brothers release
Directed by Frank Borzage
Screenplay by Laird Doyle and Casey Robinson from the play "Glorious Betsy" by Rida Johnson Young
Music and lyrics by Harry Warren and Al Dubin
Photographed by George Folsey
Gowns by Orry-Kelly
Film editor: Bill Holmes

Cast

Betsy Patterson	....Marion Davies	Isham	...............John Larkin
Captain Jerome		Pichon	.........Walter Kingsford
Bonaparte	.........Dick Powell	du Fresne	........Etienne Girardot
Napoleon Bonaparte	..Claude Rains	Cambacérès	......Halliwell Hobbes
Henry Ruggles	....Charlie Ruggles	President Thomas	
John Hathaway	...Edward Everett Horton	Jefferson	.........George Irving
		Mammy	........Hattie McDaniels
Sir Harry	........Arthur Treacher	Colored Servant	...Sam McDaniels
Charles		Pippin	.............Phillip Hurlic
Patterson	.....Henry Stephenson	*and* the Hall Johnson Choir	
Aunt Ellen	........Clara Blandick		

Story: Jerome Bonaparte is in America incognito as the emissary of his brother. At the races, he sees Betsy and it is love at first sight. He manages to sneak into her home as her French tutor but he openly defends Napoleon's policies and is discharged.

Napoleon meanwhile has been arranging a marriage for his brother with a princess. Jerome declines and enrages Napoleon. With Betsy as his intended bride, he sails for France to get his brother's blessing. In a private interview Napoleon persuades Betsy to renounce Jerome and go back home.

Eventually, Jerome gets back to Baltimore and to Betsy, still single and ready at last to be her groom.

Released June 12, 1936

Comment: New York Herald Tribune (Marguerite Tazelaar)—"Whatever satire may have been intended by the authors who named the piece, little survives on the screen except for some lapses by Miss Davies into comedy, which, since it is the best part of her dramatic equipment, she should not neglect."

New York Times—"Its chief faults are that Miss Davies is miscast and that the apocryphal script demands that Dick Powell, cast as a Bonaparte, cavort about Baltimore much in need of a haircut and warbling vacuous ditties about birds and flowers and Paris in the Spring."

CAIN AND MABEL

A Cosmopolitan Production for Warner Brothers release
Directed by Lloyd Bacon
Production numbers by Bobby Connolly
Screenplay by Laird Doyle from a story by H. C. Witwer
Photographed by George Barnes
Music and lyrics by Harry Warren and Al Dubin
Musical arrangements by Ray Heindorf
Choreography: Bobby Connell
Film editor: William Holmes

Cast

Mabel O'Dare	Marion Davies	Toddy	Pert Kelton
Larry Cain	Clark Gable	Pop Walters	William Collier, Sr.
Dodo	Allen Jenkins	Specialty	Sammy White
Reilly	Roscoe Karns	Charles Fendwick	E. E. Clive
Jake Sherman	Walter Catlett	Tom Reed	Allen Pomeroy
Ronny Cauldwell	David Carlyle	Café Proprietor	Robert Middlemass
Milo	Hobart Cavanaugh	Reed's Manager	Joseph Crehan
Aunt Mimi	Ruth Donnelly	The old maid	Eily Malyon

Story: Mabel O'Dare offers a plate of ham and eggs to an out-of-work newspaper man and loses her job as waitress. When Larry Cain loses a night's sleep in a noisy hotel, he forfeits his heavyweight championship. From then on, we follow these two losers on the way up—Cain in the ring and Mabel as a musical comedy star. Eventually they get together and go off to a little cottage in New Jersey.
Released October 18, 1936
Comment: New York Herald Tribune (Howard Barnes)—"She [Marion Davies] walks through the part, and you must be a very ardent fan to find this satisfactory."
New York Times (J.T.M.)—"Miss Davies's comedy scenes are, traditionally, her best, despite the studio's notion to the contrary. Mr. Gable's roles are becoming routine matters. He needs another 'Mutiny on the Bounty.'"

EVER SINCE EVE

A Cosmopolitan Production for Warner Brothers release
Directed by Lloyd Bacon
Screenplay by Lawrence Riley, Earl Baldwin, and Lily Hayward from a story
    by Margaret Lee and Gene Baker
Music and lyrics by M. K. Jerome and Jack Schell
Photographed by George Barnes
Gowns by Orry-Kelly
Film editor: William Holmes

Cast

Marge Winton	Marion Davies	Abbie Belldon	Louise Fazenda
Freddy Matthews	Robert Montgomery	*and* Marcia Ralston, Carol Hughes,	
"Mabel" DeCraven	Frank McHugh	Frederick Clark, Arthur Hoyt, Mary Treen, Harry Hayden, Pierre Watkin, John T. Murray, *and* William Davidson	
Sadie O'Day	Patsy Kelly		
Jake Edgall	Allen Jenkins		

Story: Marge Winton as a stenographer gets tired of the men chasing her around the office and she quits, disguises herself as an ugly duckling and goes to work for a publishing house, where only ugly girls are hired. She is sent by the wacky lady publisher to do the manuscript of a novelist, who rarely turns in any work.

Eventually, the writer sees her in her natural beauty and falls in love with her, and she attempts to live two lives for a while.

When she is thrown by reckless auto, Freddy sees that the secretary and the beauty are one and the same person and all ends happily.

Released June 24, 1937

Comment: New York Times (Frank S. Nugent)—"After playing the eye-batting ingenue for more years than it would be polite to mention, Miss Marion Davies apparently feels she has mastered the role sufficiently to begin her cycle all over again."

New York Herald Tribune (Howard Barnes)—"The chief trouble with Miss Davies's performance, aside from the material itself, is that she plays straightforwardly, establishing almost no contrast between her two impersonations. Mr. Montgomery, as the novelist, makes a more determined try for laughter, but with little success. . . . It seems to me that 'Ever Since Eve' was stopped at the start by a really bad script."

BIBLIOGRAPHY

Allen, Frederick Lewis, *Only Yesterday*, New York, 1931

Andrist, Ralph K., and the Editors of American Heritage, *The American Heritage History of the 20's and 30's*, New York, 1970

Baxter, John, *Hollywood in the Thirties*, London, 1968

Beer, Thomas, *Stephan Crane: A Study in American Letters*, New York, 1927

Behrman, S. N., *Duveen*, New York, 1952

Birmingham, Stephen, *The Right People*, Boston, 1968

Blum, Daniel, *A Pictorial History of the Talkies*, New York, 1958

Bogdanovich, Peter, *Allan Dwan: The Last Pioneer*, New York, 1971

Brownlow, Kevin, *The Parade's Gone By*, New York, 1969

Cable, Mary, and the Editors of American Heritage, *American Manners and Morals: A Picture History of How We Behaved and Misbehaved*, New York, 1969

Carlson, Oliver, *Brisbane: A Candid Biography*, New York, 1937

———, and Ernest Sutherland Bates, *Hearst: The Lord of San Simeon*, New York, 1936

Chaplin, Charles, *My Autobiography*, New York, 1964

Chase, Ilka, *Past Imperfect*, New York, 1942

Churchill, Randolph S., *Twenty-one Years*, Boston, 1965

Crowther, Bosley, *Hollywood Rajah*, New York, 1940

Davies, Marion, *Taped Reminiscences* (with Stanley Flink), unpublished, 1952, by permission, the Marion Davies Estate

Evans, Delight, "Galatea on Riverside Drive," article in *Photoplay* Magazine, October 1919, New York

Ferber, Edna, *A Peculiar Treasure*, New York, 1939

Fortune Magazine, October, 1935: *Hearst*

Fowler, Gene, *Good Night, Sweet Prince: The Life and Times of John Barrymore*, New York, 1944

———, *The Great Mouthpiece*, New York, 1931

Franklin, Joe, *Classics of the Silent Screen*, New York, 1959

Gilkes, Lillian, *Cora Crane*, Bloomington, Indiana, 1960

Gish, Lillian, *The Movies, Mr. Griffith, and Me*, New Jersey, 1969

Glyn, Anthony, *Elinor Glyn*, New York, 1955

Grey, Lita (Chaplin), with Morton Cooper, *My Life with Chaplin*, New York, 1966

Guiles, Fred Lawrence, *Norma Jean: The Life of Marilyn Monroe*, New York, 1969

Halliwell, Leslie, *The Filmgoer's Companion*, New York, 1970

Hampton, Benjamin B., *History of the American Film Industry*, New York. 1931

Head, Alice., *It Could Never Have Happened*, London, 1939

Hearst, William Randolph, *Selections: The Writings and Speeches of William Randolph Hearst*, San Francisco, 1948

Hecht, Ben, *A Child of the Century*, New York, 1954

Huxley, Aldous, *After Many a Summer Dies the Swan*, New York, 1939
Jablonski, Edward, and Lawrence D. Stewart, *The Gershwin Years*, New York, 1958
Leighton, Isabel, *The Aspirin Age*, New York, 1949
Loos, Anita, *A Girl Like I*, New York, 1966
Lundberg, Ferdinand, *Imperial Hearst*, New York, 1936
Mankiewicz, Herman, *Citizen Kane* (a screenplay, the Gregg Toland copy), unpublished version, Hollywood, 1948
Moore, Colleen, *Silent Star*, New York, 1968
Morris, Lloyd, *Incredible New York*, New York, 1951
———, *Postscript to Yesterday*, New York, 1947
Murray, Ken, *The Golden Days of San Simeon*, New York, 1971
Negri, Pola, *Memoirs of a Star*, New York, 1970
Parker, Dorothy, *Constant Reader* (Madam Glyn Lectures on "It"), New York, 1970
Parsons, Louella, *The Gay Illiterate*, New York, 1945
———, *Tell It to Louella*, New York, 1961
Phillips, Cabell, *From the Crash to the Blitz, 1929–1939*, New York, 1969
Rea, Donald William, *A Critical-Historical Account of the Planning, Production and Release of Citizen Kane*, University of Southern California, Thesis, Los Angeles, 1966
Robinson, David, *Hollywood in the Twenties*, London, 1968
Rogers, Agnes, and Frederick L. Allen, *I Remember Distinctly*, New York, 1947
Rosenberg, Bernard, and Harry Silverstein, *The Real Tinsel*, New York, 1970
Rotha, Paul, *The Film Till Now*, New York, 1951
St. Johns, Adela Rogers, *The Honeycomb*, New York, 1969
Shaw, George Bernard, *Shaw: An Autobiography 1898–1950*, edited by Stanley Weintraub, New York, 1970
Shirer, William L., *The Rise and Fall of the Third Reich*, New York, 1960
Springer, John, *All Talking! All Singing! All Dancing!*, New York, 1969
Swanberg, W. A., *Citizen Hearst*, New York, 1961
Tebbel, John, *The Life and Good Times of William Randolph Hearst*, New York, 1952
Terkel, Studs, *Hard Times*, New York, 1970
Thomas, Bob, *Thalberg: Life and Legend*, New York, 1969
Time-Life Book Staff, *This Fabulous Century: 1900 through 1950*, New York, 1969–1970
Time-Life Book Staff, John Dille, editor, *Time Capsules, 1925, 1927*, New York, 1968
Vanderbilt, Gloria, Sr. with Palma Wayne, *Without Prejudice*, New York, 1936
Vidor, King, *A Tree Is a Tree*, New York, 1953
Warner, Jack, *My First Hundred Years in Hollywood*, New York, 1965
Weinberg, Herman E., *The Lubitsch Touch*, New York, 1968
Whalen, Richard J., *The Founding Father*, New York, 1964
Williams, Henry Lionel, and Ottalie K. Williams, *Great Houses of America*, New York, 1966
Winkler, John K., *W. R. Hearst: An American Phenomenon*, New York, 1928
Wood, Leslie, *The Miracle of the Movies*, London, 1962
Wright, Cobina, Sr., *I Never Grew Up*, New York, 1952
Zierold, Norman, *The Moguls*, New York, 1969

INDEX

Academy awards, 259, 278, 315
Actor's Equity, 255
Adam and Eva, 117, 382
Adams, Jack, 301
Adamson, Harold, 220
Adlon, Louis, 175
Adoree, Renee, 208, 278
Africanus, Scipio, 182
After Many a Summer Dies the Swan (Huxley), 5, 311
After Sundown, 267
Alexander, Rita, 308
Alexander's Ragtime Band, 104
Algonquin Round Table (West), 247
"Alhambra," 311
Alias Jimmy Valentine, 225
"Ali Baba," 71
Alice in Wonderland, 269
Allom, Sir Charles, 221
Alvord, Clark, 299–300
Ambassador Hotel, 148
American, 311
American Weekly, 65
Amory, Cleveland, 322
Androcles and the Lion (Shaw), 262, 265
Angelus Temple, 175
Anglo-French pact, 219–220
Animal Kingdom, The, 259
"Anne" (*Lights of Old Broadway*), 173–174
Anti-Semitism, 277, 322–323
Apperson, Randolph, 334
April Folly, 378
Arbuckle, Roscoe ("Fatty"), 109, 361
Ardsley Art Film—Pathé, 80
Arliss, George, 123
Arthur, George K., 225
Associated Producers, Inc., 156
Astaire, Fred, 269
As Thousands Cheer, 246
Astor, Mary, 156
Astor, Vincent, 124
Astoria, Long Island, 84, 109
Avila, Miguel, 204
Ayot–St. Lawrence, 265

Babicora ranch, 304
Bachelor Father, 259, 396–397
Bad Nauheim, 48, 215, 216–217, 270, 276, 289
Baker, George, 92
Balaban & Katz theater circuit, 90
Ball, Lucille, 307
Bank holiday, 265
Bankhead, Tallulah, 349
Banky, Vilma, 193, 278
Barham, Frank, 157, 324
Barham, Mrs. Frank, 157

Barham, Guy (and Mrs.), 106, 108, 160
Barker Brothers, 181
Barrett, Elizabeth, 271, 287
The Barretts of Wimpole Street, 271, 281
Barrie, James M., 199, 202
Barrymore, Ethel, 44, 78
Barrymore, John, 44, 148, 228, 236, 259, 264
Barrymore, Lionel, 171, 234, 259
Barthelmess, Richard, 7
Baruch, Bernard, 17
Bataan, fall of, 326
The Battle of Gettysburg, 156
Baubles, Bangles and Beads, 368
Baum, Vickie, 259
Bautzer, Gregson, 332, 337, 342, 373
Baxter, Warner, 156
Beach house at Santa Monica ("Ocean House"), 106, 176–177, 188–192, 194, 197, 199, 201–202, 209, 226, 236, 256, 258, 260, 282, 292, 321, 327, 330, 350–351, 368–369
"Bear House," 245, 304, 319, 326
Beaton, Cecil, 19
Beatrice Fairfax, 85, 375
Beaumont, Harry, 246
Beautiful Lady, 25–26
Beauty's Worth, 380
Beaux Arts (Architectural School), Paris, 68
Beaux Arts Hotel (New York City), 49, 62–63, 68
Beaverbrook, Lord, 187
Beery, Wallace, 227, 259
Belasco, David, 33, 83, 125
Bell, Monta, 173
Belle of New York, 25, 117, 377
Belmont family, 56
Belmont, Mrs. Otis H. P., 221
Benchley, Robert, 41, 306
"The Bend," 324
Ben Hur, 123
Bennett, Constance, 156, 212
Bennett, Richard, 253
Benny, Jack, 361
Beranger, Lee, 253
Berengaria, the, 223
Berlin, 277
Berlin, Irving, 7, 45
Berlin, Richard, 5, 12, 266, 292–294, 295, 334, 367, 372
Bernhardt, Sarah, 33, 207, 236, 263
"Beverly Hillbillies," 373
Beverly house, the, 8, 318, 328–332, 336, 337, 339, 343, 349–352, 355–356, 359–361, 363, 366–370

Beverly of Graustark, 117, 157, 174, 188, 201–202, 208, 249, 279, 388
Bierce, Ambrose, 5
Big Broadcast, The, 267
Big House, The, 82
Big Parade, The, 208, 227, 229, 238
Bill of Divorcement, A, 259
"Billy Boone," 231
Bird of Paradise, 208, 259
Birth of a Nation, 82
Blitzkrieg, 305
Block, Paul, 40, 41, 44–48, 53, 59–61, 66, 68, 79–80, 92
Blondell, Joan, 282
Blondie, 342
"Blondie McClune," 259
Blondie of the Follies, x, 157, 202, 228, 258, 266, 398–399
Bluebird, The, 34–35
Blue Danube Waltz, 104
Boardman, Eleanor (Vidor, d'Arrast), xii, 18, 127, 159, 184, 205, 229, 251, 261, 278, 319, 335, 338, 349, 351, 354–355, 358–359, 371–372
Boettiger, Anna Roosevelt, 285, 299, 332
Boettiger, John, 285, 299
Boleslavski, Richard, 207, 272
Bolton, Guy, 66, 250
Bonfils, Martin, 218
Bonfils, Winifred, 194–195
Bon Homme Richard (ship), 20
Bonus Expeditionary Force, 258
Borah, William (Sen.), 204
Borzage, Frank, 156
Bossert Hotel (Brooklyn, N.Y.), 132
Boston Tea Party, 132
Bow, Clara, 141, 157, 187, 278, 361
Boy Meets Girl, 287
Boy Scouts of America, 332, 371
Brackett, Charles, 361
Brady, Alice, 264
"Brandon, Charles," 112–113
Brecht, Bertolt, 323
Briand, Aristide, 218
Brice, Fannie, 62, 358
Bride's Play, The, 382
Brigadoon, 267
Brisbane, Arthur, 4, 28, 111, 115, 146, 164, 185, 235, 289–295
Brisbane, Phoebe (Mrs. Arthur), 290
Broadway Melody, The, 233, 250
Broken Blossoms, 84
Brook, Clive, 156
Brooklyn, 19, 20, 21, 22, 23, 210, 373
Brooklyn Eagle, 40
Brooks, Louise, 86
"Brother, Can You Spare a Dime?, 244
Brown, Clarence, 82
Brown, Gates, 342
Brown, Capt. Horace G., 327, 338–372
"Brown House" (hotel), 277
Brown, Nacio Herb, 267
Brown of Harvard, 229
Brown, Mrs. Virginia Powell, 340, 357
Browning, Frances ("Peaches"), 64
Browning, Edward West ("Daddy"), 63–64
Bruno & Blythe, 198
Buccaneer, The, 344
Buck, Gene, 51–52, 60

Bucketshops exposé, 131–134
"Buddy" (bulldog), 188
Burden of Proof, The 376
Buried Treasure, 104, 379
Burke, Billie (Ziegfeld), 64, 77, 125, 248
Burnett, Vera, 149, 152, 157
Bushman, Francis X., 78

Cain and Mabel, 117, 285, 403
Calhoun, Eleanor, 54
California Theatre (Los Angeles), 129
Calles, President (of Mexico), 204
Calvary Cemetery (Los Angeles), 211
Campbell's Studio, N.Y.C., 64–65
Cantor, Eddie, 269
Capitol Theatre (New York City), 246, 260, 269, 270
Carillo, Leo, 108
Carioca, The, 269
Carlisle, Mary, 273
Carnival, 102
Carpentier, Georges, 236
Carroll, Lewis, 115
Cartier's, 200
Casa del Mar (at San Simeon), 149, 177
La Casa Grande, 177, 185, 301
Cashel Byron's Profession (Shaw), 263
"Caskoden, Sir Edwin," 111
Cecilia of the Pink Roses, 89–90, 114, 375
Cedars of Lebanon Hospital, 369, 371–372
Chalfin, Paul, 49
Chambers, Robert W., 86, 90, 118, 193, 212, 250
Champ, The, 208
Chandler, Harry, 265–266
Chaplin, Charlie, 52, 78, 82, 117, 128, 129, 138–139, 148, 151–162, 184, 209, 211, 219, 223, 229, 236, 248, 277, 305, 320, 353, 361, 373
Chaplin, Oona (nee O'Neill), 166
Charles II, 116, 284
"Charles Foster Kane," 57, 124, 311–312, 317
Charles the Bold, 128
Chartwell (Churchill's estate), 237
Chase, Ilka, 139, 206–207, 246
Chasen's (restaurant), 306
Chatterton, Ruth, 225
Chicago, 26, 28–29, 50, 210, 243, 373
Chicago Civic Opera, 314
Chicago Exposition of 1933, 273
Chicago *Herald-Examiner,* 243
Chicago *Tribune,* 233, 296, 313
Child of the Century, A (Hecht), 322–323
Children's Clinic (*see* Marion Davies Children's Clinic)
Chin, Chin, 35
Christian Science, 158, 208
Christie's (auction gallery), 303
Chu, Chin, Chow, 70–71
Churchill, Randolph, 236
Churchill, Winston, 56, 190, 236–237, 362
Ciano, Count Galeazzo, 274, 289–290
Cimarron, 96
"Cinderella House," 245, 319

Cinema Murder, The, 92, 100, 117, 378
Ciro's (Hollywood nightclub), 360
Citadel, The, 208
Citizen Kane, x, xii, 38, 91, 119, 145, 207, 253, 271, 307, 312–320, 351, 373
City Lights, 229
Civil War, the, 272
Claire, Ina, 39, 62
Clarendon Hotel (New York City), 164
Claridge Hotel (London), 274
Clark, Edward Hardy, 124, 204
Clements, Jack, 233
Cliquot Club Eskimos, 149
Clive, Henry, 191
Coates, Paul, 356
Cockeyed World, The, 236
Cocoanut Grove (Hollywood), 141
Cohan, George M., 39
Colette, 22, 26
College Humor, 267
Collier, Buster, 156, 273, 275, 284
Colman, Ronald, 152
Colony Club (New York City), 247
Columbia (revue?), 135
Come and Get It, 96
"Committee, The," 42–43, 291, 294–295
Communism, 261, 299
Compson, Betty, 178
Comrade X, 208
Confidential, 81
Connors, Barry, 209
Conquest, 344
Conrad, Joseph, 307
Convent of the Sacred Heart (Hastings, N.Y.), 30–31
Conversation Piece, 162
Coolidge, Calvin (Pres.), 56, 95, 190, 195, 196, 247–248
Coolidge, Mrs. Grace, 247–248
Cooper, Gary, 187, 271–273, 361
Cooper, Mrs. Gary ("Rocky"), 271
Coquette, 278
Corbett, James J., 263
Corday, Eliot (Dr.), 10, 11, 13, 342
Cosmopolitan Pictures, 80, 82, 89, 91, 100, 114, 148–149, 154–155, 208, 233, 244, 250, 279
Cosmopolitan Theatre, 124–127, 129, 173
Cotten, Joseph, 315
Court of St. James's, 253
Coward, Noel, 162
Crane, Stephen, 19
Crawford, Broderick, 361
Crawford, Joan, 119, 147, 199, 212, 234, 235, 259, 270, 278, 361
Criterion Theatre, 110–111, 113
Crocker, Harry, 148, 211, 216, 220, 251, 273, 276–277, 319, 340, 369
Crosby, Bing, 267–268, 372
Crosby, Dixie, 268
Crowd, The, 208, 229
Crowd Roars, The, 344
Crowninsheid, Frank, 36, 41
Crowther, Bosley, 271
La Cuesta Encantada, 181, 186
Curtis, Tony, 361

"Daisy" (Marion Davies' nickname), 185, 365
Damita, Lili, 269
Damon Runyon Cancer Foundation, 368
Dancing Lady, 270
Daniels, Bebe, 184–186
Danton's Death, 305
Dark Star, The, 90, 377
d'Arrast, Henri, 251, 338
Dauphin, The, 129
David Harum, 82
Davies, Ethel, 21, 23, 26, 28, 35–36, 43, 97, 104, 149, 157, 188, 209, 211, 214, 235, 319, 325, 343, 357
Davies, Marion (Marion Cecilia Douras):
  birth and childhood, 19–32
  business ability, 71, 106, 127, 201, 368, 370
  death of, 371–373
  drinking problem, 8, 42, 58, 93–94, 207, 232, 268–269, 280, 297–298, 336, 369
  education, 30–34, 71–72
  enters films, 79–80
  family background, 5, 19–32, 87–88, 93–94
  first trip to Hollywood, 96–97
  marriage to Captain Horace Brown, xii, 339, 341–342
  meeting with Hearst, 44–45
    becomes his companion, 62–63
    ordeal of Hearst's death, 3–13
    saves him from financial collapse, 294–295
  Metro-Goldwyn-Mayer years, 169–280
    leaves Metro, 279–280
  philanthropies, 191–192 199, 255
  reaction to *Citizen Kane,* 317–318
  stage career, 12, 29, 32–57, 60–63, 69–71, 77–78
  voice problem, xi, 30, 41, 44, 72, 114, 225–226
  wealth and jewels, 43, 58, 65, 83, 87, 199, 237, 244, 258, 285, 367, 373
Davies, Reine (Lederer), 21, 22–26, 28–29, 31–33, 35, 49–50, 59, 68, 78–79, 92, 103, 108–110, 149, 157, 188, 211, 280, 303, 319, 343
Davies, Rose (nee Douras, also Van Cleve, Adlon), 5, 13, 18, 21, 23, 25, 27–29, 31, 34–35, 37, 93, 97, 149, 174–175, 188, 211, 214, 218, 221, 232, 235, 254, 303, 328, 337–339, 344, 354, 357–358, 361, 372
Davis, Ann, 12
Davis, Bette, 119, 298, 364
Davis, Luther, 368
Davis, Roger, 358
Davis, Sammy, Jr., 361
Dawn, Hazel, 33
Day and Strother Mortuary, 162
Dean, Jack, 300
Debs, Eugene, 37
de Cordoba, Pedro, 80
Deering, James, 49–51, 53
de la Falaise, Marquis, 227
Delaplanque, Roger, 218
del Rio, Dolores, 218, 269, 278

DeMille, Cecil B., xi, 82, 150, 161, 321, 344
Democratic party, the, x, 46, 95, 285, 370–371
Dempster, Carol, 121
Depression of 1929, the, 237, 243–244, 256, 258
Desert Inn (Palm Springs), 106, 368, 370
Deske's Grand Hotel (Bad Nauheim), 216
Deslys, Gaby, 42
Dietrich, Marlene, 201
di Frasso, Countess Dorothy, 187, 274, 289
Dillingham, Charles, 33, 39, 45
di Misurata, Count Volpi, 275
"Dirk de Rhonde," 173–174
di San Faustino, Princess Jane, 215
"Dolores" (of the Follies), 61, 84
Donen, Stanley, 361
D'Orsay, Fifi, 189, 248, 268–269, 354
Douras, Bernard J. ("Papa Ben"), 5, 19–31, 36, 38, 43, 50, 85, 88–89, 108, 172, 214, 233, 283, 343
Douras Building (New York City), 106, 368, 370
Douras, Catherine McCann, 20
Douras, Charles, 21, 24–25, 26, 30
Douras, Daniel, 20
Douras, Rose ("Mama Rose"), 5, 16, 19–32, 33, 35–39, 41, 43–44, 47, 49–50,56–61, 70–71, 79, 85, 87–88, 92–94, 97, 102, 105, 106, 108, 140–141, 145–146, 165, 188, 200, 209–211, 223, 233, 256, 343
Dove, Billie, 200, 202, 236, 259–261
Dressler, Marie, 117, 187, 199, 209, 234
Drown, Joseph, 369
Du Barry, Madame, 285
"Duc de Douras" (ship), 20
Duel in the Sun, 208
Duke, Angier, 42
Duke, Doris, 18, 42, 371
Dumbrille, Douglas, 259
Duncan, Mary, 253
Dunne, Irene, 272
du Pompadour, Madame, 94, 192
Durante, Jimmy, 228, 260, 361
Duveen, (Lord) Joseph, 165
Dwan, Allan, 82, 90, 207, 377

Easter Egg Hunt, The (Lamkin), 362–363
Eberson, John, 89
Eckener, Hugo, 273
Edison Company, 32, 156
Edison, Thomas Alva, 32
Edwards, Cliff ("Ukelele Ike"), 234, 238
Egyptian Theatre, 165
Eidlitz, Ernest, 132–134
Einstein, Albert, 154, 190
El Capitan Theatre (Hollywood), 320
Ellis, Diana, 236
El Morocco (New York City), 360
Emerson, John, 45, 63
Empire School of Acting, 71–72
Enchantment, 379
England, 107–108, 218, 274, 275, 295, 303, 319, 325

English, Kay (Kerry), 14, 18
Europa (S.S.), 278
Ever Since Eve, 285–287, 403–404
Everything I Have Is Yours, 270
Exploits of Elaine, The, 85
"Extra Life" (Brown), 344

FBO studios, 190
Fairbanks, Douglas, Jr., 235, 270
Fairbanks, Douglas, Sr., 18, 44–45, 78, 206, 361
Fair Coed, The, 157, 198, 203, 390
"Fairy House," 319
Fallon, William J., 132–134, 136–137, 147, 154
Farrell, Charlie, 342
Farrow, John, 298, 361
Faulkner, William, 118
Fazenda, Louise, 286
Federal Bureau of Revenue, 255
"Fely" (Lights of Old Broadway), 174
Ferber, Edna, 28, 96
Ferber, Nat, 131, 137
Ferris, E. D. (Dr.), 20
Fields, Dorothy, 270
Fields, W. C., 62, 64, 219
Films in Review, 157
First National Pictures, 89, 156, 185
Fitzgerald, F. Scott, 118, 249
Fitzgerald, Zelda, 138
Fitzmaurice, Diana, 319, 337–338
Fitzmaurice, George, 319, 338
Five and Ten, 209, 253–254, 266, 397–398
Five O'Clock Girl, 250
Flagg, James Montgomery, 45
Flagler, Henry, 51
Flannery, William, 176, 189
Fleishman, Mrs. Charles, 129–130
Flink, Stanley, 15, 207, 362
Floradora Girl, The, 245, 395–396
Florence, Italy, 215
Flying Down to Rio, 269
Foley, Thomas ("Big Tom"), 68–69, 131, 136
Follies, Ziegfeld (see Ziegfeld Follies)
Fontanne, Lynn, 279
Force, Mrs. Juliana, 274–275
Ford, Frank, 156
Ford, Glenn, 372
Ford, John, 156
Forde, Hal, 66
Fortune Magazine, 291
Foundling, The (Spellman), 115
Fowler, Gene, 132–134
Fox Studios, 269
Fox theaters, 90
Fox, William, 82
Fragonard (French painter), 3, 361
France, 218–221, 251, 273, 305, 338
Franco, Generalissimo, 304–305
Franklin, Benjamin, 20
Franklin, Sidney, 157, 174, 203, 207, 249, 271, 278–279, 281
Frankovitch, Mike, 361
Franks, Bobby (Murder), 146–147
Frederick, Pauline, 231
Frederick the Great, 235
Free Soul, A, 250, 257
Freed, Arthur, 267
Freeport, L. I., 103, 108
French and Company, 164

Frisco, Joe, 244
Frohman, Charles, 33
Front Page, The, 233
Fuller & McGee, 131–132
Fulton, Robert, 123
Furness, Viscountess Thelma, 349

Gable, Clark, 202, 249, 257, 259, 264, 284, 370
"Gables, The," 245, 320
Gabor, Zsa Zsa, 351
Gabriel Over the White House, 82
Galsworthy, John, 86
Gandhi, Mahatma, 218
"Gandhi" (dachshund), 217–218, 275, 324–326, 352
Garbo, Greta, ix, 82, 104, 119, 173, 186, 199, 204, 212, 228, 259, 278, 318, 331, 344
Gardner, Ava, 361
Garner, John Nance, 256–257, 372
Gay Illiterate, The, 314
Gaynor, Janet, xi
Gentlemen Prefer Blondes, 300
George, David Lloyd, 222
George W. Lederer Filmotions, Inc., 78
Germany, 46, 68, 131, 216, 223, 238, 270–271, 275–278, 302, 305, 323, 326
Getting Mary Married, 87, 90, 117, 377
Giannini, L. M., 17
Gibson, Hoot, 186
"Gigi," 65
Gilbert, John, 184, 202, 227, 234, 331, 361
Girl from Paris, The, 55
Gish, Lillian, ix, 78, 119, 130, 148, 165, 199, 209, 212, 236
Gish sisters, 130
Glad, Gladys, 39
Glasgow, Ida Cowan (Dr.), 161
Glendinning, Ernest, 111
Glendinning, Marie, 7, 8, 10, 13, 18, 24, 34, 36, 38, 44, 59, 111, 174, 261, 303, 333, 334, 354, 355
Glyn, Elinor, 129, 157, 159, 184, 185, 187, 202, 222
Godsol, Frank Joseph, 126
Goetz, Milton, 329
Going Hollywood, x, 267, 269–270, 400
Gold Rush,The, 151, 153, 166, 209, 320
Goldwater, Barry, 372
Goldwyn Company, 126, 134, 171
Goldwyn, Frances (Mrs. Samuel), 351
Goldwyn, Samuel, 82, 126, 185, 351
Good Samaritan Hospital (Los Angeles), 280
Goodman, Daniel Carson, 121, 150, 157, 158
Gorney, Jay, 244
Gortatowsky, Jacob D., 5, 12, 331, 336–337
Goudal, Jetta, 228
Goulding, Edmund, x, 259, 281
Grace, Mary, 191, 244
Graf Zeppelin, 223, 234, 273
Graham, Sheila, 360–361
Gramercy Park (New York City), 22–23, 27–28
Grand Hotel, 259
Grant, Faith, 350

Grauman's Chinese Theatre, 233
Gray, Lawrence, 238, 245, 282, 372
Great Mouthpiece, The, 132–134
Greed, 83
Green Goddess, The, 123
Greuze (French painter), 201, 361
Grey, Lita (Chaplin), 153, 162, 165
Griffith, D. W., 80, 82–84, 109, 121, 130, 149, 156, 208, 272, 305
Groedel, Dr. Heinz, 216–217, 289
Groody, Louise (McGee), 132
Guinan, Texas, 201
"Guinevere," 56, 285
"Gwendolyn," 101
Gwynn, Nell, 116

Haines, William, 183, 187, 211, 225, 229, 230, 261, 270, 331, 359
Hale, Georgia, 153
Hall, Mordaunt, 234, 238
Hallelujah, 208
Hamlet, 236
Hampton, Benjamin B., 233
Hanes, John W., 42–43, 291
Hanfstaengl, Ernst ("Putzi"), 276–277
Harburg, Yip, 243–244
Harding, Ann, 264–265
Harding, Lyn, 111
Harding, Warren (Pres.), 37, 95, 103
Hard Times (Terkel), 243–244
Harlem film studio, 89, 103, 113, 123–124, 128
Harlow, Jean, 259
Hart, Lorenz, 270
Hart, William S., 78, 156, 161
Harvard University, 54
Hatrick, Edgar, 294
Hay, Lady Drummond, 234
Hays, Will H., 110, 111
Hays Office (Production Code Authority), 110, 147
Hayward, Lily, 149
Head, Alice E., 168, 213–215, 220–221, 265, 290
Hearst, David Whitmire (born Elbert W.), 6, 12, 48
Hearst, George (father of W.R. Hearst), 46–47, 172, 182
Hearst, George (son of W.R. Hearst), 6, 12, 14, 56, 273, 302–303, 364–365, 372
Hearst, Gretchen (Mrs. John R.), 214, 216, 273
Hearst, John Randolph, 6, 12, 16, 172, 214, 273, 284
Hearst, John Randolph, Jr. ("Bunky"), 172
Hearst, Millicent Willson, 6, 9, 14, 16–17, 23, 28, 41, 45, 48, 52, 54–57, 68, 79, 91–92, 94, 96–97, 103, 106–110, 113, 121–122, 127, 131, 134, 137, 139–140, 163, 166, 172, 182, 189, 191, 201, 214, 222, 235, 251, 294–295, 297, 365
Hearst, Phoebe Apperson, 4, 46–47, 54–56, 106–107, 124, 167, 182, 200, 215, 243, 245, 333
Hearst, Randolph Apperson, 6, 12, 48, 335

Hearst, William Randolph, ix–xi, 4–
19, 21, 40, 48–49, 287–288, 332,
353–354, 362–364
  appearance, 127–128
  aviation enthusiast, 301–302
  birthday celebrations, 283, 298,
332–333
  castle complex, 68, 83
  death and burial, 3–19, 293, 334,
337–339, 363
  devotion and love for Marion
Davies, 43, 58–59, 61–65, 68–
69, 81, 97–98, 146, 199–200,
202, 284
  dogs, 324–325
  early life, 46–47, 54
  European trips, 211–223, 273–278
  family background, 5–7, 46–47
  family relationships, 48, 52–57, 67–
69, 103, 106–108, 122, 127,
139, 185, 189
  financial status, 83, 122–123,
244, 265–266, 291–297, 299,
302
  film-making, ix, 78–85, 99–104,
109–120, 124–137, 149–150,
250, 259, 266–267, 271, 281
  first meeting with Marion Davies,
45–48
  health, 73, 94, 122, 185, 216–217,
327–328, 330–339
  marriage to Millicent Willson, 55–
57;
    (See also Hearst, Millicent
Willson)
  newspaper publishing, 57, 72, 91,
97, 99–100, 108–109, 120–121,
204–205, 220–221, 289–293,
299, 331–332, 333–334, 358
  personality, 15–16, 46, 53–54,
57–58
  political interests, x, 54, 68–69, 73,
103, 120–122, 127, 131
  will and trust agreement, 332–335
Hearst, William Randolph, Jr., 6–7,
12, 211, 216, 273, 294, 314, 333,
364–366
Hearst, Mrs. William Randolph, Jr.,
273
Hearst Corporation, 5, 331–332, 334–
337, 339
Hearst-Metrotone News, 173, 244
Hearst Organization, The, 71, 136–137,
146
Hearst press, 116, 130, 167, 169, 235,
285, 333
Hearst's "bread line," 243–244
Heartbreak House, 305
Heart of Darkness, 306
Hearts Divided, 282, 402
Hecht, Ben, 185, 233, 247, 306, 308,
322
Hecht, Mrs. Rose, 171
Heflin, Thomas (Sen.), 204
Held, Anna, 248
"Helen" (dachshund), 324–325
"Helena" (dachshund), 11, 13, 218
Henderson, Dell, 229
Henie, Sonja, 18, 349, 351
Henry, Charlotte, 269
Henry VIII, 60, 111–113, 116
Hepburn, Katharine, 71–72, 203, 259

Her Cardboard Lover, 392
Herald and Express, 13
Herald, New York, 55
Herbert, Victor, 106, 128
Herod, King, 284
Herrick, Lee, 34
Heston, Charlton, 361
High, Wide and Handsome, 343
Hill, George, 149, 151–152
Hiller, Wendy, 286
Hirsch, Oscar (and Mrs.), 108–109
His Girl Friday, 11
History of the American Film
Industry, 233
Hitler, Adolf, 276–278, 299, 302
Hohenzollern dynasty, 69
Hokinson, Helen, 322
Holland, Cecil, 264
Hollywood, 28, 95–103, 109–110, 134,
138–142, 145–149, 162, 163, 171,
191, 197, 208, 213, 229, 247, 259,
262, 267–269, 270, 281, 285, 300,
305, 314, 320–321, 329, 340, 353,
359, 361, 363–365
Hollywood Hotel, 97
Hollywood Memorial Park, 26, 211
Hollywood Reporter, The, 307, 321
Hollywood Revue (of 1929), 234, 238,
270, 394
Homestake Mine, 244
Honeycomb, The (St. Johns), 137
Hoover, Herbert C. (Pres.), 17, 190,
256, 259, 372
Hope diamond, 254
Hopper, Hedda, 3, 14, 151, 211, 314,
334–335, 337, 343, 355–357, 363,
369
Horan, Harold, 221
Horne, Lena, 361
Horton, Edward Everett, 282
Hotel Crillon, 213, 220
Hotel Los Flamingos (Acapulco),
303
Howard, Leslie, 253–254, 259
Howard, Mrs. Leslie, 254
Howard, Roy, 17
Howey, Walter, 222–223, 295–296
Hubbard, Lucien, 71
Huberth, Martin, 5, 12, 333
Huff, Jackie, 151
Hughes, Howard, 186, 200, 321
Huntington Memorial Hospital, 370
Hurst, Fannie, 209, 253
Huston, Walter, 82, 225, 259
Hutchens, Robert, 200–201
Hutton, Barbara, 252–253, 290
Huxley, Aldous, 5, 8, 311, 325
Hylan, John F., 69, 88, 124, 126, 175

Idiot's Delight, 279
I Gave Her That, 154
I.M.P. Company, 155
I Am a Fugitive from a Chain Gang,
259
Ile de France, 211
Ince, John, 158
Ince, Nell (Mrs. Thomas), 155, 160,
161
Ince, Ralph, 158
Ince, Thomas Harper, 15, 82, 126, 155–
162, 163, 171, 363, 366
"Inceville," 156

In Old Chicago, 344
Insull, Samuel, 40
Insull, Mrs, Samuel, 314–315
International Films, 80
"In the News," 324–325
Intolerance, 80, 208
Irving, Henry, 236
It (Glyn), 188
It Could Never Have Happened, 168
It's a Wise Child, 213, 266, 397

Jack-Knife Man, 208
James, Henry, 22
"Jane Packard," 66
Janice Meredith (film), 62, 130–131, 384
Janis, Elsie, 36, 39–40,
Jazz Singer, The, 223
"Jennifer Rarick," 253
"Jerry" (*chimpanzee*), 187
Jessel, George, 369
Johnson, Hiram (Sen.), 95
Johnstone, Justine, 45, 64, 66, 77, 84
Jolson, Al, 152, 154, 223–224
Jones, John Paul, 20
Joyce, Peggy Hopkins, 39, 215
Judels, Charles, 121
Julius Caesar, 305
Jungleland, 352
"Junior" (monkey), 351–352
Just You, Just Me, 238

Kael, Pauline, 307, 373
Kalmar, Bert, 250
Kane, Eddie, 184, 195, 251, 340
"Katzenjammer Kids," 28
Kaufman, Gordon, 329
Kaufman, George S., 269, 306
Keaton, Buster, 117, 234, 305
"Keely cure," 297
Keith, Ian, 156
Keith-Orpheum circuit (Vaudeville), 23
Kelly, Patsy, 269
Kempley, Chester C., 161
Kendall, Mr. & Mrs. Messmore, 364
Kennedy, Eunice (Shriver), 367
Kennedy, Jacqueline Bouvier (Mrs. John F.), 367
Kennedy, John F. (Pres.), 319–320, 367, 370–371
Kennedy, Joseph P. (Ambassador), 189, 295, 319–320, 367, 370–372
Kennedy, Patricia (Lawford), 349, 367
Kennedy, Robert F., 319–320, 370
Kennedy, Mrs. Rose, 319–320
Kennington, Tom, 350, 356
Kent, Atwater, 206
Kern, Jerome, 66
Kerry, Norman, 14, 18
Kilgour, Joseph, 80
King, Charles, 250
King, Henry, 156
King of Siam, 190, 200
Kingsley, Grace, 153
Kismet, 71, 368
Knoblock, Edward, 368
Kono, 159
Korda, Alexander, 120
Kosloff, Theodore (and the Kosloff School of Ballet), 31–32, 72, 157, 246

Kress, Samuel, 49
Kubla Khan, 311
Kurosawa, 307

"Lady Guinevere," 56, 285
La Follette, Robert (Sen.), 204
Lake, Arthur, 175, 327, 337, 340, 342
Lake, Arthur Patrick, 13, 337
Lake Havasu, Arizona, 251
Lake, Marion Rose, 337
Lake, Patricia (nee Van Cleve), xii, 13, 18, 92, 137, 174, 175, 232, 234–235, 320, 328, 337, 340, 342, 372
Lake Placid, New York, 131
Lamb, Thomas W., 89
Lamkin, Speed, 18, 166, 354, 362–363
Landon, Alf (Gov.), 285
Lane, Burton, 270
La Rocque, Rod, 194
Last Tycoon, The (a novel), 118
Las Vegas, 339, 341
Laughton, Charles, 112, 271,
Laurel (Stan) and Hardy (Oliver), 234
Lawford, Lady, 349
Lawford, Peter, 349, 367
Lawrence, James, 301
League of Nations, the, 103
Le Baron, William, 104
Le Bourget Airfield (Paris), 195
Lederer, Charles, 5, 9–13, 18, 20, 26, 33, 70–71, 88, 103, 137, 159, 171, 176, 185, 192, 202, 214, 215–216, 219, 245, 247, 256, 260, 305–307, 313–314, 320, 322–323, 328, 332, 337, 340, 342, 354, 363, 368, 372
Lederer, George, 25–26, 29, 31, 33, 78–80
Lederer, George, Jr., 26
Lederer, Maitland, 26, 28–29, 70
Lederer, Pepi, 35, 72, 88, 103, 137, 157, 188, 214, 270, 273, 275, 280, 302, 343
Lee, Davey, 224
Lely, Sir Peter, 118
Lenin, Vladimir Ilyich (Nikolai), 261
Leonard, Robert Z., x, 253
Leopold, Nathan, 147
LeRoy, Mervyn, *x*, 207, 281, 372
Leslie, George, 55
Lewis, C. Day, 307
Lewis, Jerry, 361
Lexington Road Mansion, 140–141, 145, 148, 175, 210, 303, 319, 328, 330, 350
Lido, the (Venice), 215, 290
"*Life* Goes to a Party," 361
Life Magazine, 361
Lights Club, The, 103
Lights of Old Broadway, 173, 188, 203, 208, 234, 386
Lilac Time, 126
Lindbergh, Charles A., 190, 195–198, 254
Lindner, Clarence, 79
Lippmann, Walter, 138
"Little Journeys," 71
Little Nell's Tobacco, 155
Little Old New York, 82, 122–125, 157, 173, 191, 202–203, 208, 383

Little White Cloud That Cried, The, 362
Livingston, Margaret, 160
"Liza Doolittle," 287
Lloyd, Harold, 78, 236
Lodge, Henry Cabot, 372
Loeb, Richard, 147
Loew, Marcus, 126
Loew theater circuit, 90, 246, 269
Logan, Jacqueline, 156
Lombard, Carole, 157, 202
London, 213, 220–221, 237, 251, 273–275, 290, 302, 316
London Bridge, 251
Loos, Anita, xii, 7, 22, 41, 44, 63, 71, 87, 139, 153, 184, 206, 214, 218, 258, 266, 353
Loper, Don, 360, 367
Loren, Sophia, 370
Los Angeles, 235, 243, 280, 300, 319, 327–329, 370
Los Angeles County Art Museum, xii, 231
Los Angeles Examiner, 97, 129, 169, 303, 350
Los Angeles Herald, 97, 106, 108
Los Angeles *Herald & Express,* 355
Los Angeles *Mirror,* 356
Los Angeles Times, 161, 212, 265, 366
Louis XI, 128
Louis XII, 111
Louis XIV, 284
Louis XV, 94
Love Story, 224
Lowe, Edmund, 236
"Lucy," 373
Lunt, Alfred, 279
Lynch, "Teddy," 370
Lyon, Ben, 184–187
Lyons, Leonard, 320

MacArthur, Charles, 247, 250, 306
MacArthur, Gen. Douglas, 259, 326, 371
Macbeth, 312, 315
Mackaill, Dorothy, 18, 47, 153, 155, 184, 220, 273, 275–276, 300–301, 353
MacKay, Henry S., Jr., 335
Madame Bovary, 278
Madame Sans Gêne, 227
Maeterlinck, Maurice, 34–35
Magnificent Ambersons, The, 312
Magnin, I, (dress shop), 210, 214
Maine (U.S. Navy), 19
Major, Charles, 128
"Mamie Smith," 149, 151
Mammy, 152
Manchester (U.S.S.), 332
Mankiewicz, Herman, 185, 247, 266, 306–308, 311, 314–315
Mankiewicz, Joe, 266
Mankiewicz, Sara (Mrs. Herman), 306, 314–315
Manners, J. Hartley, 266
Maraini, Antonio, 274
Marianne, 82, 237–239, 257, 258, 394–395
Marie Antoinette, 117, 249, 250, 278–279, 281
Marion Davies Building (New York City), 106, 368, 370

Marion Davies Children's Clinic, 14, 70, 191, 199, 244, 258, 327, 363, 369
Marion Davies Foundation, 258, 359
Marion Davies March, 106
Marion Davies Orchestra, 104, 152, 268
Marion, Frances, 44, 50, 99–101, 122, 126–127, 149, 174, 206, 211, 258, 261–263, 266, 267, 292, 333, 334
Markey, Gene, 261
Marx, Harpo, 215, 266
Mary of Burgundy (Princess), 128
"Mary Tudor," 111, 116
"Matt Dillon," 373
Maximilian (Prince), 129
Maxwell, Elsa, 103
Mayer, Louis B., x, 17, 130, 150, 171, 173, 187–188, 197, 203, 212, 225, 227, 230, 235, 247, 250, 255, 264, 276, 279–280, 317, 321, 331, 369
Mayer, Margaret, 172
Mayfair Club (New York City), 108
McAlpin Hotel (New York City), 132
McClintic, Judge, 136
McCloud River, 136, 245, 304, 320, 324
McCormick, Harold, 314
McCormick, Col. Robert ("Bertie"), 17, 40, 313
McHugh, Charles, 173
McHugh, Jimmy, 270
McKinley, William (Pres.), 220
McLaglen, Victor, 236
McLean, Edward Beale, 254, 338
McLean, Evalyn Walsh, 254
McPeake, James Y., 107, 221
McPherson, Aimee Semple ("Sister"), 175–176
M'divani, Alexis (Prince), 290
M'divani, David (Prince), 37
Means, Gaston B., 254
"Melanie," 162
Mellon, Andrew, 49, 190
Memphis (U.S. cruiser), 95
Menjou, Adolphe, 267
Menjou, Mrs. Katherine, 261, 267
Mercury Theatre, 305
Merrick, George, 50
"Merry Maidens, The," 55
Merry Wives of Gotham, 173
Metro Company, 126, 134
Metro-Goldwyn-Mayer, 83, 117, 119, 145, 148–150, 156, 168, 172, 173, 199, 203, 208, 224, 226–227, 229, 237, 246, 250, 253, 258–259, 261, 264, 267, 272, 278–281, 286, 289, 303, 331, 338
Metropolitan Opera House (New York City), 113, 191, 311
Mexico, 105–106, 134, 136, 162, 204–205, 244, 248, 294, 302–303, 304, 370
Milk Fund (New York City), 191
Miller Brothers 101 Ranch (Wild West Show), 156
Miller, Marilyn, 34, 246–247
Minter, Mary Miles, 109
Mix, Tom, 78, 284
Mocambo Night Club (Hollywood), 359

Monroe, Marilyn, 118–119, 121, 361, 369
Montgomery, Robert, 260, 264, 286
Montmartre Cafe (Hollywood), 141, 153
Moore, Alexander (Ambassador), 211
Moore, Colleen, xi, 126, 150, 212, 235
Moore, Matt, 80
Moore, Victor, 108
Moran, Polly, 117, 230
Morgan, Frank, 344
Morgan, Helen, 216
Morgan, Julia, 68, 124, 166, 245
Morrison, Charles, 359–362
Morrison, Marilyn, 359–362
Mother Courage (Brecht), 323
Mother Maginn, 99
Motion Picture Relief Fund, 265
Mountbatten family, 56, 222
Mountbatten, Lord Louis, 190, 275
Mouser, Floretta, 11–12, 350–351
Moving Picture World, The (periodical), 78
Mowrer, Emma, 27
Muni, Paul, 259
Murphy, Charles ("Boss"), 68
Murray, Anita, 214
Murray, James, 229
Murray, Mae, 93, 209
Murray, Mrs. Sadie, 214
Music in the Air, 278
Mussolini, Benito, 275
Mutual Company, 156
Mutual Weekly Company, 208
Mysteries of Myra, The, 85

Nagel, Conrad, 175, 203
Napoleon, 236, 282
Nast, Condé, 44
"National Magazine Company," 168
National Socialism, 277
Navy League, 359, 371
Nazis, the, 277–278, 302, 303, 305
Negri, Pola, 129, 153, 156, 193–194
    201, 209, 212, 227–228, 236, 278
Netcher, Townsend, 266
Newsweek Magazine, 313, 335
New York *American*, 48, 64, 89, 102,
    132–134, 136–137, 299
New York City, 19–95, 102–105, 131–
    133, 175–177, 233, 243, 294–299,
    316, 373
New York Criminal Court, 131–132
New York Daily News, 110, 153, 238, 296
New York Film Festival, 231
New York *Herald*, 110, 129
New York *Herald Tribune*, 239, 243
New York *Journal*, 299
New York *Journal–American*, 299
New York *Mirror*, 108–109, 302
New York *Morning Journal*, 19
New York Telegram, 110
New York Telegraph, 114
New York Times, The, 17, 66, 129–
    131, 212, 234, 238, 245, 253, 260,
    314–315
New York Tribune, 129
New Yorker Magazine, 307, 322
Neylan, John Francis, 164, 290–293, 334

Niblo, Fred, 156
19th International Biennial Art Exhibition (Venice), 274
Nixon, Richard M., 372
Nolan, Dr. Frank, 342
No, No, Nanette, 132
Normand, Mabel, 110, 126, 150, 231, 361
Norris, George (Sen.), 204
Norris, William, 111
Norvell, Mr. & Mrs. Anthony, 349
Not So Dumb, 245, 395
Novarro, Ramon, 235

O'Bannion, Dion, 146
Obregón, Alvaro (Pres.), 105
O'Brien, Pat, 82
Ocean House (*see* Beach House at Santa Monica)
O'Donnell, Rev. Father John, 303, 369, 372
Of Human Bondage, 254
Oh Boy, 66
Oil for the Lamps of China, 82
Olcott, Sidney, 123
Olympic, The (steamship), 108, 110
Oneida, The, 155, 157–163
O'Neill, Eugene, 166
On Trial, 231
Operator 13, 202, 271–272, 284, 289, 400–401
Oppenheimer, George, 269
O'Reilly, L. J., 135
Orienta Point (Mamaroneck, N.Y.), 84
Orphans of the Storm, 130
Orry-Kelly, 358
O'Sullivan, Maureen, 298
Our Big Love Scene, 267
Owen, Seena, 157

Page, Anita, 235
Page Miss Glory, 120, 281–282, 286, 401–402
Palace Hotel (San Francisco), 122, 135, 167
Palm Beach, 49–53, 103
Palm Springs, 342, 354, 368, 370
Pantages, Carmen (Considine), 14, 261, 319, 324, 333, 359
Pantages, Lloyd, 14, 215, 218, 251, 261, 313, 319
Paramount Pictures, 83–84, 89, 109, 119, 156, 193, 227, 259
Paramount Theatre (New York City), 360
Paris, 213, 218, 290
Parker, Dorothy, 41, 118, 185, 247, 306
Parsons, Harriet, 114–115, 140
Parsons, Louella O., 3, 14–15, 18, 114–
    116, 135, 140–141, 151, 157, 159,
    186, 195–197, 198, 199, 211, 262–
    264, 305, 314, 317, 355, 361
Pascal, Gabriel, 287
Past Imperfect (Chase), 139, 206–207
Patents Trust, 155
Pathé Studios, 80
"Pat O'Day," 122–123
"Patricia Pepoire," 231
Patsy, The, x, 119, 157, 203–204, 208,
    211, 213, 226, 231, 238, 271, 391

Patterson, Eleanor Medill "Cissy,"
    200–201, 290, 296
Patterson family, 313
Paul, Maury H. Biddle ("Cholly
    Knickerbocker"), 214, 221, 224
Pauley, Ed, 372
Payne, Philip, 302
Payson, Liz Whitney, 367
Pearl Harbor, 321
Peck, Orrin, 71, 96–97, 105
"Peggy Pepper," 227, 229
Pegler, Westbrook, 299, 336
Peg O'My Heart, x, 157, 250, 266–267,
    399–400
Pennington, Ann, 51, 64, 77
Pennoyer family, 222
Percy, Eileen (Ruby), 18, 45, 97, 153,
    184, 195, 220, 223, 260, 261, 273,
    283, 319, 354
Perils of Pauline, The, 85
"Peter Gunn," 373
Peters, William Frederick, 129
"Phoebe Throssel," 195, 279
Photoplay Magazine, 86, 113
Pickfair, 176, 367
Pickford, Jack, 110
Pickford, Mary, ix, 3, 14, 18, 78–79,
    83, 102, 110, 118–119, 128, 140,
    147, 150, 172, 198, 200, 206, 278,
    289, 337, 342, 354, 355, 367, 369,
    371
Pictorial Review, 302
Pidgeon, Walter, 44
Pierce Brothers Mortuary (Beverly
    Hills), 12, 210–211
Pinchot, Rosamund, 72
Pink Lady, The, 25–26, 33
Plattsburg, New York, 131
Plunket family, 222, 300–301
Plunket, Lady Dorothy, 300–301, 319
Plunket, Lord (Terence Conyngham),
    300–301, 319
Pogany, Willy, 245
Polly of the Circus, 249, 257, 258–259,
    266, 398
Polly Preferred, 227
Porter, Cole, 215
Powell, Dick, 82, 282, 372
Powell, William, 111
Power and the Glory, The, 320
Powers, Tessie, 54–55, 96
Pretty Girl Is Like a Melody, A, 84
Prevost, Marie, 84
Prince of Wales (Edward VIII, David
    Windsor), 187, 199–200
Princess Theatre, 66
Pringle, Aileen, 18, 278, 353
Prinzmetal, Myron (Dr.), 11
Private Life of Henry VIII, The, 112
Production Code Authority (Hays
    Office), 147, 311
H. M. Pulham, Esq., 208
Pygmalion, 287

Quality Street, 117, 157, 195, 198, 202–
    203, 249, 279, 287, 390
Queen Elizabeth (a film), 33
Queen Kelly, 82

RKO Pictures, 190, 305, 307, 314, 317,
    321

RKO Theater circuit, 269
Racquet Club, The (Palm Springs),
    342
Radio City Music Hall, 269, 286
Rain, 259
Rains, Claude, 282
Rapf, Harry, 198, 261
Rappe, Virginia, 109
Rashomon, 307
Rave, 81
Ray, Charles, 156
Ray, Johnny, 360
Red Dust, 259
Red Mill, The, 191, 201, 203, 208,
    388
Red Robe, The, 120
Reed, Luther, 104
Reid, Mrs. Ogden, 243
Reid, Wallace, 110, 147
Reilly, Charles A., 20, 25
Reilly, Mrs. Charles A., 20, 26, 29
Reith, Joseph, 327–328
Renaissance, the, 181
Rendigs, Charles, 132, 136
Republican party, the, 46, 95, 256, 285,
    371
Restless Sex, The, 100, 117, 379
"Rev. Davidson," 259
Revolutionary War, 130
Rhineland, the, 302
Rice, Elmer, 259
Rich, Irene, 253
Richie, John B., 157
Rin Tin Tin, 78
Ritz Hotel (New York City), 168
Ritz Tower Hotel (New York City),
    223, 224, 290, 295
"River House," 245
Riverside Drive mansion (New York
    City), 85, 88, 91, 96, 102, 177
Rivolie Theatre (New York City), 89,
    227
Rockefeller, Abby, 287, 297
Rockefeller family, 56, 287
Rockefeller, Winthrop, 287
Rockefeller, Mrs. Winthrop "Bobo,"
    287
Rodgers, Richard, 270
Rogers, Buddy, 342, 355, 367, 372
Rogers, Ginger, 269
Rogers, Will, 269
Romanoff, "Prince" Mike, 365
Romanoff's Restaurant (Beverly Hills),
    330, 364–365
Roman Scandals, 269
Roosevelt, Eleanor (Mrs. Franklin D.),
    299, 332, 336
Roosevelt, Franklin D. (Pres.), x,
    245, 256–257, 265, 285, 299, 319–
    320
Roosevelt, Theodore, 120
Rosalie, 344
Rosenberg, Dr. Alfred, 278
Rubens, Alma, 80–81, 89, 113, 120–121,
    147, 171
Rubin, Benny, 238
Ruby, Harry, 250, 283, 319
Ruggles, Charlie, 282
Runaway, Romany, 80, 82, 84, 90,
    231, 375

St. Augustine's Church (Culver City), 303
St. Clair, "Pickles," 45, 48
St. Donat's Castle, 56, 168–169, 221–222, 251, 265, 275, 293, 299, 302, 350, 364
St. Johns, Adela Rogers, 16, 137, 160–161, 233, 284
Sally, 246
Sanderson, Sybil, 54
Sands Point, Long Island, 251
San Francisco Bulletin, 164
San Francisco Examiner, 79, 84, 97
"Sanger Circus," 25, 103
San Simeon, ix, 4–5, 10, 13, 15, 28, 40, 56, 67, 94–99, 101–102, 110, 118, 124–125, 133–135, 139, 148–149, 151, 163, 167, 176, 181–188, 189–190, 194–195, 198, 200–202, 218, 222, 228, 235, 243–245, 247–248, 251–252, 258, 260–265, 267, 270–271, 280, 282, 283, 291–292, 293, 296, 299–301, 307, 311, 315–317, 318, 322–323, 325, 328–330, 334, 350–351, 354, 364, 368
Santa Barbara, 98–99
Santa Maria (Calif.), 97, 301
Santa Monica (see Beach House at Santa Monica)
Santayana, George, 247
Saratoga Springs, 49
Sargent School, 71
Saunderson, Mr. & Mrs. Alexander, 349
Savoy Hotel (London), 107, 220–221, 274
Scarface, 259
Schaefer, George J., 317
Schenck, Joseph, 17, 33, 63
Schenck, Nicholas, 277
Screen Writer's Guild, 308
Seattle Post-Intelligencer, 285
Sebastian's General Store, 98
"Second Avenue Gang," 27, 28
Selwyn, Ruth, 277
Selznick, David O., 259
Selznick, Lewis, 17, 78, 82
Sennett, Mack, 156, 227, 230
"Seymour, Jane," 60, 63
Shakespeare, William, 262
"Sharp, Becky," 21
Shaw, Charlotte, 261–265
Shaw, George Bernard, 56, 152, 183, 190, 222, 261–265, 287, 362
Shaw, Oscar, 238
Shearer, Douglas, 226
Shearer, Norma (Thalberg), 115, 117, 148, 198–199, 203, 212, 226, 234, 249–250, 257, 261, 266, 271, 279, 281
Shearn, Clarence, 299
Sheraton-Park Hotel (Washington, D.C.), 371
Sherwood, Robert E., 129, 269
Shields, Jimmy, 331, 359
Shindler Private Police, 343
Shipmates Forever, 82, 282
Shirley, Anne (Lederer), 10, 13, 337
Shore, Dinah, 361
Shoulder Arms, 82

Showboat, 96
Show People, x, 82, 119, 157, 190, 209, 225, 227, 231, 267, 271, 287, 300, 307, 392–393
Shriver, Sargent, 367
Shulsinger, Rose, 104, 114
Sills, Milton, 129
Simmons, Jean, 261
Sinatra, Frank, 366–367
Singing Fool, The, 223, 224
Singing in the Rain, 234
Skelton, Red, 361
Smiler with a Knife, The, 307
Smith, Alfred E., 68–69, 103, 122, 127, 131, 285, 299
So Big, 96
"Song of the River, The," 304
Sonny Boy, 224
Sotheby's (auction gallery), 203
Soule, Sen. Frank, 54
Soule, Katherine, 54
Spanish-American War, 19, 66
Spanish Civil War, 304–305
Spanish Falangists, 304
Spellman, Francis Cardinal, 115
Spirit of St. Louis, 196
Spreckels, Kay, 14, 18, 333, 337, 351, 355, 364–365, 370
Squaw Man, The, 156
Squibb Building (New York City), 370
Stallings, Laurence, 226, 238
Stanley, Forrest, 112
Statler Hotel (Berlin), 277
Steeger, Julius, 89
Stone, Fred, 35, 37
Stop! Look! Listen!, 45, 48
Stork Club (New York City), 360
Stradling family, 222
Strange Interlude, 117
Stranger in Paradise, 368
Street Scene, 208, 259
Strickling, Howard, 372
Sturges, Preston, 320
Styka, Tade, 274–275
Sulzberger, Arthur Hays, 17
Sulzer's Harlem River Park Casino (New York City), 85
Sumac, Yma, 361
Sunday (a play and movie), 78
Sunny, 246
Sunset Boulevard, 278, 318
"Susan Alexander," x, 207, 311–318
Svengali, 92
Swanberg, W. A., 57, 105, 293
Swanson, Gloria, 78, 84, 104, 156, 190, 212, 227, 230, 278, 318

Taka, 175
Talking pictures, 218, 223, 225–226, 238
Talmadge, Constance (Netcher), 7, 13, 18, 41, 63, 71, 108, 129, 152, 184, 228, 264, 266, 284, 319, 334, 354
Talmadge, Natalie, 7, 41
Talmadge, Norma, 7, 41, 63, 78, 119, 129, 198, 361, 369
Tammany Hall (New York City), 24, 68
Tashman, Lilyan, 38–39, 64, 77
Taylor, Estelle, 260
Taylor, Frank E., 166

Taylor, Laurette, 266
Taylor, William Desmond, 109, 231
Tazelaar, Marguerite, 239
Teapot Dome Scandal, 136
Tearle, Conway, 93
Tebbel, John, 159, 312–313
Technicolor, 174, 234, 246
Tell It to the Marines, 229
"Tell Me, Pretty Maiden," 246
Temptation, 267
Terkel, Studs, 243
Terry, Ellen, 263
Thackeray, William Makepeace, 21
Thalberg, Irving, x, 7, 17, 117–119,
    150, 173, 198–199, 212, 225, 227,
    233, 249, 250, 259, 261, 266, 271,
    278–279, 281
Theatre Owners of America, 114
Theodora Goes Wild, 272
There Goes My Heart, 344
*There's A Light in Your Eyes, Sweet-
    heart Darling,* 266
Thin Man, The, 111
Thirer, Irene, 238
This Is My Beloved, 368
Thomas, Olive, 110
Thompson, Fred, 101, 250
Three Weeks (Glyn), 188
Tibbett, Grace, 340–341
Tibbett, Lawrence, 340
Tiffany's, 47, 63, 65, 103, 176, 193,
    367
Tillie The Toiler, 389
Time Magazine, 335, 362
Todd, Thelma, 269
Toledo Blade (newspaper), 40
Tombs, The, 133
Too Much Harmony, 267
Torrent, The, 173
Tracy, Spencer, 320
Trail of '98, The, 157, 218
Treacher, Arthur, 282
Tree Is a Tree, A, 91
Trial of Mary Dugan, The, 279
Triangle Corporation, 126, 156
Trilby, 92
Truman, Harry S (Pres.), 372
Turn in the Road, The, 208
Twentieth Century, 250
Twenty-One Restaurant (New York
    City), 360

Underhill, Harriette, 129
Unger, Gladys, 238
United Artists Studio, 148, 150, 157
University of California, 171, 327
University of California Medical
    Center, 369
Urban, Gretl, 104–105, 113
Urban, Josef, 104–105, 113, 123–125
"Uriah Heep," 236

Valentino, Rudolph, 10, 141, 184, 193–
    194, 301, 373
Valley Forge, 130
Van Cleve, George, 93, 174–175, 232,
    234–235
Vanderbilt family, 56
Vanderbilt, General Cornelius, 200
Vanderbilt, George W., 49
Vanderbilt, Gertrude, 132–133, 137

Vanderbilt, Gloria, Sr., 184–185, 189
Vanderbilt, Mrs. Reginald C., 349
Vanity Fair (magazine), 41, 322
Variety, 199
Venice Amusement Park, 202, 302
Very Good, Eddie, 66
Vidor, Florence, 156, 208
Vidor, King, x, 83, 91, 157, 203–204,
    205, 207–208, 226, 229, 238, 259,
    261, 281
Vignola, Robert G., 104
Villa, Pancho, 105
Vizcaya, 49–53
Volstead Act (Prohibition), 93, 141
von Dehn, Hyatt, 367
von Dehn, Martin, 349
von Stroheim, Erich, 82–83
von Wiegand, Karl, 234

Walker, James J. (Mayor), 175
Wall Street Crash, 237, 267
Walsh, Raoul, x, 207, 372
Walska, Ganna, 314
Wanger, Walter, 266
Ward, Fanny, 23, 222, 300, 302
Warner Brothers (also Warner
    Brothers-First National), 119,
    185, 224, 272, 279–282, 285–289,
    298, 358
Warner, Harry, 261
Warner, Jack, x, 261, 271, 279–280,
    286, 298
War of the Worlds, The, 305
Warren, Dean, 369
Warren, Earl, 17, 372
Warwick Hotel (New York City), 195–
    196, 370
Washburn, Cleo, 350
Washington, George, 130
Washington *Herald,* 290, 296
Watson, Victor, 64, 131, 133–134,
    136–137
Watts Tower, 183
Wayburn, Ned, 33–34, 246
Wedding March, The, 82–83
Wedding of the Painted Doll, The,
    233–243
Weintraub, Stanley, 261
Welles, Chris, 307
Welles, Orson, x, 271, 305–308, 312–
    318
Welles, Virginia Powell (Mrs. Orson),
    306–307
We'll Make Hay While the Sun Shines,
    267
We'll Remember, 267
West, Mae, 259
Whalen, Richard J., 190
Wharton, Edith, 22
When Knighthood Was in Flower,
    106, 110–114, 116–117, 128, 191,
    201, 203, 380
When Strangers Meet, 264–265
White, Lulu, 201
White, Pearl, 85
White, Stanford, 181
White, Thomas Justin, 294
Whitney, Mrs. Harry Payne, 124
Whitney, Liz (Payson), *see* Payson,
    Liz Whitney

Whitney Museum of American Art (New York City), 274
Who?, 284
Why Was I Born? 216
Widener, Joseph Early (art collector), 49
Widener, Mrs. Jules (Ella), 51–53
Wild and Woolly, 45
Wilder, Billy, 370
Wilkerson, W. R., 321
Wilkins, Sir Hubert, 234
Williams, Bert, 60
Williams, Ella "Bill," 154, 184, 268–269, 273
Williams, Tennessee, 20–21
Willicombe, Joseph, 135, 157, 185, 220, 243, 280, 301, 319
Willson, Anita, 55
Wilson, Woodrow (Pres.), 40, 66, 103, 195, 322
Windsor, Claire, 275
Wings, 157
Winkler, John, 83
Winning of Barbara Worth, The, 275
Winslow, Herbie, 70
Winter Garden Theatre, 86, 135
Without Prejudice (Vanderbilt), 184
Wodehouse, P. G., 66
"Woman of the Day," 332
Wood, Sam, 207, 265
Woollcott, Alexander, 306
Words and Music, 78
World and His Wife, The, 113
World Film Corporation, 78

World War I, *x*, 46, 66–69, 191, 238, 259, 322–323
World War II, 135, 189, 254, 302, 304–305, 319–320, 321–324, 326–327
Wray, John Griffith, 156
Wright, Cobina, Sr., 14, 18, 343, 351, 362
Wynn, Ed, 102
Wyntoon, 4, 16, 222, 245, 251, 270–271, 293, 299, 318–320, 323–324, 326, 330, 350, 354, 364

"Xanadu," 311, 316, 318

"Yellow Peril, The," 321–322
Yes, Sir, That's My Baby, 141
Yolanda, 128–130, 384
Young Diana, The, 99, 104, 382
You Were Meant for Me, 233

Zander the Great, 148–153, 157, 169, 387
Zanuck, Darryl, 78
Ziegfeld, Florenz, 7, 27, 33, 39, 47, 51, 60–66, 84, 104, 125, 234, 248
Ziegfeld Follies, 3, 12, 27, 33, 34, 38, 45, 51, 60–66, 113, 135, 199, 210, 215, 258, 284
Ziegfeld Theatre (New York City), 64, 368
Zittell (studio manager), 92
Zukor, Adolph, 82, 84, 89
Zweig, Stefan, 278